Second Edition

The Catholic Funding Guide

A Directory of Resources for Catholic Activities

Kerry A. Robinson
Editor

The Catholic Funding Guide:
A Directory of Resources for Catholic Activities
Second Edition

Designed and typeset by Kerry A. Robinson
Cover design by Lisa Catalone of Catalone Design Co.

Copies of the *Guide* may be ordered through
FADICA, Inc.
1350 Connecticut Ave., N.W.
Suite 303
Washington, D.C. 20036-1701
or visit FADICA's website at www.fadica.org

Library of Congress Control Number: 2001129000

The Catholic Funding Guide / Kerry A. Robinson, editor.

ISBN 1-891646-02-8

© Copyright 2001, FADICA, Inc.

Table of Contents

Acknowledgements

For those uninitiated, the task of navigating the perplexing world of private philanthropy can be unsettling. *The Catholic Funding Guide* is designed to simplify the work of the non-professional fundraiser and provide that person direction in taking the first steps toward locating grant support.

This second edition of *The Catholic Funding Guide* reflects an increase of nearly 300 individual grantmaker entries from the inaugural edition published three years ago. It offers succinct information on private foundations with Catholic interests, church-sponsored funding agencies, fraternal organizations, and religious communities with grantmaking programs. Without doubt, this book will become an indispensable tool for clergy and lay volunteers alike.

In publishing this work, FADICA wishes to thank Kerry A. Robinson, the editor, who is one of the most well-informed authorities in Catholic philanthropy today. Gratitude is also expressed to Kristin M. Brantman, Shawn M. Colberg and Sharon E. Marek, who generously assisted Ms. Robinson in her research and editing tasks.

Due to the painstaking research of these four individuals, the second edition of *The Catholic Funding Guide* will lighten the burden of many grantseekers and enable donor agencies to discover many imaginative and inspiring approaches to contemporary church needs.

Dr. Francis J. Butler
President
Foundations and Donors Interested in Catholic Activities

Introduction

The Catholic Funding Guide, with 962 entries, was produced to provide information on a variety of funding sources for the full spectrum of Catholic activities. Within this *Guide* the Catholic grant seeker will find information on private and corporate foundations with a history of Catholic grant making. They are located in 45 states. Also within the *Guide* are Catholic church-based agencies that award grants, Catholic religious communities and fraternal benefit societies supporting the work of the church, and international agencies in 18 countries offering financial assistance to Catholic ministries.

This publication is intended to be a starting point for Catholic grant seekers, allowing greater access to information in one volume and saving many hours of research. The wise grant seeker will understand, however, that this is only a guide and further research will have to be conducted on those funding sources which seem to be compatible with the charity's needs. The more information one has about a funding agency and its interests, the more targeted the fundraising approach can be. The more focused the approach, the greater the likelihood of a favorable outcome.

There is a second, equally important reason for compiling this reference book. *The Catholic Funding Guide* lends testimony to the vibrant and diverse expression of Catholic stewardship throughout the world. Of course what it does not catalogue is the generosity of individual contributions of Catholics giving their time, their expertise, and their financial support to further the many ministries of the Catholic church.

An Overview of Fundraising

Many directors of Catholic nonprofit organizations believe so strongly in the importance of the organization's mission that they find themselves focusing totally on the ministry at the expense of administration. In order for an organization to be successful at its ministry, however, sound management must be present. There are many factors which contribute to the success of a nonprofit organization beyond a worthy and valued mission. The nonprofit organization must have sound leadership, adequate office and staff management, financial accountability, impeccable bookkeeping, publicity and promotion, and a long-term fundraising plan.

Fundraising is often the least favorite part of running a successful nonprofit organization. But without it, the organization cannot survive. Far too much time is wasted, often at critical moments in the life of an organization, because of inattention to fundraising.

A nonprofit organization will be successful in raising funds if it has a program worthy of support, identifies or develops a constituency with the ability to give, prepares a plan for fundraising, and then enlists leaders to carry out the plan.

Preparing a plan for fundraising is essential to establishing and maintaining financial viability for a nonprofit organization. There are four components to an overall fundraising or development plan. They include the annual fund, the special purpose gift, planned giving, and the capital campaign. Not all of these components need to be employed simultaneously and indeed some nonprofit organizations choose to implement only one or two of these fundraising components during the course of the organization's lifetime. However it is prudent to be aware of the merits of each.

The annual fund drive is the most commonly used method of fundraising. It entails developing a cadre of ongoing supporters of the organization. It is to this constituency that the organization makes annual appeals for financial support, usually through mailing solicitations and occasional benefits or special events. The special purpose gift solicitation is an effort to raise additional money in a given budget year for the purpose of obtaining a special piece of equipment, expanding a program or adding a new one, expanding staff, and so on. Typically foundations and corporate giving programs are approached for this type of support in addition to key members of one's constituency.

Planned giving is an effort to establish and build an endowment for the nonprofit organization. It appeals to individuals to bequeath assets to the nonprofit organization which will be transferred to the organization upon the individual's death. This requires forward, long-term thinking. It is unwise to ignore the merits of incorporating planned giving into one's fundraising plans since it can substantially contribute to the endowment of a nonprofit organization.

Finally, there is the capital campaign which offers an organization the opportunity to meet its considerable capital needs. It is most commonly employed to raise the necessary funds to purchase land, acquire facilities, build additional facilities, renovate and expand existing facilities, and/or increase an endowment. Capital campaigns are directed primarily at individuals, rather than corporations or foundations.

The most important source of financial support for one's organization is the organization's constituency. Religious giving accounts for more than one-half of all private philanthropy in the United States. Clearly individuals are interested in religion as a category of charitable giving. By comparison there are far fewer foundations and other funding bodies interested in religion. Nevertheless they do exist and the prudent fundraiser should be aware of those foundations which will support the organization's programs.

Applying to foundations and other funding bodies takes a good deal of preparation. However, the greater the preparation that is done up front, the higher the probability of success for the grant seeker. And with a focused approach, a great deal of time can be saved in the long run, both for grant seeker and grant maker. The following offers some practical advice to grant seekers applying to foundations. In most cases the advice pertains equally to applying for grants from church-based agencies, religious communities, fraternal benefit societies, and international funding agencies as well.

Preparation and research

A well-thought out approach to grant seeking will aid one immeasurably when it comes to writing the applications themselves. The best approach is one that involves research up front. Take advantage of the many excellent grant guides and directories that are in print and regularly updated. Examples include, *The Foundation Directory*, the *National Guide to Funding in Religion*, *Foundation Guide for Religious Grant Seekers*, and the *Fund Raiser's Guide to Religious Philanthropy*. (See additional recommendations in Section VI, page 477.) An especially helpful resource is The Foundation Center, with reference collections in Washington, D.C., New York City, San Francisco, Cleveland, and Atlanta and additional cooperating collections in various cities in every state throughout the country. (For a complete listing of Foundation Center cooperating collections in your area, see Section V, page 447.) The advantage to visiting one of The Foundation Center's cooperating collections is that they have available for the public many reference books helpful to fundraisers as well as copies of the IRS tax returns that private foundations are required by law to file. These returns provide accurate financial and funding information for each foundation.

There are two practical reasons for investing the time to thoroughly research funding organizations which have an interest in supporting Catholic activities. The first is that it will save the grant seeker a great deal of time in the long run. The second reason to invest the time in preliminary research is that it will allow the grant seeker to prepare a very thorough application which matches the funding priorities and expectations of a given funding organization.

When conducting research, the grant seeker must also make sure that the foundation funds the particular type of Catholic ministry or Catholic organization represented in the proposal. Another factor to determine is the foundation's geographical giving pattern. As a general rule, the likelihood of obtaining a grant from a foundation diminishes with distance. Some foundations limit their funding to a particular state, county, or city. A third concern for the researcher is the specific limitations a given foundation puts on its grant making. Many foundations will not support individuals or endowment funds. Some will not entertain proposals for construction or renovations. And finally, a fourth concern is the asset size of the foundation and the grant range. Each of these particulars is important to discern prior to applying to a foundation.

One final word of caution: do not be tempted to apply for a grant from a foundation when the foundation's funding requirements do not meet the organization's needs. Moreover, do not waste time sending applications to foundations that state they only fund pre-selected organizations, or to foundations which do not have a history or stated interest of supporting Catholic programs like yours, or are outside of your geographical locale. Respect the funding limitations stated by the foundation and do not ask for a dollar amount that far exceeds the range of funding for that agency. This wisdom will help the prospects for a favorable response to an organization's appeal.

Tailoring an approach to specific foundations

Once you have a list of potential donor agencies meeting all of this criteria, begin to tailor your approach to each one in turn. If the funding agency has printed guidelines or an application form that it requires, write or call for this material. The more information an applicant has at the beginning, the greater the chances of obtaining positive consideration.

Each foundation has slightly unique funding procedures, many with deadlines that fall at different times during the year. Even the largest Catholic foundations may have only one or two deadlines each year and preparation will ensure that critical deadlines are not missed.

In preparing to approach a funding agency consider, if possible, a personal visit with the foundation. A visit allows the opportunity to make personal contact and describe the organization or program in a more detailed way. Many foundations and funding agencies do not conduct personal interviews. However, representatives may call applicants once a proposal has been submitted in full.

If an application form is not required for grant consideration but simply a proposal, make sure that along with the proposal is included a brief (one or two pages is preferable) cover letter, describing the applicant organization, outlining the specific need for which funding is sought, specifying the amount requested, and describing how that money will be used to achieve the desired outcome. The important point is to be extremely concise and informative. The full proposal will elaborate and support your application.

The Proposal

Foundations requiring application forms actually make the grant seeker's task easier. Everything pertinent to the request will be included on the application form. It is more difficult to draft a proposal without guidelines. In this event, the following should always be included:

• A description of the applicant organization.

• The mission of the organization, program, or ministry.

• The problem or need and how the proposal will address it.

• A timeline for achieving the proposal's goals as well as the expected grant period. *(Virtually no foundation will award grants for deficit financing and most will not fund "after the fact" requests. This requires good organizational skills on the grant seeker's part because there is often a significant lag time between the submission of a proposal and the awarding of a grant. The grant seeker must take into account that the grant usually will only be awarded for a program or project happening after the grant money is sent.)*

• A listing of the persons involved in the project and their qualifications.

• Evidence of tax exemption.

• Financial information including a detailed budget, the amount being requested, as well as the total project cost.

• Other sources of support (both those in hand and those pending).

• A statement as to how the project or program will eventually be self-supporting.

Foundations and funding agencies with application guidelines will state any additional requirements which must be met. For instance, some Catholic foundations will require a letter of endorsement from the local bishop or religious superior as part of the proposal.

Finally, it is always helpful to have an insight into the underlying philosophy of the agency from which grant support is being sought. Accentuate and match the strengths of the applying organization to the foundation's particular interests.

Remember when appealing to foundations for grant support that foundations make up only a tiny percent of giving to charitable activities. The bulk of contributions to nonprofit organizations comes from individuals. Moreover, national and international church-related organizations contribute a sizeable amount of grant support each year as well.

Foundations recognize that they are in a position to address a wide array of social, religious, economic, and educational concerns. Foundations also strive to fund innovative solutions. Fewer and fewer foundations are interested solely in "bricks and mortar" requests. More and more foundations are looking for creative programs and strategies which, if successful, can be replicated in other areas. Attractive proposals are the ones which recognize exactly what excites a funder. Most major funders like to see evidence of collaboration with other organizations and are encouraged by a willingness on the part of the applicant to share successful programs or strategies with others. Funders also want to be reassured that an applicant is aware of any other programs or efforts addressing similar needs. A well researched, well prepared, and well written application will seek to convince grant making organizations that a decision to approve funding is a wise investment.

How To Use This Guide

The Catholic Funding Guide is divided into six sections. The first four sections are devoted to organizations that offer grant support for Catholic institutions, activities, and ministries. Each entry contains the following information, when it was available:

• The funding agency's address, telephone number, and fax.

• The principal contact.

• The geographical giving pattern.

• The special funding interest, particularly in the Catholic arena.

• Financial details, including assets, grant total, grant range, and grant average. The year for which the financial information is given is alsó noted.

• Funding limitations.

• Application guidelines.

Section I: Foundations
Section I contains entries for private and corporate foundations in the United States which have demonstrated a history of Catholic grant making. The entries are presented in alphabetical order by state. Although some foundations do not limit their grant making to a particular geographical region, the likelihood of receiving a grant from a foundation increases with proximity. Therefore, a grant seeker working for a Catholic charity in New York City would be wise to begin with the foundations located in the State of New York.

The majority of foundations which appear in this *Guide* are private foundations, which by law are required to file 990-PF tax forms, which are accessible to the public and which provide details of a foundation's funding procedures, financial information, and other pertinent information. This *Guide* contains the most current information available at the time of publication, but be advised that foundation personnel and addresses do change and occasionally funding priorities and application guidelines do as well. This makes it all the more incumbent upon the grant seeker to take the information provided in this resource and follow up on compatible leads with further, more personalized research.

This section also includes entries for corporate foundations and some corporate giving programs which have demonstrated an interest in supporting Catholic organizations. All corporate foundations listed in this *Guide* have been noted as such.

Section II: Church-based Agencies

Section II contains entries for agencies falling directly under the auspices of the Catholic church. All of the entries listed in this section have U.S. offices, although some of these are the U.S. representative of a papal agency in Rome. Many of the funding agencies listed in this section receive a substantial portion of their income from national church collections. When that information was available, it was included in the entry.

Often the only financial information available for the church-based agencies was that pertaining to grant total or grant average.

Entries are listed alphabetically by name.

Section III: Religious Communities and Fraternal Benefit Societies

Section III contains entries for both the religious communities and fraternal benefit societies which have grant making activities. Many of these organizations primarily fund the work and ministries of their own members. However, in some cases the organizations are open to receiving applications and requests for financial support from non-members.

There is a third category of funding sources included in this section; that is the funding bodies which have resulted from the sale of a religious community-sponsored hospital. Clearly we are on the cusp of a major addition to Catholic philanthropy, as healthcare systems nationwide evolve and consolidate.

Entries are listed alphabetically by name. Both those funding agencies which have resulted from the sale of a hospital and the fraternal benefit societies are noted as such.

Section IV: International Funding Agencies

Section IV contains entries for funding agencies which support Catholic activities internationally. Many of those included do not fund organizations located in the United States and the focus is predominately on developing nations. The entries are arranged alphabetically by country. U.S.-based foundations which make grants overseas are cross-referenced in this section.

All dollar amounts are listed as U.S. dollars unless otherwise noted.

The funding priority is predominately socio-economic development, although many of the funding agencies included in this section focus their grant making on missionaries and other Catholic-sponsored non-governmental organizations. Pastoral work and evangelization are also funding areas of interest. A common theme is a desire on the part of the funder to see demonstration of local support for the project. Very often an application will require a letter of endorsement from the local bishop.

Section V: The Foundation Center
Cooperating Collections Network

Section V offers a complete list of libraries and offices in each state which comprise The Foundation Center Cooperating Collection Network. The Foundation Center is an independent national service organization which provides information to the public on private philanthropic giving. The many cooperating collections throughout the country offer Foundation Center publications and sometimes 990-PF tax returns for foundations located in the immediate vicinity. Because greater research is necessary to be successful at fundraising, The Foundation Center's libraries and cooperating collections are highly recommended.

Section VI: Additional Sources of Information

Section VI provides a bibliography of very useful publications from a variety of publishers. Most of the resources recommended are grant guides and directories, which aided the research for this *Guide* tremendously and which will provide the grant seeker supplemental information.

Note: Every entry which appears in this Guide is listed alphabetically in the index.

Sources of Funding

SECTION I:
FOUNDATIONS

ALABAMA

Mildred Weedon Blount Educational & Charitable Foundation, Inc.

P.O. Box 607
Tallassee, AL 36078
Contact: Arnold B. Dopson, Chair
Geographic Giving Pattern: Primarily Alabama, with an emphasis on Elmore County.
Special Interest: Education, scholarships, Catholic church support, and Catholic agencies.
Assets: $3,541,156 (1997)
Grant Total: $112,643 and $40,000 for individuals
Grant Range: $500–$40,000
Applications: Initial approach should be by letter. The deadlines are in early May. The application address is P.O. Box 706 Tallassee, AL 36078.

The Robert and Mildred Blount Educational Charitable Foundation, Inc.

c/o Regions Bank, Trust Department
Eight Commerce Street
P.O. Box 511
Montgomery, AL 36134-0511
Contact: Regions Bank, Trust Department
Geographic Giving Pattern: Primarily Alabama.
Special Interests: Human services, substance abuse, Catholic federated giving programs, Catholic church support and Catholic agencies.
Assets: $1,616,513 (1997)
Gifts Received: $107,108

Grant Total: $99,347

Grant Range: $4,837–$32,500

Limitations: No grants to individuals.

Applications: Contributes to pre-selected organizations only. Applications are not accepted.

The Briarcliff Foundation, Inc.

P.O. Box 2623

Birmingham, AL 35202

Contact: Emmet O'Neil, II

Geographic Giving Pattern: There are no stated geographical limitations.

Special Interests: Human services, education, birth defects, Special Olympics, youth services, Catholic church support and Catholic agencies.

Assets: $2,145,639 (1998)

Grant Total: $242,233

Grant High: $24,000

Applications: Initial approach should be by letter. There are no deadlines.

The Joseph S. Bruno Charitable Foundation

P.O. Box 530727

Birmingham, AL 35253-0727

(205) 933-7822

Contact: Jera G. Stribling, Executive Director

Geographic Giving Pattern: Primarily Alabama, especially Birmingham.

Special Interest: The arts, cultural programs, education, healthcare, Catholic church support, and Catholic agencies.

Assets: $10,208,747 (1998)

Grant Total: $377,650

Grant Range: $1,000–$56,284

Limitations: No grants to individuals.

Applications: Initial approach should be by letter. An application form is not required. The deadlines are in April and October.

The Ann and Angelo Bruno Foundation
2700 Old Trace
Birmingham, AL 35243
Contact: Ronald Bruno, Chair
Geographic Giving Pattern: Primarily Birmingham, Alabama.
Special Interest: Education, healthcare, the disabled, Catholic church support, and Catholic agencies.
Assets: $4,226,101 (1998)
Grant Total: $211,174
Grant Range: $1,000–$50,000
Limitations: No grants to individuals.
Applications: Contributes to pre-selected organizations only. Applications are not accepted.

Lee Bruno Foundation
1641 Panorama Drive
Birmingham, AL 35216
Contact: Vincent Bruno, President
Geographic Giving Pattern: Primarily Birmingham, Alabama.
Special Interest: Catholic churches and social service agencies, Catholic welfare, health, and education.
Assets: $4,844,194 (1998)
Grant Total: $275,344
Grant Range: $25–$100,000
Limitations: No grants to individuals.
Applications: Contributes to pre-selected organizations only. Applications are not accepted.

The Coffey Charitable Trust
1422 Pierce Chapel Road
Wetumpka, AL 36092
Contact: David Coffey
Geographic Giving Pattern: Primarily Alabama.
Special Interests: Colleges and Catholic federated giving programs.
Assets: $87,533 (1997)
Gifts Received: $143,300
Grant Total: $56,720
Limitations: No grants to individuals.
Applications: Contributes to pre-selected organizations only. Applications are not accepted.

ALASKA

The Carr Foundation, Inc.
550 West Seventh Avenue, Suite 1540
Anchorage, AK 99501
Contact: Jacqueline Carr-Agni, Secretary-Treasurer
Geographic Giving Pattern: Limited to Alaska.
Special Interests: Higher education, community foundations, human
services, Catholic agencies and churches.
Assets: $3,196,148 (1998)
Gifts Received: $344,634
Grant Total: $356,500
Grant Range: $500–$129,500
Limitations: No grants to individuals.
Applications: Contributes to pre-selected organizations only.
Applications are not accepted.

ARIZONA

Alberta B. Farrington Foundation
7570 N. Silvercrest Way
Paradise Valley, AZ 85253-2851
Contact: Harry Cavanagh, Jr. or Mike Cavanagh
Geographic Giving Pattern: Primarily Arizona and Florida.
Special Interests: Arts and cultural programs, education, health
associations, children and youth services, recreation, and Catholic
agencies and churches.
Assets: $20,194,336 (1998)
Grant Total: $858,000
Grant Range: $1,000–$212,000
Limitations: No grants to individuals.

Elizabeth Ann Parkman Foundation
5406 Gleneagles Drive
Tucson, AZ 85718
Contact: James M. Murphy, Trustee or Elizabeth Ann Parkman,
Trustee
Geographic Giving Pattern: Primarily Tucson, Arizona.
Special Interest: Christian institutions, hospitals, medical research,
community projects, and education.

Assets: $2,069,876 (1998)
Grant Total: $142,500
Grant Range: $250–$26,500
Limitations: No grants to individuals.
Applications: Contributes to pre-selected organizations only.
Applications are not accepted.

The Pasquinelli Foundation

P.O. Box 2949
Yuma, AZ 85366-2949
(520) 783-7813
Contact: Gary J. Pasquinelli, President
Geographic Giving Pattern: National.
Special Interests: Human services, general charitable giving, and
Catholic agencies and churches.
Assets: $2,214,641 (1999)
Gifts Received: $574,588
Grant Total: $289,225
Grant Range: $100–$194,500
Limitations: No grants to individuals.
Applications: Contributes to pre-selected organizations only.
Applications are not accepted.

Southwestern Foundation for Education and Historical Preservation

P.O. Box 40380
Tucson, AZ 85717-0380
(520) 327-1215
Contact: Timothy N. Gardner, Executive Director
Geographic Giving Pattern: Limited to northern Mexico and
southwestern U.S., with an emphasis on Tucson, Arizona.
Special Interest: Education, historical preservation, Catholic church
support, and Catholic agencies.
Assets: $7,492,263 (1998)
Grant Total: $371,770
Grant Range: $1,000–$70,000
Limitations: No grants to individuals.
Applications: Initial approach should be by letter. The deadlines are
one month preceding board meetings, which occur in March and
November.

The Steele Foundation, Inc.

P.O. Box 1112
Phoenix, AZ 85001
(602) 230-2038
Contact: Bea Baker
Geographic Giving Pattern: Primarily Arizona, especially Phoenix.
Special Interest: Education, healthcare, human services and Catholic church and schools support.
Assets: $65,336,687 (1998)
Grant Total: $2,656,690
Grant Range: $1,000–$300,000
Grant Average: $5,000–$50,000
Limitations: No grants to individuals.
Applications: Contributes to pre-selected organizations only. Applications are not accepted.

ARKANSAS

Charles A. Frueauff Foundation, Inc.

Three Financial Centre
900 South Shakleford, Suite 300
Little Rock, AR 72211
(501) 219-1410
(501) 219-1416 (fax)
Contact: Sue M. Frueauff, Program Officer
Geographic Giving Pattern: National.
Special Interest: Healthcare, welfare, children, the disabled, the indigent, and higher education; some support for Catholic agencies.
Assets: $116,086,167 (1998)
Grant Total: $4,826,020
Grant Range: $2,000–$350,000
Limitations: No grants to individuals or for research. No support for individual primary or secondary schools. No loans.
Applications: Initial approach should be by proposal. Written proposals should be submitted between January 1 and March 15 or between June 1 and September 15.

Nabholz Charitable Foundation

P.O. Box 2090
Conway, AR 72033
(501) 327-7781
Contact: Robert D. Nabholz, Director
Geographic Giving Pattern: Primarily Arkansas.
Special Interest: Education, youth, Catholic church support, and Catholic agencies.
Assets: $654,649 (1999)
Gifts Received: $24,000
Grant Total: $51,250
Grant Range: $500–$10,000
Applications: Applications are not accepted.

The Wrape Family Charitable Trust

P.O. Box 193455
Little Rock, AR 72219-3455
(501) 565-9301
Contact: W. R. Wrape II, Trustee
Geographic Giving Pattern: Primarily Arkansas.
Special Interest: Catholic educational and religious organizations.
Assets: $4,460,651 (1998)
Grant Total: $282,810
Grant Range: $500–$119,500
Limitations: No grants to individuals.
Applications: Initial approach should be by letter. There are no deadlines.

CALIFORNIA

The Ahmanson Foundation

9215 Wilshire Boulevard
Beverly Hills, CA 90210
(310) 278-0770
Contact: Lee E. Walcott, Vice President and Managing Director
Geographic Giving Pattern: Primarily southern California, with an emphasis on the Los Angeles area.
Special Interest: Education, arts, humanities, medicine, health, human services, and youth organizations.

Assets: $765,246,907 (1998)
Grant Total: $50,883,144
Grant Range: $1,000–$5,500,000
Grant Average: $10,000–$25,000
Limitations: No grants to individuals or for continuing support, annual campaigns, deficit financing, or fellowships. No loans.
Applications: Initial approach should be by letter or proposal. There are no deadlines.

Anima Christi Foundation
8141 E. Kaiser Boulevard, Suite 300
Anaheim, CA 92808
(714) 282-1563 (fax)
Contact: Denise Bowman, Executive Director
Geographic Giving Pattern: Primarily Orange County, California.
Special Interests: Catholic agencies and schools, and international aid to the poor.
Assets: $645,700 (1998)
Gifts Received: $240,497
Grant Total: $514,611
Grant Range: $75–$100,000
Limitations: No grants to individuals.
Applications: Contributes to pre-selected organizations only. Applications are not accepted.

Antonini Foundation
11374 Tuxford Street
Sun Valley, CA 91352
(818) 767-8576
Contact: Marisa Antonini, President
Geographic Giving Pattern: Primarily Los Angeles, California.
Special Interests: Human services, education, hospitals, mental health, violence prevention, youth services, medical research, public affairs, women, the economically disadvantaged, and Catholic church support and Catholic agencies.
Assets: $1,172,564 (1998)
Grant Total: $60,325
Grant Range: $50–$20,000
Limitations: No grants to individuals.

Applications: Applications must be received prior to the board meeting on May 15.

Arata Brothers Trust

4061 Marsalla Court
Sacramento, CA 95820
(916) 451-5358
Contact: Renato R. Parenti, Francis B. Dillon, and Mark Sewell, Trustees
Geographic Giving Pattern: California.
Special Interest: Hospitals, education, religion, cultural awareness, social service agencies, youth, Protestant and Catholic giving, and church support.
Assets: $7,975,812 (1997)
Grant Total: $510,900
Grant Range: $1,000–$50,000
Limitations: No grants to individuals.
Applications: Initial approach should be by letter including proof of tax-exempt status. There are no deadlines.

Bob Baker Foundation, Inc.

591 Camino de la Siesta, Suite 1100
San Diego, CA 92108
(619) 297-1001
Contact: Casey Favour
Geographic Giving Pattern: Limited to San Diego, California.
Description: Bob Baker Foundation, Inc. is a corporate foundation of Bob Baker Enterprises, Inc.
Special Interest: Religious welfare organizations, higher education, the environment, healthcare, and homelessness.
Assets: $343,614 (1999)
Gifts Received: $377,500
Grant Total: $199,395
Grant Range: $100–$58,200
Limitations: No grants to individuals.
Applications: Contributes to pre-selected organizations only. Applications are not accepted.

Bank of America - Giannini Foundation

799 Market Street, #10067-5
San Francisco, CA 94103
(415) 953-3175
Contact: Caroline O. Boitano, President and Executive Director
Geographic Giving Pattern: Limited to areas of major company operations.
Description: Bank America Foundation is a company-sponsored foundation.
Special Interest: Health, human services, community and economic development, education and arts and culture.
Assets: $19,880,192 (1998)
Grant Total: $1,061,220
Grant Range: $2,500–$40,000
Grant Average: $1,000–$10,000
Limitations: No support for religious organizations for sectarian purposes.
Applications: Initial approach should be by letter or telephone, requesting application guidelines. There are no deadlines.

Arline & Thomas J. Bannan Foundation

c/o Parker, Milliken, Clark, O'Hara & Samuelian
333 S. Hope Street, 27th Floor
Los Angeles, CA 90071-1488
(213) 683-6591
Contact: Karen I. Dalby, President
Geographic Giving Pattern: Primarily California and Washington.
Special Interest: Education, hospitals, Catholic church support, and Catholic agencies.
Assets: $2,861,828 (1998)
Gifts Received: $2,068,745
Grant Total: $290,000
Grant Range: $5,000–$150,000
Limitations: No grants to individuals.
Applications: Contributes to pre-selected organizations only. Applications are not accepted.

Bellini Foundation

400 Estudillo Avenue, Suite 200
San Leandro, CA 94577
(510) 895-9932
Contact: Patrick W. Bellini, President
Geographic Giving Pattern: Primarily California.
Special Interests: Education, healthcare, children and youth services,
Catholic agencies and churches.
Assets: $6,160,871 (1999)
Grant Total: $245,500
Grant Range: $1,000–$22,000
Limitations: No grants to individuals.
Applications: Contributes to pre-selected organizations only.
Applications are not accepted.

Maribeth Benham Family Foundation

20611 Ritanna Court
Saratoga, CA 95070
Contact: Maribeth Benham, President
Geographic Giving Pattern: National.
Special Interests: Arts and cultural programs, education, human
services, Catholic agencies and churches.
Assets: $3,943,495 (1998)
Gifts Received: $4,000,000
Grant Total: $65,000
Grant Range: $500–$10,000
Limitations: No grants to individuals.
Applications: Contributes to pre-selected organizations only.
Applications are not accepted.

Burton G. Bettingen Corporation

9777 Wilshire Boulevard, Suite 615
Beverly Hills, CA 90212
(310) 276-4115
(310) 276-4693 (fax)
Contact: Patricia A. Brown, Executive Director
Geographic Giving Pattern: Primarily southern California.
Special Interest: Social services, especially with regard to children,
diocesan and church support, religious organizations, and religious
welfare.

Assets: $18,166,937 (1998)
Gifts Received: $1,482,144
Grant Total: $3,945,164
Grant Range: $200–$700,065
Grant Average: $1,000–$100,000
Limitations: No grants to individuals or for general fundraising events, conferences, seminars, dinners, or mass mailings.
Applications: Initial approach should be by letter. The deadline is December 15.

The Kathryne Beynon Foundation

199 South Los Robles Avenue, Suite 711
Pasadena, CA 91101-2460
(626) 584-8800
Contact: Robert D. Bannon, Trustee
Geographic Giving Pattern: Primarily southern California.
Special Interest: Drug abuse and alcohol programs, child welfare, Catholic church support, Catholic agencies, hospitals, and education.
Assets: $9,362,766 (1999)
Grant Total: $228,350
Grant Range: $500–$48,000
Applications: Initial approach should be by letter. There are no deadlines.

Clyde D. and Betsy A. Bruhn Trust

926 J. Street, Apartment 402
Sacramento, CA 95814-2786
Contact: Francis B. Dillon, Trustee
Special Interests: Children, youth development, healthcare, Catholic agencies and churches.
Assets: $3,334,630 (1998)
Gifts Received: $2,207,618
Grant Total: $289,938
Grant Range: $2,000–$71,985
Limitations: No grants to individuals.
Applications: Contributes to pre-selected organizations only. Applications are not accepted.

Florence E. Burgess Trust

c/o Wells Fargo Bank, Trust Tax Department
P.O. Box 63954
San Francisco, CA 94163
Contact: Wells Fargo Bank
Special Interests: Human services, Catholic agencies and churches.
Assets: $13,483,876 (1998)
Gifts Received: $62,602
Grant Total: $417,641
Grant Average: $59,663
Limitations: No grants to individuals.
Applications: Contributes to pre-selected organizations only.
Applications are not accepted.

Fritz B. Burns Foundation

4001 West Alameda Avenue, Suite 203
Burbank, CA 91505-4338
(818) 840-8802
Contact: Joseph E. Rawlinson, President
Geographic Giving Pattern: Limited to California, with an emphasis
on Los Angeles.
Special Interest: Local charities, schools, universities, churches,
hospitals, medical research facilities, welfare agencies, Catholic
religious associations, Catholic schools, and church support.
Assets: $146,851,096 (1998)
Grant Total: $5,400,800
Grant Range: $1,000–$950,000
Grant Average: $2,500–$100,000
Limitations: No grants to individuals or to private foundations.
Applications: Initial approach should be by letter. There are no
deadlines.

The John R. Cahill Foundation

425 California Street, Suite 2300
San Francisco, CA 94104
Contact: William R. Cahill, President
Geographic Giving Pattern: Primarily San Francisco, California.
Special Interest: Vocational education, children and youth services,
immigration services, Catholic agencies, and churches.

Assets: $5,175,845 (1998)
Grant Total: $263,117
Grant Range: $10,000–$68,117
Limitations: No grants to individuals.
Applications: Contributes to pre-selected organizations only. Applications are not accepted.

The Callison Foundation
969 G Edgewater Boulevard, Suite 148
Foster City, CA 94404
Contact: Gerald Hing, Secretary
Geographic Giving Pattern: Primarily the San Francisco Bay Area, California.
Special Interest: Catholic religious organizations, social welfare organizations, higher education, hospitals, youth, the arts, and cultural organizations.
Assets: $8,755,857 (1998)
Grant Total: $400,000
Grant Range: $5,000–$25,000
Limitations: No grants to individuals.
Applications: Initial approach should be by written proposal. An application form is required. The deadline is August 1.

Casillas Foundation
5655 College Avenue, Suite 250
Oakland, CA 94618
Contact: Frederic H. Clark, President
Geographic Giving Pattern: National.
Special Interest: Higher education, and Catholic organizations.
Assets: $1,415,812 (1998)
Grant Total: $77,300
Grant Range: $1,000–$15,000
Limitations: No grants to individuals.
Applications: Contributes to pre-selected organizations only. Applications are not accepted.

The William M. and Helen L. Close Family Foundation
300 N. Lake Avenue
Pasadena, CA 91101
(626) 795-8800

Contact: William M. Close, President
Special Interest: Healthcare and Catholic giving.
Assets: $5,830,438 (1998)
Gifts Received: $977,977
Grant Total: $350
Limitations: No grants to individuals.
Applications: Contributes to pre-selected organizations only.
Applications are not accepted.

Francis H. Clougherty Charitable Trust

500 Newport Center Drive, Suite 910
Newport Beach, CA 92660
(714) 644-6609
Contact: Anthony Clougherty, Trustee
Geographic Giving Pattern: Southern California.
Special Interest: Catholic higher and secondary education, Catholic
agencies, and churches.
Assets: $9,157,711 (1997)
Grant Total: $596,500
Grant Range: $2,000–$130,000
Limitations: No grants to individuals.
Applications: Contributes to pre-selected organizations only.
Applications are not accepted.

Condon Family Foundation

300 North Lake Avenue, Penthouse
Pasadena, CA 91101
Contact: Thomas J. Condon
Geographic Giving Pattern: There are no stated geographical
limitations.
Special Interests: Catholic churches and education.
Assets: $3,974,071 (1998)
Grant Total: $130,000
Grant Range: $50,000–$80,000
Limitations: No grants to individuals.
Applications: Contributes to pre-selected organizations only.
Applications are not accepted.

Dailey Family Foundation
One Capitol Mall, Suite 240
Sacramento, CA 95814
Contact: Cecilia DeLury
Geographic Giving Pattern: Primarily Southern California.
Special Interests: Human services, education, resource conservation, international affairs, Catholic church support and Catholic agencies.
Assets: $484,603 (1999)
Grant Total: $56,334
Grant Range: $50–$14,175
Limitations: No grants to individuals.
Applications: Contributes to pre-selected organizations only. Applications are not accepted.

Louise M. Davies Foundation
c/o Northern Trust
580 California Street, #1800
San Francisco, CA 94104
Contact: Donald D. Crawford, Jr., President
Geographic Giving Pattern: Primarily California, especially San Francisco.
Special Interests: Education, museums, arts and culture, natural resource conservation, Catholic church support and Catholic schools.
Assets: $2,606,588 (1998)
Grant Total: $152,500
Grant Range: $500–$25,800
Limitations: No grants to individuals.
Applications: Contributes to pre-selected organizations only. Applications are not accepted.

Georges DeBatz Trust for the Arts
601 Laurel Avenue
San Mateo, CA 94401
(415) 434-3323
Contact: Henry Howard, Trustee
Geographic Giving Pattern: Primarily California.
Special Interest: Catholic giving and the arts.
Assets: $628,416 (1997)
Grant Total: $17,700
Grant Range: $5,000–$30,000

Limitations: No grants to individuals.
Applications: Contributes to pre-selected organizations only. Applications are not accepted.

Frank C. Diener Foundation
P.O. Box 278
Five Points, CA 93624-0278
Contact: Mary Alice Diener, President
Geographic Giving Pattern: Limited to Fresno County, California.
Special Interest: Catholic religious organizations, general church funds, and human services.
Assets: $5,059,836 (1999)
Grant Total: $194,888
Grant Range: $5,000–$100,000
Limitations: No grants to individuals.
Applications: Contributes to pre-selected organizations only. Applications are not accepted.

J. Phillip and Jennifer DiNapoli Foundation
99 Almaden Boulevard, Suite 565
San Jose, CA 95113-2201
(408) 998-2460
Contact: J. Phillip DiNapoli, President
Geographic Giving Pattern: Primarily California.
Special Interests: Human services, arts and cultural programs, youth services, federated giving programs, Catholic church support and Catholic agencies.
Assets: $2,283,159 (1998)
Gifts Received: $24,995
Grant Total: $75,300
Grant Range: $100–$25,000
Applications: Initial approach should be by letter. There are no deadlines.

Carrie Estelle Doheny Foundation
707 Wilshire Boulevard, Suite 4960
Los Angeles, CA 90017
(213) 488-1122
(213) 488-1544 (fax)
Email: Doheny@Earthlink.net

www.dohenyfoundation.org
Contact: Robert A. Smith, III, President
Geographic Giving Pattern: Primarily Los Angeles, California.
Special Interest: Advancement of education, especially Catholic education, medicine, Catholic church and archdiocesan support, health and welfare of children, and aid to the needy.
Assets: $181,668,085 (1998)
Grant Total: $5,768,812
Grant Average: $5,000–$50,000
Limitations: No grants to individuals or for endowment funds, publications, travel, advertising, or radio and television programs. No scholarships.
Applications: Initial approach should be by letter. There are no deadlines.

The Drum Foundation
c/o Northern Trust of California, N.A.
580 California Street, Suite 1800
San Francisco, CA 94104
Contact: Philip Hudner, President
Geographic Giving Pattern: Primarily the Archdiocese of San Francisco, California.
Special Interest: Catholic church-related educational and charitable organizations.
Assets: $8,682,889 (1998)
Grant Total: $556,000
Grant Range: $1,000–$60,000
Limitations: No grants to individuals or for endowment funds. No matching gifts.
Applications: Contributes to pre-selected organizations only. Applications are not accepted.

Edwin & Gertrude S. Eaton Foundation
66 Cleary Court, Suite 910
San Francisco, CA 94109-6503
Contact: Evelyn T. Eaton, President
Geographic Giving Pattern: Primarily California, especially San Francisco, and France.
Special Interest: Catholic organizations including churches and missions, and a French social service organization.

Assets: $113,400 (1999)
Gifts Received: $16,950
Grant Total: $24,915
Grant Range: $50–$16,950
Limitations: No grants to individuals.
Applications: Contributes to pre-selected organizations only. Applications are not accepted.

Bettye Poetz Ferguson Foundation

425 California Street, Suite 2200
San Francisco, CA 94104
(415) 395-9700
Contact: D. Keith Bilter, Trustee
Geographic Giving Pattern: Primarily California.
Special Interest: Support for a Catholic college, social services, the arts, and music.
Assets: $1,505,881 (1998)
Gifts Received: $1,449,242
Grant Total: $815,817
Grant Range: $250–$400,000
Applications: Initial approach should be by letter. There are no deadlines.

Ernest L. and Ruth W. Finley Foundation

1400 North Dutton Avenue, Suite 12
Santa Rosa, CA 95401-1598
(707) 545-3136
Contact: Evert B. Person, Trustee
Geographic Giving Pattern: Primarily Santa Rosa, California.
Special Interest: Religious giving, performing and visual arts, and social services.
Assets: $44,662 (1998)
Gifts Received: $705,016
Grant Total: $687,612
Grant Range: $500–$500,000
Limitations: No grants to individuals.
Applications: Initial approach should be by proposal. Three copies of the proposal are requested. There are no deadlines.

Joseph I. Friedrich Foundation

1000 Town Center Drive 100
Oxnard, CA 93030
Contact: John B. Friedrich, President
Geographic Giving Pattern: Primarily California.
Special Interest: Elementary and secondary education, Catholic agencies and church support.
Assets: $1,180,127 (1999)
Grant Total: $180,275
Grant Range: $100–$76,200
Limitations: No grants to individuals.
Applications: Contributes to pre-selected organizations only. Applications are not accepted.

Furth Family Foundation

201 Sansome Street, No. 1000
San Francisco, CA 94104
(415) 433-2070
Contact: Frederick P. Furth, Manager
Geographic Giving Pattern: Primarily California.
Special Interest: Education, the arts, cultural programs, Catholic church support, and social service agencies.
Assets: $7,718,868 (1997)
Gifts Received: $1,301,250
Grant Total: $916,543
Grant Range: $25–$100,000
Limitations: No grants to individuals.
Applications: There are no deadlines for grant proposals.

David E. Gallo Foundation

P.O. Box 1130
Modesto, CA 95353
(209) 341-3788
Contact: Mary C. Gallo, Chair
Geographic Giving Pattern: National.
Special Interest: Catholic religious, educational, and charitable purposes; some support for healthcare.
Assets: $5,613,262 (1998)
Gifts Received: $5,913,675

Grant Total: $388,929
Grant Range: $24–$150,000
Limitations: No grants to individuals.
Applications: Contributes to pre-selected organizations only. Applications are not accepted.

The Ernest Gallo Foundation
P.O. Box 1130
Modesto, CA 95353
(209) 579-3204
Contact: Mrs. Ouida McCullough
Geographic Giving Pattern: Primarily California.
Special Interest: Education, healthcare, medical research, Catholic church support, and youth agencies.
Assets: $21,692,501 (1998)
Gifts Received: $4,922,500
Grant Total: $335,375
Grant Range: $1,000–$100,000
Limitations: No grants to individuals.
Applications: Initial approach should be by letter. There are no deadlines.

The Julio R. Gallo Foundation
P.O. Box 1130
Modesto, CA 95353
(209) 341-3373
Contact: Robert J. Gallo, President
Geographic Giving Pattern: Primarily California.
Special Interest: Education, Catholic church and diocesan support, religious associations, arts and culture, health, and general charitable giving.
Assets: $7,490,796 (1998)
Grant Total: $368,500
Grant Range: $250–$110,000
Limitations: No grants to individuals.
Applications: Initial approach should be by letter of request stating the purpose of the grant. There are no deadlines.

Silvio and Mary Garaventa Family Foundation
4080 Mallard Drive
Concord, CA 94520
(510) 689-8390
Contact: Silvio Garaventa, Manager
Geographic Giving Pattern: Primarily California.
Special Interest: Higher and secondary education, Catholic religious and educational institutions, church support, and youth organizations.
Assets: $3,117,096 (1999)
Gifts Received: $1,035,054
Grant Total: $56,000
Grant Range: $2,500–$21,000
Limitations: No grants to individuals.
Applications: Contributes to pre-selected organizations only. Applications are not accepted.

The Carl Gellert and Celia Berta Gellert Foundation
1169 Market Street, Suite 808
San Francisco, CA 94103
(415) 255-2829
www.fdncenter.org/grantmaker/gellert
Contact: Peter J. Brusati, Secretary
Geographic Giving Pattern: The greater San Francisco Bay Area, California.
Special Interest: Emphasis on the elderly and hospitals. Support also for Catholic churches, Catholic agencies, seminaries, higher and secondary education, medical research, drug abuse programs, community development, and social service agencies.
Assets: $14,470,978 (1998)
Grant Total: $703,920
Grant Range: $1,000–$55,000
Grant Average: $1,000–$10,000
Limitations: No grants to individuals or for seed money, emergency funds, land acquisition, or conferences. No loans or matching gifts.
Applications: Initial approach should be by letter requesting application proposal guidelines. Proposals should be submitted preferably in August or September. The deadline is October 1.

James Gleason Foundation
5 Third Street, Suite 1200
San Francisco, CA 94103
(415) 421-6995
Contact: Cressy H. Nakagawa, President, Treasurer, and Manager
Geographic Giving Pattern: Primarily the San Francisco Bay area, California.
Special Interest: Catholic welfare agencies, Protestant and Catholic church support, and Asian-American organizations.
Assets: $1,706,675 (1998)
Grant Total: $7,000
Applications: Initial approach should be by letter. The deadline is in October.

Katherine Gleason Foundation
5 Third Street, Suite 1200
San Francisco, CA 94103
(415) 421-6995
Contact: Cressy H. Nakagawa, President, Treasurer, and Manager
Geographic Giving Pattern: Primarily California.
Special Interest: Catholic religious associations, higher education, and social services.
Assets: $2,261,705 (1998)
Gifts Received: $22,000
Grant Total: $757,304
Grant Average: $10,000–$30,000
Limitations: No grants to individuals.
Applications: Contributes to pre-selected organizations only. Applications are not accepted.

John Gogian Family Foundation
2501 West 237th Street, Suite E
Torrance, CA 90505-5239
Contact: John J. Gogian, Jr., President
Geographic Giving Pattern: Primarily California.
Special Interest: Higher education, Catholic church support, Catholic agencies, social services, and youth agencies.
Assets: $15,184,704 (1997)
Grant Total: $575,005
Grant Range: $500–$185,000

Limitations: No grants to individuals.
Applications: Contributes to pre-selected organizations only.
Applications are not accepted.

Stella B. Gross Charitable Trust

c/o Bank of the West
P.O. Box 1121
San Jose, CA 95108
(408) 998-6856
Contact: Lori C. Stetzenmeyer, Trust Officer, Bank of the West
Geographic Giving Pattern: Limited to Santa Clara County,
California.
Special Interests: Arts, cultural programs, education, healthcare,
medical research, hospices, aging centers, Catholic federated giving
programs, and the disabled.
Assets: $8,485,084 (1997)
Grant Total: $260,639
Grant Range: $500–$15,000
Grant Average: $1,000–$10,000
Limitations: No grants to individuals.
Applications: Initial approach should be by letter. There are no
deadlines.

Crescent Porter Hale Foundation

220 Bush Street, Suite 1069
San Francisco, CA 94104
(415) 986-5177
Contact: Ulla Z. Davis, Executive Director
Geographic Giving Pattern: Primarily the San Francisco Bay Area,
California.
Special Interest: Emphasis on Catholic organizations. Areas of
interest include education, AIDS, children, youth, and the elderly.
Assets: $25,883,166 (1998)
Grant Total: $868,000
Grant Range: $1,000–$100,000
Grant Average: $2,000–$10,000
Limitations: No grants to individuals or for healthcare or research.
Applications: Initial approach should be by letter of intent and request
for application guidelines. There are no formal deadlines.

William H. Hannon Foundation

8055 West Manchester Boulevard, #400
Playa Del Rey, CA 90293-7990
(310) 306-0060
Contact: Kathleen Aikenhead
Geographic Giving Pattern: Primarily southern California, especially Los Angeles.
Special Interest: Education, Catholic churches, Catholic schools, medical research, and hospitals.
Assets: $15,756,159 (1998)
Gifts Received: $1,275,000
Grant Total: $664,900
Grant Range: $50–$100,000
Limitations: No grants to individuals or for private foundations.
Applications: Initial approach should be by letter. There are no deadlines.

Mark H. & Blanche M. Harrington Foundation

c/o Citizens Business Bank
225 East Colorado Boulevard, Suite 400
Pasadena, CA 91101
(626) 405-8335
Geographic Giving Pattern: Primarily California.
Special Interest: Arts and culture, education, hospitals, Catholic church support, and Catholic agencies.
Assets: $21,475,839 (1998)
Grant Total: $1,201,600
Limitations: No grants to individuals.
Applications: Initial approach should be by letter. There are no deadlines.

William R. & Virginia Hayden Foundation

110 West Las Tunas Drive, Suite A
San Gabriel, CA 91776
(626) 285-9891
(626) 285-9896 (fax)
Contact: Stanley D. Hayden, President
Geographic Giving Pattern: Primarily California, with an emphasis on Los Angeles.

Special Interest: Catholic religious and social service organizations, Catholic churches, and diocesan support.
Assets: $11,120,450 (1998)
Gifts Received: $760,248
Grant Total: $774,200
Grant Range: $100–$200,000
Limitations: No grants to individuals.
Applications: Contributes to pre-selected organizations only. Applications are not accepted.

The Hofmann Foundation
P.O. Box 907
Concord, CA 94522
(510) 682-1830
Contact: Nick Rossi
Geographic Giving Pattern: Primarily northern California, with an emphasis on the Bay Area. Some support for national organizations.
Description: The Hofmann Foundation is a corporate foundation of the Hofmann Construction Company.
Special Interest: Conservation of wildlife, education, culture, general welfare, and Catholic and Protestant churches and agencies.
Assets: $17,171,475 (1998)
Grant Total: $1,282,290
Grant Range: $100–$250,000
Grant Average: $500–$10,000
Limitations: No grants to individuals. No grants for general purposes, capital funding, operating expenses, or deficit financing.
Applications: Initial approach should be by letter not exceeding three pages. There are no deadlines. The application address is 1380 Galaxy Way, Concord, CA 94522.

The Bob & Dolores Hope Charitable Foundation
10346 Moorpark Street
North Hollywood, CA 91602-2407
Contact: Nancy Gordon, Secretary
Special Interest: Catholic giving, Catholic welfare, religious schools, hospitals, and human services.
Assets: $1,186,220 (1998)
Gifts Received: $1,507,841
Grant Total: $905,333

Grant Range: $100–$100,000
Applications: Initial approach should be by letter. There are no deadlines.

Milton Horn Art Trust

1760 Jackson
San Francisco, CA 94108-2918
Contact: Peter and Paula Ellis, Trustees
Geographic Giving Pattern: Primarily Chicago, Illinois.
Special Interests: Human services, Catholic church support and Catholic agencies.
Assets: $1,063,447 (1996)
Gifts Received: $20,000
Grant Total: $59,000
Grant Range: $28,000–$31,000
Limitations: No grants to individuals.
Applications: Contributes to pre-selected organizations only. Applications are not accepted.

The James Irvine Foundation

One Market Street
Steuart Tower, Suite 2500
San Francisco, CA 94105
(415) 777-2244
(415) 777-0869
www.irving.org
Contact: Heather Graham, Grants Manager
Geographic Giving Pattern: Limited to California.
Special Interest: Arts, healthcare, higher education, Catholic colleges, community development, Catholic and other social services, and civic culture.
Assets: $1,104,491,389 (1998)
Grant Total: $39,985,847
Grant Range: $15,000–$1,800,000
Grant Average: $150,000–$200,000
Limitations: No support for primary and secondary schools. No grants to individuals or for operating budgets, endowment funds, annual campaigns, deficit financing, films, or conferences. No support for government supported institutions. No support for purely sectarian religious activities.

Applications: Initial approach should be by letter or telephone requesting application guidelines. There are no deadlines.

J. W. and Ida M. Jameson Foundation
481 West Highland Avenue
P.O. Box 397
Sierra Madre, CA 91025
(626) 355-6973
Contact: Les M. Huhn, President
Geographic Giving Pattern: Primarily California.
Special Interest: Higher education and theological seminaries, Catholic and Protestant church support, hospitals, medical research, and youth agencies.
Assets: $16,525,801 (1999)
Grant Total: $875,000
Grant Range: $5,000–$40,000
Applications: Initial approach should be by grant proposal. The deadline is February 1.

Fletcher Jones Foundation
One Wilshire Building, Suite 2920
624 South Grand Avenue
Los Angeles, CA 90017-3335
(213) 426-6565
(213) 426-6555 (fax)
Contact: John W. Smythe, Executive Director
Geographic Giving Pattern: Primarily California.
Special Interest: Higher education, healthcare, and community services.
Assets: $172,144,152 (1998)
Grant Total: $9,372,147
Grant Range: $500–$1,000,000
Grant Average: $5,000–$50,000
Limitations: No grants to individuals or for operating funds, deficit financing, conferences, surveys, or projects supported by government agencies. No loans.
Applications: Initial approach should be by letter. Invitations to submit a formal application will be issued. There are no deadlines.

Carl N. and Margaret M. Karcher Foundation

P.O. Box 61021
Anaheim, CA 92803
Contact: Carl N. Karcher, President
Geographic Giving Pattern: Primarily Los Angeles, California.
Special Interests: Higher education, healthcare, human services, charitable giving, Catholic federated giving programs, and Catholic agencies and churches.
Assets: $400,603 (1998)
Gifts Received: $1,000
Grant Total: $676,200
Grant Range: $1,000–$150,000
Limitations: No grants to individuals.
Applications: Initial approach should be by letter including one copy of proposal. There are no deadlines.

Kinnoull Foundation

c/o J.C. Vernon Miles, Deloitte & Touche
479 Pacific Street
Monterey, CA 93940
Contact: J.C. Vernon Miles, Chair
Geographic Giving Pattern: National and international.
Special Interest: Prevention of cruelty to animals and support for the traditional teachings of the Catholic church.
Assets: $7,468,888 (1999)
Grant Total: $262,000
Grant Range: $5,000–$50,000
Limitations: No grants to individuals.
Applications: Contributes to pre-selected organizations only. Applications are not accepted.

Kirwan Family Foundation

c/o Bank of America
P.O. Box 513189, GMF
Los Angeles, CA 90051-1189
Contact: Joseph T. Gubbrud
Geographic Giving Pattern: Primarily California.
Special Interests: Education, human services, Catholic agencies and services.

Assets: $3,587,576 (1998)
Grant Total: $61,000
Grant Range: $2,000–$10,000
Limitations: No grants to individuals.
Applications: Initial approach should be by letter. There are no deadlines.

The Komes Foundation
1801 Van Ness Avenue, Suite 300
San Francisco, CA 94109
(415) 441-6462
(415) 441-6463 (fax)
Contact: Julie Garvey Komes, Trustee
Geographic Giving Pattern: Primarily northern California.
Special Interest: Education, healthcare, the arts, welfare, and Catholic giving.
Assets: $4,063,509 (1998)
Grant Total: $164,686
Grant Range: $500–$25,000
Limitations: No support for literary publications. No grants to individuals or for budget deficits, conferences, or travel.
Applications: Contributes to pre-selected organizations only. Applications are not accepted.

Walter & Francine Laband Foundation
3311 East Cameron Avenue
West Covina, CA 91791
Contact: Francine Laband, President
Geographic Giving Pattern: Primarily California.
Special Interest: Catholic educational institutions and religious organizations.
Assets: $42,337 (1999)
Gifts Received: $121,164
Grant Total: $116,519
Grant Range: 30–$51,245
Applications: Contributes to pre-selected organizations only. Applications are not accepted.

Thomas and Dorothy Leavey Foundation
4680 Wilshire Boulevard
Los Angeles, CA 90010
(323) 930-4252
Contact: Kathleen McCarthy, Chair
Geographic Giving Pattern: Primarily southern California, especially Los Angeles.
Special Interest: Hospitals, medical research, higher and secondary education, Catholic church and diocesan support, religious organizations, and general charitable giving.
Assets: $252,620,651 (1998)
Grant Total: $12,123,864
Grant Range: $1,000–$3,000,000
Grant Average: $10,000–$100,000
Applications: Initial approach should be by letter. There are no deadlines.

The Lyda-Rico DeLuca Foundation, Inc.
832 Barron Avenue
Redwood City, CA 94063
(510) 839-6527
Contact: Robert A. Gaddini, President
Geographic Giving Pattern: Primarily California.
Special Interest: Catholic secondary schools, healthcare, the disabled, social services, and youth.
Assets: $432,365 (1997)
Gifts Received: $10,000
Grant Total: $187,500
Grant Range: $1,000–$115,000
Grant Average: $10,000 or less
Limitations: No grants to individuals.
Applications: Initial approach should be by letter.

Leonardt Foundation
31200 Via Colinas, Suite 100
Westlake Village, CA 91361
(818) 707-2468
(818) 707-2776 (fax)
Contact: Felix S. McGinnis, Jr., President

Geographic Giving Pattern: National, with an emphasis on California and Ohio.
Special Interest: Catholic church support and higher education; some support for hospitals, health agencies, youth, and social services.
Assets: $2,720,712 (1996)
Grant Total: $191,250
Grant Range: $1,000–$18,450
Grant Average: $100–15,000
Limitations: No grants to individuals.
Applications: Contributes to pre-selected organizations only. Applications are not accepted.

B. C. McCabe Foundation
8152 Painter Avenue, Suite 201
Whittier, CA 90602
(562) 696-1433
(562) 698-5508 (fax)
Contact: James D. Shepard, Trustee
Geographic Giving Pattern: Primarily California and Nevada.
Special Interest: Social service organizations, food service organizations, and youth development.
Assets: $114,825,799 (1998)
Gifts Received: $160,000
Grant Total: $3,029,738
Grant Range: $2,000–$279,000
Grant Average: $10,000–$100,000
Applications: Initial approach should be by letter. There are no deadlines.

Isabel Medina Charitable Trust
c/o Wells Fargo Bank
P.O. Box 63954, MAC 0103-179
San Francisco, CA 94163
Contact: Wells Fargo Bank
Geographic Giving Pattern: National and international.
Special Interests: Human services and Catholic agencies and churches.
Assets: $5,492,667 (1998)
Gifts Received: $4,220,459
Grant Total: $45,891

Grant Range: $1,274–$6,375
Limitations: No grants to individuals.
Applications: Contributes to pre-selected organizations only.
Applications are not accepted.

The Moran Foundation
739 Vista Grande Avenue
Los Altos, CA 94024
Contact: Joseph P. Moran, President and Treasurer
Geographic Giving Pattern: Primarily California.
Special Interests: Education, healthcare, human services, civil liberties, right to life, and Catholic agencies and churches.
Assets: $11,208,720 (1998)
Grant Total: $310,038
Grant Range: $200–$43,250
Limitations: No grants to individuals.
Applications: Contributes to pre-selected organizations only.
Applications are not accepted.

Robert W. Morey & Maura Burke Morey Charitable Trust
P.O. Box 1
Tiburon, CA 94920-0799
(415) 435-2225
(415) 435-3512 (fax)
Contact: Robert W. Morey Jr., Trustee or Maura Burke Morey, Trustee
Geographic Giving Pattern: National, with an emphasis on California.
Special Interest: The Trust selects donee organizations which importantly contribute to the social fabric of democratic society. Support for secondary and higher education, Catholic schools, and other organizations.
Assets: $937,395 (1999)
Grant Total: $509,846
Grant Range: $100–$355,150
Limitations: No grants to individuals.
Applications: Initial approach should be by letter. The board meets in October.

Samuel B. Mosher Foundation

3278 Loma Riviera Drive
San Diego, CA 92110
(619) 226-6122
Contact: Robert R. Fredrickson, Secretary-Treasurer
Geographic Giving Pattern: Primarily Arizona and California.
Special Interests: Education, healthcare, youth development, arts and cultural programs, and Catholic agencies and churches.
Assets: $6,424,232 (1998)
Grant Total: $259,500
Grant Range: $500–$50,000
Grant Average: $10,000–$15,000
Limitations: No grants to individuals or for endowment funds, scholarships, fellowships, or matching gifts.
Applications: Initial approach should be by letter with one copy of proposal. There are no deadlines.

Muller Foundation

2002-168 Bayview Heights Drive
San Diego, CA 92105
Contact: Richard Vilmure, President
Geographic Giving Pattern: Primarily California.
Special Interest: Higher and secondary education, social services, Catholic churches, Catholic social services, hospitals, the arts, and cultural programs.
Assets: $9,035,643 (1998)
Grant Total: $421,750
Grant Range: $100–$12,800
Limitations: No grants to individuals.
Applications: Contributes to pre-selected organizations only. Applications are not accepted.

Peter and Pamela Mullin Family Charitable Foundation

c/o Mullin Consulting, Inc.
6422 South Figueroa Street
Los Angeles, CA 90017
Contact: Peter W. Mullin, Chair
Geographic Giving Pattern: There are no stated geographical limitations.

Special Interests: Education, federated giving programs, Catholic agencies and churches.
Assets: $997,334 (1997)
Gifts Received: $487,266
Grant Total: $1,280,000
Grant Range: $5,000–$640,000
Applications: Initial approach should be by letter. There are no deadlines.

Dan Murphy Foundation
P.O. Box 711267
Los Angeles, CA 90071
(213) 623-3120
Contact: Daniel J. Donahue, President
Geographic Giving Pattern: Primarily California, especially Los Angeles.
Special Interest: Support for activities and charities of the Catholic church including religious orders, education, social services, medical institutions, and diocesan support.
Assets: $252,779,473 (1998)
Grant Total: $13,095,177
Grant Range: $1,000–$8,432,500
Grant Average: $10,000–$50,000
Applications: Grants are generally initiated by the trustees. Initial approach should be by a one-page letter.

The Peter & Mary Muth Foundation
c/o Kushner, Smith, Joanou & Gregson, L.L.P.
2 Park Plaza, Suite 550
Irvine, CA 92614-8515
Contact: Verlyn N. Jensen, President
Geographic Giving Pattern: Primarily California.
Special Interest: Catholic giving, religious organizations, religious welfare, diocesan support, education, and other charitable activities.
Assets: $1,283,760 (1998)
Grant Total: $360,000
Grant Range: $5,000–$100,000
Limitations: No grants to individuals.
Applications: Contributes to pre-selected organizations only. Applications are not accepted.

Notre Dame Foundation Trust

1600 School Street, Suite 103
Moraga, CA 94556
Contact: Donald Potter
Geographic Giving Pattern: Primarily California.
Special Interests: Elementary education, family services Catholic church support, and Catholic agencies.
Assets: $183,905 (1997)
Gifts Received: $24,000
Grant Total: $67,975
Grant Range: $15,000–$20,000
Limitations: No grants to individuals.
Applications: Contributes to pre-selected organizations only. Applications are not accepted.

Robert Stewart Odell and Helen Pfeiffer Odell Fund

420 Montgomery Street, 5th Floor
San Francisco, CA 94104
(415) 396-3215
Contact: Eugene Ranghiasci, Vice President, Wells Fargo Bank
Geographic Giving Pattern: National, with an emphasis on San Francisco, California.
Special Interest: Higher and theological education, Protestant and Catholic church support and agencies, parochial education, religious welfare, and youth services.
Assets: $52,522,443 (1998)
Grant Total: $1,922,287
Grant Range: $1,000–$50,000
Limitations: No grants to individuals.
Applications: Initial approach should be by letter.

J. J. O'Neill Foundation

P.O. Box 8585
Rancho Santa Fe, CA 92067
Contact: Margaret H. O'Neill, Trustee
Geographic Giving Pattern: Primarily New York, New York.
Special Interest: Catholic high schools.
Assets: $2,573,401 (1998)
Grant Total: $50,000
Grant Range: $10,000–$20,000

Limitations: No grants to individuals.
Applications: Contributes to pre-selected organizations only. Applications are not accepted.

Outrageous Foundation, Inc.
2 Sixth Avenue
San Francisco, CA 94118-1324
Contact: Robert P. McGrath, President
Geographic Giving Pattern: Primarily northern California.
Special Interests: Education, theater, youth services, and Catholic agencies and churches.
Assets: $3,935,444 (1998)
Grant Total: $211,500
Grant Range: $500–$50,000
Limitations: No grants to individuals.
Applications: Contributes to pre-selected organizations only. Applications are not accepted.

Pacific Western Foundation
707 Wilshire Boulevard, Suite 6000
Los Angeles, CA 90017
(213) 830-3208
Contact: Joseph T. Nally, President
Geographic Giving Pattern: Primarily California.
Special Interest: Catholic higher and secondary education, church support, hospitals, and medical research.
Assets: $5,034,609 (1998)
Grant Total: $200,250
Grant Range: $500–$80,000
Applications: Initial approach should be by proposal. There are no deadlines.

The Ralph M. Parsons Foundation
1055 Wilshire Boulevard, Suite 1701
Los Angeles, CA 90017
(213) 482-3185
(213) 482-8878 (fax)
Contact: Christine Sisley, Executive Director
Geographic Giving Pattern: Limited to Los Angeles County, California.

Special Interests: Higher and precollegiate education, social services, cultural and civic projects, and health services for disadvantaged populations.
Assets: $320,109,197 (1998)
Grant Total: $14,561,199
Grant Range: $500–$2,000,000
Grant Average: $5,000–$15,000
Limitations: No grants to individuals. No support for sectarian religious purposes. No support for endowments.
Applications: Initial approach should be by letter. There are no deadlines.

Mary R. Payden and Joseph R. Payden Foundation

Eleven Sea Colony
Santa Monica, CA 90405
Contact: William R. Payden
Geographic Giving Pattern: Primarily California.
Special Interests: Arts and cultural programs, healthcare, human services, federated giving programs, charitable giving, Catholic church support and Catholic agencies.
Assets: $2,279,033 (1998)
Gifts Received: $564,662
Grant Total: $83,982
Grant Range: $25–$12,000
Limitations: No grants to individuals.
Applications: An application form is not required. There are no deadlines.

Thomas P. Pike Foundation

301 East Colorado, Suite 430
Pasadena, CA 91101
(626) 440-1633
Contact: Mary P. Coquillard, President
Geographic Giving Pattern: Primarily southern California.
Special Interest: Education, Catholic church support, Catholic agencies, alcoholism, and human services.
Assets: $6,606 (1998)
Grant Total: $16,851
Grant Range: $50–$1,170
Limitations: No grants to individuals. No loans.

Applications: Initial approach should be by letter. There are no deadlines.

The Riordan Foundation

300 South Grand Avenue, 29th Floor
Los Angeles, CA 90071
(213) 229-8402
(213) 229-5061 (fax)
www.riordanfnd.org
Contact: Mary Odell
Geographic Giving Pattern: Primarily California.
Special Interest: Early childhood education, prevention of illiteracy, youth development, and some Catholic giving.
Assets: $5,822,113 (1998)
Grant Total: $1,297,001
Grant Range: $185–$250,000
Grant Average: $1,000–$10,000
Limitations: No grants to individuals or for endowment funds, capital campaigns, or building funds.
Applications: Initial approach should be by letter. There are no deadlines.

Mary Stuart Rogers Foundation

c/o Stockton & Sadler
P.O. Box 3153
Modesto, CA 95353
(626) 446-2563
Contact: John Stuart Rogers, President
Geographic Giving Pattern: Primarily California.
Special Interest: Education, Catholic church and diocesan support, Catholic agencies, children, youth, and social services.
Assets: $114,063,094 (1998)
Gifts Received: $4,485
Grant Total: $10,614,380
Grant Range: $1,000–$1,500,000
Applications: Contributes to pre-selected organizations only. Applications are not accepted.

George H. Sandy Foundation
c/o Union Bank of California
P.O. Box 45000
San Francisco, CA 94145
Contact: Chester R. MacPhee, Jr.
Geographic Giving Pattern: Primarily the San Francisco Bay Area, California.
Special Interests: Activities and programs benefiting the disabled and the infirm, some support for Catholic schools and agencies.
Assets: $16,682,192 (1998)
Grant Total: $836,000
Grant Range: $1,000–$25,000
Limitations: No grants to individuals.
Applications: Initial approach should be by letter. There are no deadlines.

George W. and Faye Batton Saul Family Fund
c/o Bailard, Biehl, and Kaiser
950 Tower Lane, Suite 1900
Foster City, CA 94404-2131
Contact: Fay E. Batten Saul, President and Treasurer
Geographic Giving Pattern: Primarily the San Francisco Bay Area, California.
Special Interests: Higher education, healthcare, health association, human services, and Catholic agencies and churches.
Assets: $167,357 (1998)
Gifts Received: $150,000
Grant Total: $208,500
Grant Range: $500–$50,000
Limitations: No grants to individuals.
Applications: Contributes to pre-selected organizations only. Applications are not accepted.

Rudi Schulte Family Foundation
2927 De La Vina Street, Suite C
Santa Barbara, CA 93105-3362
Contact: Rudolf R. Schulte, President
Geographic Giving Pattern: Limited to California.

Special Interests: Human services, elementary education, mental health, counseling and support groups, rehabilitation, Catholic church support and Catholic agencies.
Assets: $1,690,707 (1997)
Gifts Received: $1,557,656
Grant Total: $25,000
Grant Range: $1,000–$5,000
Limitations: No grants to individuals.
Applications: Contributes to pre-selected organizations only. Applications are not accepted.

The Schwab Family Foundation
2233 Watt Avenue, Suite 295
Sacramento, CA 95825
(916) 484-0282
Contact: Clare M. Buckey
Geographic Giving Pattern: Primarily northern California.
Special Interests: Human services, Catholic church support, AIDS, food services, youth and family services, aging, the economically disadvantaged, and Catholic agencies.
Grant Total: $101,904 (1996)
Grant Range: $100–$49,035
Limitations: No grants to individuals.
Applications: Initial approach should be by letter. There are no deadlines.

Semper Charitable Foundation
1733 Fir Hill Drive
Saint Helena, CA 94574
(707) 963-3393
(707) 963-9881 (fax)
Contact: Mary Cunningham, President
Geographic Giving Pattern: International.
Special Interests: Sanctity of life, crisis pregnancy support, Catholic education, lay leadership in the Catholic church, early childhood education, Christian family values, truth in media, chastity, and initiatives against pornography.
Assets: $1,534,339 (1999)
Grant Total: $90,700
Grant Range: $100–$10,000

Applications: Applications are by invitation only. Contributes to pre-selected organizations only. Applications are not accepted.

The Shea Company Foundation
655 Brea Canyon Road
Walnut, CA 91789
Contact: John F. Shea, President
Geographic Giving Pattern: Primarily California.
Special Interest: Catholic church support, religious associations, education, and the disabled.
Assets: $4,810,727 (1997)
Grant Total: $241,823
Grant Range: $225–$26,250
Limitations: No grants to individuals.
Applications: Contributes to pre-selected organizations only. Applications are not accepted.

J. F. Shea Company Foundation
655 Brea Canyon Road
Walnut, CA 91789-0489
Contact: John F. Shea, President
Geographic Giving Pattern: Primarily California.
Special Interest: Catholic church support, Catholic welfare, religious associations, elementary and secondary education, and human services.
Assets: $286,537 (1997)
Gifts Received: $13,748
Grant Total: $184,040
Grant Range: $50–$50,000
Limitations: No grants to individuals.
Applications: Contributes to pre-selected organizations only. Applications are not accepted.

The Shea Foundation
655 Brea Canyon Road
Walnut, CA 91789
Contact: John F. Shea, President
Geographic Giving Pattern: Primarily California.
Special Interests: Education, hospitals, public affairs, public education, disabled, Catholic agencies and churches.

Assets: $4,810,777 (1997)
Grant Total: $241,823
Grant Range: $225–$26,250
Limitations: No grants to individuals.
Applications: Contributes to pre-selected organizations only.
Applications are not accepted.

Edmund and Mary Shea Foundation
655 Brea Canyon Road
Walnut, CA 91789
Contact: Edmund H. Shea, Jr., President
Geographic Giving Pattern: Primarily California.
Special Interest: Education, Catholic and Protestant church support
and agencies, cancer research, and the disabled.
Assets: $7,803,265 (1997)
Grant Total: $324,504
Grant Range: $100–$100,000
Limitations: No grants to individuals.
Applications: Contributes to pre-selected organizations only.
Applications are not accepted.

The John & Dorothy Shea Foundation
655 Brea Canyon Road
Walnut, CA 91789
(909) 594-0941
Contact: John F. Shea, President
Geographic Giving Pattern: Primarily California.
Special Interest: Catholic churches, archdiocesan support, and
secondary and higher education.
Assets: $15,374,816 (1997)
Grant Total: $612,862
Grant Range: $50–$232,021
Limitations: No grants to individuals.
Applications: Contributes to pre-selected organizations only.
Applications are not accepted.

Peter and Carolyn Shea Foundation
655 Brea Canyon Road
Walnut, CA 91789
Contact: Peter O. Shea, President

Geographic Giving Pattern: Primarily California.
Special Interest: Education, substance abuse services, Catholic church support, and Catholic agencies.
Assets: $3,221,347 (1998)
Grant Total: $73,015
Grant Range: $15–$25,000
Limitations: No grants to individuals.
Applications: Contributes to pre-selected organizations only. Applications are not accepted.

Y. & H. Soda Foundation

Two Theatre Square, Suite 211
Orinda, CA 94563-3346
(925) 253-2630
(925) 253-1814 (fax)
Email: jnm@silcon.com
Contact: Judith Murphy, CEO and President
Geographic Giving Pattern: Primarily Alameda and Contra Costa counties, California.
Special Interest: Education, healthcare, social services, youth, and Catholic religious organizations.
Assets: $95,444,251 (1998)
Grant Total: $4,190,087
Grant Range: $100–$560,100
Grant Average: $500–$20,000
Limitations: No grants to individuals. No support for annual fundraising drives, faculty chairs, or operating expenses. No support for animal welfare, the arts, the environment, national medical research organizations, private foundations, or political organizations.
Applications: Initial approach should be by letter. The deadlines are February 28, May 31, August 31, and November 30.

Trust Funds, Incorporated

100 Broadway, Third Floor
San Francisco, CA 94111-1404
(415) 434-3323
(415) 434-2936 (fax)
Contact: James T. Healy, President

Geographic Giving Pattern: Limited to the San Francisco Bay Area and, by exception, to projects of national or global scope which affect the Catholic church.

Special Interest: Catholic projects and institutions in the fields of religion, education, and social welfare.

Assets: $5,094,378 (1998)

Grant Total: $262,795

Grant Range: $80–$27,500

Limitations: Generally no grants to individuals. No grants for endowments, annual campaigns, or to organizations which draw substantial public support. No loans.

Applications: Initial approach should be by letter. Four copies of the proposal should be submitted. An application form is required for schools. The deadlines are quarterly.

Wayne & Gladys Valley Foundation

1939 Harrison Street, Suite 510

Oakland, CA 94612-3532

(510) 466-6060

Contact: Stephen M. Chandler, President and Executive Director

Geographic Giving Pattern: Primarily Alameda, Contra Costa and Santa Clara counties, California.

Special Interest: Catholic giving, including Catholic welfare and schools; some support for hospitals, recreation, youth, and the arts.

Assets: $343,585,786 (1998)

Grant Total: $10,431,253

Grant Range: $600–$1,000,000

Grant Average: $10,000–$200,000

Applications: Initial approach should be by letter or telephone requesting guidelines. There are no deadlines.

Von der Ahe Foundation

4605 Lankershim Boulevard, Suite 707

North Hollywood, CA 91602

Contact: William Von der Ahe, President

Geographic Giving Pattern: Primarily California.

Special Interests: Human services, arts and cultural programs, education, healthcare, alcoholism, healthcare, public administration, Catholic church support and Catholic agencies.

Assets: $8,905,590 (1998)
Grant Total: $266,850
Grant Range: $250–$50,000
Limitations: No grants to individuals.
Applications: Contributes to pre-selected organizations only.
Applications are not accepted.

Theodore Albert Von der Ahe, Jr. Trust

4605 Lankershim Boulevard, Suite 707
North Hollywood, CA 91602
Contact: Thomas R. Von der Ahe, President
Geographic Giving Pattern: Primarily California.
Special Interest: Catholic religious institutions, church support, health
and welfare services, education, and international affairs.
Assets: $8,905,590 (1998)
Grant Total: $266,850
Grant Range: $250–$50,000
Limitations: No grants to individuals.
Applications: Grants are initiated by the trustees. Applications are not
accepted.

Henry and Carol Zeiter Charitable Foundation

255 E. Weber Avenue
Stockton, CA 95202-2406
(209) 466-5566
Contact: Henry Zeiter, President
Geographic Giving Pattern: Primarily California.
Special Interests: Scholarships, Catholic church support and Catholic
agencies.
Assets: $1,516,255 (1998)
Gifts Received: $316,815
Grant Total: $54,599
Grant Range: $500–$2,000
Applications: Initial approach should be by letter. There are no
deadlines.

COLORADO

The Charter Fund
370 17th Street, Suite 5300
Denver, CO 80202-5653
(303) 572-1727
Contact: Jeanette Montoya
Geographic Giving Pattern: Limited to Colorado.
Special Interest: Education, social services, healthcare, Catholic
agencies, and Catholic churches.
Assets: $97,914 (1998)
Gifts Received: $185,000
Grant Total: $272,932
Grant Average: $100–$90,000
Applications: Unsolicited requests for grants are not considered.

Harmes C. Fishback Foundation Trust
8 Village Road
Englewood, CO 80110-4908
Contact: Katherine H. Stapleton, Treasurer
Geographic Giving Pattern: Primarily the metropolitan Denver area.
Special Interests: Higher education, museums, arts and cultural
programs, medical care, children and youth services, Catholic agencies
and churches.
Assets: $3,409,971 (1997)
Grant Total: $218,900
Grant Range: $400–$131,000
Limitations: No grants to individuals.
Applications: Initial approach should be by letter including one copy
of proposal. There are no deadlines.

The Fugere Family Foundation
45 Wild Horse Canyon
Boulder, CO 80304
Contact: James Fugere, President
Geographic Giving Pattern: Primarily Colorado.
Special Interests: Human services, the economically disadvantaged,
homelessness, Catholic church support and Catholic agencies.
Assets: $3,320,539 (1999)
Grant Total: $73,799

Grant Range: $250–$25,000
Limitations: No grants to individuals.
Applications: Contributes to pre-selected organizations only.
Applications are not accepted.

Helen K. and Arthur E. Johnson Foundation
1700 Broadway, Room 2302
Denver, CO 80290-1039
(800) 232-9931
(303) 861-4127
(303) 861-0607 (fax)
www.johnsonfoundation.net
Contact: Stan Kamprath, Executive Director or Brigit Ann Davis,
Program Officer
Geographic Giving Pattern: Limited to Colorado.
Special Interests: Education, community and social services, and
youth services.
Assets: $164,771,943 (1998)
Grant Total: $5,607,981
Grant Range: $500–$200,000
Grant Average: $5,000–$30,000
Limitations: No grants to individuals. No support for endowments.
Applications: Initial approach should be by letter or preliminary
proposal. The deadlines are January 1, April 1, July 1, and October 1.

Kenny Foundation, Inc.
1701 South 124th Street
Broomfield, CO 80020-9652
Contact: Robert Gryzmala, President and Jean M. Gryzmala,
Secretary
Geographic Giving Pattern: Limited to Colorado.
Special Interests: Education, child services, Catholic agencies and
services.
Assets: $1,062,403 (1998)
Gifts Received: $117,654
Grant Total: $349,000
Grant Range: $5,000–$202,000
Limitations: No grants to individuals.
Applications: Contributes to pre-selected organizations only.
Applications are not accepted.

Merrion Foundation

4345 Xavier Street
Denver, CO 80212
Contact: John K. Merrion, Mary Ann Merrion, or Michael P. Merrion, Managers
Geographic Giving Pattern: Primarily in Illinois.
Special Interest: Catholic organizations, education, social services, and churches.
Assets: $3,350,310 (1997)
Gifts Received: $59,000
Grant Total: $124,650
Limitations: No grants to individuals.
Applications: Contributes to pre-selected organizations only. Applications are not accepted.

The J. K. Mullen Foundation

333 Logan Street, Suite 100
Denver, CO 80203
(303) 722-3557
Contact: John F. Malo, President
Geographic Giving Pattern: Primarily Denver, Colorado.
Special Interest: Higher and secondary education, health and hospitals, Catholic-affiliated organizations, and seminaries.
Assets: $5,665,440 (1998)
Grant Total: $327,850
Grant Range: $175–$30,000
Limitations: No grants to individuals.
Applications: Initial approach should be by proposal letter or applicants may use the Colorado Common Grant Application Form. The deadline is June 1.

Priester Foundation

25 South Lane
Englewood, CO 80110
Contact: John Priester, Secretary
Geographic Giving Pattern: Giving on a national and international basis, with some emphasis on Colorado.
Special Interests: Arts and cultural programs, the economically disadvantaged, Catholic church support and Catholic agencies.

Assets: $604,506 (1997)
Gifts Received: $529,844
Grant Total: $52,250
Grant Range: $100–$13,000
Limitations: No grants to individuals.
Applications: No application forms are required. There are no deadlines.

Saeman Family Foundation, Inc.

270 St. Paul Street, Suite 300
Denver, CO 80206
(303) 316-7182
Contact: Catherine Saeman Bortle, Executive Director
Geographic Giving Pattern: Primarily Colorado.
Special Interest: Education, hospitals, children, youth, Catholic church support, and Catholic agencies.
Assets: $469,526 (1997)
Gifts Received: $947,771
Grant Total: $452,411
Grant Range: $100–$60,000
Limitations: No grants to individuals.
Applications: Contributes to pre-selected organizations only. Applications are not accepted.

Eleanore Mullen Weckbaugh Foundation

P.O. Box 3486
Englewood, CO 80155-3486
(303) 471-1301
Contact: Therese A. Polakovic, President
Geographic Giving Pattern: Primarily Colorado.
Special Interest: Catholic church support, missionary programs, welfare funds, education, hospitals, health agencies, and other charitable giving.
Assets: $10,132,043 (1998)
Grant Total: $316,000
Grant Range: $1,000–$20,000
Limitations: No grants to individuals.
Applications: Initial approach should be in writing, stating the purpose of the grant request. An application form is required. The foundation accepts the Colorado Common Grant Application Form. The deadlines

are February 1, May 1, August 1, and November 1. The application address is P.O. Box 31678, Aurora, CO 80041.

CONNECTICUT

Bodenwein Public Benevolent Foundation
c/o Sheilah Roston
Fleet Bank
777 Main Street, CTMOH22B
Hartford, CT 06115
(860) 986-7696
Contact: Marjorie Alexandre
Geographic Giving Pattern: Limited to Connecticut.
Special Interest: Social service and health agencies, arts and culture, children and youth, community development, education, Catholic church support, and Catholic agencies.
Assets: $530,935 (1998)
Grant Total: $298,946
Grant Range: $450–$20,000
Grant Average: $972–$25,000
Applications: Initial approach should be by telephone. An application form is required. The deadlines are May 15 and November 15. Applicants are limited to only one submission per year.

Burlingame Foundation
c/o Blair and Potts
P.O. Box 1214
Stamford, CT 06904-1214
Contact: Genevieve Burlingame and John Burlingame, Trustees
Geographic Giving Pattern: Primarily Massachusetts.
Special Interests: Higher education, education, human services, Catholic church support and Catholic agencies.
Assets: $1,703,802 (1997)
Gifts Received: $160,468
Grant Total: $75,900
Limitations: No grants to individuals.
Applications: Contributes to pre-selected organizations only. Applications are not accepted.

The Herman & Henrietta Denzler Charitable Trust

c/o Southport Tax and Accounting
59 Jackson Drive
Trumbull, CT 06611
(203) 888-6278
Contact: Michael J. Boyd, Trustee or Patricia Severson, Trustee
Geographic Giving Pattern: Primarily New York and Connecticut.
Special Interest: Education; aid to people in need, especially the elderly and the infirm; Catholic agencies, and church support.
Assets: $8,578,583 (1997)
Grant Total: $410,400
Grant Range: $500–$75,000
Limitations: No grant to individuals.
Applications: Initial approach should be by letter. There are no deadlines. The application address is 2 Jenny Lane, Oxford, CT 06478.

Doty Family Foundation

123-4 Richmond Hill Road
New Canaan, CT 06840
Contact: Anne Marie Paine, Secretary and Trustee
Geographic Giving Pattern: National.
Special Interest: Support for churches and charitable organizations with which members of the family are involved.
Assets: $9,356,387 (1998)
Gifts Received: $301,875
Grant Total: $740,425
Grant Range: $150–$200,000
Grant Average: $150–$12,000
Limitations: No grants to individuals.
Applications: Contributes to pre-selected organizations only. Applications are not accepted.

The Catherine and Henry J. Gaisman Foundation

44 North Stanwich Road
Greenwich, CT 06830
Contact: Catherine V. Gaisman, President
Geographic Giving Pattern: Primarily New York.
Special Interest: Hospitals, medical research, Catholic churches, and diocesan support.

Assets: $52,747,741 (1998)
Grant Total: $1,984,135
Grant Range: $200–$1,518,016
Limitations: No grants to individuals.
Applications: Contributes to pre-selected organizations only.
Applications are not accepted.

Mabel Burchard Fischer Grant Foundation

c/o Cummings & Lockwood
P.O. Box 120
Stamford, CT 06904
Contact: Malcolm J. Edgerton, Jr. and Robert A. Beer, Trustees
Geographic Giving Pattern: Primarily Connecticut.
Special Interest: Education, hospitals, Protestant and Catholic church
support, the arts, and cultural programs.
Assets: $7,589,246 (1998)
Grant Total: $285,500
Grant Range: $2,500–$10,000
Limitations: No grants to individuals.
Applications: Initial approach should be by letter. There are no
deadlines. The application address is c/o White & Case, 1155 Avenue
of the Americas, New York, NY 10036. Tel. (212) 819-8743.

The Maximilian E. & Marion O. Hoffman Foundation, Inc.

970 Farmington Avenue, Suite 203
West Hartford, CT 06107-2102
(860) 521-2949
Contact: Doris C. Chaho, President
Geographic Giving Pattern: National, with an emphasis on the
northeast.
Special Interests: Secondary and higher education, hospitals, Catholic
church support and Catholic higher educational institutions.
Assets: $42,938,577 (1997)
Grant Total: $1,851,324
Grant Range: $500–$250,000
Grant Average: $5,000–$50,000
Limitations: No grants to individuals.
Applications: An application form is required. There are no deadlines.

The Huisking Foundation, Inc.
P.O. Box 368
Botsford, CT 06404-0368
(203) 426-8618
Contact: Frank R. Huisking, Treasurer
Geographic Giving Pattern: National.
Special Interest: Catholic higher and secondary education, church and diocesan support, family support, religious welfare funds, hospitals, religious associations, conservation, the arts, museums, and animal protection.
Assets: $11,307,572 (1997)
Grant Total: $562,184
Grant Range: $200–$55,000
Limitations: No grants to individuals.
Applications: Initial approach should be by letter. Proposals should be submitted in February or August.

The John R. Kennedy Foundation, Inc.
125 Elm Street
New Canaan, CT 06840
(203) 966-5622
Contact: John R. Kennedy, President
Geographic Giving Pattern: Primarily Connecticut and New York.
Special Interest: Higher education, healthcare, social services, peace, Catholic church support, and Catholic agencies.
Assets: $6,361,128 (1994)
Grant Total: $224,115
Grant Range: $15–$50,000
Limitations: No grants to individuals.
Applications: Contributes to pre-selected organizations only. Applications are not accepted.

Keys Foundation, Inc.
P.O. Box 326
Windsor Locks, CT 06096
Contact: Raymond A. Roncari, President
Geographic Giving Pattern: Primarily Connecticut, some giving in Rome, Italy.
Special Interests: Catholic church support and Catholic agencies.
Assets: $164,916 (1996)

Grant Total: $57,900
Grant Range: $400–$25,000
Limitations: Grants to individuals awarded locally only.
Applications: Initial approach should be by letter.

John Jay Mann Foundation, Inc.

c/o Robinson & Cole
80 Field Point Road
Greenwich, CT 06830
Contact: John Jay Mann, President
Geographic Giving Pattern: Primarily Connecticut and New York.
Special Interest: Higher education, Catholic churches, Catholic agencies, hospitals, and human services.
Assets: $1,443,456 (1997)
Grant Total: $67,300
Grant Range: $300–$15,000
Applications: Grant proposals should be sent to the following address: 2200 South Ocean Lane, Fort Lauderdale, FL 33316. There are no deadlines.

The Meriden Foundation

c/o Webster Trust Co.
346 Main Street
Kensington, CT 06037-2653
(860) 829-3900
Contact: Jeffrey F. Otis, Secretary
Geographic Giving Pattern: Limited to the Meriden-Wallingford, Connecticut area.
Special Interest: Higher education, healthcare, youth and social services, Catholic church support, and Catholic agencies.
Assets: $21,474,424 (1998)
Gifts Received: $78,704
Grant Total: $768,465
Grant Range: $300–$43,492
Applications: Initial approach should be by letter. There are no deadlines.

The Napier Foundation
c/o Prudential Securities, Inc.
185 Asylum Street, City Place II
Hartford, CT 06103
Contact: Gerald B. Goldberg, Investment Advisor
Geographic Giving Pattern: Primarily Meriden, Connecticut.
Description: The Napier Foundation is a corporate foundation of the Napier Company.
Special Interest: Education, children, youth, Catholic church support, and Catholic social service agencies.
Assets: $4,300,000 (1998)
Grant Total: $150,000
Limitations: No program-related investments or loans.
Applications: Initial approach should be by letter. Nine copies of the proposal are requested. There are no deadlines. The application address is c/o Michael Consolini, Napier Park, Meriden, CT 06450.

Lucien B. and Katherine E. Price Foundation, Inc.
896 Main Street
P.O. Box 790
Manchester, CT 06040
(203) 643-4129
Contact: Rev. Francis V. Krukowski, President
Geographic Giving Pattern: Primarily Connecticut.
Special Interest: Catholic church support, religious associations, church-related schools, colleges, and hospitals.
Assets: $4,744,900 (1997)
Grant Total: $181,500
Grant Range: $500–$31,000
Applications: Initial approach should be by letter stating purpose.

Ray H. & Pauline Sullivan Foundation
c/o Fleet National Bank
777 Main Street – CTMOH18A
Hartford, CT 06115
(860) 986-4071
Contact: Sheilah B. Rostow, Vice President, Fleet National Bank
Geographic Giving Pattern: Primarily Connecticut.
Special Interest: Catholic parochial and secondary schools, scholarships, Catholic charities, churches, and diocesan support.

Assets: $14,367,334 (1998)
Grant Total: $584,785
Grant Range: $2,000–$152,810
Applications: An application form is required for scholarships and loans. The deadline is May 1.

DELAWARE

Arguild Foundation
P.O. Box 2207
1220 Market Street, 10th Floor
Wilmington, DE 19899
(302) 658-9141
Contact: Arthur G. Connolly, President
Geographic Giving Pattern: Primarily Delaware, especially Wilmington.
Special Interest: Education, welfare funds, Catholic organizations, and churches.
Assets: $6,967,829 (1997)
Grant Total: $264,108
Grant Range: $108–$15,000
Limitations: No grants to individuals.
Applications: Initial approach should be by letter. There are no deadlines.

David G. Burton, Successor Trustee
1104 Philadelphia Pike
Wilmington, DE 19809
Contact: David G. Burton, Trustee
Geographic Giving Pattern: Primarily the Delmarva Penninsula, Delaware area.
Special Interest: Catholic church support, and Catholic social, family, and human services.
Assets: $2,495,055 (1998)
Grant Total: $170,000
Grant Range: $350–$50,000
Limitations: No grants to individuals.
Applications: Initial approach should be by letter. There are no deadlines. The application address is 411 N. Rehobeth Boulevard, Milford, DE 19963. Tel. (302) 422-3041.

The Cawley Family Foundation

1100 North King Street
Wilmington, DE 19884-0141
(302) 453-6875
Contact: Charles M. Cawley, President
Geographic Giving Pattern: Primarily the East Coast, with an emphasis on Delaware.
Special Interest: Secondary and higher education, including Catholic schools and universities.
Assets: $3,054,387 (1998)
Gifts Received: $2,012,400
Grant Total: $875,400
Grant Range: $5,000–$200,000
Limitations: No grants to individuals.
Applications: Contributes to pre-selected organizations only. Applications are not accepted.

The Hazel Dell Foundation

103 Foulk Road, Suite 202
Wilmington, DE 19803
Contact: Joy S. Dunlop, President
Geographic Giving Pattern: Primarily Connecticut, New Jersey, and California.
Special Interest: Health, hospitals, education, recreation, public affairs, and local fire and police departments; some Catholic giving.
Assets: $5,689,862 (1997)
Grant Total: $140,000
Grant Range: $300–$17,000
Limitations: No grants to individuals.
Applications: Contributes to pre-selected organizations only. Applications are not accepted.

Laffey-McHugh Foundation

1220 Market Building
P.O. Box 2207
Wilmington, DE 19899-2207
(302) 658-9141
Contact: Arthur G. Connolly Jr., President
Geographic Giving Pattern: Primarily Delaware, with an emphasis on Wilmington.

Special Interest: Catholic church support and church-related institutions including schools, welfare agencies, religious associations, and child welfare agencies.
Assets: $88,353,636 (1998)
Grant Total: $3,459,233
Grant Range: $3,000–$235,000
Limitations: No grants to individuals or for operating budgets, endowment funds, research, or conferences. No loans. No program-related investments.
Applications: Initial approach should be by proposal letter. The deadlines are in April and October.

MBNA America Bank Corporate Contributions Program
MBNA America Bank, N.A.
M.S. 2811
Wilmington, DE 19884-2811
(302) 432-3551
Contact: Ralph Kuebler
Description: MBNA America Bank Corporate Contributions Program is a corporate giving program.
Special Interest: Arts and culture, higher education, libraries, public administration, Catholic agencies, and churches.
Assets: $4,338,922 (1997)
Gifts Received: $6,476,723
Grant Total: $2,549,553
Grant Range: $30–$652,500
Applications: Initial approach should be by letter or telephone requesting application guidelines. There are no deadlines.

Morania Foundation, Inc.
c/o J. P. Morgan Services, Inc.
P.O. Box 6089
Newark, DE 19714-6089
Contact: William J. McCormack, President
Geographic Giving Pattern: Primarily New York.
Special Interest: Catholic church-related institutions, foreign missions, and welfare funds.
Assets: $11,152,812 (1999)
Grant Total: $610,000
Grant Range: $2,000–$180,000

Limitations: No grants to individuals.
Applications: Initial approach should be by proposal. There are no deadlines. The application address is c/o J. P. Morgan & Co. Inc., 345 Park Avenue, New York, NY 10154. Tel. (212) 464-2597.

Raskob Foundation for Catholic Activities, Inc.

P.O. Box 4019
Wilmington, DE 19807
(302) 655-4440
(302) 655-3223 (fax)
Contact: Frederick J. Perella, Executive Vice President
Geographic Giving Pattern: National and international.
Special Interest: Institutions and organizations identified with the Catholic Church; wide spectrum of Catholic ministries and activities.
Assets: $145,528,416 (1998)
Grant Total: $6,309,493
Grant Range: $250–$85,000
Grant Average: $5,000–$15,000
Limitations: No grants to individuals or for endowment funds, deficit financing, continuing support, annual campaigns, tuition, scholarships, or building projects prior to the start or after the completion of construction.
Applications: Initial approach should be by letter or telephone requesting application guidelines and form. An application form is required. U.S. applicants must be listed in *The Official Catholic Directory.* Applications are accepted from June 8–August 8 and from December 8–February 8.

Romill Foundation

c/o Wilmington Trust Company
1100 North Market Street
Wilmington, DE 19890
Contact: Lawrence Heagney, Treasurer
Geographic Giving Pattern: Primarily Spartanburg County, South Carolina.
Special Interest: Education, community development, public interest organizations, Catholic church support, and Catholic agencies.
Assets: $2,993,850 (1997)
Gifts Received: $123,391
Grant Total: $664,624

Grant Range: $1,000–$255,000
Grant Average: $2,500–$65,000
Limitations: No grants to individuals.
Applications: Contributes to pre-selected organizations only.
Applications are not accepted.

DISTRICT OF COLUMBIA

Anthony and Anna L. Carozza Foundation
Northwest Station
P.O. Box 42133
Washington, D.C. 20015-0733
Contact: M.C. Volpe, Vice President and Treasurer
Geographic Giving Pattern: Primarily Washington, D.C.
Special Interests: Performing arts, cultural programs, secondary
education, hospitals, and Catholic federated giving programs.
Assets: $2,232,257 (1999)
Grant Total: $163,700
Grant Range: $1,000–$50,000
Limitations: No grants to individuals.
Applications: Contributes to pre-selected organizations only.
Applications are not accepted.

Mary and Daniel Loughran Foundation, Inc.
c/o Bank of America
1501 Pennsylvania Avenue, N.W., 3rd Floor
Washington, D.C. 20013
(202) 624-8251
Contact: J. Michael Brown
Geographic Giving Pattern: Limited to Washington, D.C., Virginia,
and Maryland.
Special Interest: Education, youth, social service agencies, the arts
and cultural programs; some religious giving and church support.
Assets: $15,622,359 (1998)
Grant Average: $5,000–$10,000
Limitations: No grants to individuals or for capital or endowment
funds. No loans.
Applications: Initial approach should be by proposal. Grant proposals
should be submitted between January and May. The deadline is May 1.

The Loyola Foundation, Inc.
308 C Street N.E.
Washington, D.C. 20002
(202) 546-9400
Contact: Albert G. McCarthy III, Secretary and Executive Director
Geographic Giving Pattern: National and international, primarily in developing nations.
Special Interest: Catholic overseas missionary work, church and diocesan support, and other Catholic activities of interest to the trustees.
Assets: $35,829,201 (1999)
Grant Total: $1,410,254
Grant Range: $100–$37,500
Grant Average: $500–$50,000
Limitations: Grants are made in the U.S. only to institutions or organizations of special interest to the trustees. No grants to individuals or for endowment funds, operating budgets, emergency funds, research, continuing support, deficit financing, annual budgets, scholarships, publications, or conferences. No support for minor seminaries. No loans. Large scale projects are not considered.
Applications: Initial approach should be by letter. An application form is required. U.S. applicants must be listed in *The Official Catholic Directory*. The deadlines are April 30 and October 31.

William G. McGowan Charitable Fund
P.O. Box 40515
Washington, D.C. 20016-0515
(202) 364-5030
(202) 364-3382 (fax)
Email: goodric@aol.com
www.mcgowanfund.com
Contact: Bernard Goodrich, Executive Director
Geographic Giving Pattern: Northeastern Pennsylvania; Chicago, Illinois metropolitan area; western New York State from Syracuse westward; central and northern California from north of San Luis Obispo; the area of Texas bounded by Dallas, San Antonio, and Houston; the Washington metropolitan area; and the Kansas City metropolitan area.

Special Interest: Education, medical research, and aid to underprivileged youth.
Assets: $162,906,029 (1999)
Grant Total: $7,231,347
Applications: Initial approach should be by proposal. An application form is required. The deadlines are February 1, May 1, August 1, and November 1.

McGowan Gin Rosica Family Foundation, Inc.
3626 Prospect Street, NW
Washington, D.C. 20007
Contact: Sue Gin McGowan, Secretary
Geographic Giving Pattern: Primarily Aurora, Illinois.
Special Interests: The arts, youth, social services, and Catholic programs.
Assets: $2,130,333 (1998)
Grant Total: $77,200
Grant Range: $500–$17,250
Limitations: No grants to individuals.
Applications: Contributes to pre-selected organizations only. Applications are not accepted.

FLORIDA

Anthony R. Abraham Foundation, Inc.
6600 S.W. 57th Avenue
Miami, FL 33143
(305) 665-2222
Contact: Anthony R. Abraham, Chair
Geographic Giving Pattern: Primarily Florida, especially Miami.
Special Interest: Catholic giving, church and archdiocesan support, youth agencies, medical research, and a children's hospital.
Assets: $43,307,354 (1998)
Grant Total: $1,202,341
Grant Range: $25–$545,100
Limitations: No grants to individuals.
Applications: Initial approach should be by letter. There are no deadlines.

The Amaturo Foundation, Inc.
3101 North Federal Highway, Suite 601
Fort Lauderdale, FL 33306-1042
(954) 565-1411
(954) 565-1311 (fax)
Contact: Jeanette E. Nickel, Director
Geographic Giving Pattern: Primarily Florida.
Special Interest: Catholic charities, education, child welfare, hospitals, and performing arts.
Assets: $22,164,956 (1999)
Gifts Received: $156,890
Grant Total: $1,105,061
Grant Range: $100–$163,000
Applications: Initial approach should be by written proposal. There are no deadlines for grant proposals.

J. H. Baroco Foundation, Inc.
P.O. Box 10729
Pensacola, FL 32524-0729
Contact: J. H. Baroco, Sr., President
Geographic Giving Pattern: Primarily Florida.
Special Interest: Health, education, Catholic giving, and welfare.
Assets: $3,671,490 (1998)
Gifts Received: $853,500
Grant Total: $70,000
Grant Range: $500–$15,000
Limitations: No grants to individuals.
Applications: Contributes to pre-selected organizations only. Applications are not accepted.

The Brennan Family Foundation
708 Nathan Hale Drive
Naples, FL 34108-8238
Contact: The Trustees
Geographic Giving Pattern: Primarily Massachusetts and Florida.
Special Interest: Education, Protestant and Catholic church support, and Catholic agencies.
Assets: $2,251,364 (1999)
Gifts Received: $186,000
Grant Total: $242,316

Grant Range: $100–$110,000
Limitations: No grants to individuals.
Applications: Contributes to pre-selected organizations only.
Applications are not accepted.

The Burns Foundation
150 Bradley Place, No. 212
Palm Beach, FL 33480-3826
Contact: Brian P. Burns, Director
Geographic Giving Pattern: Primarily Massachusetts.
Special Interest: Libraries, international affairs, Catholic church
support, and Catholic agencies.
Assets: $1,050,541 (1997)
Grant Total: $261,500
Grant Range: $500–$111,000
Limitations: No grants to individuals.
Applications: Contributes to pre-selected organizations only.
Applications are not accepted.

Camiccia-Arnautau Charitable Foundation, Inc.
980 North Federal Highway, Suite 402
Boca Raton, FL 33432
Contact: Bill T. Smith, Jr.
Geographic Giving Pattern: Primarily Boca Raton, Florida.
Special Interests: Human services, education, nursing homes,
Catholic church support and Catholic agencies.
Assets: $1,161,569 (1996)
Grant Total: $50,000
Grant Range: $5,000–$25,000
Limitations: No grants to individuals.
Applications: Contributes to pre-selected organizations only.
Applications are not accepted.

The Chadbourne Foundation, Inc.
17 W. Cedar Street, Suite 3
Pensacola, FL 32501
(850) 434-2244
Contact: F. Brian DeMaria, Vice President
Geographic Giving Pattern: Greater Pensacola Florida.

Special Interest: Catholic churches, parishes, religious communities, and organizations aiding the economically disadvantaged.
Assets: $6,346,326 (1999)
Grant Total: $286,266
Grant Range: $500–$50,000
Limitations: No grants to individuals.
Applications: Initial approach should be by letter. An application form is not required. The deadline is August 31.

David R. Clare and Margaret C. Clare Foundation

972 Lake House Drive
North Palm Beach, FL 33408
Contact: David R. Clare and Margaret C. Clare
Geographic Giving Pattern: National.
Special Interests: Federated giving programs and Catholic agencies and services.
Assets: $10,819,774 (1999)
Gifts Received: $1,055,054
Grant Total: $333,500
Grant Range: $2,500–$25,000
Limitations: No grants to individuals.
Applications: Contributes to pre-selected organizations only. Applications are not accepted.

Crosby Family Foundation

c/o Cummings and Lockwood
3001 Tamiami Trail North, P.O. Box 413032
Naples, FL 34101-3032
Contact: Joe Cox
Geographic Giving Pattern: Primarily Newland, North Carolina; New York, New York; and Arlington, Virginia.
Special Interests: Hospitals, healthcare, Catholic agencies and churches.
Assets: $1,462,505 (1999)
Grant Total: $102,204
Limitations: No grants to individuals.
Applications: Contributes to pre-selected organizations only. Applications are not accepted.

The Arthur Vining Davis Foundations
111 Riverside Avenue, Suite 130
Jacksonville, FL 32202-4921
(904) 359-0670
(904) 359-0675 (fax)
Email: arthurvining@msn.com
www.jvm.com/davis
Contact: Dr. Jonathan T. Howe, Executive Director
Geographic Giving Pattern: National.
Special Interest: Private higher education, hospices, healthcare,
public television, and graduate theological education.
Assets: $244,568,292 (1998)
Grant Total: $9,755,042
Grant Range: $50,000–$300,000
Grant Average: $75,000–$200,000
Limitations: No support for community chests, institutions primarily
supported by government funds, or multi-year funding projects. No
grants to individuals. No loans. And no support for institutions outside
of the U.S.
Applications: Initial approach should be by brief letter describing the
institution and program activities. There are no deadlines.

Marian Peak Deaver and Harry Gilbert Deaver Foundation
c/o First Union National Bank of Florida
77 East Camino Real
Boca Raton, FL 33432-6105
(561) 750-1040
Contact: First Union National Bank of Florida
Geographic Giving Pattern: Primarily Florida, Minnesota, and
Wisconsin.
Special Interests: Education, human services, and Catholic agencies
and churches.
Assets: $20,991,331 (1998)
Gifts Received: $250,000
Grant Total: $1,080,168
Grant Range: $2,500–$250,000
Limitations: No grants to individuals.
Applications: Generally contributes to pre-selected organizations.

Paul J. Dimare Foundation

P.O. Box 900460
Homestead, FL 33090-0460
Contact: Paul J. Dimare, Trustee
Geographic Giving Pattern: Primarily Florida.
Special Interests: Secondary and higher education, human services, Catholic agencies and churches.
Assets: $10,593,411(1998)
Gifts Received: $5,400,000
Grant Total: $32,000
Grant Range: $500–$20,000
Limitations: No grants to individuals.
Applications: Contributes to pre-selected organizations only. Applications are not accepted.

Jessie Ball duPont Fund

225 Water Street, Suite 1200
Jacksonville, FL 32202-5176
(904) 353-0890 or (800) 252-3452
(904) 353-3870 (fax)
Contact: Dr. Sherry Magill, Executive Director
Geographical Giving Pattern: Primarily the South, especially Florida, Delaware, and Virginia.
Special Interest: Higher and secondary educational institutions, cultural and historic preservation programs, social service organizations, crime and violence prevention, hospitals, health agencies, churches, church-related organizations, and youth agencies.
Assets: $298,647,823 (1998)
Gifts Received: $55,000
Grant Total: $11,287,759
Grant Range: $5,000–$250,000
Grant Average: $5,000–$50,000
Limitations: No support for organizations other than those awarded gifts by the donor from 1960–1964. No grants to individuals or generally for capital campaigns or endowments.
Applications: Initial approach should be by brief proposal or by telephone. Applicants must submit proof with initial application that a contribution was received from the donor between 1960–1964. An application form is required. There are no deadlines.

The Fortin Foundation of Florida, Inc.
125 Worth Avenue, Suite 318
Palm Beach, FL 33480-0745
(561) 832-6430
Contact: Mary Alice Fortin, President
Geographic Giving Pattern: Florida and Montana.
Special Interest: Education, social services, hospitals, youth agencies, Catholic churches, diocesan support, and Catholic welfare.
Assets: $35,500,935 (1998)
Grant Total: $1,116,600
Grant Range: $200–$350,000
Limitations: No grants to individuals.
Applications: Initial approach should be by letter. The application address is 345 Australian Avenue, No. 6, Palm Beach, FL 33480.

Robert G. Friedman Foundation, Inc.
76 Isla Bahia Drive
Fort Lauderdale, FL 33316-2331
(954) 351-9000
Contact: Robert G. Friedman, President
Geographic Giving Pattern: Primarily Florida, Michigan, Ohio, and Wisconsin.
Special Interests: Arts, education, human services, healthcare, youth services, federated giving programs, and Catholic agencies and churches.
Assets: $12,190,163 (1998)
Grant Total: $486,774
Grant Range: $200–$100,000
Applications: Initial approach should be by letter. There are no deadlines.

George A. Helow Family Foundation, Inc.
8118 Summit Ridge Lane
Jacksonville, FL 32256
Contact: George A. Helow, Chair
Geographic Giving Pattern: Primarily Jacksonville, Florida.
Special Interest: Education, healthcare, social services, Catholic church support, and Catholic agencies.
Assets: $5,243,002 (1998)
Grant Total: $344,000

Grant Range: $1,000–$67,000
Limitations: No grants to individuals.
Applications: Contributes to pre-selected organizations only.
Applications are not accepted.

Heavenly Cause Foundation

P.O. Box 900969
Homestead, FL 33090
(305) 246-2122
Contact: Edward M. Ryan, President
Geographic Giving Pattern: Primarily Pennsylvania.
Special Interest: Catholic education, church support, and Catholic
social and human services.
Assets: $6,612,454 (1998)
Grant Total: $1,304
Limitations: No grants to individuals.
Applications: Contributes to pre-selected organizations only.
Applications are not accepted.

Gordon Henke Family Foundation, Inc.

1500 South Ocean Boulevard, No. 801
Boca Raton, FL 33432
Email: mhenke@lynn.edu
Contact: Mary E. Henke, President
Geographic Giving Pattern: Primarily Florida and Wisconsin.
Special Interest: Higher and secondary education, youth, and church
support.
Assets: $2,755,131 (1999)
Grant Total: $189,900
Grant Range: $500–$77,500
Limitations: No grants to individuals and no support for private
foundations.
Applications: Initial approach should be by letter. There are no
deadlines.

The Jack Holloway Foundation, Inc.

8995 South Orange Avenue
P.O. Box 593688
Orlando, FL 32859-3688
Contact: John D. Holloway, President

Geographic Giving Pattern: Limited to Florida.
Special Interest: Higher education, Protestant and Catholic agencies and churches.
Assets: $3,831,316 (1998)
Grant Total: $234,600
Grant Range: $600–$100,000
Applications: Initial approach should be by letter. There are no deadlines.

Kelco Foundation, Inc.

2541 NW 107th Avenue
Coral Springs, FL 33065
(954) 771-8950
Contact: Susan M. Shaheen, Director
Geographic Giving Pattern: Primarily Florida, with an emphasis on Fort Lauderdale.
Special Interest: Catholic education and evangelization endeavors.
Assets: $1,362,710 (1999)
Gifts Received: $451,574
Grant Total: $370,000
Grant Range: $10,000–$275,000
Applications: Contributes to pre-selected organizations only. Applications are not accepted.

Koch Foundation, Inc.

2830 N.W. 41st Street, Suite H
Gainesville, FL 32606
(352) 373-7491
Contact: Michael Marconi, Executive Director
Geographic Giving Pattern: National and international.
Special Interest: Evangelization; Catholic religious organizations that propagate the faith, preparation of evangelists, Catholic schools which serve as a principal means of evangelization in the community, and efforts to encourage a Catholic presence in the media.
Assets: $128,119,748 (1999)
Grant Total: $10,800,711
Grant Range: $1,000–$300,000
Grant Average: $5,000–$30,000

Limitations: No grants to individuals. No support for endowment funds, deficit financing, emergency funds, scholarships, or fellowships. No loans.

Applications: Initial approach should be by letter briefly describing the project and requesting the application form, which is required. Applications should be submitted between January 1 and May 31.

The George & Mary Kremer Foundation

1100 5th Avenue South, Suite 411
Naples, FL 34102
(941) 261-2367
(941) 261-1494 (fax)
Contact: Mary Anderson Goddard, Executive Director
Geographic Giving Pattern: National.
Special Interest: Scholarship funding for needy children in Catholic elementary schools.
Assets: $64,430,530 (1999)
Grant Total: $1,980,000
Grant Average: $7,000
Applications: Initial approach should be by letter requesting application guidelines. The board meets the second Tuesday in April.

The Landegger Charitable Foundation, Inc.

219 Live Oak Street
New Smyrna Beach, FL 32170-0937
(904) 426-1755
Contact: John F. Bolt, Secretary
Geographic Giving Pattern: National, with an emphasis on New York, New York, Washington, D.C., and Florida.
Special Interest: Catholic higher education, church support, and social services.
Assets: $14,944,570 (1999)
Grant Total: $964,041
Grant Range: $500–$225,000
Limitations: No grants to individuals.
Applications: Initial approach should be by brief letter of inquiry. There are no deadlines.

Frank J. Lewis Foundation, Inc.
P.O. Box 9726
Riviera Beach, FL 33419
Contact: The Trustees
Geographic Giving Pattern: National.
Special Interest: To foster, preserve, and extend the Catholic faith. Support for educational institutions, churches, dioceses, religious orders, church-sponsored programs, social service agencies, and hospitals.
Assets: $29,711,111 (1998)
Grant Total: $2,528,788
Grant Range: $500–$200,000
Grant Average: $2,500–$25,000
Limitations: No grants to individuals or for endowment funds.
Applications: Initial approach should be by letter.

The Sumter and Ivilyn Lowry Charitable Foundation, Inc.
P.O. Box 18065
Tampa, FL 33679-8065
Contact: Ann L. Murphy, President
Geographic Giving Pattern: Primarily Tampa, Florida.
Special Interest: Education, children and youth, Catholic church support, and Catholic agencies.
Assets: $3,411,518 (1997)
Grant Total: $151,400
Grant Range: $500–$25,000
Limitations: No grants to individuals.
Applications: Initial approach should be by letter. There are no deadlines.

McKeen Fund
c/o Bessemer Trust Company of Florida
222 Royal Palm Way
Palm Beach, FL 33480
(561) 655-4030
Contact: James J. Daly
Geographic Giving Pattern: There are no stated geographical limitations.

Special Interests: Higher education, hospitals, American Red Cross, and Catholic agencies and churches.
Assets: $18,322,765 (1998)
Grant Total: $819,200
Grant Range: $1,000–$250,000
Applications: Initial approach should be by letter. There are no deadlines.

The E. F. Merkert Foundation
2359 South Ocean Boulevard
Highland Beach, FL 33487-1834
(561) 392-3210
Contact: Anna Grascia, Administrator
Geographic Giving Pattern: Primarily Massachusetts.
Special Interest: Education, human services, voluntarism, Catholic church support, and Catholic agencies.
Assets: $1,380,151 (1998)
Grant Total: $50,500
Grant Range: $1,000–$26,000
Limitations: No grants to individuals.
Applications: Initial approach should be by letter. There are no deadlines.

Curtis W. Miles Charitable Trust
c/o BankBoston - Florida N.A.
2033 Main Street
Sarasota, FL 34237
(941) 364-5215
Contact: Sid Schwalbe
Geographic Giving Pattern: Primarily Florida and Kentucky.
Special Interests: Education, human services, youth services, and Catholic agencies and churches.
Assets: $3,425,232 (1999)
Gifts Received: $23,698
Grant Total: $160,266
Grant Range: $2,000–$33,666
Limitations: No grants to individuals.
Applications: Initial approach should be by letter. There are no deadlines.

Nevins Family Foundation

6075 Pelican Bay Boulevard, Number 1006
Naples, FL 34108
Contact: M. E. Nevins and Hanna Nevins, Trustees
Geographic Giving Pattern: Primarily Florida, Washington,
Wisconsin, and Illinois.
Special Interests: Human services, Performing arts, higher education,
engineering, healthcare, youth services, Catholic church support and
Catholic agencies.
Assets: $1,051,408 (1997)
Grant Total: $70,500
Grant Range: $250–$10,000
Applications: Contributes to pre-selected organizations only.
Applications are not accepted.

Perpetual Help Foundation

67 North Bounty Lane
Key Largo, FL 33037
(305) 852-4530
Contact: Phyllis Hummel, President
Geographic Giving Pattern: National.
Special Interest: Catholic diocesan support, ministries, religious
communities, missions, and Catholic welfare.
Assets: $35,812 (1999)
Gifts Received: $181,000
Grant Total: $189,019
Grant Range: $25–$140,000
Limitations: No grants to individuals.
Applications: Contributes to pre-selected organizations only.
Applications are not accepted.

Warren P. Powers Charitable Trust

1301 Riverplace Boulevard, Suite 1904
Jacksonville, FL 32207
Contact: Jane Powers, Executive Director
Geographic Giving Pattern: Limited to the Catholic Dioceses of
Orange, California; Salt Lake City; Kansas City-Kansas; Atlanta; St.
Augustine; and Charlotte.
Special Interest: Vocations, ministry to the disabled, care of retired
clergy and religious, and the poor or homeless.

Assets: $6,456,991 (1998)
Gifts Received: $20,000
Grant Total: $1,043,870
Grant Range: $10–$100,000
Limitations: No grants to individuals.
Applications: Grants are initiated by the trustees. Contributes to pre-selected organizations only. Applications are not accepted.

Edward M. Ricci and Mary E. Lupo Charitable Trust
P.O. Box 2946
West Palm Beach, FL 33402
(561) 684-6500
Contact: Edward M. Ricci, Trustee
Geographic Giving Pattern: Primarily Washington, D.C., Maryland, and Florida.
Special Interests: Human services, secondary and higher education, Catholic church support and Catholic agencies.
Assets: $1,352,030 (1998)
Grant Total: $145,000
Grant Range: $500–$50,000
Applications: Initial approach should be by letter. There are no deadlines.

SFC Charitable Foundation, Inc.
100 S.E. 2nd Street, Suite 2800
Miami, FL 33131-2144
Contact: Howard Kaufman, President
Geographic Giving Pattern: There are no stated geographical limitations.
Special Interests: Continuing education, environment, crime prevention, food banks, human services, youth services, substance abuse, and Catholic agencies and churches.
Assets: $608,874 (1998)
Grant Total: $932,190
Grant Average: $5,000–$20,000
Limitations: No grants to individuals.
Applications: Contributes to pre-selected organizations only. Applications are not accepted.

The Vogt Family Foundation, Inc.
483 Sherbrooke Court
Venice, FL 34293-4453
(941) 493-2699
Contact: Mary Lou Vogt, President
Geographic Giving Pattern: Primarily New York.
Special Interests: Arts and cultural programs, education, hospitals, and Catholic agencies and churches.
Assets: $4,736,465 (1999)
Gifts Received: $116,230
Grant Total: $224,500
Grant Range: $1,000–$45,000
Limitations: No grants to individuals.
Applications: Contributes to pre-selected organizations only. Applications are not accepted.

Wahlert Foundation
P.O. Box 61447
Ft. Myers, FL 33906-1447
(941) 590-0683
Email: Bob16307@aol.com
Contact: R. H. Wahlert, President and Treasurer
Geographic Giving Pattern: Primarily the metropolitan Dubuque, Iowa area.
Special Interest: Education, theological education, healthcare, social services, Catholic church support, welfare organizations, and schools.
Assets: $6,852,042 (1999)
Gifts Received: $2,000
Grant Total: $471,000
Grant Range: $3,334–$450,000
Limitations: No grants to individuals. No support for publications or conferences. No matching gifts or loans.
Applications: Contributes to pre-selected organizations only. Applications are not accepted.

GEORGIA

Paul and Mary Cancellarini Charitable Trust
864 Ashfield Drive
Decatur, GA 30030
Contact: Kenneth Mattioli and Wallace Mattioli, Trustees
Geographic Giving Pattern: Primarily Connecticut.
Special Interests: Libraries, education, hospitals, nursing care,
Catholic church support and Catholic agencies.
Assets: $1,550,301 (1998)
Grant Total: $75,431
Grant Range: $5,190–$12,975
Limitations: No grants to individuals.
Applications: Contributes to pre-selected organizations only.
Applications are not accepted.

Cook Family Foundation, Inc.
2300 Windy Ridge Parkway, Suite 100 N
Atlanta, GA 30339
(770) 779-3281
(770) 779-3151 (additional telephone)
Email: cmcnabb@prgx.com
Contact: Charlene McNabb, Assistant Secretary-Treasurer
Geographic Giving Pattern: Primarily Atlanta, Georgia.
Special Interests: Human services, museums, Arts and cultural
programs, healthcare, education, disabled, youth development,
Catholic church support and Catholic agencies.
Assets: $1,341,320 (1998)
Grant Total: $3,193,730
Grant Range: $500–$3,074,380
Applications: Initial approach should be by letter. There are no
deadlines.

The Goizueta Foundation
4401 Northside Parkway, Suite 520
Atlanta, GA 30327
(404) 239-0390
Contact: Olga C. De Goizueta, Trustee
Geographic Giving Pattern: Limited primarily to the Southeast, with
an emphasis on Atlanta, Georgia.

Special Interests: Religious, educational, and charitable support.
Assets: $781,801,033 (1998)
Gifts Received: $604,616,024
Grant Total: $7,265,878
Grant Range: $5,000–$2,000,000
Applications: Contributes to pre-selected organizations only.
Applications are not accepted.

Mary E. Haverty Foundation, Inc.
c/o Bank South, N.A., Trust Department
P.O. Box 4956
Atlanta, GA 30302-4956
Contact: Rawson Haverty, Chair
Geographic Giving Pattern: Limited to Atlanta, Georgia.
Special Interests: Catholic church support and Catholic agencies.
Assets: $2,686,790 (1998)
Gifts Received: $34,063
Grant Total: $109,750
Grant Range: $500–$20,000

Donald and Marilyn Keough Foundation
200 Galleria Parkway, Suite 970
Atlanta, GA 30339
Contact: Marilyn M. Keough, President
Geographic Giving Pattern: National.
Special Interest: Irish-American associations, Catholic organizations, and higher education.
Assets: $9,014,896 (1998)
Gifts Received: $450,000
Grant Total: $541,250
Grant Range: $1,000–$200,000
Limitations: No grants to individuals.
Applications: Contributes to pre-selected organizations only.
Applications are not accepted.

Mary Ryan & Henry G. Kuhrt Foundation
c/o SunTrust Bank, Atlanta
P.O. Box 4655
Atlanta, GA 30302-4655
(404) 588-7356

Contact: Brenda Rambeau, Vice President, SunTrust Bank, Atlanta
Geographic Giving Pattern: Somewhat limited to Georgia, with an emphasis on Atlanta.
Special Interest: Catholic agencies, monasteries, convents, churches, and elementary and secondary education.
Assets: $4,810,939 (1998)
Grant Total: $200,000
Grant Range: $1,000–$10,000
Applications: Initial approach should be by letter. The grant proposal deadline is October 31.

Dorothy V. and N. Logan Lewis Foundation, Inc.
240 Third Street
P.O. Box 1606
Macon, GA 31202-0001
(912) 743-7051
Contact: Cubbedge Snow, Jr., Secretary
Geographic Giving Pattern: Primarily Macon, Georgia.
Special Interests: Elementary and secondary education and Catholic agencies and churches.
Assets: $16,021,277 (1999)
Grant Total: $565,000
Grant Range: $10,000–$150,000
Applications: Initial approach should be by letter. There are no deadlines.

Katherine John Murphy Foundation
50 Hurt Plaza, Suite 745
Atlanta, GA 30303
(404) 589-8090
Email: info@kjmurphyfoundation.org
Contact: Brenda Rambeau, Vice President
Geographic Giving Pattern: Primarily Atlanta, Georgia.
Special Interests: Arts, education, the environment, hospitals, and youth services.
Assets: $38,137,613 (1998)
Grant Total: $2,790,353
Grant Range: $264–$100,000
Limitations: No grants to individuals. No matching gifts. No loans.

Applications: Initial approach should be by letter. The deadlines are June 15 and December 15.

Patterson-Barclay Memorial Foundation, Inc.
6487 Peachtree Industrial Boulevard, Suite A
Atlanta, GA 30360
(770) 458-9888
Contact: Hugh Powell, Jr.
Geographic Giving Pattern: Primarily the Atlanta, Georgia metropolitan area.
Special Interests: Arts and cultural events, education, child development, environment, medical care, substance abuse, youth services, community development, homelessness, Catholic Federated giving programs.
Assets: $12,050,417 (1999)
Grant Total: $611,000
Grant Range: $1,000–$24,000
Grant Average: $1,000–$5,000
Limitations: No grants to individuals.
Applications: Initial approach should be by proposal. The deadline is October 1.

ILLINOIS

Ralph J. Baudhuin Foundation
c/o AMCORE Investment Group, N.A.
501 Seventh Street
P.O. Box 1537
Rockford, IL 61110-0037
Contact: Fran Baudhuin, Treasurer
Geographic Giving Pattern: Primarily Rockford, Illinois.
Special Interest: Catholic agencies, churches, and missions; some support for universities and health organizations.
Assets: $4,700,886 (1999)
Grant Total: $232,272
Grant Range: $500–$38,000
Applications: Initial approach should be by letter outlining needs to the following address: 4109 Rural Street, Rockford, IL 61110.
Tel. (815) 399-3148. There are no deadlines.

William Blair and Company Foundation

222 West Adams Street
Chicago, IL 60606
(312) 236-1600
Contact: E. David Coolidge III, Vice President
Geographic Giving Pattern: Primarily metropolitan Chicago, Illinois.
Description: The William Blair and Company Foundation is a
corporate foundation.
Special Interest: The arts, culture, higher education, healthcare,
youth, social services, Jewish and Catholic agencies, and Catholic
church support.
Assets: $5,199,358 (1999)
Grant Total: $632,317
Grant Range: $50–$20,000
Limitations: No grants to individuals.
Applications: Initial approach should be by letter. There are no
deadlines.

The Ambrose and Gladys Bowyer Foundation

16308 107th Avenue, Suite 9
Orland Park, IL 60462
(708) 873-1332
Contact: E.V. Quinn, President
Geographic Giving Pattern: Primarily Illinois, with an emphasis on
Chicago.
Special Interest: Education, hospitals, Catholic and other welfare
funds, and religious communities.
Assets: $597,855 (1998)
Grant Total: $342,000
Grant Range: $1,000–$50,000
Limitations: No grants to individuals.
Applications: Contributes to pre-selected organizations only.
Applications are not accepted.

Helen Brach Foundation

55 West Wacker Drive
Suite 701
Chicago, IL 60601
(312) 372-4417
(312) 372-0290 (fax)

Contact: Raymond F. Simon, President
Geographic Giving Pattern: Primarily the Midwest, especially
Chicago, Illinois.
Special Interest: Catholic social service agencies, schools, colleges,
retreat centers, churches, diocesan support, and the prevention of
cruelty to children and animals.
Assets: $115,983,215 (1999)
Grant Total: $3,473,675
Grant Range: $100–$100,000
Grant Average: $10,000–$25,000
Applications: Initial approach should be by letter. An application form
is required. The deadline for proposals is December 31, although the
foundation recommends submitting completed applications as early as
possible. Faxed applications are not accepted.

Fred J. Brunner Foundation

9300 King Street
Franklin Park, IL 60131
(847) 678-3232
Contact: Robert B. Wolf, Vice President
Geographic Giving Pattern: Primarily Illinois.
Special Interests: Education, health, social and youth services,
Catholic church support, and Catholic agencies.
Assets: $4,435,809 (1998)
Grant Total: $157,688
Grant Range: $250–$10,000
Limitations: No grants to individuals. No support for endowment
funds, matching gifts, fellowships or scholarships. No loans.
Applications: Initial approach should be by letter or proposal. The
deadline is December 15.

Harry F. and Elaine Chaddick Foundation, Inc.

123 West Madison Street, Suite 200
Chicago, IL 60602-4511
(312) 704-4100
Contact: Elaine M. Chaddick, President
Geographic Giving Pattern: Primarily the metropolitan Chicago
area.
Special Interests: Education, healthcare, youth development,
community services, science, and Catholic federated giving programs.

Assets: $3,250,966 (1999)
Grant Total: $162,218
Grant Range: $2,000–$60,343
Limitations: No grants to individuals.
Applications: Initial approach should be by letter including one copy of proposal. An application form is required. The deadline is April 1.

Christiana Foundation, Inc.
c/o Hinshaw, Culbertson, Moelmann, Hoban and Fuller
222 North LaSalle Street, Suite 300
Chicago, IL 60601-1081
(312) 704-3045
Contact: Jerome A. Frazel, Jr., President
Geographic Giving Pattern: Primarily Illinois and Washington.
Description: Christiana Foundation, Inc. is a corporate foundation of the Lapham-Hickey Steel Corporation.
Special Interest: Catholic community welfare organizations, secondary and higher education, and healthcare.
Assets: $1,415,638 (1999)
Grant Total: $106,690
Grant Range: $250–$20,000
Limitations: No grants to individuals.
Applications: Initial approach should be by letter. There are no deadlines.

Philip H. Corboy Foundation
30 North LaSalle Street, Suite 4200
Chicago, IL 60602
(312) 368-0500
Contact: Thomas J. Durkin, President
Geographic Giving Pattern: Primarily Chicago, Illinois.
Special Interests: Arts and cultural programs, education, healthcare, youth services, Catholic agencies and churches.
Assets: $11,797,877 (1998)
Gifts Received: $852,815
Grant Total: $475,431
Grant Range: $50–$100,000
Limitations: No grants to individuals.
Applications: Contributes to pre-selected organizations only. Applications are not accepted.

The Cottrell Foundation

10 South LaSalle, Suite 3450
Chicago, IL 60602
(312) 236-2942
Contact: Patricia Fernholz, Trustee
Geographic Giving Pattern: National.
Special Interests: Catholic organizations, including missions, refugee services, colleges, universities, and churches.
Assets: $3,744,178 (1998)
Gifts Received: $50,000
Grant Total: $198,000
Grant Range: $50–$60,000
Limitations: No grants to individuals.
Applications: Contributes to pre-selected organizations only. Applications are not accepted.

The Cuneo Foundation

9101 North Greenwood Avenue, Suite 210
Niles, IL 60714
(847) 296-3351
Contact: John F. Cuneo, Jr., President
Geographic Giving Pattern: Primarily the Chicago metropolitan area.
Special Interest: Catholic church support, church-related organizations, religious associations, welfare funds, and hospitals.
Assets: $34,816,261 (1998)
Grant Total: $623,930
Grant Range: $450–$50,000
Limitations: No grants to individuals or for scholarships, fellowships, or research funds. No loans.
Applications: Initial approach should be by proposal. There are no deadlines. The board meets in May and October.

Davies Charitable Trust

Northern Trust Bank of California, N.A.
50 S. LaSalle Street
Chicago, IL 60675
Contact: Robert Brei
Geographic Giving Pattern: Primarily northern California, especially San Francisco.

Special Interest: Education, museums, arts, culture, and natural resource conservation; some support for Catholic churches and schools.
Assets: $5,638,429 (1998)
Grant Total: $279,700
Grant Range: $500–$93,500
Limitations: No grants to individuals.
Applications: Contributes to pre-selected organizations only. Applications are not accepted.

De Santis Foundation
100 Drury Lane
Oakbrook Terrace, IL 60181-4615
Contact: Anthony De Santis, President
Geographic Giving Pattern: Primarily Chicago, Illinois.
Special Interest: Catholic giving, Catholic welfare, secondary education, and religious schools.
Assets: $1,103,342 (1997)
Gifts Received: $70,000
Grant Total: $144,000
Grant Range: $200–$20,000
Applications: Contributes to pre-selected organizations only. Applications are not accepted.

Thomas W. Dower Foundation
30 North LaSalle Street, Suite 1200
Chicago, IL 60602
(312) 236-3575
Contact: J. M. Hartigan
Geographic Giving Pattern: Primarily Illinois.
Special Interest: Education, welfare, health, hospitals, Christian organizations, Catholic agencies, and church support.
Assets: $8,077,874 (1999)
Grant Total: $401,600
Grant Range: $100–$35,000
Grant Average: Less than $10,000
Applications: Initial approach should be by letter. There are no deadlines.

Mary Kay & James D. Farley Fund

c/o Northern Trust Bank of Florida, N.A.
50 South LaSalle Street
Chicago, IL 60675
Contact: The Trustees
Geographic Giving Pattern: National.
Special Interest: Healthcare, Catholic church and diocesan support, libraries and education.
Assets: $2,896,707 (1998)
Gifts Received: $1,542,981
Grant Total: $106,750
Grant Range: $500–$13,000
Limitations: No grants to individuals.
Applications: Contributes to pre-selected organizations only. Applications are not accepted.

Father James M. Fitzgerald Scholarship Trust

c/o First of America Trust Company
301 South West Adams Street
Peoria, IL 61652
(309) 655-5322
Contact: Jo Ann Harlan, Assistant Vice President, First of America Trust Company
Geographic Giving Pattern: Limited to residents of Illinois.
Special Interest: Scholarship support for students attending Catholic schools.
Assets: $2,731,238 (1998)
Grant Total: $93,089
Limitations: No support for general purposes, capital or endowment funds, research, publications, or conferences. No loans or matching gifts.
Applications: Initial approach should be by letter indicating desire to enroll and acceptance as a seminarian. There are no deadlines.

Florik Charitable Trust

c/o Bank of America
231 S. La Salle Street
Chicago, IL 60697
(312) 828-7710
Contact: Charles Slamar, Jr.

Geographic Giving Pattern: Primarily Illinois.
Special Interest: Catholic agencies and churches.
Assets: $67,280,399 (1999)
Gifts Received: $900,610
Grant Total: $3,371,449
Grant Range: $10,000–$2,929,357
Limitations: No grants to individuals.
Applications: Initial approach should be by letter. There are no deadlines.

Foglia Family Foundation
190 South LaSalle Street, Suite 1700
Chicago, IL 60603-3411
(312) 346-4101
Contact: Patricia A. Foglia, President
Geographic Giving Pattern: Primarily Chicago, Illinois.
Special Interest: Healthcare, medical research, social services, Catholic church support, and Catholic agencies.
Assets: $4,049,067 (1999)
Gifts Received: $1,941,261
Grant Total: $2,636,222
Grant Range: $200–$1,001,000
Limitations: No grants to individuals.
Applications: Contributes to pre-selected organizations only. Applications are not accepted.

Lloyd A. Fry Foundation
135 South LaSalle Street, Suite 1910
Chicago, IL 60603
(312) 580-0310
(312) 580-0980 (fax)
Email: jdarrow@fryfoundation.org
www.fryfoundation.org
Contact: Jill C. Darrow, Executive Director
Geographic Giving Pattern: Primarily Chicago, Illinois.
Special Interest: Support for "organizations with the vision to find new solutions to persistent problems in urban Chicago, such as illiteracy, joblessness, poverty, violence and neighborhood decay."
Assets: $187,430,683 (1999)
Gifts Received: $1,363,355

Grant Total: $7,066,000
Grant Range: $500–$225,000
Grant Average: $5,000–$50,000
Limitations: No grants to individuals. No support for deficit financing, building funds, land acquisition, renovation projects, fundraising benefits, or endowment funds. No loans.
Applications: Initial approach should be by letter. The deadlines are March 1, June 1, September 1, and December 1.

FSC Foundation
555 N. Lombard Road
Addison, IL 60101
(708) 543-6310
Contact: Brother Thomas Hetland, F.S.C., Chairman
Geographic Giving Pattern: National and international.
Special Interests: Elementary and secondary education, adult education, literacy, Catholic church support, Catholic agencies and some support for missions.
Assets: $162,190 (1999)
Gifts Received: $165,000
Grant Total: $102,003
Grant Range: $800–$2,500
Applications: An application form is required along with the proposal. The deadline is September 1.

Fulk Family Charitable Trust
227 Church Road
Winnetka, IL 60093-3905
(847) 446-5086
Contact: R. Neil Fulk, Trustee
Geographic Giving Pattern: Limited to the greater Chicago area.
Special Interests: Human services, higher education, homelessness, general charitable giving, Catholic church support and Catholic agencies.
Assets: $432,960 (1999)
Gifts Received: $40
Grant Total: $50,850
Grant Range: $100–$13,750
Limitations: No grants to individuals.

Applications: Contributes to pre-selected organizations only. Applications are not accepted.

Anna C. Gamble Foundation

120 South LaSalle Street
Chicago, IL 60603
(312) 661-6862
Contact: American National Bank
Geographic Giving Pattern: There are no stated geographical limitations.
Special Interests: Human services, higher education, Catholic church support and Catholic agencies.
Assets: $2,218,961 (1998)
Grant Total: $165,000
Grant Range: $2,000–$15,000
Limitations: No grants to individuals.
Applications: Contributes to pre-selected organizations only. Applications are not accepted.

James & Zita Gavin Foundation, Inc.

161 Thorntree Lane
Winnetka, IL 60093
(708) 446-3191
Contact: James J. Gavin, Jr., President
Geographic Giving Pattern: National.
Special Interest: Catholic education and Catholic charities.
Assets: $10,960,640 (1998)
Grant Total: $648,406
Grant Average: $3,000–$120,938
Limitations: No grants to individuals.
Applications: Contributes to pre-selected organizations only. Applications are not accepted.

H. C. D. Foundation

1370 Shagbark Drive
Des Plaines, IL 60018
Contact: Harriet Dennis and Jeffrey Dennis
Geographic Giving Pattern: Primarily California and Illinois.

Special Interests: Human services, boys and girls clubs, federated giving programs, Catholic church support, Catholic agencies, and religious giving.
Assets: $1,597,238 (1998)
Grant Total: $70,030
Grant Range: $100–$9,000
Limitations: No grants to individuals.
Applications: Contributes to pre-selected organizations only. Applications are not accepted.

Mary Heath Foundation
c/o First National Bank of Oblong
P.O. Box 10
Oblong, IL 62449
(618) 592-4241
Contact: Gail M. Bailey, Administrative Officer
Geographic Giving Pattern: Limited to Illinois.
Special Interests: Public health, continuing education, schools, food banks, youth development, housing and shelter, centers and clubs, Catholic agencies and churches.
Assets: $5,218,649 (1998)
Grant Total: $166,761
Grant Range: $945–$16,182
Limitations: No grants to individuals, or for endowments, deficit reduction, financing, or political campaigns.
Applications: Initial approach should be by proposal requesting application guidelines. Six copies of the proposal are requested. The deadlines are May 1 and November 1.

Lawrence & Ada Hickey Foundation
615 Woodland Lane
Northfield, IL 60093
(312) 368-7730
Contact: Lawrence Hickey, President
Geographic Giving Pattern: Primarily Illinois.
Special Interest: Catholic churches, Catholic organizations, and higher education.
Assets: $2,461,149 (1999)
Grant Total: $288,051
Grant Range: $150–$62,600

Limitations: No grants to individuals.
Applications: Contributes to pre-selected organizations only.
Applications are not accepted.

Mercedes L. Hoag Charitable Trust
c/o First Mid-Illinois Bank and Trust
P.O. Box 499
Mattoon, IL 61938
Contact: First Mid-Illinois Bank and Trust
Geographic Giving Pattern: Primarily Illinois.
Special Interests: Human services, higher education, nursing
education, hospitals, aging, community development, Catholic church
support and Catholic agencies.
Assets: $2,466,221 (1999)
Grant Total: $105,000
Grant Range: $2,000–$20,000
Limitations: No grants to individuals.
Applications: Contributes to pre-selected organizations only.
Applications are not accepted.

KB Foundation
20 North Wacker Drive, Suite 4220
Chicago, IL 60606
Contact: M. Stein
Geographic Giving Pattern: National.
Special Interest: Catholic welfare, relief, human services, and
substance abuse programs.
Assets: $1,742,272 (1998)
Grant Total: $70,600
Grant Range: $5,000–$40,000
Limitations: No grants to individuals.
Applications: Contributes to pre-selected organizations only.
Applications are not accepted.

Kellstadt Foundation
c/o Bank of America NT & SA
231 South LaSalle Street
Chicago, IL 60697
(312) 828-1785

Contact: M. C. Ryan
Geographic Giving Pattern: Primarily Illinois, Michigan, and Kentucky.
Special Interest: Half of all grant funds are for Catholic organizations, agencies, and churches. Support also for higher education and graduate schools of business, with an emphasis on marketing.
Assets: $9,562,919 (1999)
Grant Total: $400,000
Limitations: No grants to individuals.
Applications: Initial approach should be by letter. There are no deadlines. The application address is c/o Bank of America NT & SA, 30 S. LaSalle Street, Chicago, IL 60697.

John J. Kinsella Charitable Trust
c/o Leo Burnett Company Prudential Plaza
20 North Wacker Drive, Suite 1520
Chicago, IL 60606-2903
Contact: Rockney Hudson, Trustee
Geographic Giving Pattern: Primarily Chicago, Illinois.
Special Interests: Human services, arts and cultural programs, higher education, Catholic church support and Catholic agencies.
Assets: $6,805 (1998)
Grant Total: $129,520
Grant Range: $50–$50,000
Limitations: No grants to individuals.
Applications: Contributes to pre-selected organizations only. Applications are not accepted.

Mazza Foundation
225 West Washington Street, Suite 1300
Chicago, IL 60606-3405
(312) 444-9300
Contact: Tina Lavezzorio, President
Geographic Giving Pattern: Primarily Chicago, Illinois.
Special Interest: Churches, religious organizations, social service agencies, hospitals, and education.
Assets: $40,718,504 (1999)
Grant Total: $2,106,000
Grant Range: $4,000–$500,000

Grant Average: $5,000–$50,000
Applications: There are no deadlines for grant proposals.

McIntosh Foundation, Inc.
525 Sheridan Road
Kenilworth, IL 60043-1222
Contact: William A. McIntosh, President and Treasurer
Geographic Giving Pattern: Primarily Chicago, Illinois, and New York, New York.
Special Interest: Primarily for programs of the Archdiocese of Chicago and Catholic parishes, universities, and charities.
Assets: $13,335,598 (1999)
Grant Total: $640,500
Grant Range: $5,000–$150,000
Limitations: No grants to individuals.
Applications: Contributes to pre-selected organizations only. Applications are not accepted.

Edmond and Alice Opler Foundation
180 North LaSalle, Suite 2700
Chicago, IL 60601
(312) 845-5107
Contact: Lloyd S. Kupferberg, Vice President
Geographic Giving Pattern: Primarily Illinois.
Special Interest: Higher education, healthcare, Catholic church support, and Catholic agencies.
Assets: $23,901,205 (1998)
Gifts Received: $14,156
Grant Total: $1,125,500
Grant Range: $1,000–$130,000
Applications: Initial approach should be by letter. There are no deadlines.

James M. Ragen, Jr. Memorial Fund Trust No. 1.
c/o Firstar Bank Illinois
104 North Oak Park Avenue
Oak Park, IL 60301-1387
Geographic Giving Pattern: National, with an emphasis on California and Illinois.

Special Interest: Catholic churches, social services, education, hospitals, and the economically disadvantaged.
Assets: $3,344,201 (1998)
Grant Total: $100,000
Grant Range: $2,500–$10,000
Applications: Initial approach should be by letter. An application form is required. The deadline is December 31.

The Retirement Research Foundation
8765 West Higgins Road, Suite 430
Chicago, IL 60631-4170
(773) 714-8080
(773) 714-8089
Email: info@rrf.org
www.fdncenter.org/grantmaker/rrf
Contact: Marilyn Hennessy, President
Geographic Giving Pattern: Primarily the Midwest and Florida.
Special Interest: To improve the quality of older persons in the U.S.
Assets: $202,210,408 (1998)
Grant Total: $9,503,813
Grant Range: $1,000–$150,000
Grant Average: $12,000–$40,000
Limitations: No support for endowment funds, construction, emergency funds, deficit financing, land acquisition, publications, conferences, or annual campaigns.
Applications: Initial approach should be by letter or proposal. Three copies of the proposal are required. Proposals should be submitted in January, April, or July. The deadlines are February 1, May 1, and August 1.

Arthur M. Robinson Foundation
2401 Plum Grove Road
c/o Isara # 216
Palatine, IL 60067
(847) 303-5050
Contact: The Trustees
Geographic Giving Pattern: Primarily Illinois.
Special Interests: Human services, education, boys clubs, Catholic church support and Catholic agencies.

Assets: $1,410,325 (1998)
Grant Total: $48,000
Grant Range: $1,000–$10,000
Limitations: No grants to individuals.
Applications: Contributes to pre-selected organizations only.
Applications are not accepted.

The Rooney Family Foundation
c/o Nancee Bilthusis
2101 South Wabash Avenue
Chicago, IL 60616
Contact: Philip B. Rooney, President
Geographic Giving Pattern: Primarily Illinois.
Special Interest: Education, Catholic church support, and Catholic
agencies.
Assets: $1,363,348 (1997)
Grant Total: $406,345
Grant Range: $70–$100,000
Limitations: No grants to individuals.
Applications: Initial approach should be by letter. An application form
is not required. There are no deadlines.

William G. and Mary A. Ryan Foundation
4 Westbrook Corporate Center, Suite 500
Westchester, IL 60154
Contact: The Directors
Geographic Giving Pattern: National.
Special Interests: Catholic agencies and churches.
Assets: $1,532,068 (1999)
Grant Total: $72,020
Grant Range: $100–$100,000
Limitations: No grants to individuals.
Applications: Contributes to pre-selected organizations only.
Applications are not accepted.

Sangre De Christo Charitable Trust
2000 52nd Avenue, Apartment #2
Moline, IL 61265
Contact: Bernard J. Hank, Jr., and Joyce M. Hank

Geographic Giving Pattern: There are no stated geographical limitations.
Special Interests: Higher education, youth, and Catholic agencies and churches.
Assets: $2,562,903 (1998)
Gifts Received: $284,644
Grant Total: $237,500
Grant Range: $10,000–$165,000
Limitations: No grants to individuals.
Applications: Contributes to pre-selected organizations only. Applications are not accepted.

Schiff, Hardin, and Waite Foundation
233 South Wacker Drive, Suite 7200
Chicago, IL 60606
(312) 876-1000
Contact: The Directors
Geographic Giving Pattern: Primarily Chicago, Illinois.
Special Interests: Human services, performing arts, education, food banks, fundraising, environment, Catholic church support and Catholic agencies.
Assets: $34,184 (1998)
Gifts Received: $110,420
Grant Total: $166,355
Grant Range: $105–$34,000
Limitations: No grants to individuals.
Applications: Contributes to pre-selected organizations only. Applications are not accepted.

Arthur J. Schmitt Foundation
629 Green Bay Road, Suite 1
Wilmette, IL 60091
(708) 853-0231
Contact: John A. Donahue, Executive Director
Geographic Giving Pattern: Primarily the Chicago metropolitan area.
Special Interest: Catholic educational and religious institutions and Catholic welfare.
Assets: $23,880,281 (1999)

Grant Total: $2,522,390
Grant Range: $1,000–$1,250,000
Grant Average: $2,000–$50,000
Limitations: No grants to individuals. No support for research, capital funds, or building funds. No loans or matching gifts.
Applications: Initial approach should be by proposal letter including a condensed request and supporting materials. Proposals should be submitted preferably in July, October, January, or April. Grants are awarded quarterly.

Dr. Scholl Foundation
11 South LaSalle Street, Suite 2100
Chicago, IL 60603-1302
(312) 782-5210
Contact: Pamela Scholl, President
Geographic Giving Pattern: National and international, with an emphasis on Chicago, Illinois and England.
Special Interest: Education at all levels, general charitable giving, Catholic church support, and Catholic agencies.
Assets: $205,598,216 (1998)
Grant Total: $10,378,228
Grant Range: $4,000–$500,000
Grant Average: $10,000–$100,000
Limitations: No grants to individuals. No support for public education. No support for operating budgets, deficit financing, or general support.
Applications: Initial approach should be by proposal. An application form is required. The deadline is May 15. Applications sent by fax will not be accepted.

Fred B. Snite Foundation
550 Frontage Road, Suite 3745
Northfield, IL 60093-1221
(847) 446-7705
Contact: Terrance J. Dillon, President
Geographic Giving Pattern: National, with an emphasis on Illinois and California.
Special Interest: Catholic churches, diocesan support, and church-related educational institutions.
Assets: $15,897,701 (1999)
Grant Total: $718,250

Grant Range: $1,000–$250,000
Limitations: No grants to individuals.
Applications: Initial approach should be by proposal. There are no deadlines for grant proposals.

Solo Cup Foundation
1700 Old Deerfield Road
Highland Park, IL 60035
(847) 831-4800
Contact: Ronald L. Whaley, President
Geographic Giving Pattern: National.
Special Interest: Higher and secondary education, Christian religious organizations and schools, and health associations.
Assets: $145,418 (1999)
Grant Total: $2,103,050
Grant Range: $2,500–$733,714
Applications: There are no deadlines for grant proposals.

Walter & Mary Tuohy Foundation
111 West Monroe Street, Suite 1700
Chicago, IL 60603
(312) 845-3752
Contact: John L. Tuohy, President
Geographic Giving Pattern: National.
Special Interest: Welfare, housing, and higher education; some support for Catholic churches and agencies.
Assets: $4,482,786 (1999)
Grant Total: $377,000
Grant Range: $1,000–$50,000
Grant Average: $1,000–$20,000
Applications: Applications are not accepted.

Carol Jo Vecchie Memorial Foundation
3400 Solar Avenue
Springfield, IL 62791-8348
(217) 522-6321
Contact: The Directors
Geographic Giving Pattern: There are no stated geographical limitations.

Special Interests: Hospitals, human services, and Catholic agencies and churches.
Assets: $13,099 (1998)
Gifts Received: $2,555,000
Grant Total: $2,555,389
Grant Range: $3,000–$1,050,000
Limitations: No grants to individuals.
Applications: Contributes to pre-selected organizations only. Applications are not accepted.

The Walsh Foundation
c/o Madden, Jiganti, Moore, & Sinars
190 South LaSalle Street, Suite 1700
Chicago, IL 60603
Contact: Daniel J. Walsh, President
Geographic Giving Pattern: Primarily Illinois.
Special Interests: Education, youth services, and Catholic agencies and churches.
Assets: $9,424,891 (1998)
Grant Total: $475,500
Grant Range: $1,000–$100,000
Limitations: No grants to individuals.
Applications: Contributes to pre-selected organizations only. Applications are not accepted.

Lucille and Vic Wertz Foundation
60 East Delaware Place, Suite 1480
Chicago, IL 60611
Contact: Dr. Richard T. Caleel
Geographic Giving Pattern: Primarily Michigan.
Special Interests: Hospitals, youth services, and Catholic agencies and churches.
Assets: $7,072,231 (1998)
Grant Total: $267,742
Grant Range: $5,000–$7,500
Limitations: No grants to individuals.
Applications: Contributes to pre-selected organizations only. Applications are not accepted.

W. P. and H. B. White Foundation

540 Frontage Road, Suite 3240
North Field, IL 60093
(847) 446-1441
Contact: M. Margaret Blandford, Executive Director
Geographic Giving Pattern: Primarily the metropolitan Chicago,
Illinois area.
Special Interest: Funding to organizations in the metropolitan Chicago
area that contribute to the future good of the country, primarily in the
areas of education, health, and human services, with an emphasis on
helping those most in need.
Assets: $38,180,685 (1998)
Grant Total: $2,035,250
Grant Range: $3,000–$50,000
Limitations: No grants to individuals. No support for land acquisition,
endowment funds, publicity, conferences, or deficit financing. No
matching gifts or loans.
Applications: Initial approach should be by brief letter of inquiry. The
deadlines are February 1, May 1, August 1, and November 1. The
board meets in March, June, September, and December.

Marie C. Wolf Charitable Trust

c/o Harris Trust and Savings Bank
Box 755, Tax Division
Chicago, IL 60690
(312) 461-6735
Contact: Darlene Turner, Vice President, Harris Trust and Savings
Bank
Geographic Giving Pattern: Primarily Illinois.
Special Interests: Literature, universities, education, hospitals,
science, research, and Catholic agencies and churches.
Assets: $6,279,272 (1998)
Gifts Received: $114,257
Grant Total: $300,419
Grant Range: $30,042–$120,167
Limitations: No grants to individuals.
Applications: Initial approach should be by letter. There are no
deadlines.

INDIANA

Bussing-Koch Foundation, Inc.
2905 Bayard Park Drive
Evansville, IN 47714
(812) 473-1060
Contact: Wilfred C. Bussing III, President
Geographic Giving Pattern: Primarily Indiana.
Special Interests: Catholic agencies and churches.
Assets: $10,395,402 (1999)
Grant Total: $495,274
Grant Range: $100–$50,000
Grant Average: $100–$50,000
Applications: Initial approach should be by letter including one copy of proposal. There are no deadlines.

Cornelius Family Foundation, Inc.
1055 Park Place
Zionsville, IN 46077
Contact: James M. Cornelius, President
Geographic Giving Pattern: There are no stated geographical limitations.
Special Interests: Arts and cultural programs, education, human services, Catholic agencies and churches.
Assets: $6,688,336 (1998)
Gifts Received: $147,946
Grant Total: $319,550
Grant Range: $100–$50,000
Applications: Initial approach should be by letter. There are no deadlines.

The Froderman Foundation, Inc.
4325 U.S. Highway South
P.O. Box 10039
Terre Haute, IN 47801
(812) 232-2364 (fax)
Contact: Esten Fuson, Secretary-Treasurer
Geographic Giving Pattern: Primarily Indiana.
Special Interest: Catholic and Protestant religious, educational and charitable organizations, and medicine.

Assets: $12,408,755 (1999)
Gifts Received: $500
Grant Total: $601,307
Grant Range: $643–$50,000
Applications: Initial approach should be by letter. An application form is required. There are no deadlines.

Arnold F. Habig Foundation, Inc.

1600 Royal Street
Jasper, IN 47546
(812) 482-1600
Contact: Gary P. Critser
Geographic Giving Pattern: Primarily Indiana.
Special Interest: Education, Catholic religious organizations, and church support.
Assets: $2,123,595 (1998)
Grant Total: $393,365
Grant Range: $25–$200,000
Applications: Initial approach should be by letter. There are no deadlines.

John A. Hillenbrand Foundation, Inc.

700 State Route 46 East
Batesville, IN 47006-8835
(812) 934-7000
Contact: Daniel A. Hillenbrand, President
Geographic Giving Pattern: Limited to Batesville, Indiana and surrounding areas.
Special Interest: Protestant and Catholic churches, youth programs, and higher and religious education.
Assets: $2,797,614 (1999)
Grant Total: $3,321,238
Grant Range: $1,000–$100,000
Grant Average: $2,500–$25,000
Applications: Initial approach should be by letter. There are no deadlines.

Indiana Chemical Trust
c/o Old National Trust Co.
P.O. Box 1447
Terre Haute, IN 47808-1447
(812) 462-7263
Contact: Joel Harbaugh
Geographic Giving Pattern: Primarily Vigo County, Indiana.
Description: Indiana Chemical Trust is a corporate foundation of
Terre Haute Gas Corporation, Indiana Gas and Chemical Corporation,
and Tribune-Star Publishing Company.
Special Interest: Civic, charitable, youth and educational institutions,
Catholic church support, and monasteries.
Assets: $8,702,114 (1999)
Grant Total: $486,000
Grant Range: $1,000–$150,000
Applications: Initial approach should be by letter. There are no
deadlines for grant proposals. The application address is c/o Jon
Beardsley, Old National Trust Co., P.O. Box 1447, Terra Haute, IN
47808-1447. Tel. (812) 462-7255.

Indiana Energy Foundation, Inc.
1630 North Meridian Street
Indianapolis, IN 46402
(317) 321-0357
Contact: Ron Christian
Geographic Giving Pattern: Primarily Indiana.
Special Interests: Arts, hospitals, universities, mental health
associations, athletics, medical research, federated giving programs,
Catholic agencies and churches.
Assets: $121,912 (1999)
Grant Total: $391,687
Grant Range: $1–$15,000
Applications: Initial approach should be by letter.

Irwin-Sweeney-Miller Foundation
301 Washington Street
P.O. Box 808
Columbus, IN 47202-0808
(812) 372-0251

Contact: Sarla Kalsi, Executive Director or Em Rodway, Program Officer

Geographic Giving Pattern: Primarily the Columbus, Indiana area for new funding.

Special Interest: Creative programs in social justice, education, religion, the arts, and improving family stability.

Assets: $5,510,180 (1997)

Gifts Received: $664,906

Grant Total: $1,074,047

Grant Range: $100–$331,480

Grant Average: $500–$5,000

Limitations: No grants to individuals or for deficit financing, research, fellowships, or scholarships. No loans.

Applications: Initial approach should be by letter. The deadlines are March 1 and September 1.

Jasper Office Furniture Foundation, Inc.

13th and Vine Streets

Jasper, IN 47546

(812) 482-5154

Contact: Joseph F. Steurer, President

Geographic Giving Pattern: Primarily Dubois County, Indiana.

Description: Jasper Office Furniture Foundation, Inc. is a corporate foundation of JOFCO, Inc.

Special Interest: Higher education, healthcare, human and youth services, Catholic churches, and Catholic agencies.

Assets: $742,039 (1998)

Grant Total: $76,411

Grant Range: $20–$10,000

Limitations: No grants to individuals.

Applications: Initial approach should be by letter. There are no deadlines.

Kimball International-Habig Foundation, Inc.

1600 Royal Street, GOX-201

Japer, IN 47549

(812) 482-1600

Contact: Douglas A. Habig, President

Geographic Giving Pattern: There are no stated geographical limitations.

Special Interests: Human services, arts and cultural programs, health associations, hospitals, community development, public affairs, service clubs, Catholic church support and Catholic agencies.
Assets: $2,009,942 (1999)
Gifts Received: $400,000
Grant Total: $556,634
Grant Range: $25–$25,000
Applications: There are no deadlines.

Koch Foundation, Inc.
10 South Eleventh Avenue
Evansville, IN 47744-0001
(812) 465-9600
Contact: Robert L. Koch II, President
Geographic Giving Pattern: Limited to Indiana and western Kentucky, with an emphasis on the Evansville and Vanderburgh county areas.
Special Interests: Arts and culture, education, human services, economically disadvantaged, and Catholic agencies and churches.
Assets: $19,536,476 (1998)
Gifts Received: $1,500,000
Grant Total: $1,102,870
Grant Range: $25–$212,000
Limitations: No grants to individuals (except for employee-related scholarships).
Applications: Initial approach should be by letter including one copy of proposal. There are no deadlines.

Andrew J. and Florence A. Krizman Charitable Foundation
c/o First Source Bank, Trust Department
P.O. Box 1602
South Bend, IN 46634-1602
(219) 235-2790
Contact: Mary Hugus, Trust Officer
Geographic Giving Pattern: Primarily South Bend, Indiana.
Special Interests: Historic preservation, Catholic church support and Catholic agencies.
Assets: $1,524,781 (1998)
Gifts Received: $100,000
Grant Total: $85,875

Grant Range: $1,000–$21,875
Limitations: No grants to individuals.
Applications: Contributes to pre-selected organizations only. Applications are not accepted.

Lilly Endowment, Inc.

2801 North Meridian Street
P.O. Box 88068
Indianapolis, IN 46208
(317) 924-5471
(317) 926-4431 (fax)
Contact: Sue Ellen Walker
Geographic Giving Pattern: National, for religious giving.
Special Interest: National religious research centering specifically on issues facing mainstream Protestantism, historically black churches, and the American Catholic church. Support also for theological seminaries, urban ministry, and spiritual formation.
Assets: $11,538,225,323 (1999)
Grant Total: $557,301,037
Grant Range: $485–$31,711,774
Limitations: No support for endowments.
Applications: Initial approach should be by letter, one to two pages in length. There are no deadlines.

The Walter and Mildred McComb Foundation, Inc.

1140 Lake Avenue
Fort Wayne, IN 46805
(219) 426-9494
Contact: Walter A. McComb, Director
Geographic Giving Pattern: Primarily Fort Wayne, Indiana.
Special Interests: Community development, service clubs, religion, Catholic church support and Catholic agencies.
Assets: $2,652,737 (1999)
Grant Total: $114,439
Grant Range: $200–$7,500
Limitations: No grants to individuals.

Daniel M. Niblick Family Foundation

3705 Rupp Drive
Fort Wayne, IN 46815-4525

Contact: Galen D. Maust and Barbara Stewart, Trustees
Geographic Giving Pattern: Limited to Indiana.
Special Interests: Human services, historic preservation, scholarships and financial aid, hospitals, boys and girls clubs, Catholic church support and Catholic agencies.
Assets: $5,847,479 (1999)
Grant Total: $166,500
Grant Range: $2,000–$60,000
Limitations: No grants to individuals.
Applications: Contributes to pre-selected organizations only. Applications are not accepted.

Our Sunday Visitor Institute
200 Noll Plaza
Huntington, IN 46750
(800) 348-2440
(219) 356-8400
(219) 359-0029 (fax)
Contact: Thomas J. Blee, Executive Director or Michelle J. Hogan, Executive Assistant
Geographic Giving Pattern: National.
Special Interest: Catholic church-related programs and projects which address religious literacy, contribute to the evangelization of the culture, link faith and morality particularly among the young, and explain and promote the dignity of the human person.
Assets: $29,210,057 (1999)
Grant Total: $2,295,443
Grant Range: $1,000–$100,000
Limitations: No support for capital projects or for ongoing operating expenses.
Applications: Initial approach should be by letter. Grant recipients must be registered in *The Official Catholic Directory.* The deadlines are March 15, August 15, and December 15.

M. E. Raker Foundation
6207 Constitution Drive
Fort Wayne, IN 46804
(219) 436-2182
Contact: John E. Hogan, President

Geographic Giving Pattern: Primarily Indiana, with an emphasis on Fort Wayne.
Special Interest: Catholic secondary and higher education, and youth and child development agencies.
Assets: $12,833,579 (1999)
Grant Total: $491,492
Grant Range: $972–$60,000
Limitations: No grants to individuals. No support for the arts.
Applications: An application form is required. Initial approach should be by written request. There are no deadlines.

Agnes L. Seyfert Foundation
c/o Norwest Bank Indiana, N.A.
P.O. Box 960
Fort Wayne, IN 46802
(219) 461-6451
Contact: C. V. Seyfert, Norwest Bank Indiana, N.A.
Geographic Giving Pattern: Primarily Fort Wayne, Indiana.
Special Interests: Human services.
Assets: $1,087,619 (1998)
Grant Total: $32,750
Grant Range: $500–$10,000
Limitations: No grants to individuals.
Applications: Initial approach should be by letter. There are no deadlines.

Florence M. and Paul M. Staehle Foundation
c/o Fort Wayne National Bank
P.O. Box 110
Fort Wayne, IN 46801
(219) 426-0555
Geographic Giving Pattern: Primarily Fort Wayne, Indiana.
Special Interest: Education, healthcare, Catholic church support, and Catholic social service agencies.
Assets: $4,793,681 (1997)
Grant Total: $118,099
Grant Range: $1,000–$45,000
Limitations: No grants to individuals.
Applications: Initial approach should be by letter. There are no deadlines.

United Cabinet Foundation, Inc.
58 Hannah Lane
Jasper, IN 47546-2513
(812) 482-2037
Contact: Stanley G. Krempp, President
Geographic Giving Pattern: Primarily Dubois County, Indiana.
Special Interests: Catholic church support and Catholic agencies.
Assets: $1,630,294 (1999)
Grant Total: $61,075
Grant Range: $100–$27,000
Limitations: No grants to individuals.
Applications: Initial approach should be by letter. The deadline is November 1.

Robert and Kathleen Welsh Foundation, Inc.
800 East 86th Street
Merrillville, IN 46410
Contact: The Directors
Geographic Giving Pattern: Primarily Indiana.
Special Interest: Higher education, human services, Catholic church support, and Catholic agencies.
Assets: $11,591 (1998)
Gifts Received: $725,000
Grant Total: $715,250
Grant Range: $250–$10,000
Limitations: No grants to individuals.
Applications: Contributes to pre-selected organizations only. Applications are not accepted.

IOWA

Thomas Aquinas Collins Charitable Trust
22 Sixth Avenue, N.E.
Waukon, IA 52172-1247
(319) 568-3401
Contact: Robert A. Collins, Manager
Geographic Giving Pattern: National.
Special Interest: Catholic religious purposes including religious education, pro-life activities, rosary promotion, and welfare.
Assets: $9,748 (1999)

Grant Total: $61,894
Grant Range: $10–$41,850
Applications: Initial approach should be by proposal. An application form is required. There are no deadlines.

John K. Figge and Patricia J. Figge Charitable Foundation
220 N. Main Street, Suite 600
Davenport, IA 52801
Contact: The Trustees
Special Interests: Catholic giving.
Assets: $204,960 (1998)
Grant Total: $79,197
Grant Range: $250–$15,500
Applications: Initial approach should be by letter. The application address is P.O. Box 30626, Sea Island, GA 31561.

V. O. Figge and Elizabeth Kahl Figge Charitable Foundation
710 Union Arcade Building
Davenport, IA 52801
(319) 326-2806
Contact: The Trustees
Geographic Giving Pattern: Limited to Iowa.
Special Interests: Education, healthcare, human services, Catholic agencies and churches.
Assets: $17,868,449 (1998)
Gifts Received: $3,447,264
Grant Total: $813,683
Grant Range: $5,000–$101,797
Applications: Initial approach should be by letter. There are no deadlines.

Krause Gentle Foundation
4201 Westown Parkway, Suite 220
West DesMoines, IA 50265
Contact: Dennis Folden and William A. Krause
Geographic Giving Pattern: There are no stated geographical limitations.
Special Interests: Human services, music, visual arts, animal welfare, housing and shelter, federated giving programs, muscular dystrophy,

camps, boys and girls clubs, Protestant agencies and churches, Catholic church support and Catholic agencies.
Assets: $3,179,898 (1998)
Gifts Received: $1,810,795
Grant Total: $454,683
Grant Range: $100–$102,226
Limitations: No grants to individuals.

The William C. Metz Charitable Foundation II
34 West Kings Highway
Sioux City, IA 51104
(712) 255-2200
Contact: William C. Metz, President
Geographic Giving Pattern: There are no stated geographical limitations.
Special Interests: Arts and cultural programs, higher education, human services, and Catholic agencies and churches.
Assets: $656,020 (1999)
Grant Total: $24,230
Grant Range: $30–$15,000
Limitations: No grants to individuals.
Applications: Contributes to pre-selected organizations only. Applications are not accepted.

Cynthia and Jack Rehm Private Foundation
1716 Locust Street
Des Moines, IA 50308-3032
Contact: Cynthia Rehm and Jack Rehm, Trustees
Geographic Giving Pattern: Primarily Des Moines, Iowa.
Special Interests: Colleges, universities, Catholic church support and Catholic agencies.
Assets: $1,769,789 (1999)
Gifts Received: $15,000
Grant Total: $201,858
Grant Range: $25–$62,341

Mary Louise Slattery Charitable Trust
8804 New York Avenue
Des Moines, IA 50322
Contact: Delores Nutt, Trustee

Geographic Giving Pattern: Primarily Des Moines, Iowa.
Special Interest: Hospitals, human services, Catholic church support, and Catholic agencies.
Assets: $942,365 (1998)
Grant Total: $60,000
Grant Range: $2,500–$25,000
Applications: Initial approach should be by proposal. There are no deadlines.

Clemens J. Smith Charitable Foundation

901 Sunrise
New Hampton, IA 50659
Contact: Ramona Smith-Gates, President
Geographic Giving Pattern: Limited to Epworth, Iowa.
Special Interest: Mission travel, and grants for priests or brothers to further their education.
Assets: $528,055 (1998)
Grant Total: $24,500
Grant Range: $3,500–$10,000
Applications: Initial approach should be by letter. There are no deadlines.

C. Richard Stark, Jr. and Joan E. Stark Foundation

601 Locust, Suite 1100
Des Moines, IA 50309
(515) 282-7702
Contact: C. Richard Stark, Jr. and Joan E. Stark, Directors
Geographic Giving Pattern: Primarily Iowa.
Special Interests: Elementary and secondary education and Catholic agencies and churches.
Assets: $2,899,833 (1998)
Gifts Received: $2,000,000
Grant Total: $214,000
Grant Range: $1,000–$135,000
Limitations: No grants to individuals.
Applications: Contributes to pre-selected organizations only. Applications are not accepted.

KANSAS

Daniel M. Carney Family Charitable Foundation

8100 East 22nd Street North
Building 1900
Wichita, KS 67226-2319
(316) 683-5150
Contact: Daniel M. Carney, Manager
Geographic Giving Pattern: Primarily Wichita, Kansas.
Special Interest: Education, children and youth, social services,
Catholic church support, and Catholic agencies.
Assets: $2,822,855 (1998)
Grant Total: $314,200
Grant Range: $500–$40,000
Limitations: No grants to individuals.
Applications: Initial approach should be by letter. There are no
deadlines.

Dondlinger Foundation, Inc.

P.O. Box 398
Wichita, KS 67201
(316) 945-0555
Contact: Paul J. Dondlinger, President
Geographic Giving Pattern: Primarily Wichita, Kansas.
Description: The Dondlinger Foundation, Inc. is a corporate
foundation of the Dondlinger and Sons Construction Company, Inc.
Special Interest: The arts, cultural programs, youth services, health
agencies, Catholic churches, and Catholic agencies.
Assets: $766,996 (1998)
Gifts Received: $150,000
Grant Total: $165,550
Applications: Initial approach should be by letter. There are no
deadlines. The application address is 2656 South Sheridan, Wichita,
KS 67217.

Goebel Family-Star Lumber Charitable Foundation

P.O. Box 7712
Wichita, KS 67277
(316) 942-2221
Contact: Robert L. Goebel, President

Geographic Giving Pattern: Primarily southcentral Kansas.
Description: Goebel Family-Star Lumber Charitable Foundation is a corporate foundation of Star Lumber & Supply Company, Inc.
Special Interest: Higher education, business education, healthcare, the disabled, human and youth services, and some Catholic giving.
Assets: $571,957 (1998)
Gifts Received: $176,100
Grant Total: $100,791
Grant Range: $12–$10,000
Limitations: No grants to individuals.
Applications: Initial approach should be by letter. There are no deadlines. The application address is 325 S. West Street, Wichita, KS 67213.

E. E. Newcomer Enterprises Foundation
5301 West 116th Street
Leawood, KS 66211
(816) 221-0543
Contact: Edward E. Newcomer, President
Geographic Giving Pattern: Primarily the bi-state Kansas City metropolitan area.
Special Interests: Education, Protestant services and churches, Catholic church support and Catholic agencies.
Assets: $355,690 (1999)
Gifts Received: $173,100
Grant Total: $87,000
Grant Average: $10,000
Limitations: No grants to individuals.
Applications: Contributes to pre-selected organizations only. Applications are not accepted.

John J. Sullivan, Jr. Foundation
c/o John Houlehan & Mark Henke, Trustees
4700 West 50th Place
Roeland Park, KS 66205
(913) 261-5401
Contact: John Houlehan
Geographic Giving Pattern: Primarily Kansas and Missouri.
Special Interests: Secondary and higher education and Catholic agencies and churches.

Assets: $5,382.429 (1998)
Grant Total: $380,550
Grant Range: $500–$495,000
Limitations: No grants to individuals.
Applications: Contributes to pre-selected organizations only.
Applications are not accepted.

KENTUCKY

Faragher Foundation, Inc.
618 Sunset Court
Covington, KY 41011-1126
Contact: Raymond Faragher, President
Geographic Giving Pattern: Primarily Kentucky and Cincinnati, Ohio.
Special Interests: Education, housing and shelter, Catholic church support and Catholic agencies.
Gifts Received: $106,751 (1996)
Grant Total: $108,110
Grant Range: $25,000–$58,110
Limitations: No grants to individuals.
Applications: Contributes to pre-selected organizations only.
Applications are not accepted.

Fischer Family Foundation
2670 Chancellor Drive, Suite 300
Crestview Hills, KY 41017
(606) 341-4709
Contact: Elaine M. Fischer and Henry K. Fischer
Geographic Giving Pattern: Limited to Kentucky and Ohio.
Special Interests: Fundraising, secondary and higher education, cancer research, boys clubs, the arts, Catholic agencies and churches.
Assets: $10,884,867 (1999)
Gifts Received: $2,700,000
Grant Total: $321,025
Grant Range: $100–$100,000
Limitations: No grants to individuals.
Applications: Contributes to pre-selected organizations only.
Applications are not accepted.

The Gheens Foundation, Inc.

One Riverfront Plaza, Suite 705
Louisville, KY 40202
(502) 584-4650
(502) 584-4652 (fax)
Email: lindahw@aye.net
Contact: James N. Davis, Executive Director
Geographic Giving Pattern: Primarily Kentucky, Indiana, and
Louisiana, with an emphasis on Louisville, Kentucky.
Special Interest: Higher, secondary and Catholic education, health
and social service agencies, cultural programs, Catholic churches, and
diocesan support.
Assets: $88,461,977 (1999)
Grant Total: $4,048,385
Grant Range: $4,000–$83,333
Grant Average: $5,000–$50,000
Applications: Initial approach should be by letter with a one- to two-
page outline. An application form is required. There are no deadlines.

Al J. Schneider Foundation Corporation

P.O. Box 16970
Louisville, KY 40256-0970
(502) 448-6351
Contact: Al J. Schneider, President
Geographic Giving Pattern: Primarily Kentucky.
Special Interest: Catholic religious associations, a convent, and
churches; some support for healthcare, cultural programs, youth, and
higher education.
Assets: $326,317 (1999)
Gifts Received: $202,200
Grant Total: $552,865
Grant Range: $5–$200,000
Applications: Contributes to pre-selected organizations only.
Applications are not accepted.

George P. and Henrietta D. Whipple Foundation, Inc.

509 Briar Hill Road
Louisville, KY 40206
Contact: Frank W. Burke, Sr., President
Geographic Giving Pattern: Primarily Louisville, Kentucky.

Special Interests: Human services, Catholic church support and Catholic agencies.
Assets: $1,054,020 (1999)
Grant Total: $55,500
Grant Range: $2,500–$5,000
Limitations: No grants to individuals.
Applications: Contributes to pre-selected organizations only. Applications are not accepted.

LOUISIANA

The Azby Fund
Whitney Bank Building
228 St. Charles Avenue, Suite 1311
New Orleans, LA 70130-2613
Contact: Michael S. Liebaert, Executive Director
Geographic Giving Pattern: Primarily New Orleans, Louisiana.
Special Interest: Catholic giving, church support, historic preservation, higher education, and medical sciences.
Assets: $13,795,051 (1998)
Grant Total: $736,917
Grant Range: $200–$290,266
Limitations: No grants to individuals.
Applications: Contributes to pre-selected organizations only. Applications are not accepted.

B R & R Foundation
648 Albert Hart Drive
Baton Rouge, LA 70808
Contact: Randall J. Roberts, Secretary-Treasurer
Special Interests: Historic preservation, environment, medical centers, human and family services, Catholic agencies and churches.
Assets: $4,172,802 (1998)
Grant Total: $146,600
Grant Range: $100–$40,000

Booth-Bricker Fund
826 Union Street
Suite 300

New Orleans, LA 70112
(504) 581-2430
Contact: Gray S. Parker, Chair
Geographic Giving Pattern: New Orleans, Louisiana.
Special Interest: Catholic giving, universities, hospitals, social
services, youth, the arts, and general charitable giving.
Assets: $35,676,256 (1998)
Grant Total: $1,621,536
Grant Range: $50–$117,766
Limitations: No grants to individuals. No support for operating or
maintenance expenses.
Applications: Initial approach should be by letter or proposal. There
are no deadlines. The board meets quarterly.

Joseph C. and Sue Ellen M. Canizaro Foundation

516 Northline
Metarie, LA 70005
(504) 584-5000
Contact: Joseph C. Canizaro, President and Treasurer
Geographic Giving Pattern: There are no stated geographical
limitations.
Special Interests: Human services, Catholic agencies and churches.
Assets: $2,317 (1998)
Gifts Received: $862,500
Grant Total: $851,512
Grant Range: $100–$400,00
Limitations: No grants to individuals.
Applications: Contributes to pre-selected organizations only.
Applications are not accepted.

The Maria De Renville - Franicevic Foundation

1201 South Clearview Parkway, #100
Jefferson, LA 70121
(504) 736-4636
Contact: Dr. Charles C. Mary, Jr., President
Geographic Giving Pattern: Primarily Louisiana and Pennsylvania.
Special Interests: Secondary and higher education, Catholic agencies
and churches.
Assets: $5,057,728 (1999)

Grant Total: $295,025
Grant Range: $500–$50,000
Applications: Initial approach should be by letter. There are no deadlines.

Eugenie and Joseph Jones Family Foundation
835 Union Street, Suite 333
New Orleans, LA 70112
(504) 584-1511
Contact: J. Merrick Jones, Jr., Eugenie Huger, or Susan Gundlach
Geographic Giving Pattern: Primarily Louisiana.
Special Interest: Education, healthcare, Catholic church support, and Catholic agencies.
Assets: $15,803,217 (1998)
Grant Total: $986,565
Grant Range: $200–$100,000
Limitations: No grants to individuals or for land acquisition, operating budgets, continuing support, publications, conferences, deficit financing, or emergency funds. No loans.
Applications: Initial approach should be by letter requesting guidelines. The board meets quarterly.

Libby-Dufour Fund
c/o M. Cleland Powell II
Whitney Bank Building
228 St. Charles Avenue
New Orleans, LA 70130-2615
(504) 586-7421
Contact: M. Cleland Powell, President
Geographic Giving Pattern: Limited to New Orleans, Louisiana.
Special Interest: Christian charities, churches, church-related education, and Christian welfare funds; some support for hospitals and medical centers.
Assets: $10,455,516 (1998)
Grant Total: $415,000
Grant Range: $5,000–$50,000
Limitations: No grants to individuals or for endowment funds or operating budgets.

Applications: Initial approach should be by proposal, with full explanation of why the charity needs the grant. There are no deadlines. The board meets quarterly.

J. Edgar Monroe Foundation (1976)

228 Saint Charles Avenue, Suite 1402
New Orleans, LA 70130
(504) 529-3539
Contact: Robert J. Monroe, President
Geographic Giving Pattern: Primarily Louisiana.
Special Interest: The arts, culture, historic preservation, higher and parochial education, diocesan support, churches, and religious organizations.
Assets: $12,094,387 (1997)
Grant Total: $1,057,090
Grant Range: $45–$725,000
Grant Average: $100–$50,000
Limitations: No grants to individuals.
Applications: Initial approach should be by proposal. An application form is not required. The board meets quarterly.

Reily Foundation

640 Magazine Street
New Orleans, LA 70130-3406
(504) 524-6131
Contact: H. Eustis Reily
Geographic Giving Pattern: Primarily the New Orleans, Louisiana area.
Special Interest: The arts, culture, education, human services, diocesan support, Protestant and Catholic churches and agencies.
Assets: $9,704,751 (1998)
Gifts Received: $2,150,000
Grant Total: $1,581,750
Grant Range: $900–$334,000
Limitations: No grants to individuals.
Applications: Initial approach should be by proposal. An application form is required. There are no deadlines.

The Louis P. Saia Foundation

1405 Bayou Black Drive
Houma, LA 70360
(504) 876-0660
Contact: Louis P. Saia, Jr.
Geographic Giving Pattern: Primarily Louisiana.
Special Interests: Human services, education, hospitals, Catholic church support and Catholic agencies.
Assets: $1,403,031 (1998)
Grant Total: $53,600
Grant Range: $350–$12,000
Applications: Initial approach should be by letter or telephone. There are no deadlines.

Stuller Family Foundation

818 Bayou Tortue Road
Broussard, LA 70518
Contact: Matthew G. Stuller, Trustee
Geographic Giving Pattern: Primarily Lafayette, Louisiana.
Special Interests: Catholic agencies and churches.
Assets: $16,207,563 (1998)
Gifts Received: $2,845,030
Grant Total: $1,618,560
Grant Range: $250–$800,000
Applications: Initial approach should be by proposal.

Fanny Edith Winn Educational Trust

P.O. Drawer 730
Crowley, LA 70527-0730
(318) 783-7000
Contact: The Trustees
Geographic Giving Pattern: Primarily Louisiana.
Special Interest: Education, and Protestant and Catholic church support and agencies.
Assets: $4,422,541 (1998)
Grant Total: $199,000
Grant Range: $1,000–$37,200
Applications: An application form is not required. There are no deadlines for grant proposals.

MAINE

McCarthy Family Foundation
Route 96
East Boothbay, ME 04544-9806
Contact: Eugene G. McCarthy, President
Geographic Giving Pattern: National and international.
Special Interest: Catholic theological education, religious orders, and church support.
Assets: $2,157,536 (1998)
Gifts Received: $250,000
Grant Total: $336,909
Grant Range: $613–$120,000
Limitations: No grants to individuals.
Applications: Contributes to pre-selected organizations only. Applications are not accepted.

MARYLAND

The Abell Foundation, Inc.
111 S. Calvert Street, Suite 2300
Baltimore, MD 21202-6174
(410) 547-1300
(410) 539-6579 (fax)
Email: abell@abell.org
www.abell.org
Contact: Robert C. Embry, Jr., President
Geographic Giving Pattern: Limited to Maryland, with an emphasis on Baltimore.
Special Interest: Education, economic development, human services, and homelessness.
Assets: $267,402,753 (1999)
Grant Total: $12,951,129
Grant Range: $15,000–$1,500,000
Grant Average: $5,000–$50,000
Limitations: No grants to individuals. No support for housing or medical facilities.
Applications: Initial approach should be by letter, requesting guidelines. An application form is required. The deadlines are January 1, March 1, May 1, August 1, September 1, and November 1.

Charles S. Abell Foundation, Inc.

8401 Connecticut Avenue, Suite 1111
Chevy Chase, MD 20815
(301) 652-2224
(301) 652-4614 (fax)
Contact: W. Shepherdson Abell, Secretary-Treasurer
Geographic Giving Pattern: Primarily Washington, D.C. and Maryland.
Special Interest: Church-related food and shelter centers, social service agencies, women, children, and Catholic federated giving programs.
Assets: $21,483,485 (1998)
Grant Total: $666,840
Grant Range: $10,000–$40,000
Limitations: No grants to individuals.
Applications: Initial approach should be by proposal, not exceeding two pages. The deadlines are in February, May, August, and November.

Angelos Scholarship Foundation

100 North Charles Street, 22nd Floor
Baltimore, MD 21201
(410) 426-3200
Contact: Peter G. Angelos, President
Geographic Giving Pattern: Primarily Baltimore, Maryland.
Special Interests: Higher education and Catholic agencies and churches.
Assets: $6,299,524 (1998)
Gifts Received: $8,164,507
Grant Total: $2,980,500
Grant Range: $1,000–$330,000
Applications: Initial approach should be by letter. There are no deadlines.

Darby Foundation

P.O. Box 1660
Easton, MD 21601
(908) 522-8435
Contact: Nicholas Brady, Trustee

Geographic Giving Pattern: Primarily New York, New Jersey, and Washington, D.C.

Special Interest: Museums, libraries, historical societies, social services, Catholic church support, and Catholic agencies.

Assets: $2,012,342 (1999)

Grant Total: $154,000

Grant Range: $1,000–$50,000

Applications: Initial approach should be by letter. There are no deadlines.

Eiserer-Hickey Foundation, Inc.

9101 Sligo Creek Parkway

Silver Spring, MD 20901

(301) 587-6300

Contact: Leonard A. C. Eiserer, President

Geographic Giving Pattern: Primarily Maryland.

Special Interests: Human services, education, food distribution, federated giving programs, the economically disadvantaged, meals on wheels, homelessness, Catholic church support and Catholic agencies.

Assets: $783,946 (1999)

Grant Total: $89,000

Grant Range: $1,000–$25,000

Limitations: No grants to individuals.

Applications: Contributes to pre-selected organizations only. Applications are not accepted.

France-Merrick Foundation

The Exchange

1122 Kenilworth Drive, Suite 118

Towson, MD 21204

(410) 832-5700

(410) 832-5704 (fax)

Contact: Robert W. Schaefer, Executive Director

Geographic Giving Pattern: Primarily the Baltimore, Maryland metropolitan area.

Special Interest: Higher education, civic and cultural affairs, historic preservation, healthcare, social services, Catholic schools, and diocesan support.

Assets: $239,141,281 (1999)

Grant Total: $8,218,235
Grant Range: $1,000–$600,000
Grant Average: $5,000–$50,000
Limitations: No grants to individuals.
Applications: Initial approach should be by letter describing the organization and the purpose for which funds will be used. An application form is not required. There are no deadlines.

The James M. Johnston Trust for Charitable and Educational Purposes
2 Wisconsin Circle
Chevy Chase, MD 20815
(301) 907-0135
Contact: Julia Sanders, Office Manager
Geographic Giving Pattern: Primarily Washington, D.C. and North Carolina.
Special Interest: Higher, secondary and Catholic education, including training of nurses and faculty salaries.
Assets: $104,615,027 (1998)
Grant Total: $3,855,630
Grant Range: $5,000–$130,000
Limitations: No grants to individuals. No support for building funds, endowment funds or operating budgets.
Applications: Initial approach should be by letter. The deadline is October 15.

Joseph S. Keelty Foundation
61 East Padonia Road
P.O. Box 528
Timonium, MD 21094
(410) 252-8600, ext. 18
Contact: James Keelty Jr., President
Geographic Giving Pattern: Primarily Maryland and Virginia.
Special Interest: Higher, secondary and Catholic education, and Catholic religious organizations.
Assets: $1,152,436 (1999)
Gifts Received: $100,000
Grant Total: $133,400
Limitations: No grants to individuals.

Applications: Contributes to pre-selected organizations only. Applications are not accepted.

The Marion I. and Henry J. Knott Foundation, Inc.
3904 Hickory Avenue
Baltimore, MD 21211
(410) 235-7068
(410) 889-2577 (fax)
Email: knott@knottfoundation.org
www.knottfoundation.org
Contact: Gregory Cantori, Executive Director
Geographic Giving Pattern: Limited to the greater Baltimore, Maryland area, particularly the Baltimore Catholic Archdiocese.
Special Interest: Catholic activities including education, healthcare, and social and human services.
Assets: $47,037,416 (1998)
Grant Total: $1,637,580
Grant Range: $5,000–$213,280
Grant Average: $10,000–$50,000
Limitations: No support for pro-choice causes, public education, organizations in operation for less than one year, public sector agencies, environmental organizations, daycare centers, or single disease organizations. No grants to individuals. No support for scholarship funds, annual giving appeals, or political activities.
Applications: Initial approach should be by telephone or letter requesting application guidelines. The deadlines are February 1 and August 1.

The Linehan Family Foundation, Inc.
515 Fairmount Avenue, Suite 900
Towson, MD 21286
Contact: Darielle D. Linehan, President
Geographic Giving Pattern: Primarily Baltimore, Maryland.
Special Interests: Education, Catholic agencies and churches.
Assets: $4,733,456 (1999)
Grant Total: $570,800
Grant Range: $50–$80,000
Limitations: No grants to individuals.
Applications: Contributes to pre-selected organizations only. Applications are not accepted.

The William and Mary McCormick Foundation, Inc.
9520 Baltimore Boulevard
College Park, MD 20740-1322
(301) 474-9500
Contact: William J. McCormick, Jr., President
Geographic Giving Pattern: Primarily Maryland and Massachusetts.
Description: The William and Mary McCormick Foundation, Inc. is a corporate foundation of Jordan-Kitt Music, Inc.
Special Interest: Education, legal services, Catholic agencies and churches.
Assets: $303,363 (1999)
Gifts Received: $32,000
Grant Total: $10,600
Grant Range: $100–$2,500
Applications: There are no deadlines for grant proposals.

George W. McManus Foundation, Inc.
3703 Greenway
Baltimore, MD 21218
(410) 243-3703
Contact: The Trustees
Geographic Giving Pattern: Primarily the Baltimore metropolitan area.
Special Interests: Education, speech and hearing centers, legal services, human services, and Catholic agencies and churches.
Assets: $5,189,984 (1998)
Grant Total: $60,590
Grant Range: $15–$10,400
Limitations: No grants to individuals.
Applications: Contributes to pre-selected organizations only. Applications are not accepted.

The Thomas F. and Clementine L. Mullan Foundation, Inc.
2330 West Joppa Road, Suite 210
Lutherville, MD 21093
(410) 494-9200
Contact: Thomas F. Mullan III, President and Treasurer
Geographic Giving Pattern: Primarily Baltimore, Maryland.
Special Interest: Hospitals and health agencies, higher and secondary education, Catholic church support, and social services.

Assets: $3,348,820 (1998)
Grant Total: $161,761
Grant Range: $100–$17,400
Limitations: No grants to individuals.
Applications: Contributes to pre-selected organizations only.
Applications are not accepted.

The W. O'Neil Foundation

5454 Wisconsin Avenue, Suite 730
Chevy Chase, MD 20815
(301) 656-5848
(301) 656-2304 (fax)
Contact: Helene O'Neil Cobb, President
Geographic Giving Pattern: National and international through U.S.-based charities.
Special Interest: Basic needs of the poor and emergency relief, primarily through Catholic agencies.
Assets: $49,159,648 (1999)
Grant Total: $2,405,750
Grant Range: $1,500–$50,000
Limitations: No grants to individuals or for endowment funds, capital campaigns, church or school renovations, administrative overhead, conferences, or seminars. No matching gifts or loans.
Applications: Initial approach should be by letter of inquiry. There are no deadlines.

John A. Quinn Foundation, Inc.

5020 Nicholson Court, Suite 207 A
Kensington, MD 20895-1007
Contact: Eileen S. Quinn, President
Geographic Giving Pattern: Primarily the greater metropolitan Washington, D.C. area.
Special Interest: Education, Catholic church support, and Catholic agencies.
Assets: $2,681,472 (1999)
Grant Total: $287,000
Grant Range: $2,500–$136,950
Limitations: No grants to individuals.
Applications: Contributes to pre-selected organizations only.
Applications are not accepted.

Stephalee Foundation, Inc.
12320 Parklawn Drive
Rockville, MD 20852-1786
(301) 984-2410
Contact: Lawrence J. Cain, Jr., Manager
Geographic Giving Pattern: Primarily Maryland.
Special Interests: Higher education Catholic church support and
Catholic agencies.
Assets: $89,236 (1999)
Gifts Received: $54,888
Grant Total: $45,000
Limitations: No grants to individuals.
Applications: Contributes to pre-selected organizations only.
Applications are not accepted.

The Sullivan Family Foundation
6441 Cloisters Gate Drive
Baltimore, MD 21212
(410) 377-8777
Contact: Michael D. Sullivan
Special Interests: Catholic giving.
Assets: $897,160 (1999)
Grant Total: $78,940
Grant Range: $300–$20,040
Applications: There are no deadlines.

MASSACHUSETTS

The George I. Alden Trust
370 Main Street, Room 1250
Worcester, MA 01608-1714
(508) 798-8621
(508) 791-6545 (fax)
Contact: Francis H. Dewey III, Chair
Geographic Giving Pattern: National.
Special Interest: Private, independent education, primarily colleges.
Some support for secondary schools, historic preservation, and youth
services.
Assets: $184,810,449 (1998)

Grant Total: $6,947,000
Grant Range: $5,000–$1,000,000
Grant Average: $10,000–$100,000
Limitations: No grants to individuals. No loans.
Applications: Initial approach should be by proposal letter. There are no deadlines.

Birmingham Foundation
Ten Post Office Square
Suite 600 South
Boston, MA 02109-4603
(617) 573-5226
Contact: Paul J. Birmingham, Trustee
Geographic Giving Pattern: Primarily Massachusetts, especially Boston.
Special Interest: Catholic welfare funds, education, and social service agencies.
Assets: $6,806,384 (1999)
Grant Total: $536,150
Grant Range: $750–$100,000
Limitations: No grants to individuals.
Applications: Contributes to pre-selected organizations only. Applications are not accepted.

Patrick Carney Foundation
Batterymarch Park II
Quincy, MA 02169
(617) 472-1000
Contact: Patrick Carney
Geographic Giving Pattern: Primarily Massachusetts.
Special Interests: Higher education, hospitals, human and social services, Catholic church support and Catholic agencies.
Assets: $166,901 (1999)
Gifts Received: $61,100
Grant Total: $60,632
Grant Range: $60–$20,000
Limitations: No grants to individuals.
Applications: Initial approach should be by letter providing information regarding qualified charitable status and intended use of grant. There are no deadlines.

S. Casey and C. Casey Coyne Fund

P.O. Box 454
Harwich Port, MA 02646
(508) 432-3200
Contact: Richard Cain, State Street Bank and Trust Company
Geographic Giving Pattern: Primarily Massachusetts.
Special Interests: Human services, healthcare, Catholic church support and Catholic agencies.
Assets: $1,917,030 (1999)
Grant Total: $93,000
Grant Range: $2,500–$6,500
Applications: Contributes to pre-selected organizations only. Applications are not accepted.

Warren Cross Foundation

c/o Warren Investments
177 Worcester Street, Suite 303
Wellesley Hills, MA 02181
(617) 235-8997
Contact: Patricia Cross, Trustee
Geographic Giving Pattern: Primarily Massachusetts.
Special Interests: Human services, arts and cultural programs, education, healthcare, Catholic church support and Catholic agencies.
Assets: $847,744 (1999)
Gifts Received: $21,788
Grant Total: $259,637
Grant Range: $35–$100,000
Limitations: No grants to individuals.
Applications: Contributes to pre-selected organizations only. Applications are not accepted.

Irene E. and George A. Davis Foundation

1 Monarch Place
Springfield, MA 01144
(413) 734-8336
(413) 734-7845 (fax)
Email: davisfoun@aol.com
Contact: Mary E. Walachy, Executive Director
Geographic Giving Pattern: Primarily western Massachusetts.

Description: The Irene E. and George A. Davis Foundation is a corporate foundation of the American Saw and Manufacturing Company.
Special Interest: Higher education and Catholic institutions including churches, social services, hospitals, and community funds.
Assets: $64,314,907 (1998)
Gifts Received: $4,006,314
Grant Total: $3,390,979
Grant Range: $100–$500,000
Grant Average: $1,000–$50,000
Limitations: No grants to individuals or for deficit financing, equipment, endowment funds, scholarships, research, publications, or conferences. No matching gifts or loans.
Applications: Initial approach should be by proposal. An application form is required. The deadlines are February 1, May 1, August 1, and November 1.

DeMatteo Charitable Foundation
131 Messina Drive
Braintree, MA 02184
Contact: M. John DeMatteo, Trustee
Geographic Giving Pattern: Primarily Massachusetts.
Special Interests: Children and youth services and Catholic agencies and churches.
Assets: $456,726 (1998)
Grant Total: $306,150
Grant Range: $50–$200,000
Limitations: No grants to individuals.
Applications: Initial approach should be by letter with description and purpose of organization and intended use of requested gift. There are no deadlines.

V. Eugene and Rosalie DeFreitas Foundation
c/o Eastern Bank & Trust Company
94 Pleasant Street
Malden, MA 02148
(781) 388-3074
Contact: Robert M. Wallask, Vice President, Eastern Bank & Trust Company
Geographic Giving Pattern: National.

Special Interest: Protestant and Catholic colleges and seminaries for the purpose of teaching and training Christian missionaries, particularly for foreign missions.
Assets: $10,974,621 (1999)
Grant Total: $546,000
Grant Range: $20,000–$50,000
Limitations: No grants to individuals.
Applications: Initial approach should be by letter requesting an application form and guidelines. An application form is required. The deadline is July 1.

The Paul A. Duchaine Family Charitable Trust Foundation
25 Agawam Road
Sharon, MA 02067
Contact: The Trustees
Geographic Giving Pattern: There are no stated geographical limitations.
Special Interests: Education Catholic church support and Catholic agencies.
Assets: $1,796,088 (1998)
Grant Total: $73,250
Grant Range: $250–$50,000
Limitations: No grants to individuals.
Applications: Contributes to pre-selected organizations only. Applications are not accepted.

Egan Family Foundation
87 Elm Street
Hopkinton, MA 01748
Contact: Catherine E. Walker, Executive Director
Geographic Giving Pattern: Limited to Massachusetts.
Special Interests: Education, health associations, Catholic agencies and churches.
Assets: $16,691,223 (1998)
Grant Total: $1,235,225
Grant Range: $250–$1,005,000
Limitations: No grants to individuals.
Applications: Contributes to pre-selected organizations only. Applications are not accepted.

Aubert J. Fay Charitable Fund
P.O. Box 668
Lowell, MA 01852
Contact: Stephen L. Gervais, Trustee
Geographic Giving Pattern: Limited to Lowell, Massachusetts.
Special Interests: Hospitals, education, children and youth services, Catholic federated giving programs, Catholic agencies and churches.
Assets: $5,756,553 (1999)
Grant Total: $173,000
Grant Range: $500–$10,000
Limitations: No grants to individuals.
Applications: Initial approach should be by letter. There are no deadlines.

Flatley Foundation
50 Braintree Hill Office Park, Suite 400
Braintree, MA 02184-8754
Contact: Thomas J. Flatley, Trustee
Geographic Giving Pattern: Primarily Massachusetts.
Special Interest: Education, international affairs, social services, Protestant and Catholic church support, and Catholic agencies.
Assets: $110,481,839 (1998)
Gifts Received: $19,205,356
Grant Total: $2,331,500
Grant Range: $500–$1,010,000
Limitations: No grants to individuals.
Applications: Contributes to pre-selected organizations only. Applications are not accepted.

The Lawrence H. Hyde Charitable Trust
637 Main Street
Harwich Port, MA 02646
(508) 430-0104
Contact: Lawrence H. Hyde, Jr., President
Geographic Giving Pattern: Primarily Massachusetts and Michigan.
Special Interests: Catholic agencies and churches in impoverished areas.
Assets: $1,960,144 (1998)
Grant Total: $231,000
Grant Range: $8,000–$63,000

Limitations: No grants to individuals.
Applications: Contributes to pre-selected organizations only.
Applications are not accepted.

Leclerc Charity Fund
19 Water Street
Leominster, MA 01453-3216
(508) 537-0715
Contact: Raymond Leclerc, Manager
Geographic Giving Pattern: Primarily Massachusetts.
Special Interest: Catholic religious organizations and churches;
support also for schools for the deaf and blind.
Assets: $5,367,066 (1999)
Gifts Received: $200,000
Grant Total: $195,145
Grant Range: $100–$21,900
Limitations: No grants to individuals.
Applications: Contributes to pre-selected organizations only.
Applications are not accepted.

The Lynch Foundation
c/o Sullivan & Worcester
One Post Office Square, 25th Floor
Boston, MA 02109
(617) 338-2800
Contact: J. Frederick Bush, Secretary
Geographic Giving Pattern: National, with an emphasis on
Massachusetts.
Special Interest: Healthcare, hospitals, medical research, and
Catholic organizations.
Assets: $41,725,868 (1998)
Grant Total: $2,879,586
Grant Range: $5,000–$500,000
Limitations: No grants to individuals.
Applications: Initial approach should be by letter. An application form
is required.

William E. Maloney Foundation
271 Massachusetts Avenue
Lexington, MA 02173
(781) 862-3400
Contact: John W. Maloney, Trustee
Geographic Giving Pattern: Primarily Massachusetts.
Special Interests: Education, youth services, federated giving
programs, Catholic church support and Catholic agencies.
Assets: $8,035 (1999)
Grant Total: $50,775
Grant Range: $1,000–$21,000
Limitations: No grants to individuals.
Applications: Initial approach should be by proposal. There are no
deadlines.

Catherine McCarthy Memorial Trust Fund
P.O. Box 896
Lawrence, MA 01842
(978) 686-6151
Contact: Thomas F. Caffrey, Trustee
Geographic Giving Pattern: Primarily Massachusetts, with an
emphasis on the greater Lawrence area.
Special Interest: Higher education, social services, Catholic church
support, and Catholic agencies.
Assets: $5,506,387 (1999)
Grant Total: $303,838
Grant Range: $500–$60,500
Limitations: No grants to individuals. No support for national health
organizations, private foundations, annual campaigns, operating funds,
or standard educational programs.
Applications: Initial approach should be by letter or proposal of no
more than ten pages. There are no deadlines.

The 1991 Corcoran Foundation
100 Grandview Road, Suite 207
Braintree, MA 02184-2600
(617) 849-0011
Contact: John M Corcoran, Jr. and Thomas Corcoran, Trustees
Geographic Giving Pattern: Primarily Massachusetts.

Special Interests: Human services, education, Catholic church
support and Catholic agencies.
Assets: $3,595,204 (1999)
Gifts Received: $977,398
Grant Total: $118,800
Grant Range: $100–$10,000
Limitations: No grants to individuals.
Applications: Contributes to pre-selected organizations only.
Applications are not accepted.

Oxford Fund, Inc.
675 Massachusetts Avenue
Cambridge, MA 02139
(617) 576-8012
Contact: Robert W. MacPherson, President
Geographic Giving Pattern: Primarily Massachusetts.
Special Interests: Human services, opera, secondary and higher
education, disasters, fire prevention and control, Catholic federated
giving programs, and Christian church support and Catholic agencies.
Assets: $1,410,265 (1999)
Grant Total: $67,250
Grant Range: $250–$60,000
Limitations: No grants to individuals.
Applications: Contributes to pre-selected organizations only.
Applications are not accepted.

Joseph Perini Memorial Foundation
73 Mount Wayte Avenue
Framingham, MA 01701
(508) 628-2000
Contact: Joseph R. Perini III, Secretary
Geographic Giving Pattern: Primarily Massachusetts.
Description: Perini Memorial Foundation, Inc. is a corporate
foundation of Perini Corporation.
Special Interest: Education, family and social services, Catholic
church support, religious associations, youth, and healthcare.
Assets: $3,637,044 (1998)
Grant Total: $148,825
Grant Range: $100–$12,000

Applications: Initial approach should be by letter. The deadline is in November. The application address is c/o Selection Committee, P.O. Box 31, Framingham, MA 01701.

Sawyer Charitable Foundation
200 Newbury Street, 4th Floor
Boston, MA 02116
(617) 267-2414
Contact: Carol S. Parks, Executive Director
Geographic Giving Pattern: Primarily the greater New England area.
Special Interest: Catholic welfare funds, Catholic agencies, churches, education, health agencies, and the disabled.
Assets: $7,455,299 (1999)
Gifts Received: $700,000
Grant Total: $349,000
Grant Range: $150–$150,000
Limitations: No grants to individuals or for operating budgets or building funds.
Applications: Initial approach should be by proposal, including proof of 501(c) status. The deadline is October 15.

Blanche M. Walsh Charity Trust
174 Central Street, Suite 329
Lowell, MA 01852
(508) 454-5654
Contact: Robert F. Murphy, Jr., Trustee
Geographic Giving Pattern: National.
Special Interest: Giving is limited to Catholic organizations, including educational institutions and welfare organizations.
Assets: $2,583,695 (1999)
Grant Total: $155,530
Grant Range: $1,000–$4,000
Grant Average: $1,500
Limitations: No grants to individuals or for endowment funds, continuing support, annual campaigns, or deficit financing. No matching gifts or loans.
Applications: Initial approach should be by letter prior to November 1. An application form is required. The deadline for grant applications is December 1.

John A. White Trust
186 Pleasant Street
East Walpole, MA 02032
Contact: Mary E. Garrity, Trustee
Geographic Giving Pattern: Primarily the greater Boston, Massachusetts area.
Special Interest: Catholic social service organizations.
Assets: $15,660 (1999)
Gifts Received: $81,679
Grant Total: $93,500
Grant Range: $500–$14,000
Limitations: No grants to individuals.
Applications: There are no deadlines.

MICHIGAN

The Ave Maria Foundation
30 Frank Lloyd Wright Drive
P.O. Box 373
Ann Arbor, MI 48106-0373
(313) 930-1855
Contact: Joseph E. Davis, Program Director
Geographic Giving Pattern: Primarily Michigan.
Special Interest: Religion, Catholic church support, secondary and higher education, missionary support, and social services.
Assets: $249,587,494 (1998)
Grant Total: $17,763,944
Limitations: No grants to individuals.
Applications: Contributes to pre-selected organizations only. Applications are not accepted.

Cadillac Products Inc. Foundation
5800 Crooks Road
Troy, MI 48098-2830
Contact: Roger K. Williams, Treasurer
Geographic Giving Pattern: Primarily Michigan and Phoenix, Arizona.
Description: The Cadillac Products, Inc. Foundation is a corporate foundation.

Special Interest: Education, children, youth, Catholic agencies, and churches.
Assets: $770,301 (1998)
Gifts Received: $200,000
Grant Total: $46,000
Grant Range: $1,000–$28,000
Applications: Initial approach should be by letter. There are no deadlines.

Bernard J. & Camille Cebelak Foundation

P.O. Box 790
Ada, MI 49301
(616) 454-9495
Contact: Camille L. Cebelak, President
Geographic Giving Pattern: Primarily Grand Rapids, Michigan.
Special Interest: Education, medical research, Catholic church support, and Catholic agencies.
Assets: $4,225,703 (1998)
Gifts Received: $50,044
Grant Total: $190,000
Grant Range: $1,000–$40,000
Limitations: No grants to individuals.
Applications: Contributes to pre-selected organizations only. Applications are not accepted.

Peter J. & Constance M. Cracchiolo Foundation

24055 Jefferson Avenue, Suite 200
St. Clair Shores, MI 48080-1514
(810) 445-8111
Contact: Peter J. Cracchiolo, President
Geographic Giving Pattern: Primarily Michigan.
Special Interest: Hospitals, human services, Catholic church support, and Catholic agencies.
Assets: $7,458,775 (1999)
Grant Total: $259,310
Grant Range: $100–$60,325
Limitations: No grants to individuals.
Applications: Contributes to pre-selected organizations only. Applications are not accepted.

Raymond M. & Jane E. Cracchiolo Foundation
24055 Jefferson Avenue, Suite 200
St. Clair Shores, MI 48080-1514
(810) 445-8111
(810) 445-8112 (fax)
Contact: Raymond M. Cracchiolo, President
Geographic Giving Pattern: Limited to Michigan.
Special Interest: Youth, child welfare, and Christian religious organizations.
Assets: $3,130,317 (1999)
Grant Total: $99,914
Grant Range: $1,000–$25,000
Limitations: No grants to individuals.
Applications: Contributes to pre-selected organizations only. Applications are not accepted.

Thomas and Carol Cracchiolo Foundation
24055 Jefferson Avenue, Suite 200
St. Clair Shores, MI 48080-1514
(810) 445-8111
Contact: Thomas A. Cracchiolo, President
Geographic Giving Pattern: Primarily Michigan.
Special Interest: Health associations, children and youth, Catholic church support, and Catholic agencies.
Assets: $8,275,384 (1999)
Grant Total: $298,685
Grant Range: $100–$69,300
Limitations: No grants to individuals.
Applications: Contributes to pre-selected organizations only. Applications are not accepted.

Opal Dancey Memorial Foundation
45 South Street
Creswell, MI 48422
Contact: Rev. Gary Imms
Geographic Giving Pattern: Primarily the Midwest.
Special Interest: Seminaries and schools of theology.
Assets: $2,394,206 (1999)
Grant Total: $120,000

Applications: Initial approach should be by letter. An application form is required. The deadline is June 15.

DeSeranno Educational Foundation, Inc.
21777 Hoover Road
Warren, MI 48089
Contact: Edward Miller
Special Interest: Catholic organizations, schools, colleges and churches, and some scholarship support.
Assets: $15,061,506 (1998)
Grant Total: $119,681
Grant Range: $500–$41,681
Applications: Initial approach should be by letter. There are no deadlines.

The Drake/Quinn Family Charitable Foundation
7178 Aqua Fria Court, Southeast
Grand Rapids, MI 49456
(616) 940-1972
(616) 942-1687
(616) 940-9820 (fax)
Email: mjqdrake@iserv.net
Contact: Marilyn J. Q. Drake, President
Geographic Giving Pattern: Primarily Grand Rapids, Michigan.
Special Interests: Arts and cultural programs, housing, youth, Catholic agencies and churches.
Assets: $4,476,707 (1998)
Gifts Received: $149,986
Grant Total: $136,702
Grant Range: $25–$31,000
Applications: Contributes to pre-selected organizations only. Applications are not accepted.

Benson and Edith Ford Fund
100 Renaissance Center, 34th floor
Detroit, MI 48243
(313) 259-7777
Contact: David M. Hempstead, Secretary
Geographic Giving Pattern: Primarily Michigan.

Special Interest: Healthcare, human services, education, the arts, culture, Catholic church support, and Catholic agencies.
Assets: $47,745,487 (1998)
Gifts Received: $6,842,346
Grant Total: $2,258,934
Grant Range: $1,000–$1,055,000
Grant Average: $5,000–$50,000
Limitations: No grants to individuals.
Applications: Initial approach should be by letter. There are no deadlines.

The Richard Fortuna Foundation
14461 Levan Road
Livonia, MI 48154-5022
(734) 464-4764
Contact: Reverend George Fortuna, Trustee
Geographic Giving Pattern: Primarily Michigan.
Special Interests: Higher education, American Red Cross, Catholic church support and Catholic agencies.
Assets: $316,698 (1998)
Grant Total: $41,819
Grant Range: $565–$38,000
Applications: Initial approach should be by proposal. There are no deadlines.

Freiheit Foundation
161 Ottawa Northwest, Suite 301A
Grand Rapids, MI 49503
Contact: Peter Neguyen, Assistant
Geographic Giving Pattern: Primarily Michigan, Virginia, and Washington, D.C.
Special Interest: Catholic giving, religious education, religious communities, religious welfare, and public affairs.
Assets: $3,709,383 (1997)
Gifts Received: $1,000,000
Grant Total: $1,125,500
Grant Average: $2,500–$150,000
Limitations: No grants to individuals.

Applications: Contributes to pre-selected organizations only. Applications are not accepted.

Granger Foundation
P.O. Box 22187
Lansing, MI 48909-2187
(517) 393-1670
Contact: Alton L. Granger, Trustee
Geographic Giving Pattern: Primarily Michigan.
Special Interest: General charitable giving, social services, and Protestant and Catholic church support and agencies.
Assets: $16,487,457 (1998)
Gifts Received: $737,963
Grant Total: $944,942
Grant Range: $1,290–$100,000
Grant Average: $5,000–$10,000
Limitations: No grants to individuals.
Applications: Initial approach should be by letter. An application form is required. Four copies of the proposal are requested. There are no deadlines.

Herrick Foundation
840 West Long Lake Road, Suite 200
Troy, MI 48098-6358
(248) 267-3321 and
(248) 879-3021
(248) 879-2001 (fax)
Contact: Jan Maloney, Administrator
Geographic Giving Pattern: National, with emphasis on Michigan.
Special Interest: Higher education, church support, youth, health and welfare agencies, hospitals, and libraries.
Assets: $228,002,591 (1999)
Grant Total: $13,584,295
Grant Average: $5,000–$100,000
Limitations: No grants to individuals. No support for international organizations.
Applications: Initial approach should be by letter. There are no deadlines.

Myrtle E. & William G. Hess Charitable Trust
c/o Banc One Investment Management Group
611 Woodward Avenue
Detroit, MI 48226
(313) 225-3124
(313) 225-3948 (fax)
Email: Therese_Thorn@em.fcnbd.com
Contact: Therese M. Thorn, Vice President
Geographic Giving Pattern: Limited to Oakland County, Michigan.
Special Interest: Catholic churches, religious orders, welfare, education, religious schools, social services, youth programs, and hospitals.
Assets: $9,160,497 (1999)
Grant Total: $664,700
Grant Range: $5,000–$110,000
Applications: Initial approach should be by grant proposal. Two copies are requested. Proposals must be received by March 1.

Jones Foundation
936 Sycamore Avenue
Holland, MI 49424
Contact: Walter T. Jones, President
Geographic Giving Pattern: Primarily Michigan.
Special Interests: Education, boys and girls clubs, human services, and Catholic agencies and churches.
Assets: $828,933 (1998)
Gifts Received: $237,124
Grant Total: $708,500
Grant Range: $500–$202,000
Limitations: No grants to individuals.
Applications: Contributes to pre-selected organizations only. Applications are not accepted.

W. K. Kellogg Foundation
One Michigan Avenue East
Battle Creek, MI 49017-4058
(616) 968-1611
(616) 968-0413 (fax)
www.wkkf.org
Contact: Karen E. Lake, Director, Communications and Marketing

Geographic Giving Pattern: National and international.
Special Interests: Health, food systems, rural development, youth and education, higher education, philanthropy and voluntarism.
Assets: $6,387,840,996(1999)
Gifts Received: $769,365
Grant Total: $202,919,594
Grant Average: $5,000–$1,000,000
Limitations: No grants to individuals. No support for sectarian religious purposes. No grants for operating budgets. No loans.
Applications: Initial approach should be by letter of one to two pages. There are no deadlines.

Kowalski Sausage Company Charitable Trust
c/o NBD Bank
611 Woodward Avenue
Detroit, MI 48226
(313)225-4294
Contact: John Todd, NBD Bank, N.A.
Geographic Giving Pattern: Primarily Michigan.
Description: Kowalski Sausage Company Charitable Trust is a corporate foundation.
Special Interest: Education, the arts, cultural programs, healthcare, medical research, Catholic churches, and Catholic agencies.
Assets: $1,216,594 (1999)
Grant Total: $20,500
Grant Range: $5,000–$29,000
Limitations: No grants to individuals.
Applications: Initial approach should be by grant proposal. There are no deadlines.

The Kresge Foundation
3215 W. Big Beaver Road
P.O. Box 3151
Troy, MI 48084
(248)643-9630
(248) 643-0588 (fax)
www.kresge.org
Contact: John E. Marshall, III, President
Geographic Giving Pattern: Primarily Michigan.

Special Interests: Human services, science, higher education, humanities, arts and culture, environment, healthcare, and public affairs.
Assets: $2,203,399,210 (1998)
Grant Total: $105,791,792
Grant Range: $80,000–$4,000,000
Grant Range: $100,000–$500,000
Limitations: No grants to individuals. No support for church building projects, endowment funds, scholarships, or general purposes. No loans.
Applications: Initial approach should be by letter or telephone. There are no deadlines.

Arnold G. And Martha M. Langbo Foundation
111 Capital Avenue, Southwest
Battle Creek, MI 49015
(802) 253-0996
Contact: Martha M. Langbo, President
Geographic Giving Pattern: Primarily Michigan.
Special Interests: Human services, higher education, federated giving programs, Catholic church support and Catholic agencies.
Assets: $834,736 (1998)
Grant Total: $86,860
Grant Range: $100–$13,250
Applications: Initial approach should be by letter. There are no deadlines.

Lutjens Family Foundation
c/o John P. Schneider
333 Bridge Street, Northwest, Suite 800
Grand Rapids, MI 49504
Contact: Eric Schmitt, Director
Geographic Giving Pattern: Primarily Michigan.
Special Interests: Orchestra, American Red Cross, Catholic church support and Catholic agencies.
Assets: $445,911 (1997)
Gifts Received: $1,614
Grant Total: $52,100
Grant Range: $500–$50,000
Limitations: No grants to individuals.

Applications: Contributes to pre-selected organizations only. Applications are not accepted.

MSJ Foundation
333 Bridge Street, N.W., Suite 800
Grand Rapids, MI 49504
Contact: John Schneider
Geographic Giving Pattern: Primarily Grand Rapids, Michigan.
Special Interest: Secondary education, Catholic church support, and Catholic agencies.
Assets: $2,646,876 (1998)
Grant Total: $16,183
Limitations: No grants to individuals.
Applications: Contributes to pre-selected organizations only. Applications are not accepted.

Manat Foundation
26877 Northwestern Highway, Suite 413
Southfield, MI 48034
Contact: Manuel and Natalie Charach, Manager
Geographic Giving Pattern: Primarily Washington D.C., Michigan, and New York.
Special Interests: Hospitals, human services, youth services, Catholic agencies and churches.
Assets: $3,673,481 (1998)
Gifts Received: $401,000
Grant Total: $404,495
Grant Range: $500–$125,000
Limitations: No grants to individuals.
Applications: Contributes to pre-selected organizations only. Applications are not accepted.

W. D. and Prudence McIntyre Foundation
900 Tower Building, First Floor Annex
Troy, MI 48908
(313) 222-3183
Contact: Don Korn, Trust Officer, Bank One Trust Co.
Geographic Giving Pattern: Primarily Michigan.
Special Interests: Human services Catholic church support and Catholic agencies.

Assets: $1,322,765 (1999)
Grant Total: $62,860
Grant Range: $360–$10,000
Limitations: No grants to individuals.
Applications: Initial approach should be by letter. There are no deadlines. The application address is 611 Woodward Drive, Detroit, MI 48226.

Molloy Foundation, Inc.
P.O. Box 200
St. Clair Shores, MI 48080
(810) 775-5660
Contact: Therese M. Molloy, President
Geographic Giving Pattern: Primarily Michigan.
Special Interest: Education, religion, and social services.
Assets: $1,170,625 (1999)
Grant Total: $54,900
Grant Range: $100–$12,000
Applications: Initial approach should be by proposal. There are no deadlines.

Pellerito, Manzella, Certa and Cusmano Family Foundation
30295 Embassy Street
Beverly Hills, MI 48205
Contact: Frank A. Pellerito, Trustee
Geographic Giving Pattern: Primarily Michigan.
Special Interests: Human services, education, youth services, Catholic church support and Catholic agencies.
Assets: $655,502 (1998)
Grant Total: $43,604
Grant Range: $40–$72,000
Applications: Initial approach should be by proposal or telephone. There are no deadlines.

Edgar and Elsa Prince Foundation
190 River Avenue, Suite 300
Holland, MI 49423
Contact: Elsa D. Prince, President
Geographic Giving Pattern: Primarily Michigan.

Special Interest: Protestant and Catholic church support, education, and agencies.
Assets: $91,463,309 (1998)
Grant Total: $9,480,382
Grant Range: $200–$1,125,000
Grant Average: $5,000–$100,000
Limitations: No grants to individuals.
Applications: Contributes to pre-selected organizations only. Applications are not accepted.

Sage Foundation
P.O. Box 1919
Brighton, MI 48116-5634
(810) 227-7660
Contact: Melissa Sage Fadim, President
Geographic Giving Pattern: National.
Special Interest: Emphasis on higher and secondary education and hospitals. Support also for the disabled, Catholic religious and charitable organizations, churches, and cultural programs.
Assets: $58,676,484 (1998)
Grant Total: $2,643,620
Grant Range: $1,000–$250,000
Grant Average: $10,000–$25,000
Applications: Initial approach should be by letter requesting application guidelines. There are no deadlines.

Sehn Foundation
3515 Brookside
Bloomfield Hills, MI 48302-2911
(248) 642-6595
Contact: Francis J. Sehn, President
Geographic Giving Pattern: Primarily Detroit, Michigan.
Special Interest: Education, healthcare, Catholic agencies, and church support.
Assets: $4,541,151 (1998)
Grant Total: $192,137
Grant Range: $500–$14,000
Limitations: No grants to individuals.
Applications: Contributes to pre-selected organizations only. Applications are not accepted.

Seymour and Troester Foundation
20630 Harper Avenue, Suite 117
Harper Woods, MI 48225
(313) 886-9840
Contact: B. A. Seymour, Jr., President
Geographic Giving Pattern: Primarily Michigan.
Special Interest: Grants largely for Catholic higher and secondary educational institutions, and Catholic charitable organizations.
Assets: $2,621,638 (1998)
Grant Total: $93,000
Grant Range: $1,000–$25,000
Limitations: No grants to individuals.
Applications: Contributes to pre-selected organizations only. Applications are not accepted.

Michael T. & Nancy E. Timmis Foundation
200 Talon Centre
Detroit, MI 48207-4274
(313) 396-4200
Contact: Michael T. O. Timmis, President
Geographic Giving Pattern: Primarily Michigan.
Special Interest: Catholic churches, diocesan support, Christian evangelism, missionary work, welfare, religious education, and hunger relief.
Assets: $8,947,631 (1997)
Gifts Received: $454,150
Grant Total: $571,280
Grant Range: $100–$160,000
Limitations: No grants to individuals.
Applications: Contributes to pre-selected organizations only. Applications are not accepted.

The Thomas J. Tracy Family Foundation
525 North Woodward Avenue, Suite 1300
Bloomfield Hills, MI 48304-2969
(248) 540-8091
Contact: Thomas J. Tracy, President
Geographic Giving Pattern: Primarily Michigan, with an emphasis on Detroit.

Special Interest: Catholic religious organizations and Irish cultural organizations.
Assets: $337,486 (1999)
Gifts Received: $877,534
Grant Total: $540,000
Limitations: No grants to individuals.
Applications: Contributes to pre-selected organizations only. Applications are not accepted.

Vlasic Foundation
710 North Woodward, # 100
Bloomfield Hills, MI 48304-2852
(248) 642-3380
Contact: Robert J. Vlasic, President
Geographic Giving Pattern: Primarily Michigan.
Special Interest: Cultural programs, health agencies, hospitals, social services, and Catholic organizations.
Assets: $4,207,302 (1999)
Grant Total: $424,686
Limitations: No grants to individuals.
Applications: Contributes to pre-selected organizations only. Applications are not accepted.

John W. and Rose E. Watson Foundation
c/o Citizens Bank, Saginaw
101 North Washington Avenue
Saginaw, MI 48607
(517) 799-7910
Contact: Jean Seaman, Vice President
Geographic Giving Pattern: Limited to Saginaw, Michigan.
Special Interest: Scholarship awards for students graduating from a Catholic high school in Saginaw, children, youth, Catholic church support, and Catholic agencies.
Assets: $7,826,993 (1998)
Gifts Received: $335
Grant Total: $184,000 and $188,489 for individuals.
Grant Range: $500–$14,000
Applications: An application form is required. The deadline is a month prior to the start of an academic year. The application address is 5800 Weiss Street, Saginaw, MI 48602.

Wolohan Family Foundation
1100 River Forest
Saginaw, MI 48603
(517) 793-4505
Contact: Patricia A. Niederstadt, President
Geographic Giving Pattern: Primarily Michigan.
Special Interest: Higher education, Catholic church support, and Catholic agencies.
Assets: $9,612,261 (1998)
Grant Total: $385,175
Grant Range: $1,000–$75,000
Limitations: No grants to individuals.
Applications: Contributes to pre-selected organizations only. Applications are not accepted.

MINNESOTA

Adams-Mastrovich Family Foundation
c/o Norwest Bank Minnesota, N.A.
733 Marquette Avenue
Minneapolis, MN 55479-0046
(612) 667-8517
Contact: Halsey H. Halls, Vice President, Norwest Bank Minnesota, N.A.
Geographic Giving Pattern: Giving limited to Los Angeles, California and South Dakota.
Special Interests: Arts and cultural programs, higher education, Catholic agencies and churches, hospitals, and religious federated giving programs.
Assets: $34,152,856 (1998)
Grant Total: $1,165,500
Grant Range: $3,000–$157,000
Limitations: No grants to individuals.
Applications: Initial approach should be by letter requesting application guidelines. The deadline is August 1.

Charles and Ellora Alliss Educational Foundation
c/o First Trust, N.A.
P.O. Box 64704
St. Paul, MN 55164

(651) 244-4581
Contact: John Bultena, Secretary
Geographic Giving Pattern: Limited to Minnesota.
Special Interest: Scholarship programs at educational institutions.
Assets: $109,885,521 (1998)
Grant Total: $4,754,760
Grant Range: $9,760–$661,440
Grant Average: $80,000–$164,000
Limitations: No grants to individuals or for general purposes, capital funds, endowment funds, research, or operating budgets. No matching gifts or loans.
Applications: Initial approach should be by letter. Proposals should be submitted in August or September.

The Andreas Foundation
c/o Andreas Office
P.O. Box 3584
Mankato, MN 56002-3584
Contact: Michael D. Andreas, Vice President
Geographic Giving Pattern: National.
Special Interest: Higher and secondary education, civil rights, cultural programs, youth agencies, hospitals, Catholic churches, diocesan support, and religious education.
Assets: $54,981,626 (1998)
Gifts Received: $3,500,000
Grant Total: $7,664,594
Grant Range: $100–$2,000,007
Grant Average: $1,000–$5,000
Limitations: No grants to individuals.
Applications: Contributes to pre-selected organizations only. Applications are not accepted.

Aquinas Foundation
2115 Summit Avenue
St. Paul, MN 55105-1096
(651) 962-6688
Contact: Terrence J. Murphy, President
Geographic Giving Pattern: Primarily Minneapolis and St. Paul, Minnesota.

Special Interest: Education, human services, Catholic church support, and Catholic agencies.
Assets: $3,415,849 (1999)
Grant Total: $556,886
Grant Range: $55–$188,430
Limitations: No grants to individuals.
Applications: Contributes to pre-selected organizations only. Applications are not accepted.

Gordon and Margaret Bailey Foundation
1325 Bailey Road
St. Paul, MN 55119
Contact: Margaret Bailey, Vice President
Geographic Giving Pattern: Primarily Minnesota.
Special Interests: Human services, medical care, rehabilitation, nursing services, Catholic church support and Catholic agencies.
Assets: $2,458,605 (1997)
Gifts Received: $300,000
Grant Total: $86,955
Applications: Initial approach should be by letter. There are no deadlines.

The Barry Foundation
2104 Hastings Avenue
Newport, MN 55055
Contact: B. John Barry, President
Geographic Giving Pattern: Primarily Minnesota.
Special Interest: Education, healthcare, social services, Catholic church support, and Catholic agencies.
Assets: $9,442,121 (1998)
Grant Total: $398,520
Grant Range: $35–$50,000
Limitations: No grants to individuals.
Applications: Contributes to pre-selected organizations only. Applications are not accepted.

Otto Bremer Foundation
445 Minnesota Street, Suite 2000
St. Paul, MN 55101-2107
(612) 227-8036

(612) 227-2522 (fax)
Email: obf@bfsi.com
www.fdncenter.org/grantmaker/bremer
Contact: John Kostishack, Executive-Director
Geographic Giving Pattern: Limited to cities in Minnesota, North Dakota, and Wisconsin where there are Bremer Bank affiliates.
Special Interest: Emphasis on rural poverty and combating racism; support also for post-secondary education, human services, health, religion, and community affairs.
Assets: $294,888,232 (1998)
Grant Total: $13,498,782
Grant Range: $500–$250,000
Grant Average: $4,000–$40,000
Limitations: No support for national health organizations. No grants to individuals or for endowment funds, medical research, or professorships.
Applications: Initial approach should be by letter or telephone. Submit proposal at least three months before funding decision is desired.

The Bush Foundation

E-900 First National Bank Building
332 Minnesota Street
St. Paul, MN 55101
(651) 227-0891
(651) 297-6485 (fax)
Email: pampusch@bushfound.org
Contact: Anita M. Pampusch, President
Geographic Giving Pattern: Minnesota, North Dakota, and South Dakota; nationally for college support.
Special Interest: Education, the arts, humanities, healthcare, women and girls, religiously-affiliated colleges and universities, and Catholic social service programs.
Assets: $814,007,902 (1999)
Grant Total: $35,247,357
Grant Range: $4,000–$1,000,000
Grant Average: $40,000–60,000
Limitations: No support for private foundations, operating support, or construction of hospitals, church sanctuaries, daycare centers, or buildings in public colleges and universities. No loans.

Applications: Initial approach should be by letter or telephone requesting detailed list of application requirements. Two copies of the proposal are required.

Patrick and Aimee Butler Family Foundation
E-1420 U.S. Bank Building
332 Minnesota Street
St. Paul, MN 55101-1369
(651) 222-2565
Email: bff@worldnet.att.net
Contact: Kerrie Blevins, Program Director
Geographic Giving Pattern: Primarily Minnesota, especially St. Paul-Minneapolis.
Special Interest: Catholic colleges and universities, social service organizations, and diocesan support.
Assets: $49,591,395 (1998)
Grant Total: $1,427,200
Grant Range: $500–$254,200
Limitations: No grants to individuals. No support for elementary and secondary education, health, hospitals, employment programs, or vocational programs. No loans.
Applications: Initial approach should be by letter or telephone requesting an application form. The board meets in June and October.

The Catholic Aid Association Foundation
3499 North Lexington Avenue
St. Paul, MN 55126-8098
(651) 490-0170
(651) 490-0746 (fax)
www.catholicaid.com
Contact: Michael F. McGovern, President
Geographic Giving Pattern: Primarily Iowa, Minnesota, North Dakota, South Dakota, and Wisconsin. Some support for national Catholic efforts and international mission efforts.
Special Interest: Disaster relief in the upper midwest, chastity and abstinence programs, and support for Catholic schools and religious education programs for media center and curriculum development.
Assets: $456,734 (1998)
Grant Total: $86,301
Grant Average: $1,120

Grant Range: $250–$5,000
Applications: Initial approach should be by letter.

The Catholic Community Foundation in the Archdiocese of St. Paul and Minneapolis

328 West Kellogg Boulevard
St. Paul, MN 55102-1997
(651) 290-1613
(651) 290-1609 (fax)
Email: ccFendow@archspm.org
Contact: The Directors
Geographic Giving Pattern: Primarily St. Paul and Minneapolis, Minnesota.
Special Interests: Human services, education, Catholic church support and Catholic agencies.
Assets: $53,353,226 (1997)
Gifts Received: $12,692,296
Grant Total: $3,701,595
Grant Range: $305,841 and less.
Applications: An application form is required.

The Charisma Foundation

c/o Huttener & Krenn, PA
7900 Xerxes Avenue South, Suite 928
Minneapolis, MN 55431
Contact: J. M. Felton, President and Treasurer
Geographic Giving Pattern: Primarily Minnesota.
Special Interests: Education, substance abuse, children and family services, women's advocacy, economic development, and Catholic agencies, services and missions.
Assets: $64,443 (1999)
Gifts Received: $1,237,925
Grant Total: $1,293,000
Grant Range: $4,500–$36,000
Limitations: No grants to individuals.
Applications: Contributes to pre-selected organizations only. Applications are not accepted.

Charity, Inc.

c/o Totinos
P.O. Box 21055
Minneapolis, MN 55421-0055
(612) 576-6979
Contact: Mrs. Deanna Hulme
Geographic Giving Pattern: Primarily Minnesota.
Special Interest: Human services, Catholic church support, and Catholic agencies.
Assets: $8,726,752 (1998)
Gifts Received: $389,139
Grant Total: $183,438
Grant Range: $250–$50,000
Limitations: No grants to individuals.
Applications: Initial approach should be by letter. There are no deadlines.

The Coss Foundation

P.O. Box 17
Cannon Falls, MN 55009
Contact: Lawrence M. Coss, President
Geographic Giving Pattern: Limited to Minnesota.
Special Interests: Arts and cultural programs, education, diabetes research, Catholic agencies and churches.
Assets: $19,635,031 (1997)
Gifts Received: $7,528,200
Grant Total: $456,631
Grant Range: $250–$130,000
Limitations: No grants to individuals.
Applications: Contributes to pre-selected organizations only. Applications are not accepted.

John & Clara Dolan Foundation

19562 Waterford Court
Shorewood, MN 55331
(612) 470-0904
Contact: John F. Dolan, President
Geographic Giving Pattern: Primarily Minnesota.
Special Interest: Catholic organizations, seminaries, and colleges.
Assets: $734,687 (1999)

Gifts Received: $161,610
Grant Total: $136,245
Grant Range: $200–$76,385
Applications: Initial approach should be by letter. There are no deadlines.

Flaherty Family Foundation
11800 Singletree Lane, Number 210
Eden Prairie, MN 55344-5397
Contact: Edward F. Flaherty
Geographic Giving Pattern: Primarily Minnesota.
Special Interests: Human services, education, youth services, Catholic church support and Catholic agencies.
Assets: $28,749 (1998)
Gifts Received: $190,000
Grant Total: $171,139
Limitations: No grants to individuals.
Applications: Contributes to pre-selected organizations only. Applications are not accepted.

Frey Foundation
c/o Wabash Management, Inc.
4005 IDS Center, 80th South 8th Street
Minneapolis, MN 55402
Contact: James R. Frey, Director
Geographic Giving Pattern: Primarily Minnesota, especially Minneapolis-St. Paul.
Special Interest: Catholic church support, Catholic welfare, and education.
Assets: $5,498,363 (1998)
Grant Total: $23,000
Grant Range: $1,000–$12,000
Limitations: No grants to individuals.
Applications: Initial approach should be by letter. An application form is required. The deadlines are February 15, May 15, August 15, and November 15.

The Gilligan Foundation

P.O. Box 24735
Edina, MN 55424
Contact: Peter J. Gilligan, President
Geographic Giving Pattern: Primarily Minneapolis, Minnesota.
Special Interests: Homelessness, health association, human services, food services, and Catholic federated giving programs.
Assets: $3,603,778 (1999)
Gifts Received: $312,813
Grant Total: $122,000
Grant Range: $1,000–$20,000
Limitations: No grants to individuals.
Applications: Contributes to pre-selected organizations only. Applications are not accepted.

Green Tree Financial Corporation

345 Saint Peter Street
600 Landmark Towers
Saint Paul, MN 55102-1639
(651) 293-3497
Contact: Ed Finn, President
Geographic Giving Pattern: Primarily Minnesota.
Special Interests: Arts and cultural programs, child development, education, cancer research, human services, boys and girls clubs, family services, federated giving programs, Catholic agencies and churches.
Assets: $0 (1999)
Gifts Received: $216,233
Grant Total: $216,233
Grant Range: $25–$50,000
Limitations: No grants to individuals.
Applications: Contributes to pre-selected organizations only. Applications are not accepted.

Hiawatha Education Foundation

2001 Theurer Boulevard
Winona, MN 55987
(507) 453-8765
Contact: Robert A. Kierlin, President

Geographic Giving Pattern: Primarily Minnesota, especially Winona and Rochester.
Special Interest: Catholic high schools and colleges.
Assets: $52,863,735 (1999)
Gifts Received: $5,409,875
Grant Total: $9,493,840
Grant Range: $500–$2,055,000
Applications: Initial approach should be by letter. There are no deadlines.

Father Kasal Charitable Foundation, Inc.

c/o Minnesota Trust
107 W. Oakland Avenue
P.O. Box 463
Austin, MN 55912
(507) 437-3231
(507) 437-8376 (fax)
Contact: Warren F. Plunkett, Chair and President
Geographic Giving Pattern: Primarily the Midwest and Italy.
Special Interest: Catholic church activities and education.
Assets: $2,443,764 (1996)
Grant Total: $52,000
Grant Range: $7,500–$30,000
Applications: Contributes to pre-selected organizations only. Applications are not accepted.

Kent Family Charitable Trust

c/o Norwest Bank Minnesota, N.A.
733 Marquette Avenue
Minneapolis, MN 55479-0053
Contact: Edward J. Callahan, Norwest Bank Minnesota, N.A.
Geographic Giving Pattern: Primarily Minnesota.
Special Interests: Education, Catholic agencies and churches.
Assets: $4,512,950 (1999)
Grant Total: $427,000
Grant Range: $1,000–$10,000
Limitations: No grants to individuals.
Applications: Contributes to pre-selected organizations only. Applications are not accepted.

Kopp Family Foundation

7701 France Avenue South, Suite 500
Edina, MN 55435-3201
(612) 841-9896
(612) 841-9893 (fax)
Email: koppff@koppfamilyfdtn.org
www.koppfamilyfdtn.org
Contact: Elizabeth Wheeler, Administrator
Geographic Giving Pattern: Primarily Minnesota.
Special Interest: Education, children, youth, Catholic church support,
and Catholic agencies.
Assets: $17,799,333 (1998)
Gifts Received: $3,653,125
Grant Total: $1,161,850
Grant Range: $100–$60,000
Limitations: No grants to individuals.
Applications: Initial approach should be by letter. There are no
deadlines.

Ida C. Koran Trust

c/o U.S. Bank, N.A.
P.O. Box 64704
St. Paul, MN 55164-0704
Contact: S. Bartley Osborn, Trustee or Richard F. Rintelmann,
Trustee
Geographic Giving Pattern: Primarily Minnesota.
Special Interest: Archdiocesan support, Catholic churches, and
Catholic agencies.
Assets: $38,202,814 (1998)
Grant Total: $1,103,630
Grant Range: $1,000–$20,000
Applications: Contributes to pre-selected organizations only.
Applications are not accepted.

The McKnight Foundation

600 TCF Tower
121 S. 8th Street
Minneapolis, MN 55402
(612) 333-4220
(612) 332-3833 (fax)

Email: info@mcknight.org
www.mcknight.org
Contact: Carol Berde, Executive Vice President
Geographic Giving Pattern: Primarily Minnesota.
Special Interest: Human and social services, and scientific research programs.
Assets: $1,891,340,406 (1998)
Grant Total: $72,262,002
Grant Range: $2,500–$500,000
Grant Average: $10,000–$250,000
Limitations: No support for religious organizations for sectarian purposes. No grants to individuals.
Applications: Initial approach should be by 2- to 4-page letter. The deadlines are February 15, May 15, August 15, and November 15 for human service and other general grants.

Richard F. McNamara Family Foundation
7808 Creekridge Circle, Suite 200
Minneapolis, MN 55439
(612) 944-3533
Contact: Richard F. McNamara and James L. Reissner, Directors
Geographic Giving Pattern: Limited to Minnesota.
Special Interests: Education, human services, Catholic agencies and churches.
Assets: $3,069,331 (1998)
Gifts Received: $1,175,000
Grant Total: $152,725
Grant Range: $100–$50,000
Limitations: No grants to individuals.
Applications: Contributes to pre-selected organizations only. Applications are not accepted.

1988 Irrevocable Cochrane Memorial Trust
c/o U.S. Bank, N.A., Tax Services Department
P.O. Box 64713
St. Paul, MN 55164-0713
(651) 244-1039
Contact: John L. Jerry
Geographic Giving Pattern: Limited to the Washington, D.C. area.

Special Interest: Religious, scientific, literary and educational purposes, Catholic church support, and Catholic agencies.
Assets: $7,457,587 (1998)
Gifts Received: $7,256
Grant Total: $214,000
Grant Range: $10,000–$25,000
Limitations: No grants to individuals.
Applications: Initial approach should be by letter. There are no deadlines.

The Casey Albert T. O'Neil Foundation
c/o U.S. Bank, N.A.
P.O. Box 64713
St. Paul, MN 55164-0713
(651) 244-0935
Contact: Nancy H. Frankenberry
Geographic Giving Pattern: The metropolitan St. Paul-Minneapolis, Minnesota area.
Special Interest: Catholic religious associations and missions, health agencies, and aid to disabled children.
Assets: $16,379,017 (1999)
Grant Total: $716,000
Grant Range: $750–$40,000
Limitations: No grants to individuals or for deficit financing, capital campaigns, endowment or scholarship funds, research, special projects, publications, or conferences. No matching gifts or loans.
Applications: Initial approach should be by proposal letter. There are no deadlines. The application address is c/o U.S. Bank, N.A., P.O. Box 64704, St. Paul, MN 55164.

I. A. O'Shaughnessy Foundation, Inc.
W-1271 First Bank Building
332 Minnesota Street
St. Paul, MN 55101
(651) 244-4954
Contact: John Bultena, Secretary-Treasurer
Geographic Giving Pattern: National, with an emphasis on Minnesota, Illinois, Kansas, and Texas.

Special Interest: Secondary, higher and Catholic education, cultural programs, social services, medical research, and Catholic religious organizations.
Assets: $88,730,505 (1998)
Grant Total: $4,205,430
Grant Range: $2,500–$416,250
Grant Average: $2,000–$200,000
Limitations: No grants to individuals. No loans. No support for religious missions or individual parishes.
Applications: Grants are usually initiated by the directors. Initial approach should be by letter. Applications must be in written form. There are no deadlines.

The Elizabeth C. Quinlan Foundation, Inc.
5217 Wayzata Boulevard, Suite 200
St. Louis Park, MN 55416
(612) 544-5367
Contact: Kathy Iverson
Geographic Giving Pattern: Limited to Minnesota, with an emphasis on the Twin Cities metropolitan area.
Special Interest: Catholic institutions, higher education, church support, the arts, cultural programs, and social services.
Assets: $4,666,539 (1998)
Grant Total: $125,125
Grant Range: $300–$20,000
Limitations: No grants to individuals. No support for political, fraternal, or sports organizations. No grants for goodwill advertising or benefit funding. No loans.
Applications: Initial approach should be by letter. The deadline is September 1. Proposals preferably should be submitted in May or June.

Gerald Rauenhorst Family Foundation
10350 Bren Road West
Minnetonka, MN 55343
(612) 656-4695
(612) 333-5425 (fax)
Contact: John H. Agee, Vice President and Manager
Geographic Giving Pattern: National, with an emphasis on Minnesota.

Special Interest: Higher education, Catholic church support, church-related institutions, general charitable giving, and healthcare.
Assets: $30,127,420 (1998)
Grant Total: $1,599,920
Grant Range: $5,000–$201,508
Limitations: No grants to individuals.
Applications: Contributes to pre-selected organizations only. Applications are not accepted.

The Saint Paul Foundation, Inc.
600 Norwest Center
55 East Fifth Street
St. Paul, MN 55101-2703
(651) 224-5463
(651) 224-8123 (fax)
Email: inbox@tspf.org
www.tpsf.org
Contact: Paul A. Verret, President
Geographic Giving Pattern: Limited to the metropolitan Saint Paul, Minnesota area.
Special Interest: Humanities, arts and culture, education, healthcare, human services, children adn youth, community development, and minorites.
Assets: $3497,387,279 (1998)
Gifts Received: $28,824,940
Grant Total: $21,979,779
Grant Average: $100–$100,000
Limitations: No grants for annual operating budgets or endowment funds.
Applications: Initial approach should be by letter. An application form is required.

The Sayer Charitable Foundation
4700 Lyndale Avenue North
Minneapolis, MN 55430
Contact: Michael Scott Sayer, Treasurer
Geographic Giving Pattern: Primarily Minnesota.
Special Interests: Education, the economically disadvantaged, and Catholic agencies and churches.
Assets: $4,620,219 (1998)

Gifts Received: $2,616,768
Grant Total: $87,350
Grant Range: $500–$30,000
Applications: Initial approach should be by letter requesting guidelines. The deadline is in July.

Sexton Foundation

P.O. Box 178, RR No. 1
Grey Eagle, MN 56336
(320) 285-4321
Contact: M. Yvonne Sexton, President
Geographic Giving Pattern: Primarily St. Cloud, Minnesota and Lewisville, Texas.
Special Interest: Catholic churches and colleges.
Assets: $11,216,586 (1999)
Gifts Received: $762,116
Grant Total: $385,225
Grant Range: $1,000–$95,000
Limitations: No grants to individuals and no support for private foundations.
Applications: There are no deadlines for grant proposals.

Sieben Foundation, Inc.

c/o Adler Trust Company
10350 Bren Road West
Minnetonka, MN 55343
Contact: Mark Rauenhorst, C.E.O.
Geographic Giving Pattern: Primarily Minnesota.
Special Interests: Higher education, substance abuse, human services, Catholic federated giving programs, and Catholic agencies and services.
Assets: $18,850,863 (1997)
Gifts Received: $9,261,000
Grant Total: $505,000
Grant Range: $2,500–$45,000
Limitations: No grants to individuals.
Applications: Contributes to pre-selected organizations only. Applications are not accepted.

Valley News Charity Fund
1305 Stadium Road
Mankato, MN 56001
Contact: The Trustees
Geographic Giving Pattern: Primarily Mankato, Minnesota.
Description: Valley News Charity Fund is a corporate foundation of Valley News Company.
Special Interest: Education, health, human services, youth services, Catholic agencies, and churches.
Assets: $1,066,941 (1999)
Grant Total: $70,782
Grant Range: $20–$3,000
Limitations: No grants to individuals.
Applications: Contributes to pre-selected organizations only. Applications are not accepted.

The Wasie Foundation
U.S. Bank Place, Suite 4700
601 Second Avenue South
Minneapolis, MN 55402-4319
(612) 332-3883
Contact: Lea M. Johnson, Program Officer and Office Manager
Geographic Giving Pattern: Limited to Minnesota.
Special Interest: Primarily for the education of American students of Polish ancestry through the establishment of endowed scholarship programs at post-secondary institutions. Support also for Catholic universities and colleges, children, and schizophrenia.
Assets: $33,783,945 (1998)
Gifts Received: $300
Grant Total: $1,104,991
Grant Range: $427–$500,000
Limitations: No grants to individuals.
Applications: Initial approach should be by letter requesting application guidelines. Deadlines vary.

MISSOURI

Andrews McMeel Universal Foundation
4520 Main Street, Suite 700
Kansas City, MO 64111
(816) 932-6700
Contact: Kathleen Andrews, Vice President and Secretary
Geographic Giving Pattern: Primarily Kansas City, Missouri.
Special Interest: Art museums, education, health, children's services, and Catholic churches and agencies.
Assets: $5,446,280 (1998)
Grant Total: $444,238
Grant Range: $50–$71,428
Applications: Initial approach should be by proposal. There are no deadlines.

The Edward L. Bakewell, Jr. Family Foundation
c/o Bakewell Corporation
7800 Forsyth Boulevard, 8th Floor
St. Louis, MO 63105
(314) 862-5555
Contact: Thomas J. Bannister, Secretary
Geographic Giving Pattern: Primarily Missouri.
Description: The Edward L. Bakewell, Jr. Family Foundation is a corporate foundation of the Bakewell Corporation.
Special Interest: Historic preservation, arts and culture, higher education, conservation, healthcare, substance abuse programs, Catholic churches, and Catholic agencies.
Assets: $531,059 (1998)
Grant Total: $24,565
Grant Range: $50–$1,833
Applications: Initial approach should be by proposal. Two copies are requested. An application form is required. Applications are accepted from September 1 through November 30.

Patrick D. & Catherine E. Barron Charitable Foundation
609 Cepi Drive
Chesterfield, MO 63005
Contact: Patrick D. Barron, Trustee
Geographic Giving Pattern: Primarily Missouri.

Special Interest: Catholic and Protestant giving, family services, and youth ministries.
Assets: $2,370,112 (1998)
Grant Total: $105,799
Grant Range: $2,000–$50,000
Limitations: No grants to individuals.
Applications: Contributes to pre-selected organizations only. Applications are not accepted.

August A. Busch III Charitable Trust
911 Washington Avenue, Seventh Floor
St. Louis, MO 63101
(314) 231-2800
Contact: Thomas E. Lowthar
Geographic Giving Pattern: Primarily St. Louis, Missouri.
Special Interests: Education, animal welfare, human and youth services, Catholic federated giving programs, Catholic agencies and churches.
Assets: $2,691,516 (1998)
Gifts Received: $39,490
Grant Total: $317,991
Grant Range: $350–$100,000
Limitations: No grants to individuals.
Applications: Initial approach should be by proposal. There are no deadlines.

The Charles Foundation
c/o NationsBank, N.A.
100 North Broadway
St. Louis, MO 63102
(314) 466-4284
Contact: E. Crabtree
Geographic Giving Pattern: Primarily St. Louis, Missouri.
Special Interests: Theological education, international relief, Catholic agencies and churches.
Assets: $3,590,973 (1998)
Gifts Received: $1,400,872
Grant Total: $76,000

Grant Range: $1,000–$75,000
Applications: Initial approach should be by proposal. There are no deadlines.

The Caleb C. and Julia W. Dula Educational and Charitable Foundation

112 South Hanley Road
St. Louis, MO 63105-3418
(314) 726-2800
(314) 863-3821 (fax)
Contact: James F. Mauze
Special Interest: Limited to charities the Dulas have supported during their lifetime, with an emphasis on higher and secondary education, hospitals, libraries, social service agencies, child welfare, Protestant and Catholic church support, cultural programs, and historic preservation.
Assets: $45,672,064 (1998)
Grant Total: $2,100,200
Grant Range: $5,000–$150,000
Limitations: No grants to individuals. No loans.
Applications: Initial approach should be by proposal letter. The deadlines are April 1 and October 1.

Enright Foundation, Inc.

7508 Main Street
Kansas City, MO 64114
(816) 361-4942
Contact: Kathleen Cassidy, President
Geographic Giving Pattern: Primarily Missouri.
Special Interest: Catholic religious organizations, church support, hospitals, child welfare, and social service agencies.
Assets: $5,151,891 (1999)
Grant Total: $193,515
Grant Range: $100–$30,000
Limitations: No grants to individuals. No grants for scholarships.
Applications: Contributes to pre-selected organizations only. Applications are not accepted.

W. Fairleigh Enright Charitable Trust

P.O. Box 308
St. Joseph, MO 64501
Geographic Giving Pattern: Limited to St. Joseph, Missouri.
Special Interests: Human services, Catholic agencies, and community organizations.
Assets: $4,865,175 (1998)
Grant Total: $205,000
Grant Range: $5,000–$50,000
Limitations: No grants to individuals.
Applications: Contributes to pre-selected organizations only. Applications are not accepted.

Fabick Charitable Trust, Inc.

One Fabick Drive
Fenton, MO 63026-2928
(314) 343-5900
Contact: Dave Kramer
Geographic Giving Pattern: Primarily Missouri.
Description: Fabick Charitable Trust, Inc. is a corporate foundation of the John Fabick Tractor Company.
Special Interest: Higher education, church support, religious organizations, hospitals, and community funds.
Assets: $22,952 (1998)
Grant Total: $127,750
Grant Range: $750–$50,000
Applications: Initial approach should be by proposal letter. The deadline is October 15.

The Catherine Manley Gaylord Foundation

1015 Locust Street, Suite 555
St. Louis, MO 63101
(314) 421-0181
(314) 621-6522 (fax)
Contact: Donald E. Fahey, Manager
Geographic Giving Pattern: The metropolitan St. Louis, Missouri area.
Special Interest: Protestant and Catholic church support, youth and child welfare agencies, civic affairs, social services, music, the arts, and higher education.

Assets: $6,393,166 (1999)
Grant Total: $232,290
Grant Range: $100–$31,000
Limitations: No grants to individuals. No loans.
Applications: Contributes mostly to pre-selected organizations. Initial approach should be by letter requesting application guidelines. There are no deadlines.

Hauck Charitable Foundation

1031 Executive Parkway
Saint Louis, MO 63141
(314) 851-9200
Contact: The Trustees
Geographic Giving Pattern: Primarily St. Louis, Missouri.
Special Interests: Arts and cultural programs, human services, education, economically disadvantaged, and Catholic agencies and churches.
Assets: $5,422,571 (1999)
Grant Total: $206,870
Grant Range: $200–$11,500
Limitations: No grants to individuals.
Applications: Contributes to pre-selected organizations only. Applications are not accepted.

William T. Kemper Foundation

P.O. Box 13095
Kansas City, MO 64199-3095
(816) 234-2985
Contact: Michael D. Fields, Executive Director
Geographic Giving Pattern: Primarily Missouri, Kansas, and western Illinois.
Special Interest: Education, health and human services, civic and economic development, the arts, Christian agencies, and church support.
Assets: $270,022,764 (1999)
Grant Total: $12,172,682
Grant Range: $200–$500,000
Grant Average: $250–$600,000

Limitations: No grants to individuals. No support for political purposes, veterans' or fraternal organizations, private foundations, fundraising activities, or endowment funds.
Applications: Initial approach should be by proposal. There are no deadlines.

McDonnell Foundation, Inc.

310 West 49th Street, Apartment #1005
Kansas City, MO 64112-2425
(816) 753-7142
Contact: T. R. Brous
Geographic Giving Pattern: Primarily New York.
Special Interests: Universities, Jewish federated giving programs and Catholic agencies and churches.
Assets: $5,622,863 (1998)
Grant Total: $170,200
Grant Range: $250–$35,000
Limitations: No grants to individuals.
Applications: Contributes to pre-selected organizations only. Applications are not accepted.

The McGee Foundation

4800 Main Street, Suite 458
Kansas City, MO 64112-2510
(816) 931-1515
Contact: Joseph J. McGee, Jr., President
Geographic Giving Pattern: Limited to the greater Kansas City, Missouri area.
Special Interest: Care for the sick, education, and other benevolent, charitable, religious, or scientific institutions.
Assets: $11,362,475 (1999)
Grant Total: $647,500
Grant Range: $1,000–$50,000
Limitations: No support for visual or performing arts, historic preservation, community development, rehabilitation, public information programs, united appeals, or national organizations with wide support. No grants to individuals or for endowment funds, research, publications, or conferences. No multi-year grants or loans.
Applications: Initial approach should be by letter. There are no deadlines.

Miller-Mellor Association

708 East 47th Street
Kansas City, MO 64110
(816) 561-4307
Contact: James L. Miller, Secretary-Treasurer
Geographic Giving Pattern: Primarily Missouri, especially Kansas City.
Special Interest: Catholic church support, higher education, cultural programs, and health services.
Assets: $4,456,779 (1999)
Grant Total: $107,830
Grant Range: $1,000–$11,000
Applications: Initial approach should be by letter or proposal. There are no deadlines.

James C. and Elise S. Moloney Family Charitable Foundation

8690 Moloney Cabin Ridge Road
Barnhart, MO 63012
Contact: James C. Moloney, President
Geographic Giving Pattern: Primarily St. Louis, Missouri.
Special Interests: Catholic church support and Catholic agencies.
Assets: $104,633 (1998)
Grant Total: $24,984
Applications: Contributes to pre-selected organizations only. Applications are not accepted.

Orscheln Industries Foundation, Inc.

P.O. Box 280
Moberly, MO 65270
(660) 263-4900
Contact: Brent Bradshaw
Geographic Giving Pattern: Primarily Missouri.
Description: Orscheln Industries Foundation, Inc. is a corporate foundation.
Special Interest: Catholic church support, religious organizations, community funds, higher education, and scholarships.
Assets: $18,174,788 (1998)
Grant Total: $1,234,124
Grant Range: $25–$106,000
Grant Average: $1,000–$30,000

Applications: Initial approach should be by letter to contact listed above at the following address: P.O. Box 266, Moberly, MO 65270. Tel: (660) 263-8300. The deadline is April 1.

The Pendergast-Weyer Foundation
9300 E. 155th Street
Kansas City, MO 64149
(816) 322-8440
Contact: R. Kenneth Burnett, President
Geographic Giving Pattern: Limited to towns and cities in Missouri.
Special Interest: Catholic churches, religious orders, hospitals, and schools.
Assets: $8,626,260 (1999)
Grant Total: $183,224
Grant Range: $2,000–$262,000
Grant Average: $1,000–10,000
Limitations: No support for clergymen, chanceries, or church foundations. No grants to individuals or for annual campaigns, seed money, building funds, land acquisition, endowment funds, research, publications, or conferences. No matching gifts or loans.
Applications: Initial approach should be by letter. The deadlines are April 10 and September 10.

PMJ Foundation
720 Olive Street, Suite 2400
St. Louis, MO 63101-2396
(314) 345-6000
Contact: Matthew Perlow, President
Geographic Giving Pattern: Primarily St. Louis, Missouri; some giving in Naples, Florida.
Special Interest: Christian organizations, ministries, and churches; some support for social services and higher education.
Assets: $1,106,774 (1999)
Grant Total: $287,445
Grant Range: $100–$14,000
Limitations: No grants to individuals.
Applications: Contributes to pre-selected organizations only. Applications are not accepted.

A. J. Schwartze Community Foundation
238 Madison
Jefferson City, MO 65102
(573) 634-1221
Contact: Michael W. Prenger, Trust Officer, Central Trust Bank
Geographic Giving Pattern: Primarily Missouri.
Special Interests: Education, community development, government and public administration, and Catholic agencies and churches.
Assets: $11,556,161 (1999)
Grant Total: $507,958
Grant Range: $1,000–$20,000
Limitations: No grants to individuals.
Applications: Initial approach should be by proposal. The deadline is in February.

The Shaughnessy Family Foundation
6767 Southwest Avenue
Saint Louis, MO 63143
(314) 781-7820
Contact: Joseph F. Shaughnessey
Geographic Giving Pattern: There are no specified geographical limitations.
Special Interests: Catholic agencies and churches.
Assets: $383,852 (1998)
Gifts Received: $200,000
Grant Total: $201,000
Grant Range: $1,000–$100,000
Limitations: No grants to individuals.
Applications: Contributes to pre-selected organizations only. Applications are not accepted.

Ruth M. and Francis A. Stroble Charitable Foundation
9880 Waterbury Drive
St. Louis, MO 63124
(314) 821-5410
Contact: Francis A. Stroble and Ruth M. Stroble, Trustees
Geographic Giving Pattern: Primarily Missouri.
Special Interests: Human services, education, hospitals, Catholic federated giving programs, Catholic church support and Catholic agencies.

Assets: $1,998,428 (1998)
Grant Total: $134,450
Limitations: No grants to individuals.
Applications: Initial approach should be by letter.

Sycamore Tree Trust

c/o A. G. Edwards Trust Company
2 North Jefferson
St. Louis, MO 63103
(314) 289-4200
Contact: Gregory Ranalletta, Associate Vice President, A.G.
Edwards Trust Company
Geographic Giving Pattern: Primarily Missouri.
Special Interest: Catholic church support, religious associations,
religious welfare, the arts, cultural programs, and higher education.
Assets: $32,266 (1997)
Gifts Received: $340,339
Grant Total: $1,379,154
Grant Range: $50–$283,259
Limitations: No grants to individuals. No support for scholarships or
fellowships. No loans.
Applications: Contributes to pre-selected organizations only.
Applications are not accepted.

Vatterott Foundation

10449 St. Charles Rock Road
St. Ann, MO 63074
(314) 427-4000
Contact: Claire Vatterott Hundelt, Trustee
Geographic Giving Pattern: Primarily St. Louis, Missouri.
Special Interest: Catholic churches, schools, and charitable
organizations.
Assets: $1,756,385 (1999)
Grant Total: $52,450
Grant Range: $100–$6,000
Applications: Contributes to pre-selected organizations only.
Applications are not accepted.

Walter and Jean Voelkerding Charitable Trust

P.O. Box 81
Dutzow, MO 63342
(314) 433-5520
Contact: William J. Zollmann, III, Trustee
Geographic Giving Pattern: Primarily North Dakota and Warren County, Missouri.
Special Interest: Catholic youth ministry, Catholic social services, educational institutions, and church support.
Assets: $3,210,330 (1999)
Grant Total: $169,000
Grant Range: $50,000–$56,250
Limitations: No grants to individuals.
Applications: Contributes to pre-selected organizations only. Applications are not accepted.

NEBRASKA

Thomas D. Buckley Trust

P.O. Box 647
Chappell, NE 69129
(308) 874-2212
Contact: Dwight E. Smith
Geographic Giving Pattern: Primarily Nebraska, particularly Chappell, and surrounding counties.
Special Interest: Community development programs, Christian churches, civic affairs, hospitals, health services, and education.
Assets: $15,167,346 (1999)
Grant Total: $618,133
Grant Range: $25–$50,000
Grant Average: $500–$10,000
Limitations: No grants to individuals.
Applications: Initial approach should be by letter requesting an application form. An application form is required. There are no deadlines.

Ron and Carol Cope Foundation
c/o National Bank of Commerce
1248 O Street
Lincoln, NE 68508
Contact: Carol I. Cope
Geographic Giving Pattern: Primarily Nebraska.
Special Interest: Education, Catholic church support, and Catholic agencies.
Assets: $12,400,384 (1999)
Gifts Received: $2,109,800
Grant Total: $242,000
Grant Range: $5,500–$110,000
Applications: Initial approach should be by letter. There are no deadlines. The application address is 4622 Parklane Drive, Kearney, NE 68847.

May L. Flanagan Foundation
P.O. Box 6155
Lincoln, NE 68506
(402) 476-9200
Contact: Edwin C. Perry
Geographic Giving Pattern: Limited to Lincoln, Nebraska
Special Interests: Community development, Catholic church support and Catholic agencies.
Assets: $0 (1998)
Gifts Received: $60,828
Grant Total: $60,828
Grant Range: $1,000–$10,000
Limitations: No grants to individuals.
Applications: An application form is required. The deadline is October 1.

Hickey Family Foundation
13310 I Street
Omaha, NE 68137
(402) 330-7099
Contact: Bonnie Hicky, President
Geographic Giving Pattern: There are no stated geographical limitations.

Special Interests: Education, conservation, youth services, Catholic agencies and services.
Assets: $3,243,473 (1999)
Gifts Received: $1,059,547
Grant Total: $123,700
Grant Range: $1,000–$49,000
Limitations: No grants to individuals.
Applications: Contributes to pre-selected organizations only. Applications are not accepted.

Clifford J. Miller Charitable Foundation
8990 West Dodge Road, Suite 220
Omaha, NE 68114-3395
(402) 391-3939
Contact: Donna M. Johansen, President
Geographic Giving Pattern: Primarily Omaha, Nebraska.
Special Interests: Catholic high schools.
Assets: $475,690 (1999)
Grant Total: $270,000
Grant Range: $5,000–$25,000
Limitations: No grants to individuals.
Applications: Contributes to pre-selected organizations only. Applications are not accepted.

Peed Foundation
P.O. Box 82545
Lincoln, NE 68510-2545
(402) 479-8900
Contact: Thomas Peed, President and Rhonda Peed, Director
Geographic Giving Pattern: Primarily Lincoln, Nebraska
Special Interest: Catholic giving, Catholic welfare, Catholic schools, and education.
Assets: $344,529 (1999)
Limitations: No grants to individuals.
Applications: There are no deadlines for application proposal letters.

Soener Foundation
1026 Mercer Park Road
Omaha, NE 68131-1219
(402) 551-9128

Contact: Robert L. Soener, President
Geographic Giving Pattern: Primarily Omaha, Nebraska.
Special Interests: Human services, elementary and secondary education, higher education, healthcare, Catholic church support and Catholic agencies.
Assets: $1,954,706 (1999)
Grant Total: $101,632
Grant Range: $500–$11,808
Limitations: No grants to individuals.
Applications: Contributes to pre-selected organizations only. Applications are not accepted.

Paul, John, Anton, and Doris Wirth Foundation, Inc.

R.R. 2, Box 283
Nebraska City, NE 68410
(402) 873-4331
Contact: Anton Wirth, Treasurer
Geographic Giving Pattern: Primarily Nebraska City, Nebraska.
Special Interests: Human services, education, Catholic church support and Catholic agencies.
Assets: $628,042 (1999)
Gifts Received: $105,067
Grant Total: $53,423
Grant Range: $50–$1,000
Limitations: No grants to individuals.
Applications: Contributes to pre-selected organizations only. Applications are not accepted.

NEVADA

The Bennett Foundation

Executive Offices
2535 S. Las Vegas Boulevard
Las Vegas, NV 89109
(702) 737-2888
Contact: William G. Bennett, President
Geographic Giving Pattern: Primarily Nevada.
Special Interest: Health and human services, Jewish agencies and temples, and Catholic agencies and churches.

Assets: $12,392,249 (1998)
Grant Total: $1,528,800
Grant Range: $500–$502,000
Applications: Initial approach should be by letter. There are no deadlines.

The Boyd Foundation
2950 South Industrial Road
Las Vegas, NV 89109-1100
Contact: William S. Boyd, President
Geographic Giving Pattern: Primarily Las Vegas, Nevada.
Special Interest: Museums, higher education, medical research, social services, Catholic church support, and Catholic agencies.
Assets: $4,142,316 (1997)
Gifts Received: $359,000
Grant Total: $155,300
Grant Range: $100–$30,000
Applications: Initial approach should be by letter. An application form is required. There are no deadlines.

Frank and Victoria Fertitta Foundation, Ltd.
2960 West Sahara Avenue, Suite 200
Las Vegas, NV 89102
(702) 367-9969
Contact: The Trustees
Geographic Giving Pattern: Primarily Nevada.
Special Interest: Education, economic development, Catholic church support, and Catholic agencies.
Assets: $204,423 (1997)
Grant Total: $1,317,333
Grant Range: $10,000–$50,000
Applications: Initial approach should be by letter. There are no deadlines.

Conrad N. Hilton Foundation
100 West Liberty Street, Suite 840
Reno, NV 89501
(775) 323-4221
(775) 323-4150 (fax)
Email: foundation@hiltonfoundation.org

www.hiltonfoundation.org
Contact: Steven M. Hilton, President
Geographic Giving Pattern: National.
Special Interest: Substance abuse prevention, the multi-handicapped blind, water development in Ghana, Catholic welfare, religious communities, and churches. A special area of interest is the work of Catholic Sisters which is funded through the Conrad N. Hilton Fund for Sisters. (See entry in Section IV: International Funding Agencies, page 439.)
Assets: $519,169,747 (1999)
Gifts Received: $12,714,456
Grant Total: $18,620,969
Grant Range $1,000–$2,200,000
Grant Average: $1,000–$300,000
Limitations: No support for medical research, the arts, the elderly, political lobbying, or legislative activities. No grants to individuals or for general fundraising events. No loans.
Applications: Initial approach should be by letter. There are no deadlines.

Joshua Foundation

499 Melrose Heights Street
Henderson, NV 89012
Contact: Forest Purdy, Jr., Manager
Geographic Giving Pattern: There are no stated geographical limitations.
Special Interests: Youth services, Goodwill Industries, Catholic church support and Catholic agencies.
Assets: $3,311,824 (1997)
Grant Total: $40,440
Limitations: No grants to individuals.
Applications: No application forms are required. There are no deadlines.

E. L. Wiegand Foundation

Wiegand Center
165 West Liberty Street, Suite 200
Reno, NV 89501
(775) 333-0310
Contact: Kristen A. Avansino, President and Executive Director

Geographic Giving Pattern: Primarily Nevada and adjoining western states including California, Arizona, Oregon, Idaho, Utah, and Washington.

Special Interest: Education, health, medical research especially when children benefit, civic and community affairs, cultural programs, and Catholic institutions.

Assets: $106,415,022 (1998)

Gifts Received: $24,998

Grant Total: $4,756,301

Grant Range: $1,000–$250,000

Grant Average: $10,000–$100,000

Limitations: No grants to individuals. No support for endowment funds, debt reduction, operating funds, general fundraising, emergency funding, or film presentations. No support for groups receiving significant aid from the United Way or public tax funds. No loans or multi-year funding.

Applications: Initial approach should be by letter requesting informational brochure. An application form is required. There are no deadlines.

NEW HAMPSHIRE

Hogan Foundation

21 Prentiss Way

Exeter, NH 03833

(603) 778-2549

Contact: Coleman F. Hogan, Trustee

Geographic Giving Pattern: Primarily New Hampshire.

Special Interests: Human services, Elementary and secondary education, healthcare, rehabilitation, higher education, Catholic church support and Catholic agencies.

Assets: $649,526 (1999)

Grant Total: $60,875

Grant Range: $50–$25,000

Limitations: No grants to individuals.

Applications: An application form is not required. There are no deadlines.

The Darald and Julie Libby Foundation
300 North River Road, Suite 611
Manchester, NH 03104
(603) 647-0446
Contact: Darald Libby and Julie Libby, Trustees
Geographic Giving Pattern: Primarily New Hampshire and Connecticut.
Special Interests: Human services, education, youth services, Native Americans, Catholic church support and Catholic agencies.
Assets: $210,747 (1998)
Grant Total: $146,756
Grant Range: $1,000–$75,000
Applications: An application form is not required. There are no deadlines.

Annie Rowell Charitable Remainder Trust
c/o Bank of New Hampshire, N.A.
P.O. Box 477
Concord, NH 03302-0477
(603) 229-5791
Contact: Bank of New Hampshire, N.A.
Geographic Giving Pattern: Primarily New Hampshire.
Special Interests: Higher education, Catholic agencies and churches.
Assets: $6,642,961 (1999)
Grant Total: $365,447
Grant Average: $121,816
Limitations: No grants to individuals.
Applications: Contributes to pre-selected organizations only. Applications are not accepted.

Annie Rowell Intervivos Trust
c/o Bank of New Hampshire, N.A.
P.O. Box 477
Concord, NH 03302-0477
(603) 229-5791
Contact: Bank of New Hampshire, N.A.
Geographic Giving Pattern: National.
Special Interests: Hospitals, religion, and Catholic agencies and churches.

Assets: $22,157,227 (1999)
Grant Total: $1,385,679
Grant Average: $423,499
Limitations: No grants to individuals.
Applications: Contributes to pre-selected organizations only.
Applications are not accepted.

Smith Family Foundation, Inc.
c/o Wescott, Millham, and Dyer
28 Bowman Street, P.O. Box 1700
Laconia, NH 03247
(978) 687-3774
Contact: The Directors
Geographic Giving Pattern: Primarily Lakeport, New Hampshire.
Special Interests: Elementary and secondary education, higher education, colleges, Catholic church support and Catholic agencies.
Assets: $373,933 (1998)
Grant Total: $17,690
Grant Range: $2,000–$40,000
Limitations: No grants to individuals.
Applications: Contributes to pre-selected organizations only.
Applications are not accepted.

NEW JERSEY

Elsie E. & Joseph W. Beck Foundation
1129 Broad Street
Shrewsbury, NJ 07702
(732) 389-0330
Contact: John P. Keegan, Secretary
Geographic Giving Pattern: Primarily New Jersey.
Special Interest: Higher and secondary education, especially Catholic education.
Assets: $7,568,078 (1998)
Grant Total: $345,000
Grant Range: $2,000–$40,000
Limitations: No grants to individuals.
Applications: Contributes to pre-selected organizations only.
Applications are not accepted.

Robert E. Brennan Foundation, Inc.

c/o Moore Stephens, PC
340 North Avenue, East, Suite 6
Cranford, NJ 07016-2461
(908) 272-7000
Contact: Robert E. Brennan, President
Geographic Giving Pattern: Primarily New Jersey.
Special Interest: Catholic and Jewish organizations, religious schools, religious welfare, higher and secondary education, social services, and health associations.
Assets: $171,520 (1997)
Grant Total: $7,250
Grant Range: $250–$2,000
Limitations: No grants to individuals.
Applications: Contributes to pre-selected organizations only. Applications are not accepted.

Brunetti Foundation

1655 U.S. Highway 9
Old Bridge, NJ 08857
(732) 727-3300
Contact: John J. Brunetti, President
Geographic Giving Pattern: Primarily New Jersey, New York, and Florida.
Special Interest: A military academy, higher education, medical research, hospitals, and some support for Catholic churches.
Assets: $4,055,505 (1998)
Grant Total: $250,888
Grant Range: $250–$36,578
Limitations: No grants to individuals.
Applications: Contributes to pre-selected organizations only. Applications are not accepted.

Charles Edison Fund

101 South Harrison Street
East Orange, NJ 07018
(973) 675-9000
Contact: John P. Keegan, President
Geographic Giving Pattern: National, with an emphasis on New Jersey, Indiana, and New Hampshire.

Special Interest: Historic preservation, foundation-sponsored exhibits at museums, science-education teaching kits, and colleges and universities, including Catholic schools.
Assets: $41,587,275 (1997)
Gifts Received: $4,234
Grant Total: $1,378,550
Grant Range: $100–$125,000
Limitations: No grants to individuals. No grants for building or endowment funds, scholarships, or fellowships. No matching gifts or loans.
Applications: Initial approach should be by letter or proposal. Deadlines fall in February, May, August, and November.

The Roberta and Thomas Ferguson Family Foundation, Inc.
c/o Dillon, Bitar & Luther
53 Maple Avenue
P.O. Box 398
Morristown, NJ 07960-0398
Contact: Mary Powers, Director
Geographic Giving Pattern: National, with an emphasis on New Jersey.
Special Interest: Higher education, Catholic schools and universities, church support, and other charitable giving.
Assets: $1,788,473 (1998)
Grant Total: $254,500
Grant Range: $1,000–$50,000
Applications: Initial approach should be by letter. There are no deadlines.

The Hackett Foundation, Inc.
12 Minneakoning Road
Flemington, NJ 08822
(908) 237-0615
Contact: Alice T. Hackett, Grants Chair
Geographic Giving Pattern: National, especially New Jersey, New York, and Pennsylvania, and developing nations in Africa, Asia, Latin America, and the Pacific.
Special Interest: Emphasis on Catholic missions; support also for Catholic health and social service agencies.
Assets: $20,364,118 (1999)

Grant Total: $833,855
Grant Range: $700–$54,874
Grant Average: $1,000–$20,000
Limitations: No grants to individuals or for land acquisition, endowment funds, matching gifts, scholarships, fellowships, research, demonstration projects, publications, salaries, or conferences. No loans.
Applications: Initial approach should be by letter. An application form is required. The deadline is the 10th of every month. The application address is 33 Second Street, Raritan, NJ 08869.

The Hyde and Watson Foundation
437 Southern Boulevard
Chatham, NJ 07928
(973) 966-6024
(973) 966-6404 (fax)
Contact: Hunter W. Corbin, President
Geographic Giving Pattern: The metropolitan New York, New York area.
Special Interest: Support for capital projects, in the broad fields of health, education, religion, social services, arts and humanities.
Assets: $90,631,608 (1998)
Grant Total: $4,010,300
Grant Range: $3,000–$100,000
Grant Average: $5,000–$25,000
Limitations: No grants to individuals or for deficit financing, annual campaigns, operating budgets, or general endowments.
Applications: Initial approach should be by letter. The deadline for preliminary appeals is February 15 and September 15.

The International Foundation
170 Changebridge Road Unit C5-4
Montville, NJ 07045
(973) 227-6107
(973) 227-6821 (fax)
Contact: Dr. Edward A. Holmes, Grants Chair
Geographic Giving Pattern: International, especially Asia, the Caribbean, Latin America, the Middle East, the Philippines, the South Pacific, and southern Africa, through U.S.-based tax-exempt nonprofits.

Special Interest: Agriculture, health, education, and social development; support also for missions and Catholic international development efforts.
Assets: $36,702,471 (1998)
Grant Total: $1,293,500
Grant Average: $5,000–$45,000
Limitations: No grants to individuals or for endowment funds, operating budgets, scholarships, fellowships, video productions, or conferences. No matching gifts or loans.
Applications: Initial approach should be by letter requesting application guidelines. Two copies of the proposal are requested. An application form is required. A self addressed stamped envelope is requested for replying.

The Ix Foundation
308 Pitney Avenue
Spring Lake, NJ 07762
Contact: Personnel Manager
Geographic Giving Pattern: New Jersey and areas of company operations in New York, New York; Lexington, North Carolina; and Charlottesville, Virginia.
Description: The Ix Foundation is a corporate foundation of Frank Ix and Sons, Inc.
Special Interest: The arts, education, Catholic church support, welfare, health agencies, and human services.
Assets: $1,724,935 (1998)
Grant Total: $45,090
Grant Range: $100–$13,000
Applications: An application form is required. There are no deadlines.

The Robert Wood Johnson Foundation
Route 1 and College Road East
P.O. Box 2316
Princeton, NJ 08543-2316
(609) 452-8701
Email: mail@rwjf.org
www.rwjf.org
Contact: Richard J. Toth, Director, Office of Proposal Management
Geographic Giving Pattern: National.
Special Interests: Health and healthcare.

Assets: $7,867,784,532 (1998)
Gifts Received: $9,460,844
Grant Total: $309,416,070
Limitations: No grants to individuals or for operating expenses, endowment funds, capital costs or equipment. No support for programs or institutions concerned solely with a specific disease or basic biomedical research.
Applications: Initial approach should be by preliminary letter of no more than five pages. There are no deadlines.

Quentin J. Kennedy Foundation, Inc.
22 Oldsmith Road
Tenafly, NJ 07670
(201) 391-1776
Contact: Quentin J. Kennedy, President
Geographic Giving Pattern: Primarily New York and New Jersey.
Special Interest: Catholic organizations including welfare agencies, hospitals, and higher educational institutions.
Assets: $13,127,427 (1998)
Grant Total: $1,999,100
Grant Range: $250–$260,000
Limitations: No grants to individuals.
Applications: Contributes to pre-selected organizations only. Applications are not accepted.

The James Kerney Foundation
P.O. Box 6698
Trenton, NJ 08648-0698
(609) 924-0369 (fax)
Contact: T. Lincoln Kerney II, President
Geographic Giving Pattern: Limited to Trenton, New Jersey and surrounding areas.
Special Interests: Art and cultural programs, education, youth services, community development, Catholic agencies and churches, and the economically disadvantaged.
Assets: $4,453,831 (1999)
Grant Total: $249,000
Grant Range: $200–$50,000
Limitations: No grants to individuals, or for operating budgets, architectural drawings or conceptual plans.

Applications: The New York and New Jersey common application form is accepted. Initial approach should be by letter including one copy of proposal. The deadline is July 1.

The Lebensfeld Foundation
c/o VIS, Inc.
15 Exchange Place
Jersey City, NJ 07302-3912
(201) 946-2600
Contact: Joseph F. Arrigo, Secretary-Treasurer
Geographic Giving Pattern: Primarily New York and Pennsylvania.
Special Interest: The arts, culture, education, hospitals, Catholic church support, and Catholic agencies.
Assets: $40,703,388 (1999)
Grant Total: $2,432,500
Grant Average: $500–$500,000
Limitations: No grants to individuals.
Applications: There are no deadlines for grant proposals.

Maneely Fund, Inc.
900 Haddon Avenue, Suite 432
Collingswood, NJ 08108
(609) 854-5400
Contact: James E. O'Donnell, President
Geographic Giving Pattern: Primarily New York, New Jersey, and Pennsylvania.
Special Interest: Music, the arts, culture, education, healthcare, human services, Catholic church support, and Catholic agencies.
Assets: $3,967,077 (1999)
Grant Total: $212,365
Grant Range: $100–$13,000
Limitations: No grants to individuals.
Applications: Initial approach should be by letter. There are no deadlines.

The Dorothy J. and Lawrence P. Marron Foundation
50 North Franklin Turnpike, Room 209
Ho-Ho-Kus, NJ 07423
(201) 445-2929
Contact: Arthur J. Werger, Treasurer

Geographic Giving Pattern: Primarily northern New Jersey.
Special Interests: Human services, mental health, Catholic federated giving programs, Catholic church support and Catholic agencies.
Assets: $5,823 (1998)
Grant Total: $79,800
Grant Range: $300–$10,000
Limitations: No grants to individuals.
Applications: Initial approach should include two copies of proposal. There are no deadlines.

Nicholas Martini Foundation

777 Passaic Avenue
Clifton, NJ 07012
(973) 594-1899
(973) 890-1477 (fax)
Contact: William J. Martini, President
Geographic Giving Pattern: Primarily the city of Pasaic, and Essex and Bergen counties, New Jersey.
Special Interest: Public health, welfare, education, community development, the arts, humanities, and some Catholic giving.
Assets: $14,198,811 (1998)
Grant Total: $299,500
Grant Range: $300–$25,000
Limitations: No grants to individuals.
Applications: Initial approach should be by letter on organizational letterhead. The deadline varies.

Mary's Pence

402 Main Street, Suite 210
Metuchen, NJ 08840
(732) 452-9611
(732) 452-9612 (fax)
www.maryspence.org
Contact: Karen M. Flotte, National Coordinator
Geographic Giving Pattern: Primarily North, South, and Central America.
Special Interests: Human services, civil rights, women, Catholic church support and Catholic agencies.
Assets: $264,379 (1998)
Grant Total: $53,150

Grant Range: $600–$1,500
Applications: Initial approach should be a letter or telephone call with a short description of ministry. The deadline is June 26.

Robert and Dorothy McCaffrey Foundation, Inc.
730 Central Avenue
Murray Hill, NJ 07974
Contact: Robert McCaffrey, President
Geographic Giving Pattern: Primarily New Jersey and Massachusetts.
Special Interests: Human services, elementary and secondary and higher education, family services, women, health associations, Catholic church support and Catholic agencies.
Assets: $575,791 (1998)
Grant Total: $90,000
Grant Range: $1,000–$12,000
Limitations: No grants to individuals.
Applications: Contributes to pre-selected organizations only. Applications are not accepted.

The Mulholland Foundation
150 Werimus Lane
Hillsdale, NJ 07642
(201) 664-2148
Contact: James S. Mulholland, Jr., Treasurer
Geographic Giving Pattern: National.
Special Interests: Catholic agencies and churches.
Assets: $578,524 (1998)
Grant Total: $435,942
Grant Range: $500–$429,442
Limitations: No grants to individuals.
Applications: Initial approach should be by letter outlining charitable purposes.

Paragano Family Foundation, Inc.
899 Mountain Avenue
Springfield, NJ 07081
(973) 376-1010
Contact: Nazario Paragano, Trustee
Geographic Giving Pattern: Primarily New Jersey.

Special Interest: Catholic churches, Catholic agencies, religious orders, and youth services.
Assets: $5,140,163 (1998)
Grant Total: $195,525
Grant Average: $1,000–$75,000
Applications: There are no deadlines for proposals. The application address is 365 South Street, Morristown, NJ 07960. Tel. (973) 292-8550.

The Pick Foundation, Inc.
330 South Street
P.O. Box 1975
Morristown, NJ 07962-1975
(973) 540-0968
Contact: Kurt T. Borowsky, Chair
Geographic Giving Pattern: Primarily New Jersey.
Special Interests: Human services, vocational education, higher education, youth services, Catholic church support and Catholic agencies.
Assets: $848,761 (1998)
Grant Total: $80,115
Grant Range: $100–$9,400
Limitations: No grants to individuals.
Applications: An application form is not required. There are no deadlines.

Jacob and Sophie Rice Foundation
220 Trenton Boulevard
Sea Girt, NJ 08750
Contact: Patricia Hamilton, President
Geographic Giving Pattern: Primarily New York.
Special Interest: Education, healthcare, hospitals, and Jewish and Catholic welfare funds.
Assets: $3,607,753 (1998)
Grant Total: $173,500
Grant Range: $1,000–$25,000
Limitations: No grants to individuals.
Applications: Initial approach should be by letter. There are no deadlines.

The Sandy Hill Foundation
330 South Street
P.O. Box 1975
Morristown, NJ 07962-1975
(973) 540-9020
Contact: Maria Sapol
Geographic Giving Pattern: Primarily New Jersey, New York, and Pennsylvania.
Special Interest: Education, social services, health, Catholic churches, diocesan support, and Catholic schools.
Assets: $37,468,672 (1998)
Grant Total: $2,073,351
Grant Range: $100–$200,000
Grant Average: $5,000–$25,000
Limitations: No grants to individuals.
Applications: Initial approach should be by letter. There are no deadlines.

Turrell Fund
21 Van Vleck Street
Montclair, NJ 07042-2358
(973) 783-9358
(973) 783-9283 (fax)
Email: Turrell@bellatlantic.net
Contact: E. Belvin Williams, Executive Director
Geographic Giving Pattern: Limited to Essex, Union, Hudson and Passaic counties, New Jersey and Vermont.
Special Interest: Support for organizations dedicated to service or care of children and youth under 12 years of age, with emphasis on the needy and disadvantaged.
Assets: $159,184,721 (1998)
Grant Total: $8,778,539
Grant Range: $2,000–$265,000
Grant Average: $5,000–$50,000
Limitations: No grants to individuals. No support for advocacy work or for endowments, conferences or research. No loans.
Applications: Contributes to pre-selected organizations only. Applications are not accepted.

Victoria Foundation, Inc.
40 South Fullerton Avenue
Montclair, NJ 07042
(973) 783-4450
(973) 783-6664 (fax)
Email: CMCFarvic@aol.com
Contact: Catherine M. McFarland, Executive Officer
Geographic Giving Pattern: Limited to New Jersey, with an emphasis on Newark.
Special Interest: Urban activities, education, children and youth, and Catholic elementary and secondary schools.
Assets: $225,978,744 (1998)
Grant Total: $9,812,204
Grant Range: $634–$1,000,000
Grant Average: $300–$100,000
Limitations: No grants to individuals. No support for publications or conferences.
Applications: Initial approach should be by two-page letter or proposal. An application form is required. The deadlines are February 1 and August 1.

Frank Visceglia Foundation
300 Raritan Center Parkway
Edison, NJ 08818-7815
(908) 225-2200
Contact: Peter C. Visceglia, President
Geographic Giving Pattern: Primarily New Jersey and New York.
Special Interest: Catholic schools, churches, colleges, and religious orders.
Assets: $5,620,981 (1998)
Grant Total: $218,835
Grant Range: $115–$10,000
Limitations: No grants to individuals.
Applications: Contributes to pre-selected organizations only. Applications are not accepted.

Vollmer Foundation, Inc.
217 Gravel Hill Road
Kinnelon, NJ 07405
(973) 492-2309

Contact: Albert L. Ennist, Assistant Secretary
Geographic Giving Pattern: Limited to Venezuela.
Special Interest: Health, higher education, and Catholic church support.
Assets: $7,807,353 (1999)
Grant Total: $522,967
Grant Range: $1,623–$350,000
Grant Average: $4,000–$20,000
Limitations: No grants to individuals or for building funds. No matching gifts or loans.
Applications: Contributes to pre-selected organizations only. Applications are not accepted.

Alberto Vollmer Foundation, Inc.
35 West 43rd Street
Bayonne, NJ 07002
(201) 339-8997
Contact: Edward M. Philips
Geographic Giving Pattern: Primarily Caracas, Venezuela.
Special Interest: Higher education, medical research, Catholic church support, and Catholic agencies.
Assets: $11,777,707 (1998)
Grant Total: $587,331
Grant Range: $1,000–$150,000
Limitations: No grants to individuals.
Applications: Contributes mostly to pre-selected organizations only. Applications are not accepted.

NEW MEXICO

The Frost Foundation, Ltd.
511 Armijo Street, Suite A
Santa Fe, NM 87501
(505) 986-0208
(505) 986-0430 (fax)
Contact: Mary Amelia Whited-Howell, President
Geographic Giving Pattern: National.
Special Interest: Social services, the environment, and education including Catholic universities.

Assets: $38,867,214 (1999)
Grant Total: $0
Grant Average: $10,000–$100,000
Limitations: No grants to individuals or for operating expenses, medical research, building funds, endowment funds, or scholarships. No loans.
Applications: Initial approach should be by letter or telephone. The deadlines are June 1 and December 1.

Lannan Foundation

313 Read Street
Santa Fe, NM 87501
(505) 986-8160
(505) 986-8195 (fax)
www.lannan.org
Contact: Linda Hughes, Administrator
Geographic Giving Pattern: National.
Special Interest: Visual and literary arts, especially of the Native American communities. Some miscellaneous giving, including diocesan support through the United States Catholic Conference.
Assets: $227,088,924 (1998)
Grant Total: $17,190,370
Grant Range: $50–$3,296,200
Limitations: No grants to individuals.
Applications: Applications and letters of intent are not accepted while the foundation reviews its grantmaking procedure.

NEW YORK

The Alberto Foundation

55 Old Turnpike Road, Suite 212
Nanuet, NY 10954
(973) 483-5154
Contact: Charles M. Alberto, President
Geographic Giving Pattern: Primarily New Jersey.
Special Interests: Higher education, hospitals, Catholic church support and Catholic agencies.
Assets: $1,495,859 (1998)
Grant Total: $75,025
Grant Range: $250–$10,000

Limitations: No grants to individuals.
Applications: Contributes to pre-selected organizations only.
Applications are not accepted.

Altman Foundation

220 East 42nd Street, Suite 411
New York, NY 10017-5806
(212) 682-0970
Contact: Jane B. O'Connell, President
Geographic Giving Pattern: Limited to New York, with an emphasis on the five boroughs of New York City.
Special Interest: Education, private voluntary hospitals, health centers, artistic and cultural institutions for outreach projects, social welfare programs for the disadvantaged, youth programs, and youth ministry.
Assets: $220,958,701 (1998)
Grant Total: $8,670,264
Grant Range: $5,000–$266,000
Limitations: No grants to individuals or for building funds.
Applications: Initial approach should be by proposal letter, three to five pages in length, describing the project. An application form is not required. There are no deadlines.

Altman/Kazickas Foundation

c/o B. Strauss Association, Ltd.
307 5th Avenue, 8th Floor
New York, NY 10016-6517
Contact: Roger C. Altman, Trustee
Geographic Giving Pattern: National.
Special Interests: Art and historical societies, Christian agencies and church support.
Assets: $2,853,500 (1999)
Gifts Received: $2,067,168
Grant Total: $837,942
Grant Range: $25–$200,000
Limitations: No grants to individuals.
Applications: Contributes to pre-selected organizations only.
Applications are not accepted.

American Chai Trust
c/o Perlman and Perlman
220 Fifth Avenue, 7th Floor
New York, NY 10001
Contact: Clifford Perlman, Trustee
Geographic Giving Pattern: Primarily the New York, New York metropolitan area.
Special Interests: Human services, arts and cultural programs, literacy, family services, youth, AIDS research, hospitals, disabled, aging, food services, the economically disadvantaged, homelessness, cancer research, health associations, substance abuse, vocational education, education, community development, Catholic church support and Catholic agencies.
Assets: $1,886,291 (1999)
Grant Total: $81,682
Grant Average: $500–$5,000
Limitations: No grants to individuals or for building funds.
Applications: Initial approach should be a letter requesting application criteria. There are no deadlines.

The Baker Foundation
485 Washington Avenue
Pleasantville, NY 10570
(914) 747-1550
Contact: Mary Catherine Baker, Secretary
Geographic Giving Pattern: Primarily the metropolitan New York, New York area.
Special Interest: Catholic organizations, homeless issues, churches, seminaries, and child welfare.
Assets: $2,818,213 (1999)
Grant Total: $108,900
Grant Range: $500–$10,000
Limitations: No grants to individuals.
Applications: Contributes to pre-selected organizations only. Applications are not accepted.

The Boisi Family Foundation

c/o The Beacon Group
399 Park Avenue, 17th Floor
New York, NY 10022
(212) 339-9100
Contact: Geoffrey T. Boisi and Norine I. Boisi, Trustees
Geographic Giving Pattern: Primarily New York.
Special Interests: Human services, arts and cultural programs,
education, Catholic church support and Catholic agencies.
Assets: $2,779,884 (1999)
Gifts Received: $1,039,798
Grant Total: $505,050
Grant Range: $200–$80,000
Limitations: No grants to individuals, or for scholarships. No loans.
Applications: Contributes to pre-selected organizations only.
Applications are not accepted.

Booth Ferris Foundation

c/o Morgan Guaranty Trust Company of New York
60 Wall Street, 46th Floor
New York, NY 10260-0001
(212) 809-1630
Contact: Hildy J. Simmons, M.D., Trustee
Geographic Giving Pattern: National, with an emphasis on the
metropolitan New York, New York area for social service and cultural
organizations.
Special Interest: Private education, especially theological education,
small colleges, independent secondary schools, social services, and
cultural programs.
Assets: $259,303,863 (1998)
Grant Total: $11,079,500
Grant Range: $25,000–$300,000
Grant Average: $50,000–$250,000
Limitations: No support for federated campaigns, community chests,
or for work with specific diseases or disabilities. No grants to
individuals or for research. Generally no grants to educational
institutions for scholarships, fellowships, or unrestricted endowments.
No loans.
Applications: Initial approach should be by proposal, accompanied by
an annual report and financial data. There are no deadlines.

The Brennan Charitable Foundation, Inc.
131 Tulip Avenue
Floral Park, NY 11001
(516) 354-1900
Contact: John O. Brennan, Secretary
Geographic Giving Pattern: Primarily New York, New York.
Special Interests: Catholic secondary education.
Assets: $3,499,078 (1998)
Gifts Received: $12,000
Grant Total: $272,464
Limitations: No grants to individuals.
Applications: Initial approach should be by letter. There are no deadlines.

Brooklyn Benevolent Society
488 Atlantic Avenue
Brooklyn, NY 11217
(718) 875-2066
Contact: Cornelius A. Heany, Secretary
Geographic Giving Pattern: Limited to New York, New York, with an emphasis on the borough of Brooklyn.
Special Interest: Catholic secondary and higher education, children, and youth.
Assets: $6,791,301 (1999)
Grant Total: $409,500
Grant Average: $500–$12,500
Limitations: No grants to individuals.
Applications: Initial approach should be by brief letter of inquiry, describing program. The deadline is October 30.

The Robert Brunner Foundation, Inc.
c/o Capramont, Ltd.
63 Wall Street, Suite 1903
New York, NY 10005
(212) 344-0050
Contact: Eugene C. Rainis, Secretary and Treasurer
Geographic Giving Pattern: Primarily the District of Columbia, New York, New York, and Belgium.
Special Interest: Catholic institutions, principally educational and religious organizations founded by the donor.

Assets: $11,584,675 (1998)
Grant Total: $366,000
Grant Average: $4,000–$288,000
Applications: Contributes to pre-selected organizations only. Applications are not accepted.

J. Homer Butler Foundation

P.O. Box 1841
Old Chelsea Station
New York, NY 10011
(718) 273-3100
(718) 442-5088 (fax)
Contact: Dorothy Montalto, Secretary
Geographic Giving Pattern: National and international.
Special Interest: Catholic churches, schools, seminaries, charitable organizations, international missions, social services, and leprosy.
Assets: $5,100,022 (1998)
Grant Total: $162,100
Grant Range: $1,000–$20,000
Grant Average: $1,000–$3,000
Limitations: International missions are funded through U.S.-based religious communities.
Applications: Initial approach should be by letter. An application form is required. The deadlines are June 30 and December 31.

Byrne Foundation

240 Onieda Street
Syracuse, NY 13202-3373
Contact: James Coughlin
Geographic Giving Pattern: Primarily Syracuse, New York.
Special Interests: Higher education, hospitals, general charitable giving, Catholic church support and Catholic agencies.
Assets: $130,496 (1999)
Gifts Received: $66,000
Grant Total: $81,600
Grant Range: $250–$5,000
Applications: Initial approach should be by letter requesting a pre-grant inquiry form. There are no deadlines.

Helen & Robert Cahill Foundation, Inc.

c/o Goldstein Golub Kessler & Company
812 Park Avenue
New York, NY 10036
Contact: Robert L. Cahill, Jr., President
Geographic Giving Pattern: Primarily New York, New York.
Special Interest: Catholic churches, religious orders and charitable organizations.
Assets: $248,970 (1998)
Gifts Received: $211,094
Grant Total: $163,550
Grant Range: $100–$29,250
Limitations: No grants to individuals.
Applications: Contributes to pre-selected organizations only. Applications are not accepted.

The Louis Calder Foundation

230 Park Avenue, Room 1525
New York, NY 10169
(212) 687-1680
www.lcfnyc.org
Contact: Allison Sargent, Grant Program Manager
Geographic Giving Pattern: Generally restricted to New York, New York.
Special Interests: Programs that promote health, education, and welfare of New York City children and youth.
Assets: $179,279,261 (1999)
Grant Total: $7,363,092
Grant Range: $2,000–$250,000
Grant Average: $15,000–$50,000
Limitations: No grants to individuals. No support for building or endowment funds.
Applications: Initial approach should be by letter. The NYRAG Common Application Form is acceptable. The deadline is March 31.

The Thomas and Agnes Carvel Foundation

35 East Grassy Sprain Road
Yonkers, NY 10710
(914) 793-7300
Contact: Ann McHugh

Geographic Giving Pattern: Primarily New York, especially Westchester County, and New Jersey.
Special Interest: Children's rehabilitation, family health services, diocesan and church support, Catholic medical centers, and religious education.
Assets: $40,975,556 (1999)
Gifts Received: $22,304,500
Grant Total: $1,571,400
Grant Range: $1,000–$400,000
Applications: Initial approach should be by letter. The deadline is October 1.

The Center for Educational Programs, Inc.

355 Lexington Avenue, 3rd Floor
New York, NY 10017
Contact: M. Guzman, Executive Vice President
Geographic Giving Pattern: Primarily New York, New York.
Special Interest: Education, Catholic agencies, and churches.
Assets: $8,306,851 (1999)
Grant Total: $435,834
Limitations: No grants to individuals.
Applications: Contributes to pre-selected organizations only. Applications are not accepted.

The Charitable Foundation of the Burns Family, Inc.

c/o Allen & Brown
60 East 42nd Street, Suite 1760
New York, NY 10165-0006
(212) 697-3723
Contact: Randal B. Borough, President
Geographic Giving Pattern: Primarily New York, New Jersey, Charlotte, North Carolina, and Sheridan, Wyoming.
Special Interest: Education, social services, and Protestant and Catholic church support and agencies.
Assets: $4,181,153 (1999)
Grant Total: $125,500
Grant Average: $500–$14,000
Limitations: No grants to individuals.
Applications: Contributes to pre-selected organizations only. Applications are not accepted.

Joseph and Josephine Ciricleo Trust

22 Claudet Way
Eastchester, NY 10709-1539
(914) 636-4099
Contact: Joseph Ciricleo and Josephine Ciricleo, Trustees
Geographic Giving Pattern: Primarily New York.
Special Interests: Education, health associations, Catholic church support and Catholic agencies.
Assets: $85,488 (1999)
Grant Total: $42,545
Grant Range: $200–$10,000
Limitations: No grants to individuals.
Applications: Contributes to pre-selected organizations only. Applications are not accepted.

Clark Charitable Fund

c/o The Chase Manhattan Bank, N.A.
1211 Avenue of the Americas
New York, NY 10036
(212) 270-9094
Contact: The Chase Manhattan Bank, N.A.
Geographic Giving Pattern: The metropolitan New York, New York area.
Special Interest: Income distributed to the parent body of major religious denominations for aid to needy churches; support also for health, welfare, youth, and the aged.
Assets: $8,977,316 (1998)
Grant Total: $256,000
Grant Average: $5,000–$21,334
Applications: Initial approach should be by written proposal. The deadline is October 31.

Coleman Foundation

c/o Goldman Sachs & Company, Tax Department
85 Broad Street
New York, NY 10004-2408
(212) 902-6897
Contact: Francis Coleman, Jr.
Geographic Giving Pattern: Primarily New York.

Special Interest: Secondary education, general charitable giving,
Catholic church support, and Catholic agencies.
Assets: $642,041 (1999)
Gifts Received: $99,975
Grant Total: $118,704
Grant Average: $100–$25,000
Limitations: No grants to individuals.
Applications: Applications are not accepted.

Coles Family Foundation

c/o Goldman, Sachs & Company, Tax Department
85 Broad Street
New York, NY 10004
(212) 902-6897
Contact: Michael H. Coles
Geographic Giving Pattern: New York.
Special Interest: Catholic giving, church support, child welfare, higher
and other education, cultural programs, and foreign policy.
Assets: $5,204,014 (1999)
Gifts Received: $326,909
Grant Total: $831,092
Grant Average: $50–$100,000
Limitations: No grants to individuals.
Applications: Applications are not accepted.

Constans Culver Foundation

c/o The Chase Manhattan Bank, N.A.
1211 Avenue of the Americas, 34th Floor
New York, NY 10036
(212) 789-4115
Contact: The Trustees
Geographic Giving Pattern: Primarily New York.
Special Interest: Protestant and Catholic church support, civic and
cultural organizations, higher and insurance education, the
disadvantaged, housing issues, and health associations.
Assets: $8,043,408 (1998)
Grant Total: $260,200
Grant Range: $500–$25,000
Limitations: No grants to individuals or for endowment funds.

Applications: Initial approach should be by proposal letter. Proposals are preferred in September.

Beatrice P. Delany Charitable Trust
c/o The Chase Manhattan Bank, N.A.
1211 Avenue of the Americas, 34th Floor
New York, NY 10036
Contact: John H. F. Enteman
Geographic Giving Pattern: Primarily the Chicago, Illinois metropolitan area.
Special Interest: Education, hospitals, health organizations, and Catholic organizations.
Assets: $170,045,515 (1998)
Grant Total: $18,000,000
Grant Range: $5,000–$1,650,000
Grant Average: $5,000–$100,000
Limitations: No grants to individuals.
Applications: Initial approach should be by letter. There are no deadlines. The application address is c/o Chase Manhattan Bank, 1211 6th Avenue, New York, NY 10036.

Dolan Family Foundation
c/o William A. Frewin, Jr.
One Media Crossways
Woodbury, NY 11797
(516) 393-1900
Contact: Marianne Dolan Weber, President
Geographic Giving Pattern: National and international.
Special Interest: Support for a science laboratory, the disabled, Catholic churches, and Catholic schools.
Assets: $33,041,252 (1998)
Grant Total: $2,557,244
Grant Range: $534–$784,284
Grant Average: $100,000–$295,000
Limitations: No grants to individuals.
Applications: Contributes to pre-selected organizations only. Applications are not accepted.

The Max and Victoria Dreyfus Foundation, Inc.

50 Main Street, Suite 1000
White Plains, NY 10606
(914) 682-2008
Contact: Lucy Gioia, Office Administrator
Geographic Giving Pattern: National.
Special Interests: Hospitals, medical research, education, health and social services, cultural programs, and some Catholic giving.
Assets: $91,171,833 (1997)
Grant Total: $3,989,200
Grant Range: $1,000–$51,750
Grant Average: $1,000–$10,000
Limitations: No grants to individuals.
Applications: Initial approach should be by 3-page letter. The deadlines are March 15, July 15, and November 15.

Walter A. Duffy Perpetual Charitable Trust

c/o Manufacturers and Traders Trust Company
P.O. Box 22900
Rochester, NY 14692
(716) 258-8215
Contact: Trust Officer
Geographic Giving Pattern: There are no stated geographical limitations.
Special Interests: Catholic federated giving programs Catholic church support and Catholic agencies.
Assets: $987,814 (1999)
Grant Total: $28,888
Grant Range: $100–$2,869
Limitations: No grants to individuals.
Applications: Contributes to pre-selected organizations only. Applications are not accepted.

Sarita Kenedy East Foundation, Inc.

c/o Cahill, Gordon and Reindel
80 Pine Street, 17th Floor
New York, NY 10005-1702
(212) 701-3292
Contact: John H. Young
Geographic Giving Pattern: National.

Special Interest: Catholic organizations, agencies, churches, and monasteries.
Assets: $18,110,506 (1999)
Grant Total: $689,250
Grant Average: $1,000–$150,000
Limitations: No grants to individuals.
Applications: Contributes primarily to pre-selected organizations. Initial approach should be by letter. The deadline is November 1.

Education for Youth Society

c/o Spear, Leeds & Kellogg
120 Broadway
New York, NY 10271
Contact: William G. Peskoff
Geographic Giving Pattern: National.
Special Interest: Education, hospitals, human services, and Catholic institutions.
Assets: $16,417,518 (1999)
Gifts Received: $24,093,354
Grant Total: $10,846,816
Grant Average: $25–$1,520,500
Limitations: No grants to individuals.
Applications: Contributes to pre-selected organizations only. Applications are not accepted.

Blanche T. Enders Charitable Trust

c/o The Chase Manhattan Bank, N.A.
1211 Sixth Avenue, 38th Floor
New York, NY 10036
(212) 789-4073
Contact: John Boncada, Vice President
Geographic Giving Pattern: Primarily New York, New York.
Special Interest: Child welfare, social services, Catholic religious and welfare institutions, education, animal welfare, health associations, hospitals, and organizations for the blind.
Assets: $7,305,334 (1999)
Grant Total: $212,000
Grant Range: $2,000–$10,000
Limitations: No grants to individuals.

Applications: Initial approach should be by letter. The deadline is in October.

The William Ewing Foundation
150 Broadway, Suite 1011
New York, NY 10036
(212) 852-1000
Contact: William Ewing, Jr., Trustee
Geographic Giving Pattern: Colorado and New York, with an emphasis on the New York, New York metropolitan area.
Special Interests: Culture, spirituality, education, Catholic church support and Catholic agencies.
Assets: $2,717,193 (1999)
Grant Total: $111,900
Limitations: No grants to individuals.
Applications: Initial approach should be by letter. There are no deadlines.

Fahey Family Foundation
c/o Goldman Sachs & Company, Tax Department
85 Broad Street
New York, NY 10004
(212) 902-6897
Contact: The Trustees
Geographic Giving Pattern: Primarily New York.
Special Interest: Arts and culture, education, healthcare, children and youth, Catholic church support, and Catholic agencies.
Assets: $2,536,532 (1999)
Grant Total: $306,782
Grant Range: $250–$50,000
Limitations: No grants to individuals.
Applications: Contributes to pre-selected organizations only. Applications are not accepted.

The Robert J. and Martha B. Fierle Foundation
1920 Liberty Building, 420 Main Street
Buffalo, NY 14202-3687
(716) 856-2112
Contact: James E. Kelly, Manager
Geographic Giving Pattern: Primarily Buffalo, New York.

Special Interests: Human services, higher education, music, federated giving programs, Catholic church support and Catholic agencies.
Assets: $649,597 (1999)
Grant Total: $65,200
Grant Range: $1,000–$10,000
Limitations: No grants to individuals.
Applications: Contributes to pre-selected organizations only. Applications are not accepted.

Galasso Foundation
74 N. Aurora Street
Lancaster, NY 14086
(716) 686-0995
Email: galasso@rdinet
Contact: Marta G. Powers, Administrator
Geographic Giving Pattern: National, with an emphasis on upstate New York.
Special Interests: Education, healthcare, family services and Catholic organizations and activities.
Assets: $11,163,484 (1998)
Gifts Received: $50,000
Grant Total: $446,680
Grant Range: $150–$50,000
Limitations: No grants to individuals.
Applications: Contributes to pre-selected organizations only. Applications are not accepted.

Louis V. Gerstner, Jr. Foundation, Inc.
c/o Bessemer Trust Company, N.A., Tax Department
630 5th Avenue
New York, NY 10111
(212) 708-9216
Contact: Louis V. Gerstner, Jr., President
Geographic Giving Pattern: Primarily New York.
Special Interest: Education, and Protestant and Catholic church support and agencies.
Assets: $8,069,191 (1999)
Gifts Received: $210,000
Grant Total: $480,110

Grant Range: $250–$100,000
Limitations: No grants to individuals.
Applications: Contributes to pre-selected organizations only.
Applications are not accepted.

Golub Charitable Trust
c/o Citibank, N.A.
One Court Square, 22nd Floor
Long Island City, NY 11120
Contact: Citibank N.A.
Geographic Giving Pattern: Primarily New York, New York.
Special Interests: Higher education, health associations, human services, and Catholic agencies and churches.
Assets: $4,458,810 (1998)
Grant Total: $61,209
Grant Range: $5,563–$32,000
Applications: Contributes to pre-selected organizations only.
Applications are not accepted.

The Gordon Fund
c/o Sullivan & Crowell
125 Broad Street
New York, NY 10004-2498
(212) 558-4000
(212) 558-3064 (fax)
Contact: James I. Black, III
Geographic Giving Pattern: Primarily New York, Massachusetts, California, and Connecticut.
Special Interest: Education, theological education, healthcare, and cultural and environmental programs; some support for Catholic churches, dioceses, and youth ministry.
Assets: $10,728,952 (1998)
Grant Total: $3,673,500
Grant Range: $500–$1,000,000
Grant Average: $1,000–$50,000
Limitations: No grants to individuals.
Applications: Initial approach should be by written proposal, including an outline of the purpose of the grant. There are no deadlines.

Gorilowich Family Foundation

c/o The Bank of New York, Tax Department
One Wall Street, 28th Floor
New York, NY 10286
Contact: Theodore J. Vittoria, Jr., The Bank of New York
Geographic Giving Pattern: Primarily New York.
Special Interest: Theological education, Catholic church support, and Catholic agencies.
Assets: $4,926,973 (1999)
Grant Total: $201,702
Grant Average: $7,779–$38,896
Limitations: No grants to individuals.
Applications: Contributes to pre-selected organizations only. Applications are not accepted.

Mary P. Dolciani Halloran Foundation

711 Third Avenue, 19th Floor
New York, NY 10017-5516
(212) 687-4900
Contact: James. J. Halloran, President
Geographic Giving Pattern: National.
Special Interests: Elementary and secondary education, healthcare, human services, Catholic agencies and churches.
Assets: $7,954,136 (1999)
Grant Total: $181,500
Grant Range: $1,800–$20,000
Limitations: No grants to individuals.
Applications: Contributes to pre-selected organizations only. Applications are not accepted.

The Healey Family Foundation

85 Broad Street, Tax Department
New York, NY 10004
Contact: Thomas J. Healey, Trustee
Geographic Giving Pattern: Primarily the northeast, with an emphasis on New York.
Special Interest: General charitable giving, education, and Catholic organizations and diocesan support.
Assets: $1,438,646 (1998)
Gifts Received: $466,929

Grant Total: $100,439
Grant Average: $100–$25,000
Limitations: No grants to individuals.
Applications: Contributes to pre-selected organizations only.
Applications are not accepted.

The Hearst Foundation, Inc.

888 Seventh Avenue, 45th Floor
New York, NY 10106-0057
(212) 586-5404
(212) 586-1917 (fax)
www.fndcenter.org/grantmaker/hearst
Contact: Robert M. Frehse, Jr., Vice President and Executive
Director, Grant Programs east of the Mississippi; or Thomas Eastham,
Vice President and Western Director, Grant Programs west of the
Mississippi.
Geographic Giving Pattern: Limited to the United States and its
territories.
Special Interest: Poverty, minorities, education, theological education,
healthcare, cultural organizations, and human and family services.
Assets: $283,685,795 (1998)
Grant Total: $9,505,000
Grant Range: $15,000–$100,000
Grant Average: $25,000–$50,000
Limitations: No grants to individuals. No grants for media projects,
conferences, workshops, seminars, special events, or advertising for
fundraising. No support for public policy, building projects, and multi-
year grants. No loans.
Applications: Initial approach should be by letter or proposal, not
exceeding five pages. The foundation will accept the NYRAG
Common Application Form. Applications should include a one-page
executive summary. There are no deadlines. Proposals for projects
east of the Mississippi should be sent to the address listed above.
Proposals for projects west of the Mississippi should be sent to
Thomas Eastham, Western Director, 90 New Montgomery Street,
Suite 1212, San Francisco, CA 94105. Tel: (415) 543-0400.

The William Randolph Hearst Foundation

888 Seventh Avenue, 45th Floor
New York, NY 10106-0057
(212) 586-5404
(212) 586-1917 (fax)
www.fndcenter.org/grantmaker/hearst
Contact: Robert M. Frehse, Jr., Vice President and Executive
Director, Grant Programs east of the Mississippi; or Thomas Eastham,
Vice President and Western Director, Grant Programs west of the
Mississippi.
Geographic Giving Pattern: Limited to the United States and its
territories.
Special Interest: Poverty, minorities, education, theological education,
healthcare, cultural organizations, and human and family services.
Assets: $618,965,626 (1998)
Grant Total: $20,377,900
Grant Range: $10,000–$250,000
Grant Average: $10,000–$50,000
Limitations: No grants to individuals. No grants for media projects,
conferences, workshops, seminars, special events, or advertising for
fundraising. No support for public policy, building projects, and multi-
year grants. No loans.
Applications: Initial approach should be by letter or proposal. The
foundation will accept the NYRAG Common Application Form. There
are no deadlines. Proposals for projects east of the Mississippi should
be sent to the address listed above. Proposals for projects west of the
Mississippi should be sent to Thomas Eastham, Western Director, 90
New Montgomery Street, Suite 1212, San Francisco, CA 94105. Tel:
(415) 543-0400.

Hoffman Article 5 Charitable Trust

c/o Chase Manhattan Bank, N.A.
One Chase Manhattan Plaza, 5th Floor
New York, NY 10081
Contact: Patricia A. Gallagher and Robert Warshaw, Chase
Manhattan Bank, N.A.
Geographic Giving Pattern: There are no stated geographic
limitations.
Special Interests: Catholic agencies and churches.
Assets: $11,271,638 (1997)

Gifts Received: $13,179,970
Grant Total: $2,000,000
Grant Range: $500,000–$1,500,000
Limitations: No grants to individuals.
Applications: Contributes to pre-selected organizations only.
Applications are not accepted.

Homeland Foundation, Inc.
c/o AMCO
667 Madison Avenue, 20th Floor
New York, NY 10021
(212) 949-0949
(212) 949-0543 (fax)
Contact: E. Lisk Wyckoff, Jr., Treasurer
Geographic Giving Pattern: National and international.
Special Interest: Catholic diocesan support, Catholic welfare
organizations in the U.S. and abroad, educational institutions, missions,
and seminary support.
Assets: $103,319,907 (1998)
Grant Total: $4,167,117
Grant Range: $2,000–$625,603
Grant Average: $2,000–$200,000
Limitations: No grants to individuals.
Applications: Initial approach should be by letter. There are no
deadlines. The application address is 230 Park Avenue, New York,
NY 10017.

Josephine Lawrence Hopkins Foundation
61 Broadway, Suite 2100
New York, NY 10006
(212) 480-0400
Contact: William P. Hurley, Vice President
Geographic Giving Pattern: Primarily New York, New York.
Special Interest: Catholic giving, church support, youth agencies,
education, and cultural programs.
Assets: $3,854,935 (1999)
Grant Total: $158,500
Grant Range: $1,000–$30,000
Limitations: No grants to individuals. No loans.

Applications: Contributes to pre-selected organizations only. Applications are not accepted.

Hugoton Foundation
900 Park Avenue, Suite 17E
New York, NY 10021
(212) 734-5447
Contact: Joan K. Stout, President
Geographic Giving Pattern: Primarily New York, New York and Miami, Florida.
Special Interest: Hospitals, healthcare, medical research, education, religious welfare, Catholic churches, diocesan support, and Catholic schools.
Assets: $44,992,319 (1998)
Grant Total: $1,972,900
Grant Range: $1,000–$400,000
Grant Average: $5,000–$25,000
Limitations: No grants to individuals.
Applications: Initial approach should be by written proposal. There are no deadlines.

The Humanitas Foundation
1114 Avenue of the Americas, 28th Floor
New York, NY 10036
(212) 704-2300
(212) 704-2301 (fax)
Contact: Peter S. Robinson, Executive Vice President
Geographic Giving Pattern: National.
Special Interest: Emphasis on Catholic organizations and service agencies.
Assets: $452,825 (1998)
Gifts Received: $671,850
Grant Total: $680,400
Grant Range: $1,000–$135,750
Grant Average: $5,000–$25,000
Limitations: No support for schools, universities, or stewardship. No grants to individuals or for scholarships, endowments, or large capital campaigns. No grants awarded outside of the U.S.

Applications: Initial approach should be by letter requesting funding priorities and application guidelines. Deadlines are January 30 and July 15.

The Jarx Foundation, Inc.
c/o Janet Moses
P.O. Box 407
Harrison, NY 10528
(914) 925-7780
Contact: James R. Capra, President
Geographic Giving Pattern: Primarily New York, New York; the West Indies, and El Salvador.
Special Interests: Catholic agencies and churches.
Assets: $864,872 (1998)
Gifts Received: $586,880
Grant Total: $407,668
Grant Range: $1,000–$135,750
Limitations: No grants to individuals.
Applications: Contributes to pre-selected organizations only. Applications are not accepted.

Joy Family Foundation
107-111 Goundry Street
North Tonawanda, NY 14120
(716) 892-6665
(716) 695-1074 (fax)
Email: info@joyfamilyfoundation.org
www.joyfamilyfoundation.org
Contact: Marsha J. Sullivan, Executive Director
Geographic Giving Pattern: Primarily Buffalo, New York and Genesse, Erie, and Niagara counties, New York.
Special Interest: Children, youth, education, healthcare, social and family services, Catholic church support, and Catholic agencies.
Assets: $7,973,199 (1998)
Gifts Received: $115,662
Grant Total: $455,246
Grant Range: $300–$25,000
Applications: Initial approach should be by letter. An application form is required. There are no deadlines.

The John M. and Mary A. Joyce Foundation
37 Seminary Road
Bedford, NY 10506
(914) 287-6117
Contact: Timothy J. Joyce, Vice President and Treasurer
Geographic Giving Pattern: Primarily New York.
Special Interest: Catholic giving, public health, welfare, and education.
Assets: $7,423,827 (1999)
Grant Total: $277,850
Grant Average: $1,000–$60,000
Limitations: No grants to individuals.
Applications: Contributes to pre-selected organizations only. Applications are not accepted.

Keyser Family Foundation
c/o Bessemer Trust Company
630 Fifth Avenue
New York, NY 10111
(212) 708-9216
Contact: John P. Keyser and Elizabeth I. Keyser, Directors
Geographic Giving Pattern: National, with an emphasis on Chicago, Illinois.
Special Interests: Secondary and higher education, Catholic church support and Catholic agencies.
Assets: $898,812 (1998)
Gifts Received: $982,994
Grant Total: $91,500
Grant Range: $500–$25,000
Limitations: No grants to individuals.
Applications: Contributes to pre-selected organizations only. Applications are not accepted.

John W. and Mary M. Koessler Foundation, Inc.
c/o Paul Hilbert Associates
100 Corporate Parkway, Suite 410
Amherst, NY 14226
(716) 831-9044
Contact: John W. Koessler, Jr., President
Geographic Giving Pattern: Primarily Buffalo, New York.

Special Interests: Secondary education Catholic church support and Catholic agencies.
Assets: $2,083,549 (1998)
Grant Total: $140,000
Grant Range: $40,000–$100,000
Limitations: No grants to individuals.
Applications: Initial approach should be by letter. There are no deadlines.

The Stefano La Sala Foundation, Inc.

141 Parkway Road, Suite 28
Bronxville, NY 10708-3605
Contact: A. Stephen La Sala, Director
Geographic Giving Pattern: Primarily New York, New York.
Special Interest: Higher and secondary education, hospitals, Catholic church support, and social service agencies.
Assets: $3,472,835 (1998)
Grant Total: $168,015
Grant Range: $2,500–$32,500
Limitations: No grants to individuals. No support for private foundations.
Applications: Contributes to pre-selected organizations only. Applications are not accepted.

James T. Lee Foundation, Inc.

c/o Grubb and Ellis, Inc.
55 East 59th Street, 11th Floor
New York, NY 10022
(212) 326-4923
Contact: Raymond T. O'Keefe, President
Geographic Giving Pattern: Primarily New York.
Special Interest: Higher education, medical education, hospitals, religious associations, and child welfare.
Assets: $6,868,600 (1999)
Grant Total: $555,000
Grant Range: $2,500–$32,500
Limitations: No grants to individuals or for operating budgets, seed money, capital or endowment funds, publications, or conferences. No loans.

Applications: Contributes to pre-selected organizations only. Applications are not accepted.

George Link, Jr. Foundation

c/o Emmet, Marvin & Martin
1290 Avenue of the Americas, 5th Floor
New York, NY 10271
(201) 846-8481
Contact: Michael J. Catanzaro, Vice President
Geographic Giving Pattern: Primarily New York, New Jersey, and Massachusetts.
Special Interest: Catholic hospitals, educational institutions, churches, and monasteries.
Assets: $44,063,893 (1998)
Grant Total: $1,976,000
Grant Range: $2,000–$100,000
Grant Average: $10,000–$35,000
Applications: Initial approach should be by proposal. Five copies are requested. There are no deadlines.

The Henry Luce Foundation, Inc.

111 West 50th Street, Room 4601
New York, NY 10020
(212) 489-7700
(212) 581-9541 (fax)
Email: hlf@hluce.org
www.hluce.org
Contact: John Wesley Cook, President
Geographic Giving Pattern: National and international; international activities limited to East and Southeast Asia.
Special Interest: Grants for specific projects in the broad areas of Asian affairs, higher education, scholarship, theology, American arts, and public affairs.
Assets: $938,307,513 (1998)
Gifts Received: $53,383
Grant Total: $33,628,028
Grant Range: $500–$2,250,000
Limitations: No support for journalism or media projects. No grants to individuals (except for Luce Scholars Program), or for endowment

funds, domestic building funds, general operating support, or annual fund drives. No loans.

Applications: Initial approach should be by letter requesting application guidelines.

The Manning and Napier Foundation, Inc.

1100 Chase Square
Rochester, NY 14604
(716) 325-6880
Contact: Foundation Coordinator
Geographic Giving Pattern: Primarily New York.
Special Interest: Education, healthcare, human services, and Catholic agencies and organizations.
Assets: $25,712 (1998)
Gifts Received: $82,100
Grant Total: $89,892
Grant Range: $50–$10,000
Limitations: No grants to individuals.
Applications: Initial approach should be by letter. There are no stated deadlines.

Marquis George MacDonald Foundation, Inc.

c/o Chase Manhattan Bank, N.A.
270 Park Street
New York, NY 10017-2070
(212) 552-3993
Contact: Donna M. Bowers, Administrator
Geographic Giving Pattern: There are no stated geographical limitations.
Special Interests: Arts and cultural programs, education, environment, cancer research, substance abuse, the aging, community development, Catholic agencies and churches.
Assets: $9,487,901 (1998)
Gifts Received: $3,500
Grant Total: $402,453
Grant Range: $226–$15,000
Limitations: No grants to individuals. No matching gifts or loans.
Applications: Contributes to pre-selected organizations only. Applications are not accepted.

The Marcelle Foundation
Eight Devon Court
Voorheesville, NY 12186
Contact: Ann W. Marcelle, President
Geographic Giving Pattern: Primarily Albany, New York.
Special Interests: Human services, Catholic church support and Catholic agencies.
Assets: $782,788 (1998)
Gifts Received: $10,000
Grant Total: $102,300
Grant Range: $1,000–$50,000
Limitations: No grants to individuals.
Applications: Contributes to pre-selected organizations only. Applications are not accepted.

The Charles A. Mastronardi Foundation
c/o Morgan Guaranty Trust Co.
345 Park Avenue
New York, NY 10154
(212) 464-2773
Contact: Charles M. Davidson
Geographic Giving Pattern: Primarily New York.
Special Interest: Catholic church support, educational institutions, hospitals, health, and child welfare.
Assets: $24,127,343 (1998)
Grant Total: $1,019,625
Grant Range: $2,000–$135,250
Grant Average: $2,500–$50,000
Limitations: No grants to individuals.
Applications: Applications are not accepted.

Mathis-Pfohl Foundation
5-46 46th Avenue
Long Island City, NY 11101
(718) 748-4800
Contact: James M. Pfohl, President
Geographic Giving Pattern: There are no stated geographical limitations.
Special Interests: Arts and cultural programs, education, human services, and Catholic agencies and churches.

Assets: $9,272,910 (1998)
Grant Total: $355,725
Grant Range: $100–$50,000
Applications: Initial approach should be by letter. There are no deadlines.

The Mattison Foundation
60 Heights Road
Plandome, NY 11030-1413
Contact: William C. Mattison, Jr., President
Geographic Giving Pattern: Primarily the greater metropolitan New York, New York, including Long Island.
Special Interests: Higher education, hospitals, Catholic church support and Catholic agencies.
Assets: $860,871 (1996)
Gifts Received: $105,000
Grant Total: $101,600
Grant Range: $1,000–$50,000
Limitations: No grants to individuals.
Applications: Contributes to pre-selected organizations only. Applications are not accepted.

The McCaddin-McQuirk Foundation, Inc.
P.O. Box 5001
New York, NY 10185
(314) 298-3502
Contact: John J. Caffrey
Geographic Giving Pattern: National and international, especially Canada, South America, Africa, Asia, and the Pacific.
Special Interest: To foster educational opportunities for poorer students to be priests, deacons, catechists, or lay teachers of the Catholic Church in the United States or elsewhere.
Assets: $3,430,735 (1998)
Grant Total: $189,650
Grant Range: $900–$18,000
Applications: Initial approach should be by letter. Applications must be made through a bishop, rector, or head of a seminary. The deadline is December 1.

James J. McCann Charitable Trust and McCann Foundation, Inc.

35 Market Street
Poughkeepsie, NY 12601
(914) 452-3085
Contact: John J. Gartland, Jr., President
Geographic Giving Pattern: Limited to Poughkeepsie and Dutchess County, New York.
Special Interest: Education, Catholic secondary schools and colleges, (including scholarship funds), church and diocesan support, religious associations, hospitals, recreation, civic projects, social services, and cultural programs.
Assets: $30,545,812 (1999)
Grant Total: $698,453
Grant Range: $100–$3,700,000
Grant Average: $2,500–$50,000
Limitations: No grants to individuals or for operating budgets, emergency funds, endowment funds, or deficit financing. No matching gifts or loans.
Applications: Initial approach should be by letter or proposal. The trustees meet in January and July.

The McCarthy Charities, Inc.

P.O. Box 1090
Troy, NY 12181-1090
(618) 273-6037
Contact: Robert P. McCarthy, Treasurer
Geographic Giving Pattern: Primarily Troy and Albany, New York.
Special Interest: Catholic church support, church-related education, and Catholic welfare agencies; support also for community funds, social service agencies, and hospitals.
Assets: $18,428,645 (1998)
Grant Total: $679,060
Grant Range: $50–$60,000
Grant Average: $500–$10,000
Limitations: No grants to individuals.
Applications: Contributes to pre-selected organizations only. Applications are not accepted.

Mary A. and John M. McCarthy Foundation
c/o KCG Capital Advisors
880 Third Avenue, 8th Floor
New York, NY 10022
Contact: Stephen J. McCarthy, Trustee
Geographic Giving Pattern: Primarily the mid-Atlantic and
Northeast regions, with emphasis on the greater Washington, D.C.
area; Boston, Massachusetts; and New York, New York.
Special Interest: Arts and culture, healthcare, animal welfare,
Catholic church support, and Catholic agencies.
Assets: $6,587,595 (1999)
Gifts Received: $235,000
Grant Total: $199,500
Grant Range: $10,000–$25,000
Grant Average: $5,000–$25,000
Limitations: No grants to individuals.
Applications: Contributes to pre-selected organizations only.
Applications are not accepted.

The McEwen Family Foundation
c/o US Trust Company of New York
114 West 47th Street
New York, NY 10036
(212) 852-3834
Contact: Arthur I. McEwen and Jane E. McEwen, Trustees
Geographic Giving Pattern: There are no stated geographical
limitations.
Special Interests: Catholic church support and Catholic agencies.
Assets: $20,965 (1998)
Grant Total: $2,915
Grant Range: $100–$32,200
Limitations: No grants to individuals.
Applications: Contributes to pre-selected organizations only.
Applications are not accepted.

McMullen Family Foundation
c/o Gilmartin Poster & Shafto
1 William Street, 5th Floor
New York, NY 10004

Contact: John J. McMullen, Sr.
Geographic Giving Pattern: Primarily New Jersey; some giving in Ireland.
Special Interests: Primary, secondary and higher education.
Assets: $18,883,680 (1999)
Grant Total: $764,777
Grant Range: $255–$160,000
Limitations: No grants to individuals.
Applications: Contributes to pre-selected organizations only. Applications are not accepted.

Lorraine J. McNally Trust

P.O. Box 643
16 Harlem Street
Glen Falls, NY 12801-0643
(518) 793-3451
Contact: Thomas M. Lawson
Geographic Giving Pattern: Primarily New York.
Special Interests: Human services, elementary and secondary education, Catholic church support and Catholic agencies.
Assets: $3,178,015 (1999)
Grant Total: $60,000
Grant Range: $1,000–$4,000
Limitations: No grants to individuals.
Applications: Initial approach should be by letter.

William M. & Miriam F. Meehan Foundation, Inc.

120 East 87th Street, Suite R4L
New York, NY 10128
(212) 534-8607
(212) 426-7472 (fax)
Contact: John D. O'Leary, Executive Director
Geographic Giving Pattern: Primarily New York, New York.
Special Interest: Catholic church support, religious welfare, social services, education, environment, health, youth, and child welfare.
Assets: $11,921,353 (1998)
Gifts Received: $84,856
Grant Total: $513,874
Grant Range: $200–$30,400
Limitations: No grants to individuals.

Applications: Contributes to pre-selected organizations only.
Applications are not accepted.

The Meriweather Foundation
c/o Cleary Gottlieb et al.
One Liberty Plaza
New York, NY 10006
Contact: Steven Loeb, Esq.
Geographic Giving Pattern: There are no stated geographical
limitations.
Special Interests: Arts and cultural programs, healthcare, human
services, and Catholic agencies and churches.
Assets: $2,114,808 (1997)
Gifts Received: $1,089,779
Grant Total: $470,700
Grant Range: $100–$50,000
Limitations: No grants to individuals.
Applications: Contributes to pre-selected organizations only.
Applications are not accepted.

Merlin Foundation
c/o Schulte, Roth and Zabel
900 Third Avenue
New York, NY 10022
Contact: William D. Zabel
Geographic Giving Pattern: National, with an emphasis on New
York.
Special Interests: Arts and cultural programs, education, healthcare,
recreation, international human rights, Catholic agencies and churches.
Assets: $5,603,589 (1998)
Grant Total: $236,150
Grant Range: $100–$50,000
Limitations: No grants to individuals.
Applications: Contributes to pre-selected organizations only.
Applications are not accepted.

Montague Family Charitable Foundation
P.O. Box 810
Buffalo, NY 14226-0810
Contact: William P. Montague, Chair

Geographic Giving Pattern: Primarily New York.
Special Interests: Human services, Higher education, hospitals, Catholic church support and Catholic agencies.
Assets: $368,192 (1998)
Grant Total: $66,700
Grant Range: $500–$50,000
Limitations: No grants to individuals.
Applications: Initial approach should be by letter. The deadline is November 30.

The Muccia Family Fund
c/o First Manhattan Company
437 Madison Avenue
New York, NY 10022
(212) 756-3300
Contact: Carrol A. Muccia, Jr., Chair
Geographic Giving Pattern: There are no stated geographical limitations.
Special Interests: Education Catholic church support and Catholic agencies.
Assets: $1,207,591 (1998)
Grant Total: $115,550
Grant Range: $100–$50,000
Limitations: No grants to individuals.
Applications: Contributes to pre-selected organizations only. Applications are not accepted.

Agnus Noster Foundation
272 Madison Avenue, #300
New York, NY 10016
Contact: Gayle Susan Marra, President
Geographic Giving Pattern: There are no stated geographical limitations.
Special Interests: Catholic agencies and churches.
Assets: $3,721,039 (1999)
Grant Total: $106,500
Grant Range: $10,000–$38,500
Limitations: No grants to individuals.
Applications: Contributes to pre-selected organizations only. Applications are not accepted.

The Joseph C. Nugent Family Charitable Trust

c/o Bankers Trust Company
P.O. Box 1297, Church Street Station
New York, NY 10008
(212)454-3931
Contact: Bankers Trust Company
Geographic Giving Pattern: Primarily New York, New York.
Special Interests: Human services, higher education, youth services, residential and custodial care, Catholic church support and Catholic agencies.
Assets: $3,547,003 (1999)
Grant Total: $156,900
Grant Range: $100–$36,250
Limitations: No grants to individuals.
Applications: Contributes to pre-selected organizations only. Applications are not accepted.

John F. O'Brien Foundation

P.O. Box 11567
Loudonville, NY 12211-0567
Contact: Rosanna Biondo, Trustee
Geographic Giving Pattern: Primarily Albany, New York.
Special Interests: Human services, elementary and secondary education, hospitals, Catholic church support and Catholic agencies.
Assets: $1,480,625 (1999)
Grant Total: $107,000
Grant Range: $5,000–$50,000
Applications: An application form is not required. There are no deadlines.

The Jonathan & Shirley O'Herron Foundation

c/o Lazard Freres & Company, LLC
30 Rockefeller Plaza
New York, NY 10020-1902
(212)632-6507
Contact: Jonathan O'Herron, President
Geographic Giving Pattern: Primarily Massachusetts, Connecticut, Vermont, and New York.
Special Interest: Catholic churches, education, hospitals, and social services.

Assets: $255,669 (1999)
Gifts Received: $245,750
Grant Total: $523,250
Grant Average: $250–$30,000
Limitations: No grants to individuals.
Applications: Initial approach should be by letter describing the organization and its activities. There are no deadlines.

Cyril F. and Marie E. O'Neil Foundation
c/o Siegel, Sacks & Company
630 Third Avenue
New York, NY 10017
(212) 682-6640
Contact: Ralph O'Neil, President
Geographic Giving Pattern: Primarily New York and Ohio.
Special Interest: Higher and secondary education, missions, Catholic church support, and welfare.
Assets: $7,242,835 (1999)
Grant Total: $504,270
Grant Range: $500–$42,000
Limitations: No grants to individuals.
Applications: Contributes to pre-selected organizations only. Applications are not accepted.

William and Joyce O'Neill Foundation
c/o The Chase Manhattan Bank
One Chase Manhattan Plaza, 5th Floor
New York, NY 10081
Contact: Lawrence Greenberg
Geographic Giving Pattern: No stated geographical limitations.
Special Interest: Catholic education and church support.
Assets: $884,430 (1998)
Gifts Received: $207
Grant Total: $12,000
Limitations: No grants to individuals.
Applications: Initial approach should be by letter. The application address is c/o Chase Manhattan Bank, 251 Royal Way, Palm Beach, FL 33480.

The O'Sullivan Children Foundation, Inc.
355 Post Avenue
Westbury, NY 11590
(516) 334-3209
(516) 334-3949 (fax)
Contact: Kevin P. O'Sullivan, President
Geographic Giving Pattern: Primarily the greater metropolitan New York, New York area.
Special Interest: Catholic organizations including churches, hospitals, health associations, youth organizations, welfare agencies, and missions.
Assets: $5,438,646 (1998)
Gifts Received: $76,840
Grant Total: $390,095
Grant Range: $50–$60,000
Limitations: No grants to individuals.
Applications: Contributes to pre-selected organizations only. Applications are not accepted.

The Old Mill Foundation, Inc.
c/o Martin and Seinger and Company
225 Broadway, Room 1501
New York, NY 10007
Contact: Annabelle G. Coleman or Denis P. Coleman, Jr., Directors
Special Interest: Education, health, Catholic church and diocesan support, Catholic welfare, and cultural programs.
Assets: $509,974 (1999)
Grant Total: $481,448
Grant Range: $60–$160,000
Limitations: No grants to individuals.
Applications: Contributes to pre-selected organizations only. Applications are not accepted.

Theresa and Edward O'Toole Foundation
1 Wall Street, 28th Floor
New York, NY 10286
(212) 635-1622
Contact: Stella Lau, Vice President, The Bank of New York
Geographic Giving Pattern: Primarily New York, New Jersey, and Florida.

Special Interest: Catholic churches, Catholic welfare funds, hospitals, higher education, Native Americans, and aging.
Assets: $55,772,330 (1999)
Grant Total: $1,970,000
Applications: Initial approach should be by letter. There are no deadlines. The application address is Personal Trust Administration, 1 Wall Street, 23rd Floor, New York, NY 10286.

Pascucci Family Foundation
270 South Service Road, Suite 45
Melville, NY 11747-0888
(516) 622-9419
Contact: Christopher S. Pascucci or Ralph P. Pascucci, Managers
Geographic Giving Pattern: There are no stated geographical limitations.
Special Interests: Education, healthcare, human services, youth, Catholic agencies and churches.
Assets: $13,624,422 (1999)
Grant Total: $956,206
Grant Range: $1,000–$122,500
Limitations: No grants to individuals.
Applications: Contributes to pre-selected organizations only. Applications are not accepted.

The Vincent and Harriet Palisano Foundation
2100 Main Place Tower
Buffalo, NY 14202
(716) 853-1621
Contact: James M. Beardsley, Trustee
Geographic Giving Pattern: Primarily Buffalo, New York.
Special Interest: Higher and secondary education including scholarships, and Catholic associations.
Assets: $4,964,713 (1999)
Grant Total: $300,000
Grant Range: $1,500–$20,000
Limitations: No grants to individuals.
Applications: Contributes to pre-selected organizations only. Applications are not accepted.

Richard C. and Karen E. Penfold Family Foundation, Inc.

4588 South Park Avenue
Blasdell, NY 14219
Contact: The Directors
Geographic Giving Pattern: National, with emphasis on New York.
Special Interests: Education, health associations, human services, and Catholic agencies and churches.
Assets: $3,772,703 (1999)
Grant Total: $400,018
Grant Range: $25–$250,000
Limitations: No grants to individuals.
Applications: Contributes to pre-selected organizations only. Applications are not accepted.

The Pinkerton Foundation

630 Fifth, Suite 1755
New York, NY 10111
(212) 332-3385
(212) 332-3399 (fax)
Email: pinkfdn@mindspring.com
Contact: Joan Colello, Executive Director
Geographic Giving Pattern: Primarily the metropolitan New York, New York area.
Special Interest: Family and youth services, learning disabled children and adults, and Catholic religious welfare organizations.
Assets: $154,280,125 (1998)
Gifts Received: $17,100
Grant Total: $5,054,309
Grant Average: $6,000–$150,000
Limitations: No support for religious education, medical research, the media, or the direct provision of healthcare. No grants to individuals or for emergency assistance.
Applications: Initial approach should be by letter. An application form is required. The foundation accepts the NYRAG Common Application Form. The deadlines are February 1 and September 1.

The Ponagansett Foundation, Inc.

c/o Patterson, Belknap, Webb & Tyler
1133 Avenue of the Americas, Suite 2200
New York, NY 10036-6710

(212) 336-2000
Contact: Mary B. Shea, President
Geographic Giving Pattern: Primarily New York.
Special Interest: Education, Catholic church support, and Catholic agencies.
Assets: $3,271,811 (1999)
Grant Total: $127,515
Grant Range: $25–$10,000
Limitations: No grants to individuals.
Applications: Contributes to pre-selected organizations only. Applications are not accepted.

The Generoso Pope Foundation

211 West 56th Street, Suite 5-E
New York, NY 10019
(212) 765-4156
Contact: Anthony Pope, Vice President
Geographic Giving Pattern: Primarily the metropolitan New York, New York area and Westchester County.
Special Interest: Catholic church and diocesan support, religious associations, monasteries, welfare funds, higher and secondary education, and hospitals.
Assets: $52,485,101 (1999)
Grant Total: $1,162,020
Grant Range: $1,000–$103,000
Grant Average: $1,000–$50,000
Limitations: No grants to individuals.
Applications: Initial approach must be by proposal letter. There are no deadlines.

The Purchase Fund

c/o Barry Strauss Associates, Ltd.
307 5th Avenue, 8th Floor
New York, NY 10016-6517
(212) 779-4700
Contact: Peter M. Flanigan, Manager
Geographic Giving Pattern: National, with an emphasis on New York.
Special Interests: Theater, education, human services, Catholic agencies and churches.

Assets: $598,056 (1999)
Grant Total: $290,879
Grant Range: $100–$130,334
Limitations: No grants to individuals.
Applications: Contributes to pre-selected organizations only.
Applications are not accepted.

Leslie C. Quick, Jr. & Regina A. Quick Charitable Trust Foundation

c/o AMCO
667 Madison Avenue, 20th Floor
New York, NY 10021
(407) 655-8000
Contact: Leslie C. Quick, Jr., Trustee
Geographic Giving Pattern: Primarily Florida and New York.
Special Interest: Higher education, Christian churches, missionary work, diocesan support, and hospitals.
Assets: $7,847,926 (1999)
Grant Total: $1,224,892
Grant Range: $250–$170,000
Limitations: No grants to individuals.
Applications: Contributes to pre-selected organizations only.
Applications are not accepted.

Jacob L. Reiss Foundation

c/o The Bank of New York, Tax Department
One Wall Street, 28th Floor
New York, NY 10286
(212) 635-1520
Geographic Giving Pattern: Primarily New York and New Jersey.
Special Interest: Hospitals, human services, Catholic church support, and Catholic agencies.
Assets: $6,428,110 (1999)
Grant Total: $247,000
Grant Range: $1,000–$33,000
Limitations: No grants to individuals.
Applications: Contributes to pre-selected organizations only.
Applications are not accepted.

Richard A. Rendich Foundation
c/o U.S. Trust Company of New York
114 West 47th Street
New York, NY 10036
(212) 852-3683
Contact: Carolyn Larke, Assistant Vice President, U.S. Trust
Company of New York or Linda R. Francisovich, Senior Vice
President, U.S. Trust Company of New York
Geographic Giving Pattern: Primarily New York, Pennsylvania, and
New Jersey.
Special Interest: Education of needy persons of the Catholic faith,
especially young seminarians, through loans, gifts, and scholarships.
Assets: $3,820,051 (1997)
Gifts Received: $12,159
Grant Total: $137,000
Grant Range: $3,000–$20,000
Applications: Applications are not accepted.

May Ellen and Gerald Ritter Foundation
9411 Shore Road
Brooklyn, NY 11209-6755
(718) 836-4080
Contact: Emma A. Daniels, President
Geographic Giving Pattern: New York.
Special Interest: Health agencies and Catholic welfare funds.
Assets: $11,430,055 (1999)
Grant Total: $601,700
Grant Range: $500–$150,000
Grant Average: $1,000–$25,000
Limitations: No grants to individuals.
Applications: Initial approach should be by letter and proposal. There
are no deadlines.

The Mary Gordon Roberts Fund
c/o Sullivan and Cromwell
125 Broad Street
New York, NY 10004-2498
(212) 558-4000
Contact: Mary Gordon Roberts, Trustee

Geographic Giving Pattern: Primarily New York, New York.
Special Interests: Education, performing arts, human services,
Catholic agencies and churches.
Assets: $1,077,746 (1999)
Gifts Received: $588,016
Grant Total: $804,750
Grant Range: $250–$500,000
Limitations: No grants to individuals.
Applications: Initial approach should be by letter. There are no
deadlines.

Peter B. & Adeline W. Ruffin Foundation, Inc.

8 W. 38th Street, Room 905
New York, NY 10018
(212) 302-2810
Contact: Edward G. McAnaney, President
Geographic Giving Pattern: Primarily New York, New Jersey,
Connecticut, Pennsylvania, Virginia, and Washington, D.C.
Special Interest: Healthcare, human services, Catholic churches,
Catholic agencies, and education, including Catholic colleges and
parochial schools.
Assets: $51,525,688 (1999)
Gifts Received: $16,380,390
Grant Total: $1,986,000
Grant Range: $1,000–$50,000
Limitations: No grants to individuals.
Applications: Contributes to pre-selected organizations only.
Applications are not accepted.

Santa Maria Foundation, Inc.

P.O. Box 604138
Bay Terrace, NY 11360-4138
Contact: Margaret Devine
Geographic Giving Pattern: Primarily New York.
Special Interest: Catholic agencies, churches, missionary programs,
the economically disadvantaged, and education.
Assets: $9,366,625 (1998)
Gifts Received: $560,660
Grant Total: $379,500
Grant Range: $2,000–$100,000

Limitations: No grants to individuals.
Applications: Initial approach should be by letter. Applicant organizations must be listed in *The Official Catholic Directory*. The deadline is November 1.

Elias Sayour Foundation, Inc.
183 Madison Avenue, Suite 502
New York, NY 10016
(212) 686-7560
Contact: Mary Jane Gosen, Vice President
Special Interest: Catholic church support, welfare funds, religious organizations, hospitals, and general charitable giving.
Assets: $2,323,402 (1999)
Grant Total: $98,350
Grant Range: $100–$10,000
Applications: Initial approach should be by letter. There are no deadlines.

Mario and Annunziatina Sbarro Family Foundation, Inc.
c/o Parker, Chapin, Flattau and Klimpl
1211 Avenue of the Americas
New York, NY 10036
(212) 704-6253
Contact: Carol F. Burger
Geographic Giving Pattern: Primarily Philadelphia, Pennsylvania.
Special Interests: Cancer research Catholic church support and Catholic agencies.
Assets: $130,297 (1998)
Grant Total: $10,300
Grant Range: $250–$5,000
Limitations: No grants to individuals.
Applications: Contributes to pre-selected organizations only. Applications are not accepted.

Priscilla & Richard J. Schmeelk Foundation, Inc.
1003 Park Boulevard
Massapequa, NY 11762
(516) 795-1400
Contact: Richard J. Schmeelk, President and Treasurer
Geographic Giving Pattern: Primarily New York, New York.

Special Interest: Education, healthcare, children, youth, Catholic church support, and Jewish and Catholic agencies.
Assets: $4,923,119 (1999)
Grant Total: $751,770
Grant Range: $2,500–$32,500
Limitations: No grants to individuals.
Applications: Contributes to pre-selected organizations only. Applications are not accepted.

The Kilian J. and Caroline F. Schmitt Foundation, Inc.

1 HSBC Plaza
Rochester, NY 14604
(716) 264-0030
Contact: Robert H. Fella, President
Geographic Giving Pattern: Primarily the Rochester, New York metropolitan area.
Special Interests: Education, human services, the aged, and Protestant and Catholic agencies and churches.
Assets: $12,350,712 (1999)
Grant Total: $609,100
Grant Range: $500–$165,000
Limitations: No grants to individuals.
Applications: Initial approach should be by letter. An application form is required. There are no deadlines.

Society of the Friendly Sons of Saint Patrick in the City of New York

80 Wall Street, #712
New York, NY 10005-3601
(212) 269-1770
Contact: Victor D. Ziminsky, Jr., President
Geographic Giving Pattern: Primarily New York, New York.
Special Interest: Catholic giving and Catholic welfare.
Assets: $1,727,042 (1998)
Grant Total: $110,000
Grant Range: $500–$25,000
Applications: Contributes to pre-selected organizations only. Applications are not accepted.

Edward L. & Joan B. Steiniger Charitable Foundation

One Court Square, PBG Tax Dept., 22nd Floor
Long Island City, NY 11120
(718) 248-1201
Contact: Richard Monaghan
Geographic Giving Pattern: Primarily New York, New York.
Special Interest: Catholic schools, secondary and higher education, and theological education.
Assets: $27,391,659 (1998)
Gifts Received: $25,175
Grant Total: $1,343,202
Applications: Initial approach should be by letter. The deadline is December 31. The application address is c/o Citibank, N.A., 153 E. 53rd Street, 5th Floor, New York, NY 10043.

Martha Washington Straus and Harry H. Straus Foundation, Inc.

8 Sky Meadow Farm
Lincoln Avenue
Port Chester, NY 10573
(212) 533-6246
Contact: Roger J. King, Treasurer
Geographic Giving Pattern: Primarily New York, New York and the metropolitan Washington, D.C. area.
Special Interest: Health, hospitals, medical research, and education; some support for Jewish and Christian purposes, Catholic churches, and religious institutions.
Assets: $8,512,828 (1998)
Gifts Received: $34,599
Grant Total: $503,500
Grant Range: $100–$17,000
Limitations: No grants to individuals.
Applications: Contributes to pre-selected organizations only. Applications are not accepted.

The Peter & Caroline Striano Foundation, Inc.

65-45 Fresh Meadow Lane
Flushing, NY 11365-2011
(718) 539-4300
Contact: Peter Striano, President

Geographic Giving Pattern: Primarily New York and New Jersey.
Special Interest: Catholic church support, Catholic welfare, child welfare, and education.
Assets: $312,471 (1998)
Gifts Received: $100
Grant Total: $232,073
Grant Range: $25–$17,000
Applications: Contributes to pre-selected organizations only. Applications are not accepted.

The Sullivan Family Foundation

1100 Park Avenue
New York, NY 10128
Contact: Thomas A. Sullivan, President
Geographic Giving Pattern: Primarily New York.
Special Interest: Higher and medical education, hospitals, Catholic church support, and general charitable giving.
Assets: $2,743,339 (1998)
Gifts Received: $77,891
Grant Total: $392,110
Grant Range: $1,000–$180,000
Limitations: No grants to individuals.
Applications: Contributes to pre-selected organizations only. Applications are not accepted.

Joseph R. Takats Foundation

135 Delaware Avenue, Penthouse Suite
Buffalo, NY 14202-2410
(716) 854-5034
Contact: The Trustees
Geographic Giving Pattern: Primarily Buffalo, New York.
Special Interests: Human services, elementary and secondary education, hospitals, health associations, Catholic church support and Catholic agencies.
Assets: $1,717,100 (1999)
Grant Total: $82,399
Grant Range: $100–$4,000
Limitations: No grants to individuals.
Applications: Contributes to pre-selected organizations only. Applications are not accepted.

The Robert Mize & Isa White Trimble Family Foundation
c/o Allen and Brown
60 East 42nd Street, Suite 1760
New York, NY 10165
(212) 697-3723
Contact: Daniel J. Ashley, President
Geographic Giving Pattern: Primarily New York.
Special Interest: Hospitals, child welfare, social services, Catholic
religious agencies, and Catholic welfare organizations.
Assets: $2,752,090 (1999)
Grant Total: $138,500
Grant Average: $1,000–$17,500
Limitations: No grants to individuals. No support for scholarships or
fellowships. No loans.
Applications: Contributes to pre-selected organizations only.
Applications are not accepted.

Tripifoods Foundation
c/o Hodgson, Russ, Andrews, Woods & Good
1800 One M&T Plaza
Buffalo, NY 14203
(716) 856-4000
Contact: Carl J. Tripi, Trustee
Geographic Giving Pattern: Primarily Buffalo, New York.
Description: Tripifoods Foundation is a corporate foundation of
Tripifoods, Inc.
Special Interest: Education, food services, human services, Catholic
churches, and Catholic agencies.
Assets: $168,796 (1998)
Gifts Received: $43,000
Grant Total: $33,500
Grant Range: $250–$7,000
Limitations: No grants to individuals.
Applications: Contributes to pre-selected organizations only.
Applications are not accepted.

The Waldorf Family Foundation, Inc.
17 Beach Drive
Huntington, NY 11743
(631) 423-9500

Contact: The Officers
Geographic Giving Pattern: Primarily New Jersey and the New York City metropolitan area.
Special Interests: Catholic agencies and churches.
Assets: $265,949 (1998)
Gifts Received: $150,000
Grant Total: $268,375
Grant Range: $240–$83,495
Limitations: No grants to individuals.
Applications: Contributes to pre-selected organizations only. Applications are not accepted.

The Wasily Family Foundation, Inc.
181 Smithtown Boulevard
Nesconset, NY 11767
(631) 979-2142
Contact: Patrick N. Moloney, Secretary
Geographic Giving Pattern: Primarily New York, New York.
Special Interests: Television, healthcare, AIDS, human services, youth, hospices, the disabled, Native Americans, and Catholic agencies and churches.
Assets: $18,303,262 (1998)
Gifts Received: $1,837,000
Grant Total: $555,000
Grant Range: $10,000–$25,000
Applications: Initial approach should be by letter. There are no deadlines.

The Wikstrom Foundation
1 East Avenue, NYRO MO3A
Rochester, NY 14604
Contact: William A. McKee, Vice President
Geographic Giving Pattern: Primarily New York.
Special Interest: Cultural programs, higher education, programs for the elderly, and Catholic organizations, including church support.
Assets: $1,729,044 (1998)
Grant Total: $128,500
Grant Average: $500–$25,000
Limitations: No grants to individuals. No loans.

Applications: Initial approach should be by letter. There are no deadlines.

NORTH CAROLINA

Baird Foundation
c/o Wachovia Bank, N.A.
P.O. Box 3099
Winston-Salem, NC 27150-7153
(336) 732-5252
Contact: Wachovia Bank, N.A.
Geographic Giving Pattern: Limited to Georgia.
Special Interests: Catholic agencies and churches, religion.
Assets: $8,729,745 (1998)
Grant Total: $291,079
Grant Range: $15,265–$17,031
Limitations: No grants to individuals.
Applications: Contributes to pre-selected organizations only. Applications are not accepted.

The Donald D. Lynch Family Foundation
108 Artillery Lane
Raleigh, NC 27615
(919) 846-0830
Contact: Donald D. Lynch, Executive Director
Geographic Giving Pattern: There are no stated geographical limitations.
Special Interests: Catholic charitable organizations.
Assets: $922,399 (1999)
Grant Total: $51,397
Grant Range: $3,500–$4,120
Applications: Initial approach should be in writing.

The RosaMary Foundation
c/o Wachovia Bank & Trust Co., N.A.
P.O. Box 3099
Winston-Salem, NC 27150-7153
(336) 732-5252
Contact: Louis M. Freeman, Chair

Geographic Giving Pattern: Primarily the greater New Orleans, Louisiana area.

Special Interests: Education, including Catholic schools, social services, civic affairs, and cultural programs.

Assets: $50,108,015 (1998)

Grant Total: $1,965,967

Grant Range: $1,000–$345,000

Limitations: No grants to individuals.

Applications: Initial approach should be by proposal, no more than three pages in length. An application form is required. The deadline is March 1 and October 15. The application address is P.O. Box 51299, New Orleans, LA 70151. Tel (504) 895-1984.

Sabates Foundation

800 East Boulevard

Charlotte, NC 28203

(704) 372-9527

Contact: Dominic Cappelli, Director

Geographic Giving Pattern: Primarily Charlotte, North Carolina.

Special Interests: Human services, higher education, hospitals, and health associations, Catholic church support and Catholic agencies.

Assets: $15,186 (1999)

Grant Total: $37,000

Grant Range: $1,000–$30,000

Limitations: No grants to individuals.

Applications: Initial approach should be by letter. The deadline is June 30.

Sarah H. Sutherland Charitable Trust

c/o Southern National Bank of North Carolina

P.O. Box 2887

Wilson, NC 27894

Email: rhand@BBTnet.com

Contact: Ray Hand, Vice President, Branch Banking and Trust Company

Geographic Giving Pattern: Primarily North Carolina.

Special Interests: Universities and Catholic agencies and churches.

Assets: $5,895,042 (1998)

Grant Total: $236,848

Grant Range: $1,000–$52,140

Limitations: No grants to individuals.
Applications: Contributes to pre-selected organizations only.
Applications are not accepted.

OHIO

Emma Leah and Laura Belle Bahmann Foundation
8041 Hosbrook Road, Suite 210
Cincinnati, OH 45236-2907
(513) 891-3799
Contact: John T. Gatch, Executive Director
Geographic Giving Pattern: Primarily Cincinnati, Ohio.
Special Interests: Ear and throat diseases, care for the aging,
Catholic agencies and churches.
Assets: $11,479,952 (1998)
Gifts Received: $935
Grant Total: $586,503
Grant High: $52,140 and $2,740 for individuals.
Limitations: No grants to individuals.
Applications: Contributes to pre-selected organizations only.
Applications are not accepted.

Frances E. Bidenharn Trust
c/o Bank One Trust Company, N.A.
774 Park Meadow Road
Westerville, OH 43081-2871
(330) 433-8354
Contact: Bank One Trust Company, N.A.
Geographic Giving Pattern: Giving on a national basis with an
emphasis on Ohio and Pennsylvania.
Special Interests: Higher education Catholic church support and
Catholic agencies.
Assets: $2,796,804 (1998)
Grant Total: $76,624
Grant Range: $10,942–$10,950
Limitations: No grants to individuals.
Applications: Contributes to pre-selected organizations only.
Applications are not accepted.

Borden Foundation, Inc.

c/o Borden Inc., Tax Dept.
180 East Broad Street, 29th Floor
Columbus, OH 43215-3799
(614) 225-4580
Contact: Frankie L. Nowlin, President
Geographic Giving Pattern: Primarily in areas of company
operations, with an emphasis on Columbus, Ohio.
Special Interest: Disadvantaged children, community affairs, higher
education, diocesan support, and Catholic social service agencies.
Assets: $1,541,186 (1998)
Grant Total: $1,801,763
Grant Range: $25–$203,429
Grant Average: $100–$250,000
Limitations: No grants to individuals or for deficit financing, building
funds, land acquisition, renovations, endowment funds, scholarships,
research, or publications. No support for advertisements, membership
drives, or conferences. No loans.
Applications: Initial approach should be by letter. There are no
deadlines.

Eva L. and Joseph M. Bruening Foundation

627 Hanna Building
1422 Euclid Avenue
Cleveland, OH 44115-1901
(216) 621-2632
(216) 621-8198 (fax)
Contact: Janet E. Narten, Executive Director
Geographic Giving Pattern: Limited to the greater Cleveland, Ohio
area.
Special Interest: Catholic education, social services, the elderly, the
disabled, the disadvantaged, and healthcare; some support for
churches and dioceses.
Assets: $73,304,880 (1999)
Grant Total: $4,609,168
Grant Range: $200–$125,000
Grant Average: $5,000–$100,000
Limitations: No grants to individuals or for annual campaign appeals,
mass mailings, endowments, general operating expenses, research,
publications, or seminars.

Applications: Initial approach should be by written proposal. Two copies are requested. The deadlines are March 1, July 1, and November 1.

The Cloyes-Myers Foundation
3200 National City Center
Cleveland, OH 44114
Contact: John D. Drinko
Geographic Giving Pattern: Limited to Ohio.
Description: The Cloyes-Myers Foundation is a corporate foundation of Cloyes Gear & Products, Inc.
Special Interest: Higher education, human services, Catholic churches, and Catholic agencies.
Assets: $65,141 (1998)
Grant Total: $1,000
Limitations: No grants to individuals.
Applications: Contributes to pre-selected organizations only. Applications are not accepted.

Justin F. Coressel Charitable Trust
c/o Terry Melton
101 Clinton Street, Suite 2000
Defiance, OH 43512
Contact: Justin F. Coressel, Director
Geographic Giving Pattern: Primarily Defiance, Ohio.
Special Interest: Higher education, healthcare, youth, community development, Catholic church support, and Catholic agencies.
Assets: $3,233,519 (1998)
Grant Total: $162,500
Grant Range: $1,000–$15,000
Limitations: No grants to individuals.
Applications: Initial approach should be by letter. There are no deadlines. The application address is 500 East High Street, Defiance, OH 43512. Tel. (419) 782-6677.

Charles H. Dater Foundation, Inc.
302 Gwynne Building
602 Main Street
Cincinnati, OH 45202

(513) 241-1234
Email: BruceA.Krone@Dater.org
Contact: Bruce A. Krone, Secretary
Geographic Giving Pattern: Primarily the greater Cincinnati, Ohio area.
Special Interest: Social and family services, with emphasis on children and the disadvantaged.
Assets: $58,494,367 (1999)
Grant Total: $2,472,500
Grant Average: $5,000–$100,000
Applications: Initial approach should be by letter. An application form is required. There are no deadlines.

The DeBartolo Family Foundation
7620 Market Street
Youngstown, OH 44512-6052
(330) 965-2000
Contact: The Trustees
Geographic Giving Pattern: Primarily Youngstown, Ohio.
Special Interest: Catholic churches and education.
Assets: $2,575,251 (1998)
Grant Total: $129,100
Grant Range: $250–$7,500
Limitations: No grants to individuals.
Applications: Contributes to pre-selected organizations only. Applications are not accepted.

The Thomas J. Emery Memorial
c/o Frost and Jacobs
2500 PNC Center
Cincinnati, OH 45202
(513) 651-8377
Contact: Lee Crooks, Foundation Administrator
Geographic Giving Pattern: Primarily Cincinnati, Ohio.
Special Interest: Arts and culture, healthcare, and education, including Catholic schools.
Assets: $2,575,251 (1998)
Grant Total: $129,100
Grant Range: $250–$7,500

Limitations: No grants to individuals.
Applications: Initial approach should be by letter. Two copies of the proposal are requested. There are no deadlines. The application address is 201 East 5th Street, Cincinnati, OH 45202.

The Father's Table
1085 Fairington Drive
Sidney, OH 45365
Contact: John M. Garmhausen, Trustee
Description: Gilardi Foundation is a corporate foundation of A.M. Gilardi & Sons, Inc.
Special Interest: Healthcare, right to life, neighborhood centers, and Catholic federated giving programs.
Assets: $6,157 (1997)
Gifts Received: $105,000
Grant Total: $100,000
Grant Range: $5,000–$40,000
Applications: Contributes to pre-selected organizations only. Applications are not accepted.

John D. Finnegan Foundation
c/o Mahoning National Bank of Youngstown, Trust Department
P.O. Box 479
Youngstown, OH 44501
(330) 742-7035
Contact: David Sabine, Senior Vice President and Senior Trust Officer.
Geographic Giving Pattern: Primarily Youngstown, Ohio.
Special Interest: Catholic religious organizations and welfare agencies, higher education, and care of the aged.
Assets: $6,345,514 (1998)
Grant Total: $230,000
Grant Range: $1,000–$75,000
Limitations: No grants to individuals. No support for operating budgets, scholarships, or fellowships. No matching grants or loans.
Applications: Initial approach should be by letter or proposal. Submit proposals between January and March, preferably.

H & H Foundation

P.O. Box 1888
Lima, OH 45802-1888
(419) 331-1040
Contact: Leo J. Hawk, President
Geographic Giving Pattern: Primarily Ohio.
Special Interest: Catholic giving, church support, missions, Catholic schools, and other charitable giving.
Assets: $1,162,245 (1998)
Gifts Received: $500,000
Grant Total: $449,453
Grant Range: $332–$100,000
Limitations: No grants to individuals.
Applications: Initial approach should be by proposal. There are no deadlines. The application address is 2301 Baton Rouge Avenue, Lima, OH 45805

H. C. S. Foundation

1801 East 9th Street, Suite 1035
Cleveland, OH 44114-3103
(216) 781-3502
Contact: The Trustees
Geographic Giving Pattern: Limited to Ohio.
Special Interest: Catholic education, high schools, colleges and universities. Support also for health organizations, and maternity and infant care.
Assets: $96,768,843 (1998)
Grant Total: $3,848,000
Grant Range: $3,000–$1,000,000
Grant Average: $25,000–$100,000
Limitations: No grants to individuals.
Applications: Applications should be in writing. There are no deadlines.

Richard M. and Yvonne Hamlin Foundation

3560 West Market Street, Suite 300
Akron, OH 44333
(330) 665-2900
Contact: The Trustees

Geographic Giving Pattern: Primarily Ohio.
Special Interests: Ballet, higher education, healthcare, federated giving programs, Catholic agencies and churches.
Assets: $5,277,994 (1998)
Gifts Received: $443,174
Grant Total: $153,450
Grant Range: $100–$50,000
Applications: An application form is required.

Homan Foundation
7609 Coldstream Drive
Cincinnati, OH 45255
(606) 341-6450
Contact: Walter E. Homan, Trustee
Geographic Giving Pattern: Primarily Ohio, Kentucky, and Florida.
Special Interest: Catholic schools and churches, and other charitable, scientific, and literary organizations.
Assets: $1,911,637 (1998)
Grant Total: $186,050
Grant Range: $200–$42,500
Limitations: No grants to individuals.
Applications: Initial approach should be by proposal. The deadline is November 15. The application address is P.O. Box 17350, Edgewood, KY 41017.

Hubert Foundation
9555 Dry Fork Road
Harrison, OH 45030-1994
(513) 367-8600
Contact: The Trustees
Geographic Giving Pattern: Primarily Cincinnati, Ohio.
Special Interest: Catholic churches, Catholic programs, secondary education, low income housing programs, civic affairs, and community projects.
Assets: $12,367,268 (1999)
Grant Total: $316,843
Grant Range: $50–$46,000
Limitations: No grants to individuals.
Applications: Contributes to pre-selected organizations only. Applications are not accepted.

Joseph E. and Mary E. Keller Foundation
105 Collingwood Avenue
Dayton, OH 45419
(937) 299-2418
Contact: John C. Keyes, Trustee
Geographic Giving Pattern: National.
Special Interest: Catholic giving, higher education, and healthcare.
Assets: $3,330,319 (1998)
Grant Total: $397,600
Grant Range: $1,000–$275,000
Limitations: No grants to individuals.
Applications: Contributes to pre-selected organizations only.
Applications are not accepted.

The KRW Foundation
1400 North Point Tower
1001 Lakeside Avenue
Cleveland, OH 44114-1152
(216) 523-1900
Contact: George J. Durkin
Geographic Giving Pattern: Primarily Ohio.
Special Interests: Human services, elementary and secondary
education, higher education, Catholic church support and Catholic
agencies.
Assets: $1,156,377 (1998)
Gifts Received: $87,359
Grant Total: $98,950
Grant Range: $100–$40,000
Limitations: No grants to individuals.
Applications: Contributes to pre-selected organizations only.
Applications are not accepted.

The Frances and Jane S. Lausche Foundation
1942 Brushview Drive
Richmond Heights, OH 44143
(216) 943-0989
Contact: Madeline Debevec
Geographic Giving Pattern: Eastern Europe.
Special Interest: Higher education, human services, Catholic church
support, and Catholic agencies.

Assets: $2,817,567 (1998)
Grant Total: $124,039
Grant Range: $146–$20,000
Limitations: No grants to individuals.
Applications: Initial approach should be by letter. There are no deadlines.

The LaValley Foundation
5800 Monroe Street, Building F
Sylvania, OH 43560
(419) 882-0081
Contact: Richard G. LaValley, President
Geographic Giving Pattern: Primarily northwestern Ohio and southeastern Michigan.
Special Interest: Catholic church support, Catholic schools, and aid to school-aged youth.
Assets: $14,026,402 (1998)
Grant Total: $408,038
Grant Range: $1,000–$333,200
Applications: Contributes to pre-selected organizations only. Applications are not accepted.

Lehner Family Foundation Trust
c/o Jane Lehner
35 South River Road
Monroe Falls, OH 44262
(330) 688-6616
Contact: Rick Burke, Manager
Geographic Giving Pattern: Limited to Ohio.
Special Interests: Animal welfare, home healthcare, Catholic agencies and churches.
Assets: $11,209,369 (1998)
Grant Total: $140,500
Grant Range: $500–$50,000
Limitations: No grants to individuals.
Applications: Contributes to pre-selected organizations only. Applications are not accepted.

Carl H. Lindner Foundation
49 East Fourth Street, Suite 521
Cincinnati, OH 45202
Contact: Carl H. Lindner, Jr.
Geographic Giving Pattern: Primarily Ohio.
Special Interests: Theological education, religion, Protestant agencies and churches, and Catholic agencies and churches.
Assets: $12,280,648 (1997)
Gifts Received: $3,071
Grant Total: $2,209,461
Limitations: No grants to individuals.
Applications: Contributes to pre-selected organizations only. Applications are not accepted.

Joseph L. & Sarah S. Marcum Foundation
475 Oakwood Drive
Hamilton, OH 45013
(513) 867-3870
Contact: Joseph L. Marcum, Chair
Geographic Giving Pattern: Primarily Ohio.
Special Interests: Higher education, human services, arts and cultural programs, and Catholic agencies and churches.
Assets: $5,869,290 (1998)
Grant Total: $210,750
Grant Range: $100–$60,100
Limitations: No grants to individuals.
Applications: Contributes to pre-selected organizations only. Applications are not accepted.

Marian Foundation
3800 Norbrook Drive
Columbus, OH 43220
(614) 457-4154
Contact: William Huber, President
Geographic Giving Pattern: Primarily Columbus, Ohio.
Special Interest: Catholic welfare and youth organizations.
Assets: $2,128,953 (1999)
Grant Total: $100,000
Grant Range: $1,000–$10,400

Limitations: Grants do not exceed $7,500.
Applications: Initial approach should be by proposal including proof of tax exemption. The deadline is March 1. The application address is P.O. Box 21748, Columbus, OH 43221.

Mathile Family Foundation
6450 Sandlake Road
Dayton, OH 45414
(937) 264-4600
(937) 264-4635 (fax)
Email: kippy.king@cymi.com
Contact: Kippy Ungerleider King, Grants Associate
Geographic Giving Pattern: Primarily Dayton, Ohio; some support for Missouri and New Mexico.
Special Interest: Human needs, children, pre-collegiate education, free enterprise education, Catholic diocesan support, Indian missions, and Catholic social services.
Assets: $32,616,169 (1998)
Gifts Received: $1,637,841
Grant Total: $4,189,132
Grant Range: $900–$238,423
Grant Average: $2,500–$100,000
Limitations: No grants to individuals or for endowment funds.
Applications: Initial approach should be by letter, proposal, or telephone. The deadlines are February 1, May 1, August 1, and November 1.

The Maynard Family Foundation
P.O. Box 277
3200 Gilchrist Road
Mogadore, OH 44269-0277
(330) 733-6291
Contact: Pamela E. Loughry
Geographic Giving Pattern: Primarily Ohio.
Special Interests: Human services, secondary education, healthcare, youth services, federated giving programs, Catholic church support and Catholic agencies.
Assets: $1,722,138 (1998)
Grant Total: $100,138
Grant Range: $50–$26,863

Applications: Initial approach should be by letter. The deadlines are December 31, March 30, June 30 and September 30.

The Arthur B. McBride, Sr. Family Foundation
2069 West Third Street
Cleveland, OH 44113
(216) 861-3448
Contact: The Trustees
Geographic Giving Pattern: Primarily Cleveland, Ohio.
Special Interests: Higher education, hospitals, medical research, human services, Catholic agencies and churches.
Assets: $9,004,691 (1998)
Grant Total: $408,500
Grant Range: $1,000–$25,000
Limitations: No grants to individuals.
Applications: Contributes to pre-selected organizations only. Applications are not accepted.

McDonald Investments Foundation
800 Superior Avenue
Cleveland, OH 44114
(216) 443-2300
(216) 443-8452 (fax)
Email: tclevidence@mcdinvest.com
Contact: Thomas G. Clevidence, Chair
Geographic Giving Pattern: Primarily in areas of company operations, with an emphasis on Cleveland, Ohio.
Special Interests: Arts and cultural organizations, education, human services, and diocesan support of Catholic Charities.
Assets: $1,098,352 (1999)
Gifts Received: $528,000
Grant Total: $991,970
Grant Range: $100–$35,000
Limitations: Religious and welfare support is restricted to local arms of United Way, United Jewish Welfare Fund, and Catholic Charities.
Applications: Initial approach should be by letter. There are no deadlines.

The McKeever Foundation, Inc.
c/o C. J. Monastra & Co., Inc.
20102 Chagrin Boulevard
Shaker Heights, OH 44122
(216) 392-8298
Contact: Jerome McKeever, Trustee
Geographic Giving Pattern: Primarily Ohio.
Special Interests: Education Catholic church support and Catholic agencies.
Assets: $1,196,485 (1998)
Grant Total: $130,350
Grant Range: $250–$30,000
Applications: Initial approach should be by letter. There are no deadlines.

Mill-Rose Foundation, Inc.
c/o Mill-Rose Company
7995 Tyler Boulevard
Mentor, OH 44060
(440) 946-5727
Contact: Paul M. Miller, Trustee
Geographic Giving Pattern: Primarily Ohio.
Description: Mill-Rose Foundation, Inc. is a corporate foundation of the Mill-Rose Company.
Special Interest: Arts and culture, education, healthcare, human services, Catholic churches, and Catholic agencies.
Assets: $39,924 (1999)
Grant Total: $230,193
Grant Range: $50–$51,500
Limitations: No grants to individuals.
Applications: Initial approach should be by letter. There are no deadlines.

The Murphy Family Foundation
25800 Science Park Drive
P.O. Box 22747
Beachwood, OH 44112
(216) 831-7320
(216) 831-2296 (fax)
Email: jtmcmpany@aol.com

Contact: Rita M. Carfagna, President
Geographic Giving Pattern: Primarily Ohio, with an emphasis on greater Cleveland.
Special Interest: Poverty, hunger, shelter, education, Protestant and Catholic churches, and welfare.
Assets: $5,685,866 (1999)
Grant Total: $454,517
Grant Range: $1,000–$20,000
Limitations: No grants to individuals. No support for health or disability-related programs. No support for the arts.
Applications: Initial approach should be by letter requesting application guidelines. The deadlines are January 15, April 15, August 15, and November 15.

John P. Murphy Foundation
Tower City Center, 924 Terminal Tower
50 Public Square
Cleveland, OH 44113-2203
(216) 623-4770
(216) 623-4773 (fax)
Contact: Herbert E. Strawbridge, President and Treasurer
Geographic Giving Pattern: Primarily the greater Cleveland, Ohio area.
Special Interest: Higher education, community development, health, civic affairs, social services, and youth.
Assets: $68,459,481 (1999)
Grant Total: $3,620,915
Grant Range: $1,000–$4,500,000
Grant Average: $10,000–$25,000
Limitations: No grants to individuals or for endowment funds. No loans.
Applications: Initial approach should be by letter or telephone. An application form is required. Eight copies of the proposal are requested.

T. R. Murphy Residuary Trust
50 North Fourth Street
P.O. Box 1030
Zanesville, OH 43702-1030
(740) 454-2591

Contact: R. William Geyer, Trustee
Geographic Giving Pattern: Limited to Muskingum County, Ohio.
Special Interest: Support for three local Catholic high schools and scholarships to worthy graduates.
Assets: $4,744,548 (1998)
Grant Total: $44,827 and $117,102 for individuals.
Applications: An application form is required for scholarships. The deadline is May 1.

The M. G. O'Neil Foundation
c/o Gencorp
175 Ghent Road
Fairlawn, OH 44333-3300
(330) 869-4412
Contact: M.G. O'Neil, President
Geographic Giving Pattern: Primarily Ohio.
Special Interest: Catholic organizations, community funds, and social service agencies.
Assets: $3,735,629 (1998)
Grant Total: $537,025
Grant Range: $100–$75,000
Limitations: No grants for conferences, seminars, or special projects.
Applications: Initial approach should be by letter. There is no deadline for grant proposals.

The O'Neill Brothers Foundation
3550 Lander Road
Cleveland, OH 44124
(216) 464-2121
Contact: Robert K. Healey, President
Geographic Giving Pattern: Primarily Cleveland, Ohio.
Special Interest: Education, healthcare, animal welfare, youth, community development, Catholic church support, and Catholic agencies.
Assets: $1,290,347 (1998)
Grant Total: $155,935
Grant Range: $100–$20,000
Limitations: No grants to individuals.
Applications: Initial approach should be by letter. There are no deadlines.

The F. J. O'Neill Charitable Corporation

3550 Lander Road
Cleveland, OH 44124
(216) 464-2121
Contact: Hugh O'Neill, President
Geographic Giving Pattern: Primarily the greater Cleveland, Ohio area.
Special Interest: Catholic religious organizations, church support, medical research, and higher and secondary education.
Assets: $60,555,797 (1998)
Grant Total: $13,695,740
Grant Range: $1,000–$200,000
Grant Average: $25,000–$100,000
Limitations: No grants for scholarships, fellowships, or prizes.
Applications: An application form is required.

The Corinne F. O'Neill Charitable Corporation

3550 Lander Road
Cleveland, OH 44124
(216) 464-2121
Contact: The Trustees
Geographic Giving Pattern: Primarily Cleveland, Ohio.
Special Interest: Catholic organizations and human services.
Assets: $1,027,771 (1998)
Grant Total: $268,000
Grant Average: $500–$50,000
Limitations: No grants to individuals.
Applications: Contributes to pre-selected organizations only. Applications are not accepted.

The William J. and Dorothy K. O'Neill Foundation, Inc.

30195 Chagrin Boulevard, Suite 310
Cleveland, OH 44124
(216) 831-9667
(216) 831-3779 (fax)
Email: oneillfdn@aol.com
www.oneillfdn.org
Contact: William J. O'Neill, Jr., President and Christine E. Henry, Director
Geographic Giving Pattern: Primarily Ohio, especially Cleveland.

Special Interest: Catholic organizations, education, health, and Catholic church support.
Assets: $6,755,716 (1998)
Gifts Received: $92,888
Grant Total: $825,169
Grant Range: $500–$72,000
Grant Average: $5,000–$25,000
Applications: Initial approach should be by letter or telephone. Deadlines are six weeks prior to quarterly board meetings. The board meets in March, June, September and December. Organizations are restricted to submitting only one application per year.

Ranch Foundation
1400 North Point Tower
1001 Lakeside Drive
Cleveland, OH 44114-1152
(216) 523-1900
Contact: George E. Wasmer
Geographic Giving Pattern: Primarily Cleveland, Ohio.
Special Interests: Human services, secondary education, hospitals, higher education, Catholic church support and Catholic agencies.
Assets: $1,585,730 (1998)
Grant Total: $162,935
Grant Range: $50–$52,340
Limitations: No grants to individuals.
Applications: Contributes to pre-selected organizations only. Applications are not accepted.

Roan Foundation
1001 Lakeside Avenue East, #1400
Cleveland, OH 44114-1152
(216) 523-1900
Contact: William A. Rawlings, Jr.
Geographic Giving Pattern: Primarily Cleveland, Ohio.
Special Interests: Human services, secondary education, animal welfare, federated giving programs, education, Catholic church support and Catholic agencies.
Assets: $1,073,878 (1998)
Grant Total: $88,651
Grant Range: $500–$10,000

Limitations: No grants to individuals.
Applications: Contributes to pre-selected organizations only.
Applications are not accepted.

Helen L. and Marie F. Rotterman Trust

1300 Courthouse Plaza Northeast
P.O. Box 220 Dayton, OH 45402-0220
(937) 222-2500
Contact: Jeffrey B. Shulman, Trustee
Geographic Giving Pattern: National.
Special Interests: Higher education, women, Catholic agencies and churches.
Assets: $3,636,102 (1999)
Grant Total: $141,570
Grant Range: $7,865–$94,380
Applications: Initial approach should be by letter.

Saint Gerard Foundation

c/o William E. Reichard
25109 Detroit Road
Westlake, OH 44145
(440) 356-3438
Contact: Elizabeth C. Mooney, Treasurer
Geographic Giving Pattern: National.
Special Interest: Conservative public policy organizations, Catholic church support, Catholic agencies, and higher and secondary education.
Assets: $596,953 (1998)
Grant Total: $356,900
Grant Range: $25–$100,000
Limitations: No grants to individuals.
Applications: Contributes to pre-selected organizations only.
Applications are not accepted.

Jacob G. Schmidlapp Trust No. 1 and No. 2

c/o Fifth Third Bank
Fifth Third Center, ML 1090C7
Foundation Office
Cincinnati, OH 45263
(513) 579-6034

Contact: Laura J. Baumann, Foundation Officer
Geographic Giving Pattern: Primarily the greater Cincinnati, Ohio area.
Special Interest: Relief of sickness and suffering, care of young children, care of the helpless and afflicted, education, and child care training.
Assets: $62,221,532 (1998)
Grant Total: $3,223,796
Grant Average: $5,000–$100,000
Limitations: No grants to individuals or for deficit financing. No support for sectarian religious purposes or political purposes. No loans.
Applications: Initial approach should be by letter. The deadlines are February 1, May 1, August 1, and November 1.

Schmidt-Messmer Perpetual Charitable Trust

c/o Bank One, Kentucky, N.A.
774 Park Meadow
Westerville, OH 43081
Contact: Bank One, Kentucky, N.A.
Geographic Giving Pattern: Primarily Kentucky.
Special Interests: Literature, hospitals, aging, housing and shelter, Catholic church support and Catholic agencies.
Assets: $2,401,509 (1998)
Gifts Received: $4,226
Grant Total: $76,346
Grant Average: $10,791
Limitations: No grants to individuals.
Applications: Contributes to pre-selected organizations only. Applications are not accepted.

The I. J. Van Huffel Foundation

SNB Trust Department
108 Main Avenue, SW
Warren, OH 44481
(330) 841-0238
Contact: William Hanshaw
Geographic Giving Pattern: Primarily Ohio.
Special Interest: Education, Catholic and Protestant agencies, church support, hospitals, social service agencies, the arts, and cultural programs.

Assets: $3,259,059 (1998)
Grant Total: $103,000
Grant Average: $500–$13,000
Applications: There are no deadlines.

Dr. Frank Vecchio and Helen Williams Vecchio Foundation

925 Euclid Avenue, Suite 1100
Cleveland, OH 44115-1475
(216) 696-4087
Contact: Michael Elliot, Trustee
Geographic Giving Pattern: Primarily Ohio.
Special Interests: Elementary and secondary education, healthcare, Catholic church support and Catholic agencies.
Assets: $2,251,813 (1998)
Grant Total: $97,500
Grant Range: $1,000–$50,000
Limitations: No grants to individuals.
Applications: Initial approach should be by letter. There are no deadlines.

Zembrodt Family Foundation, Inc.

3023 East Kemper Road, Building 9
Cincinnatti, OH 45241
Contact: Cyril Zembrodt, President
Geographic Giving Pattern: Primarily the greater Cincinnatti, Ohio area including northern Kentucky.
Special Interests: Secondary education, human services, and Catholic agencies and churches.
Assets: $4,686,390 (1998)
Gifts Received: $620,000
Grant Total: $297,488
Grant Range: $2,000–$297,488
Limitations: No grants to individuals.
Applications: Contributes to pre-selected organizations only. Applications are not accepted.

OKLAHOMA

Fulton and Susie Collins Foundation
1924 South Utica, Suite 800
Tulsa, OK 74104
(918) 748-9860
Contact: Suzanne M. Collins, Trustee
Geographic Giving Pattern: Primarily Tulsa, Oklahoma.
Special Interest: Arts and culture, education, healthcare, Catholic church support, and Catholic agencies.
Assets: $7,904,631 (1998)
Gifts Received: $1,188,957
Grant Total: $429,961
Grant Range: $50–$250,000
Limitations: No grants to individuals.
Applications: There are no deadlines for grant proposals.

The J. E. and L. E. Mabee Foundation, Inc.
3000 Mid-Continent Tower
401 South Boston, 30th Floor
Tulsa, OK 74103-4017
(918) 584-4286
Contact: John H. Conway, Jr., Vice Chair
Geographic Giving Pattern: Limited to Arkansas, Kansas, Missouri, New Mexico, Oklahoma, and Texas.
Special Interest: Christian religious organizations, higher education, and healthcare.
Assets: $756,591,508 (1999)
Grant Total: $40,026,246
Grant Range: $10,000–$3,000,000
Grant Average: $50,000–$400,000
Limitations: No grants to individuals. No support for research, endowment funds, scholarships, fellowships, or operating expenses. No loans.
Applications: Initial approach should be by proposal. An application form is not required. The deadlines are March 1, June 1, September 1, and December 1.

John E. Rooney Charitable Trust

2400 Mid-Continent Tower
Tulsa, OK 74103
Contact: John E. Rooney, Trustee
Geographic Giving Pattern: Primarily Tulsa, Oklahoma.
Special Interest: Arts and cultural programs, higher education, human services, and Catholic agencies and churches.
Assets: $152,907 (1998)
Grant Total: $78,083
Grant Range: $82–$22,750
Limitations: No grants to individuals.
Applications: Contributes to pre-selected organizations only. Applications are not accepted.

Maxine Ann Stanley Fund

c/o Bank One Trust Company, N.A.
P.O. Box 1
Tulsa, OK 74193
Contact: Bank One Trust Company
Geographic Giving Pattern: Primarily Oklahoma.
Special Interests: Heart and circulatory diseases and Catholic agencies and churches.
Assets: $3,832,721 (1998)
Grant Total: $137,260
Grant Range: $1,825–$138,809
Limitations: No grants to individuals.
Applications: Contributes to pre-selected organizations only. Applications are not accepted.

Warren Charite

P.O. Box 470372
Tulsa, OK 74147-0372
(918) 492-8100
Contact: W. R. Lissau, Vice President
Geographic Giving Pattern: Primarily Oklahoma.
Special Interest: Primarily local Catholic healthcare facilities, schools, and other Catholic organizations; some support for community groups.
Assets: $7,157,502 (1998)
Grant Total: $461,800
Grant Range: $250–$184,000

Limitations: No grants to individuals.
Applications: Initial approach should be by letter. There are no deadlines.

The William K. Warren Foundation
P.O. Box 470372
Tulsa, OK 74147-0372
(918) 492-8100
Contact: W. R. Lissau, President
Geographic Giving Pattern: Primarily Oklahoma.
Special Interest: Catholic healthcare facilities, education, social services, and a medical research program.
Assets: $403,160,749 (1998)
Gifts Received: $43,882,909
Grant Total: $26,467,500
Grant Average: $1,000–$50,000
Limitations: No grants to individuals.
Applications: Initial approach should be by letter. There are no deadlines.

OREGON

Chiles Foundation
111 SW Fifth Avenue
Suite 4050
Portland, OR 97204-3643
(503) 222-2143
Contact: Earle M. Chiles, President
Geographic Giving Pattern: National, with an emphasis on Oregon, especially Portland, and the Pacific Northwest.
Special Interest: Education, religious education, medical research and advancement, divinity schools, church support, and monasteries.
Assets: $24,768,993 (1998)
Grant Total: $1,745,667
Grant Range: $500–$561,700
Grant Average: $500–$305,500
Limitations: No grants to individuals or for deficit financing, mortgage reduction, litigation projects, or conferences already in progress. No loans.

Applications: Initial approach should be by telephone requesting an application form.

Clark Foundation

255 Southwest Harrison Street, GA 2
Portland, OR 97201
(503) 223-5290
Contact: Jean Ameele, Administrator
Geographic Giving Pattern: Primarily Portland, Oregon.
Special Interest: Cultural programs, youth agencies, secondary education, the environment, and medical care. Emphasis on building funds for higher educational institutions, churches, and religious associations.
Assets: $75,222 (1998)
Gifts Received: $1,903,134
Grant Total: $1,738,499
Grant Range: $500–$100,000
Grant Average: $1,000–$25,000
Limitations: No grants to individuals or for research or endowment funds. No matching gifts or loans.
Applications: Initial approach should be by letter. There are no deadlines.

The Collins Foundation

1618 S. W. 1st Avenue, Suite 305
Portland, OR 97201-5708
(503) 227-7171
Contact: Jerry E. Hudson, Executive Vice President
Geographic Giving Pattern: Limited to Oregon, with an emphasis on Portland.
Special Interest: Higher education, youth, hospices and health agencies, social welfare and Catholic, Protestant, Jewish and interfaith religious giving.
Assets: $177,037,780 (1999)
Grant Total: $7,155,330
Grant Range: $5,000–$1,000,000
Grant Average: $5,000–$100,000
Limitations: No grants to individuals or for deficit financing, endowment funds, general purposes, scholarships, fellowships, operating budgets, annual campaigns, or annual fundraising activities.

Applications: Initial approach should be by letter. There are no deadlines.

A. J. Frank Family Foundation
P.O. Drawer 79
Mill City, OR 97360
(503) 897-2371
Contact: Douglas Highberger
Geographic Giving Pattern: Primarily Oregon.
Special Interest: Catholic church support, welfare funds, and secondary education.
Assets: $7,289,107 (1999)
Gifts Received: $5,000
Grant Total: $394,181
Grant Range: $100–$91,468
Limitations: No grants to individuals.
Applications: Initial approach should be by letter. The deadlines are August 15 and December 15.

B. P., Lester and Regina John Foundation
1000 Southwest Vista Avenue, Suite 116
Portland, OR 97205
(503) 223-4590
(503) 223-9920 (fax)
Contact: Patricia J. Abraham, President
Geographic Giving Pattern: Primarily Portland, Oregon.
Special Interests: Healthcare, human services, homelessness, Catholic agencies and churches.
Assets: $4,206,015 (1998)
Grant Total: $79,500
Grant Range: $500–$25,000
Limitations: No grants to individuals.
Applications: Contributes to pre-selected organizations only. Applications are not accepted.

Helen John Foundation
16727 Northwest Norwalk Drive
Beaverton, OR 97007
(503) 645-4719
Contact: James G. Condon

Geographic Giving Pattern: Primarily Oregon and Washington.
Special Interests: Human services, secondary and elementary education, higher education, Protestant churches and agencies, Catholic church support and Catholic agencies.
Assets: $1,655,975 (1999)
Grant Total: $71,750
Grant Range: $1,000–$8,350
Limitations: No grants to individuals.
Applications: Contributes to pre-selected organizations only. Applications are not accepted.

Lora L. & Martin N. Kelley Family Foundation Trust
P.O. Box 31
Wilsonville, OR 97070
(503) 226-1331
Contact: Martin N. Kelley, Manager
Geographic Giving Pattern: Primarily Omaha, Nebraska, Oregon, and Montana.
Special Interest: Museums, performing arts, conservation, housing, Catholic church support, and Catholic agencies.
Assets: $24,987,106 (1999)
Gifts Received: $15,006,250
Grant Total: $828,300
Grant Range: $5,000–$330,000
Limitations: No grants to individuals.
Applications: Contributes to pre-selected organizations only. Applications are not accepted.

Maybelle Clark Macdonald Fund
5200 SW Macadam Avenue, #470
Portland, OR 97201
(503) 291-9575
Contact: Maybelle Clark Macdonald, President
Geographic Giving Pattern: Primarily Oregon.
Special Interest: Local cultural programs, Catholic church support, education, and youth agencies.
Assets: $1,782,678 (1999)
Gifts Received: $979,375
Grant Total: $538,656
Grant Range: $200–$277,000

Limitations: No grants to individuals.
Applications: Initial approach should be by letter. There are no deadlines.

Harry A. Merlo Foundation, Inc.
121 South West Morrison, Suite 450
Portland, OR 97204
(503) 221-3030
Contact: Gary R. Maffei, Vice President
Geographic Giving Pattern: Primarily Oregon.
Special Interest: Education, children and youth, community development, Catholic church support, Catholic agencies, and Catholic federated giving programs.
Assets: $5,587,476 (1999)
Gifts Received: $1,693
Grant Total: $338,877
Grant Range: $100–$100,000
Applications: Initial approach should be by letter.

Harry and Dorothy Murphy Foundation
8835 Southwest Canyon Lane, Suite 210
Portland, OR 97225
(503) 223-1332
(503) 203-1581 (fax)
Contact: Edward N. Murphy, President
Geographic Giving Pattern: Primarily Oregon.
Special Interests: Human services, higher education, youth services, Catholic church support and Catholic agencies.
Assets: $1,303,365 (1999)
Grant Total: $71,196
Grant Range: $40–$52,000
Limitations: No grants to individuals.
Applications: Initial approach should be by letter. The deadline is December 31st.

Share-It-Now Foundation
661 East 18th Avenue
Eugene, OR 97401
(541) 683-4975
Contact: Martha B. Russell, Trustee

Geographic Giving Pattern: Primarily California, New York, and Oregon.

Special Interests: The environment, sustainability, and Catholic agencies and church support.

Assets: $831,933 (1998)

Grant Total: $69,617

Grant Range: $100–$1,730

Limitations: No grants to individuals.

Applications: Initial approach should be by letter. There are no deadlines.

St. Martin de Porres Trust

1100 Southwest Sixth Avenue, Suite 1504
Portland, OR 97204-3705
(503) 248-9535

Contact: Eugene E. Feltz and Harold D. Christianson, Trustees

Geographic Giving Pattern: Primarily Oregon.

Special Interests: Education Catholic church support and Catholic agencies.

Assets: $2,736,990 (1997)

Gifts Received: $495,947

Grant Total: $77,000

Grant Range: $500–$5,000

Applications: Initial approach should be by letter. There are no deadlines.

PENNSYLVANIA

Avery Foundation

c/o Crown, Cork, & Seal Co., Inc.
1 Crown Way
Philadelphia, PA 19154-4599
(215) 698-5100

Contact: William J. Avery, Trustee

Geographic Giving Pattern: Primarily Pennsylvania.

Special Interests: Education, human services, Catholic agencies and churches.

Assets: $573,661 (1998)

Grant Total: $251,366

Grant Range: $150–$44,438
Limitations: No grants to individuals.
Applications: Initial approach should be by letter. There are no deadlines.

The Patsy and Rose H. Billera Foundation
P.O. Box 788
Allentown, PA 18105-0788
(610) 433-7501
Contact: Joseph Billera, President
Geographic Giving Pattern: Primarily Pennsylvania.
Special Interests: Human services, healthcare, higher education, hospitals, Catholic church support and Catholic agencies.
Assets: $546,223 (1999)
Gifts Received: $66,045
Grant Total: $74,375
Grant Range: $1,160–$15,195
Limitations: No grants to individuals.
Applications: Contributes to pre-selected organizations only. Applications are not accepted.

Brooks Foundation
c/o PNC Bank, #18406-8   P2-PTPP-26-3
2 PNC Plaza, 620 Liberty Avenue
Pittsburgh, PA 15222-2705
(412) 762-3390
Contact: John Colbertson, Vice President, PNC Bank, N.A.
Geographic Giving Pattern: Primarily Pittsburgh, Pennsylvania.
Special Interest: Communications, art and culture, education, and Protestant and Catholic church support and agencies.
Assets: $5,968,230 (1999)
Grant Total: $254,000
Grant Range: $250–$18,500
Limitations: No grants to individuals.
Applications: Initial approach should be by letter. There are no deadlines.

Michael A. Bruder Foundation

P.O. Box 600
600 Reed Road
Broomall, PA 19008-0600
(610) 353-5100
Contact: Thomas A. Bruder
Geographic Giving Pattern: Primarily Pennsylvania, Illinois, Indiana, and Ohio.
Description: The Michael A. Bruder Foundation is a corporate foundation of M.A. Bruder & Sons, Inc.
Special Interest: Higher education, hospitals, and scholarships.
Assets: $727,710 (1999)
Grant Total: $54,693
Grant Range: $943–$6,250
Applications: There are no deadlines for grant proposals.

The Cain Foundation

One Monroe Street at Radcliffe
P.O. Box 205
Bristol, PA 19007-0205
(215) 788-9277
Contact: George P. Cain and May Cain, Trustees
Geographic Giving Pattern: Primarily Pennsylvania.
Special Interests: Catholic church support and Catholic agencies.
Assets: $448,987 (1999)
Gifts Received: $200,000
Grant Total: $31,050
Grant Range: $1,500–$5,000
Limitations: No grants to individuals.
Applications: Contributes to pre-selected organizations only. Applications are not accepted.

The Calihan Foundation

600 Grant Street, Suite 4606
Pittsburgh, PA 15219-2702
(412) 227-6900
Contact: Victoria L. Pacoe, Secretary
Geographic Giving Pattern: Primarily Pittsburgh, Pennsylvania.
Special Interests: Performing arts, federated giving programs, education, Catholic agencies and support.

Assets: $1,285,787 (1999)
Gifts Received: $799,857
Grant Total: $318,457
Grant Range: $50–$30,000
Limitations: No grants to individuals.
Applications: Initial approach should be by letter. There are no deadlines.

The Caritas Foundation
700 Hobbs Road
Wayne, PA 19087
(610) 527-0325
Contact: Rev. Peter Toscani, O.S.A., Trustee
Special Interest: Education, Catholic church support, and Catholic social service agencies.
Assets: $1,411,286 (1998)
Gifts Received: $62,105
Grant Total: $43,916
Grant Range: $50–$31,700
Limitations: No grants to individuals.
Applications: Initial approach should be by letter. There are no deadlines.

Gunard Berry Carlson Memorial Foundation, Inc.
P.O. Box 526
Thorndale, PA 19372
(610) 384-2800
Contact: Barbara C. Travaglini, Secretary-Treasurer
Geographic Giving Pattern: Primarily Pennsylvania.
Special Interests: Higher education, secondary education, Catholic church support and Catholic agencies.
Assets: $1,620,277 (1999)
Gifts Received: $3,445
Grant Total: $96,300
Grant Range: $500–$15,000
Limitations: No grants to individuals.
Applications: An application for in required. There are no deadlines.

Colonial Oaks Foundation

P.O. Box 6829
850 N. Wyommissing Boulevard, Suite 200
Wyomissing, PA 19610
(610) 988-2400
(610) 371-1101 (fax)
Contact: Christine M. Auman, Executive Director
Geographic Giving Pattern: Primarily Berks County, Pennsylvania.
Special Interest: Education, culture, Catholic church support, and Catholic social service agencies.
Assets: $17,500,394 (1998)
Gifts Received: $1,627,000
Grant Total: $584,850
Grant Range: $250–$130,000
Limitations: No grants to individuals.
Applications: Initial approach should be by letter. There are no deadlines. The application address is P.O. Box 5936, Wyomissing, PA 19610-5936.

Connelly Foundation

One Tower Bridge, Suite 1450
West Conshohocken, PA 19428
(610) 834-3222
(610) 834-0866 (fax)
Email: info@connellyfnd.org
www.connellyfnd.org
Contact: Victoria K. Flaville, Vice President
Geographic Giving Pattern: Philadelphia, Pennsylvania, and the surrounding Delaware Valley area.
Special Interest: Education, health, human services, culture, and civic affairs.
Assets: $315,682,501 (1998)
Grant Total: $20,410,868
Grant Range: $250–$5,000,000
Grant Average: $5,000–$50,000
Limitations: No grants to individuals or for research.
Applications: Initial approach should be by written proposal. Guidelines are available. Applicants may use the Delaware Valley Grantmakers Application Form. There are no formal deadlines.

Copernicus Society of America

P.O. Box 385
Fort Washington, PA 19034
(215) 628-3632
Contact: P. Erik Nelson
Geographic Giving Pattern: Primarily Pennsylvania and Poland.
Special Interest: Support and advancement of the Polish culture and heritage, historic preservation, Catholic church support, and Catholic agencies.
Assets: $7,391,411 (1999)
Grant Total: $473,094
Grant Range: $125–$125,000
Limitations: No grants to individuals. No support for operating budgets, annual campaigns, seed money, emergency funds, deficit financing, building funds, land acquisition, equipment, materials, fellowships, or research. No matching gifts or loans.
Applications: Contributes to pre-selected organizations only. Applications are not accepted.

The Crossroads Foundation

234 Edelweiss Drive
Pittsburgh, PA 15090
(412) 621-9422
Contact: Matt Stalder
Geographic Giving Pattern: Primarily Pittsburgh, Pennsylvania.
Special Interest: Catholic churches, schools, and welfare organizations.
Assets: $117,059 (1999)
Gifts Received: $384,528
Grant Total: $197,087
Grant Range: $8,600–$58,242
Limitations: No grants to individuals.
Applications: Contributes to pre-selected organizations only. Applications are not accepted.

Charles A. Dailey Foundation

5602 Bonaventure Drive
Erie, PA 16505
(814) 838-4619

Contact: Charles A. Dailey
Geographic Giving Pattern: Primarily Erie, Pennsylvania.
Special Interests: Human services, education, federated giving programs, Catholic church support and Catholic agencies.
Assets: $1,268,137 (1999)
Grant Total: $49,450
Grant Range: $50–$30,000
Limitations: No grants to individuals.
Applications: Contributes to pre-selected organizations only. Applications are not accepted.

Di Loreto Foundation

1031 Old Cassatt Road
Berwyn, PA 19312
(610) 647-1280
Contact: Richard Di Loreto, President
Special Interests: Catholic institutions.
Assets: $0 (1998)
Gifts Received: $62,500
Grant Total: $62,750
Grant Range: $250–$15,000
Limitations: No grants to individuals.
Applications: Initial approach should be by letter. There are no deadlines. The application address is P.O. Box 784, Southeastern, PA 19399.

Donahue Family Foundation, Inc.

718 Bigelow Corporate Center
Bigelow Square
Pittsburgh, PA 15219-1945
(412) 471-6420
(412) 471-9011 (fax)
Contact: William J. Donahue, Executive Vice President
Geographic Giving Pattern: Southwestern Pennsylvania.
Special Interest: Catholic education and social service agencies.
Assets: $3,248,157 (1998)
Grant Total: $217,448
Grant Range: $5,000–$57,715
Applications: Contributes to pre-selected organizations only. Applications are not accepted.

Mary J. Donnelly Foundation

Center City Tower
650 Smithfield Street, Suite 1810
Pittsburgh, PA 15222
(412) 471-5828
(412) 471-0736 (fax)
Contact: Thomas J. Donnelly, Trustee
Geographic Giving Pattern: Primarily Pennsylvania.
Special Interest: Catholic educational, welfare, and religious organizations.
Assets: $4,024,573 (1999)
Grant Total: $641,145
Grant Range: $5,000–$250,000
Limitations: No grants to individuals or for endowment funds. No matching gifts or loans.
Applications: Initial approach should be by letter. Three copies of the grant proposal are requested. There are no deadlines.

The Eustace Foundation

308 East Lancaster Avenue, 3rd Floor
Wynnewood, PA 19096
Contact: J. Eustace Wolfington, Trustee
Geographic Giving Pattern: Primarily Pennsylvania.
Special Interest: Education, human services, Catholic church support, Catholic agencies, and Catholic federated giving programs.
Assets: $12,199,856 (1998)
Gifts Received: $500,000
Grant Total: $384,295
Grant Range: $25–$57,250
Limitations: No grants to individuals.
Applications: Contributes to pre-selected organizations only. Applications are not accepted.

IGN Foundation

1701 Market Street
Philadelphia, PA 19103-2921
Contact: Frank S. Polizzi, Trustee
Geographic Giving Pattern: Primarily Philadelphia, Pennsylvania.
Special Interest: Catholic church support and Catholic agencies.

Assets: $6,872,950 (1999)
Grant Total: $161,000
Grant Range: $5,000–$50,000
Limitations: No grants to individuals.
Applications: Initial approach should be by letter. The application address is 435 Devon Park Drive, Suite 510, Wayne, PA 19087. There are no deadlines.

The J. D. B. Fund
404 South Swedesford Road
P.O. Box 157
Gwynedd, PA 19436-0157
(215) 699-2233
Contact: Paul J. Corr, Manager
Geographic Giving Pattern: Primarily the Philadelphia, Pennsylvania area.
Special Interest: Education, conservation, the environment, Catholic churches, diocesan support, and Catholic agencies.
Assets: $3,295,243 (1999)
Grant Total: $156,356
Grant Average: $50–$20,000
Limitations: No grants to individuals.
Applications: Initial approach should be by letter. There are no deadlines.

Jomar Foundation
19 Short Road
Doylestown, PA 18901
Contact: Joseph A. Murphy, President
Geographic Giving Pattern: Primarily Ohio and Virginia.
Special Interests: Hospitals, Catholic agencies and churches.
Assets: $2,518,912 (1999)
Grant Total: $498,916
Grant Average: $5,000–$10,000
Limitations: No grants to individuals.
Applications: Contributes to pre-selected organizations only. Applications are not accepted.

T. James Kavanagh Foundation

P.O. Box 609
Broomal, PA 19008
(610) 356-0743
(610) 356-4606 (fax)
Contact: Brenda S. Brooks, CEO
Geographic Giving Pattern: Limited to Pennsylvania and southern New Jersey.
Special Interest: At least 60 percent of funding for Catholic churches, Catholic welfare agencies, and religious associations. Additional support for Catholic schools and environmental aid.
Assets: $14,679,206 (1999)
Grant Total: $405,611
Grant Range: $1,000–$13,000
Limitations: No grants outside of the U.S. including Catholic organizations with missions overseas. No grants to individuals or for endowment funds, seed money, deficit financing, land acquisition, publications, or scholarships. No matching gifts or loans. No support for private foundations, conferences, or fellowships.
Applications: An application form is required with the proposal. Grant proposals should be submitted preferably by the end of February, July, or October.

Kate M. Kelley Foundation

108 North Dithridge Street
Pittsburgh, PA 15213
(412) 343-9200
Contact: Rev. Leo V. Vanyo, Trustee
Geographic Giving Pattern: Primarily Pittsburgh, Pennsylvania.
Special Interest: Catholic church support and church-related education.
Assets: $5,118,218 (1998)
Grant Total: $1,097,000
Grant Range: $1,000–$75,000
Limitations: No grants to individuals.
Applications: Contributes to pre-selected organizations only. Applications are not accepted.

Paul E. Kelley Foundation

233 East Lancaster Avenue, Suite 102
Ardmore, PA 19003
(610) 649-1448
(610) 649-1498 (fax)
Email: superpac@bellatlantic.net
Contact: Paul E. Kelley, Jr., Vice President
Geographic Giving Pattern: Primarily Pennsylvania, with an emphasis on Philadelphia.
Special Interests: Education, Catholic secondary and higher education, community funds, health and hospitals, and arts and culture.
Assets: $23,543,564 (1998)
Grant Total: $969,100
Grant Range: $150–$300,000
Applications: Initial approach should be by letter. An application form is required.

E. Roy Knoppel Charitable Trust

Paoli Executive Green
41 Leopard Road, Suite 200
Paoli, PA 19301
(610) 651-0156
Contact: Joseph E. Greene, Jr., Trustee
Geographic Giving Pattern: Primarily Pennsylvania.
Special Interests: Human services, museums, legal services, special populations, Catholic church support and Catholic agencies.
Assets: $349,439 (1998)
Grant Total: $165,000
Grant Range: $2,500–$50,000
Limitations: No grants to individuals.
Applications: Initial approach should be by letter. There are no deadlines.

Samuel P. Mandell Foundation

1735 Market Street, Suite 3410
Philadelphia, PA 19103-7501
(215) 979-3400
Contact: Seymour Mandell, Trustee
Geographic Giving Pattern: Primarily Pennsylvania.

Special Interests: Religious funds, hospitals, medical research, health associations, education, arts and culture, community affairs and the environment.
Assets: $28,774,722 (1998)
Grant Total: $1,472,132
Grant Range: $50–$205,750
Limitations: No grants to individuals. No support for private operating foundations.
Applications: Initial approach should be by letter. There are no deadlines.

The Maronda Foundation
11 Timberglen Drive
Imperial, PA 15126
(724) 695-1200
Contact: William J. Wolf, President
Geographic Giving Pattern: Primarily Pennsylvania.
Special Interests: Human services, elementary and secondary education, youth services, Catholic church support and Catholic agencies.
Assets: $1,776,730 (1998)
Grant Total: $373,214
Grant Range: $466–$165,687
Limitations: No grants to individuals.
Applications: Contributes to pre-selected organizations only. Applications are not accepted.

John C. and Lucine O. B. Marous Charitable Foundation
33 Eaton Road
Pittsburgh, PA 15238
Contact: John C. Marous, Jr., President
Geographic Giving Pattern: Primarily Pennsylvania.
Special Interests: Federated giving programs, theological education, Catholic church support and Catholic agencies.
Assets: $229,577 (1998)
Grant Total: $99,600
Grant Range: $100–$31,500
Limitations: No grants to individuals.
Applications: Contributes to pre-selected organizations only. Applications are not accepted.

The Rocco and Barbara Martino Foundation, Inc.

512 Watch Hill Road
Villanova, PA 19085
Contact: Rocco L. Martino
Geographic Giving Pattern: National, with an emphasis on Pennsylvania.
Special Interests: Catholic agencies and churches, and higher education.
Assets: $3,444,676, (1998)
Gifts Received: $13,405
Grant Total: $163,210
Grant Range: $200–$50,200
Limitations: No grants to individuals.
Applications: Contributes to pre-selected organizations only. Applications are not accepted.

The Rev. Raymond J. and Rev. Terrence F. McNulty Memorial Endowment Fund

c/o PNC Bank, N.A. P2-PTPP-08-4
Pittsburgh, PA 15222-2705
(412) 762-2000
Contact: PNC Bank, N.A.
Geographic Giving Pattern: Primarily Philadelphia, Pennsylvania.
Special Interest: Scholarship support awarded directly to Catholic elementary and secondary schools.
Assets: $401,562 (1998)
Grant Total: $24,705
Grant Average: $8,235
Limitations: No grants to individuals.
Applications: Contributes to pre-selected organizations only. Applications are not accepted.

John McShain Charities, Inc.

The Wynnewood House, #200
300 E. Lancaster Avenue
Wynnewood, PA 19096-2105
(610) 896-8994
Contact: Sr. Pauline Mary McShain, SHCJ
Geographic Giving Pattern: Primarily Philadelphia, Pennsylvania.

Special Interest: Catholic higher and secondary education, Catholic church and diocesan support, social welfare, and cultural programs.
Assets: $59,422,771 (1999)
Grant Total: $2,533,779
Grant Range: $50–$250,000
Grant Average: $2,000–$100,000
Limitations: No grants to individuals.
Applications: Initial approach should be by letter. There are no deadlines.

Matthew T. Mellon Foundation

c/o Mellon Bank, N.A.
P.O. Box 185
Pittsburgh, PA 15230-9897
(412) 234-1398 or
(412) 234-5892
Contact: Leonard B. Richards
Geographic Giving Pattern: Primarily New York, New York.
Special Interests: Elementary and secondary education, healthcare, human services, and Catholic agencies and churches.
Assets: $4,188,099 (1999)
Grant Total: $161,000
Grant Range: $5,500–$100,000
Applications: Initial approach should be by letter or telephone requesting application guidelines. The application address is 3 Mellon Bank Center, Pittsburgh, PA 15259.

The Morris Charitable Trust

440 Parkview Drive
Wynnewood, PA 19096-1640
Contact: Michael J. Morris, Trustee
Geographic Giving Pattern: Primarily Philadelphia, Pennsylvania.
Special Interests: Education, theological education, human services, Catholic federated giving programs, and Catholic agencies and churches.
Assets: $1,702,338 (1999)
Grant Total: $209,450
Grant Range: $200–$118,120
Limitations: No grants to individuals.

Applications: Initial approach should be by letter. There are no deadlines.

The Mullen Family Foundation

204 Coventry Lane
Media, PA 19063
(610) 565-5617
Contact: John J. Mullen, Trustee
Geographic Giving Pattern: Primarily Philadelphia, Pennsylvania.
Special Interests: Hospitals, cancer and Catholic agencies and churches.
Assets: $736,926 (1998)
Grant Total: $47,800
Grant Range: $300–$10,000
Applications: Initial approach should be by letter. An application form is required. There are no deadlines.

The Pew Charitable Trusts

One Commerce Square
2005 Market Street, Suite 1700
Philadelphia, PA 19103-7077
(215) 575-9050
(215) 575-4939 (fax)
Email: info@pewtrusts.com
www.pewtrusts.com
Contact: Dr. Luis E. Lugo, Program Director for Religion
Geographic Giving Pattern: National.
Special Interest: In religion support is given to promote the development and application of Judeo-Christian values and to encourage better understanding of how those values shape our lives and civic responsibilities. Support is also given to strengthen religious scholarship, foster international understanding, and develop the ministry of congregations in their communities.
Assets: $4,734,121,560 (1998)
Grant Total: $161,055,093
Limitations: No grants to individuals or for endowment funds, deficit financing, scholarships, or fellowships, except those identified or initiated by the trusts. No support for political organizations, capital campaigns, construction, or equipment.

Applications: Contact the foundation for specific application procedure, guidelines, and limitations in the religious program area. Initial approach should be by a two to three-page letter of inquiry. There are no set deadlines.

John Charles and Kathryn S. Redmond Foundation

P.O. Box 1146
Blue Bell, PA 19422
Contact: John C. Redmond, III, President
Geographic Giving Pattern: Primarily Pennsylvania.
Special Interests: Higher education, elementary and secondary education, Catholic church support and Catholic agencies.
Assets: $1,409,301 (1998)
Grant Total: $50,500
Grant Range: $500–$5,000
Limitations: No grants to individuals.
Applications: Contributes to pre-selected organizations only. Applications are not accepted.

Kal and Lucille Rudman Foundation

c/o Asher & Co.
1845 Walnut Street, Suite 1300
Philadelphia, PA 19103-4714
Contact: Lucille Rudman and Solomon Rudman
Geographic Giving Pattern: Primarily Cherry Hill, New Jersey and Philadelphia, Pennsylvania.
Special Interests: Arts and cultural programs, universities, human services, and Catholic agencies and churches.
Assets: $3,685,413 (1997)
Gifts Received: $231,653
Grant Total: $84,300
Grant Range: $300–$32,000
Limitations: No grants to individuals.
Applications: Contributes to pre-selected organizations only. Applications are not accepted.

Ryan Memorial Foundation

P.O. 426
Pittsburgh, PA 15230
Contact: The Trustees

Geographic Giving Pattern: Primarily Pennsylvania.
Special Interests: Arts and cultural programs, education, hospitals, youth development, international affairs, business, federated giving programs, and Catholic agencies and churches.
Assets: $8,048,488 (1998)
Grant Total: $320,648
Grant Range: $500–$83,228
Limitations: No grants to individuals.
Applications: Contributes to pre-selected organizations only. Applications are not accepted.

St. Marys Catholic Foundation

1935 State Street
St. Marys, PA 15857
(814) 781-4222
(814) 781-4223 (fax)
Contact: Richard J. Reuscher, Secretary-Treasurer
Geographic Giving Pattern: Primarily Erie Diocese, Pennsylvania, with an emphasis on the St. Marys area.
Special Interest: Catholic schools (all levels) and religious associations.
Assets: $13,460,000 (1999)
Gifts Received: $110,000
Grant Total: $590,344
Grant Range: $1,000–$227,732
Limitations: No grants to individuals or for endowment funds, scholarships, or fellowships. No loans.
Applications: Contributes to pre-selected organizations only. Applications are not accepted.

The Donald B. and Dorothy L. Stabler Foundation

c/o Dauphin Deposit Bank & Trust Company
213 Market Street
Harrisburg, PA 17101
Contact: William King, Chair
Geographic Giving Pattern: Primarily Pennsylvania, with an emphasis on Harrisburg.
Special Interest: Education, hospitals, Catholic church support, and Catholic agencies.
Assets: $13,764,576 (1999)

Grant Total: $610,750
Grant Range: $500–$66,000
Limitations: No grants to individuals. No support for research programs, land acquisition, special projects, seed money, publications, conferences, deficit financing, or emergency funds. No loans.
Applications: Initial approach should be by letter. An application form is required. There are no deadlines.

The Stewart Foundation
P.O. Box 902
York, PA 17405
(717) 771-3502
Contact: Gary A. Stewart, President
Geographic Giving Pattern: Primarily York, Pennsylvania.
Special Interests: Healthcare, community development and a Catholic high school.
Assets: $844,604 (1999)
Grant Total: $224,766
Grant Range: $200–$100,000
Limitations: No grants to individuals.
Applications: Contributes to pre-selected organizations only. Applications are not accepted.

James M. and Margaret V. Stine Foundation
c/o Robert J. Weinberg
3000 Two Logan Square Peper Hamilton
Philadelphia, PA 19103-2799
(215) 981-4444
Contact: Margaret V. Stine, President and Treasurer
Geographic Giving Pattern: Primarily Pennsylvania.
Special Interests: Higher education, animal welfare, and Catholic agencies and churches.
Assets: $24,381,979 (1998)
Grant Total: $1,391,053
Grant Range: $253–$600,000
Limitations: No grants to individuals.
Applications: Contributes to pre-selected organizations only. Applications are not accepted.

Harry C. Trexler Trust
33 South Seventh Street, Suite 205
Allentown, PA 18101-2406
(610) 434-9645
(610) 437-5721 (fax)
Contact: Thomas H. Christman, Executive Director
Geographic Giving Pattern: Limited to Lehigh County, especially
Allentown, Pennsylvania.
Special Interest: Hospitals, churches, youth agencies, social services,
and Catholic diocesan support.
Assets: $137,993,764 (2000)
Grant Total: $4,288,375
Grant Range: $2,000–$514,725
Limitations: No grants to individuals or for endowment funds,
research, scholarships, or fellowships. No loans.
Applications: Initial approach should be by letter. The deadline is
December 1.

USA Waste/Chambers Development Foundation For Pittsburgh Charities
1500 Ardmore Boulevard, #407
Pittsburgh, PA 15221
(412) 244-6120
Contact: Nancy Barnhart
Geographic Giving Pattern: Primarily Pittsburgh, Pennsylvania.
Special Interests: Hospitals, higher education, pediatrics, science,
Catholic church support and Catholic agencies.
Assets: $1,880,004 (1999)
Grant Total: $500,000
Grant Range: $450–$264,417
Applications: Initial approach should be by letter. There are no
deadlines.

The Leo Yochum Foundation
2024 Blairmont Drive
Pittsburgh, PA 15241
Contact: Leo Yochum, Chair and President
Geographic Giving Pattern: Primarily Pennsylvania with an
emphasis on York.

Special Interests: Higher education, hospitals, youth services, Catholic church support and Catholic agencies.
Assets: $38,482 (1998)
Gifts Received: $250,000
Grant Total: $128,765
Grant Range: $500–$20,000
Limitations: No grants to individuals.
Applications: Contributes to pre-selected organizations only. Applications are not accepted.

RHODE ISLAND

David and Betsey Kilmartin Charitable Foundation, Inc.
247 Farnum Road
Glocester, RI 02814
(401) 949-1166
Contact: David F. Kilmartin, President
Geographic Giving Pattern: Primarily New England.
Description: Kilmartin Industries Charitable Foundation, Inc. is a corporate foundation.
Special Interest: Health associations, Catholic agencies, and churches.
Assets: $706,178 (1999)
Grant Total: $39,047
Grant Range: $200–$14,000
Limitations: No grants to individuals.
Applications: Initial approach should be by typed, double-spaced letter. There are no deadlines.

SOUTH CAROLINA

John Sam Lay Trust
1108 Roe Ford Road
Greenville, SC 29617
Contact: The Trustees
Geographic Giving Pattern: There are no stated geographical limitations.
Special Interests: Higher education, colleges, Catholic church support and Catholic agencies.
Assets: $243,312 (1997)

Grant Total: $100,000
Grant Range: $5,000–$45,000
Limitations: No grants to individuals.
Applications: Contributes to pre-selected organizations only. Applications are not accepted.

The Simpson Foundation
c/o Wachovia Bank of South Carolina
1401 Main Street, Suite 501
Columbia, SC 29226-9365
(803) 765-3671
Contact: C. Gerald Lane, Vice President and Trust Officer, Wachovia Bank
Geographic Giving Pattern: Primarily South Carolina.
Special Interests: Historic preservation, arts and cultural programs, education, healthcare, medical research, Catholic federated giving programs, and Protestant federated giving programs.
Assets: $10,403,770 (1999)
Grant Total: $180,350
Grant Range: $500–$10,000
Limitations: No grants to individuals, for scholarships or loans.
Applications: Initial approach should be by letter or proposal. Five copies of the proposal are requested. The deadlines are April 1 and October 1.

Security's Lending Hand Foundation
204 East Main Street
Spartanburg, SC 29306
(864) 582-8193
Contact: Susan A. Bridges, Chair
Geographic Giving Pattern: National.
Special Interests: Hospitals, food banks, boys and girls clubs, youth, hospices, federated giving programs, Protestant agencies and churches, and Catholic agencies and churches.
Assets: $359 (1998)
Gifts Received: $61,727
Grant Total: $327,200
Grant Range: $100–$20,500
Limitations: No grants to individuals.

Applications: Contributes to pre-selected organizations only. Applications are not accepted.

SOUTH DAKOTA

Alpha & Omega Family Foundation
c/o Norwest Bank South Dakota, N.A.
101 N. Phillips Avenue
Sioux Falls, SD 57104
Contact: J. R. Mahoney, President
Geographic Giving Pattern: Primarily Minnesota.
Special Interest: Education, scholarship support and Catholic organizations.
Assets: $31,949,556 (1998)
Grant Total: $1,537,758
Grant Average: $7,516–$1,000,000
Limitations: No grants to individuals.
Applications: Contributes to pre-selected organizations only. Applications are not accepted.

Dakota Charitable Foundation, Inc.
P.O. Box 8303
Rapid City, SD 57709
(605) 341-3620
Contact: Ray J. Hillenbrand, Director
Geographic Giving Pattern: Primarily Rapid City, South Dakota.
Special Interest: Human services, Catholic church support, and Catholic agencies.
Assets: $6,472,878 (1999)
Grant Total: $373,000
Grant Average: $1,000–$52,000
Limitations: No grants to individuals.
Applications: Contributes to pre-selected organizations only. Applications are not accepted.

Maas Foundation
P.O. Box 7
Watertown, SD 57201
(605) 882-2853
Contact: George E. Maas, President

Geographic Giving Pattern: Primarily Minnesota.
Special Interest: Higher education, Catholic church support, and Catholic agencies.
Assets: $7,535,612 (1998)
Grant Total: $197,000
Grant Range: $1,000–$85,000
Limitations: No grants to individuals.
Applications: Contributes to pre-selected organizations only. Applications are not accepted.

TENNESSEE

The Assisi Foundation of Memphis, Inc.
6077 Primacy Parkway, Suite 253
Memphis, TN 38119
(901) 684-1564
(901) 684-1997 (fax)
Contact: Barry J. Flynn, Executive Director
Geographic Giving Pattern: Limited to Memphis and Shelby County, Tennessee.
Special Interest: Healthcare, education, community development, civic affairs, cultural programs, and religious organizations.
Assets: $5,030,512 (1998)
Gifts Received: $7,000,000
Grant Total: $6,391,908
Grant Range: $1,000–$701,123
Grant Average: $10,000–$50,000
Limitations: No grants to individuals. No support for endowments or building funds.
Applications: Initial approach should be by letter on organizational letterhead, requesting application. Eight copies of the proposal are requested. The deadlines are March 1, June 1, September 1, and December 1.

Association for the Care of Aging Population – The Care Foundation
5100 Wheelis Drive, Suite 106
Memphis, TN 38117
(901) 763-1762
Contact: Matthew T. Bond and George T. Johnson, Directors

Geographic Giving Pattern: Primarily Memphis, Tennessee.
Special Interests: Higher education, healthcare, Catholic agencies and churches.
Assets: $1,671,577 (1998)
Grant Total: $669,700
Grant Range: $1,000–$500,000
Limitations: No grants to individuals.
Applications: Contributes to pre-selected organizations only. Applications are not accepted.

Justin and Valerie Blair Potter Foundation
One NationsBank Plaza
Nashville, TN 37239-1697
(615) 749-3164
Contact: Otis Goodin, Trust Officer
Geographic Giving Pattern: Primarily Tennessee.
Special Interests: Archives, medical care, athletics, equestrianism, boys and girls clubs, civil liberties, right to life, and Catholic agencies and churches.
Assets: $28,336,255 (1998)
Grant Total: $1,108,250
Grant Range: $25,000–$391,875
Applications: Initial approach should be by letter. There are no deadlines.

Kate Collins Roddy and J. P. Roddy, Sr. Foundation, Inc.
6701 Baum Drive, Suite 250
Knoxville, TN 37919
Contact: Thomas Roddy, Executive Director
Geographic Giving Pattern: Primarily Tennessee.
Special Interests: Education, youth services, healthcare clinics, zoological societies, Catholic church support and Catholic agencies.
Assets: $1,890,298 (1997)
Gifts Received: $366,164
Grant Total: $78,680
Grant Range: $1,500–$5,000
Applications: The initial approach should be by letter. The deadline is October 31.

TEXAS

The Beretta Foundation

1250 N.E. Loop 410, Suite 235
San Antonio, TX 78209
(210) 805-9505
(210) 805-8713 (fax)
Email: jbt@txdirect.net
Contact: Jacqueline Beretta, Chair
Geographic Giving Pattern: Primarily San Antonio, Texas.
Special Interest: Museums, higher education, Catholic church support, and Catholic agencies.
Assets: $2,614,044 (1996)
Grant Total: $119,433
Grant Range: $250–$33,000
Grant Average: $100–$50,000
Limitations: No grants to individuals.
Applications: There are no deadlines for grant proposals.

The Mr. and Mrs. Joe W. Bratcher, Jr. Foundation

c/o H. Davis Hughes
1400 Franklin Plaza
111 Congress Avenue
Austin, TX 78701
(512) 479-9730
Contact: Joe W. Bratcher, Jr., President
Geographic Giving Pattern: Primarily Austin, Texas.
Special Interests: Hospitals, federated giving programs, Catholic church support and Catholic agencies.
Assets: $361,283 (1998)
Grant Total: $105,000
Grant Range: $5,000–$25,000
Limitations: No grants to individuals.
Applications: Initial approach should be by letter. The deadline is September 30.

The Burkitt Foundation

P.O. Box 2558
Houston, TX 77252-8037
(713) 216-1451

Contact: Cornelius O. Ryan, President
Geographic Giving Pattern: Primarily southwestern U.S., with an emphasis on Texas, New Mexico, Arizona, and Louisiana.
Special Interest: Private higher and secondary education, churches, religious organizations, and social services, with an emphasis on Catholic-sponsored programs.
Assets: $12,518,807 (1999)
Grant Total: $362,496
Grant Range: $2,000–$92,800
Limitations: No grants to individuals or for endowment funds. No support for deficit financing. No loans.
Applications: Initial approach should be by letter. The deadlines are February 15 and August 15.

Harry S. and Isabel C. Cameron Foundation
c/o Bank of America
P.O. Box 2518
Houston, TX 77252-2518
(713) 247-7865
Contacts: Diane Guiberteau
Geographic Giving Pattern: Primarily Texas, with an emphasis on Houston.
Special Interest: Education, Catholic church and diocesan support, health, social services, and youth agencies.
Assets: $39,751,060 (1999)
Grant Total: $1,956,498
Grant Range: $500–$213,000
Grant Average: $1,000–$15,000
Limitations: No grants to individuals or for operating budgets or endowment funds. No matching gifts or loans.
Applications: Contributes to pre-selected organizations only. Applications are not accepted.

The James R. Dougherty, Jr., Foundation
P.O. Box 640
Beeville, TX 78104-0640
(512) 358-3560
(512) 358-9693 (fax)
Contact: Daren R. Wilder, Assistant Secretary

Geographic Giving Pattern: Primarily Texas and overseas through U.S.-based Catholic organizations.
Special Interest: Catholic church-related institutions, education, cultural programs, and general charitable purposes.
Assets: $9,373,754 (1998)
Grant Total: $680,035
Grant Range: $100–$18,334
Grant Average: $1,000–$5,000
Limitations: No grants to individuals. No loans.
Applications: Proposals should be sent ten days prior to board meetings which are held semiannually.

The Gorges Foundation

P.O. Box 3547
Harlingen, TX 78551-3547
Contact: Matt Gorges, Chair
Geographic Giving Pattern: Primarily Cameron County, Texas.
Special Interests: Higher education, public libraries, Christian agencies and churches, and Catholic agencies and churches.
Assets: $1,701,500 (1998)
Grant Total: $220,669
Grant Average: $2,500–$10,000
Limitations: No grants to individuals.
Applications: Initial approach should be by detailed letter. There are no deadlines. The board meets on May 15.

Ed Haggar Family Foundation

16051 Addison Road
Addison, TX 75001
(214) 956-4254
Contact: E. R. Haggar, Director
Geographic Giving Pattern: Primarily Texas.
Special Interest: Education, healthcare, and Catholic educational institutions, agencies, churches, and campus ministry programs.
Assets: $9,521,468 (1999)
Grant Total: $509,840
Grant Range: $100–$62,000
Grant Average: $500–$20,000

Applications: Proposal letters should be one to three pages in length. There are no deadlines. The application address is 6113 Lemmon Avenue, Dallas, TX 75209.

The Curtis & Doris K. Hankamer Foundation
9039 Katy Freeway, Suite 530
Houston, TX 77024-1623
(713) 461-8140
Contact: Gregory A. Herbst
Geographic Giving Pattern: Primarily Houston, Texas.
Special Interest: Cancer research, geriatrics fellowships at a local medical school, ministry programs, Protestant and Catholic church support, and Catholic agencies.
Assets: $9,364,832 (1998)
Grant Total: $692,000
Grant Range: $10,000–$100,000
Limitations: No grants to individuals.
Applications: Contributes to pre-selected organizations only. Applications are not accepted.

The Robert and Marie Hansen Family Foundation
3300 South Gessner Road
Houston, TX 77036-5100
(713) 735-3274
Contact: John P. Hansen, Director
Geographic Giving Pattern: There are no stated geographical limitations.
Special Interests: Human services, secondary education, libraries, health associations, Catholic church support and Catholic agencies.
Assets: $1,785,436 (1998)
Grant Total: $84,068
Grant Range: $50–$15,000
Limitations: No grants to individuals.
Applications: There are no applications or deadlines.

William E. and Natoma Pyle Harvey Charitable Trust
2001 Kirby, P.O. Box 4886
Houston, TX 77210-4886
(713) 831-5582
Contact: Bob Fisher

Geographic Giving Pattern: Primarily Houston, Texas.
Special Interests: Human services, museums, higher education, Catholic church support and Catholic agencies.
Assets: $2,290,572 (1998)
Grant Total: $99,000
Grant Range: $2,500–$10,000
Limitations: No grants to individuals.
Applications: An application form is required. The deadline is April 30.

Houston Endowment, Inc.
600 Travis, Suite 6400
Houston, TX 77002-3007
(713) 238-8100
(713) 238-8101 (fax)
www.houstonendowment.org
Contact: H. Joe Nelson, III, President
Geographic Giving Pattern: Primarily Houston, Texas.
Special Interest: For the support of any charitable, educational, or religious undertaking.
Assets: $1,461,119,551 (1999)
Grant Total: $63,906,488
Grant Range: $2,500–$2,500,000
Limitations: No grants to individuals. No loans. No grants for fundraising activities. No grants outside of the U.S.
Applications: Initial approach should be by letter. There are no deadlines.

The John G. and Marie Stella Kenedy Memorial Foundation
1700 First City Tower II
Corpus Christi, TX 78478
(512) 887-6565
(512) 887-6582 (fax)
Contact: Judy Gilbreath, Office Manager
Geographic Giving Pattern: Primarily southern Texas.
Special Interest: Ninety percent of grants issued are restricted to Catholic activities including churches, dioceses, social services, and pastoral ministry. Additional support for education, the arts, humanities, youth, and health.
Assets: $185,252,017 (1998)

Grant Total: $1,126,690
Grant Average: $50,000 or less
Limitations: No grants to individuals or for operating budgets, annual fund drives, deficit financing, endowments, or general funds. The foundation does not entertain requests over $500,000.
Applications: An application form is required. The deadlines are May 1 and November 1.

Arnold J. and Irene B. Kocurek Family Foundation, 1986
562 PR 2635
Rio Medina, TX 78066
(830) 751-2881
Contact: Arnold J. Kocurek
Geographic Giving Pattern: Primarily Texas, with an emphasis on San Antonio.
Special Interests: Human services, education, medical research, theological schools, youth services, homelessness, religious federated giving, disadvantaged, Catholic church support and Catholic agencies.
Assets: $99,222 (1999)
Grant Total: $69,000
Grant Range: $1,000–$6,000
Applications: The initial approach should be by letter. There are no deadlines.

MBC Foundation
9826 Marek Road
Houston, TX 77038-3225
(713) 681-9213
Contact: Ralph S. Marek, Secretary
Geographic Giving Pattern: Primarily Houston, Texas.
Special Interests: Human services and Catholic federated giving programs.
Assets: $5,241,231 (1998)
Grant Total: $151,876
Grant High: $151,876
Limitations: No grants to individuals.
Applications: Contributes to pre-selected organizations only. Applications are not accepted.

The Kathryn O'Connor Foundation

One O'Connor Plaza, Suite 1100
Victoria, TX 77901
(361) 578-6271
Contact: D. H. Braman, Jr., President
Geographic Giving Pattern: Limited to Texas, with an emphasis on
Victoria and Refugio counties.
Special Interest: Catholic church and diocesan support, religious
schools, and the relief of poverty.
Assets: $6,400,049 (1998)
Grant Total: $360,367
Grant Range: $3,000–$150,000
Grant Average: $10,000–$50,000
Limitations: No grants to individuals. No matching gifts or loans.
Applications: Initial approach should be by proposal. There are no
deadlines.

Rockwell Fund, Inc.

1360 Post Oak Boulevard, Suite 1825
Houston, TX 77056
(713) 629-9022
(713) 629-7702 (fax)
www.rockfund.org
Contact: R. Terry Bell, President
Geographic Giving Pattern: Primarily Texas, with an emphasis on
Houston.
Special Interest: Charitable, religious, educational, medical, arts and
humanities, and civic purposes.
Assets: $123,663,968 (1998)
Grant Total: $3,399,415
Grant Range: $1,000–$100,000
Limitations: No grants to individuals. No loans.
Applications: Initial approach should be by letter. An application form
is required. The deadlines are February 1, May 1, August 1, and
November 1.

San Antonio Area Foundation
P.O. Box 120366
San Antonio, TX 78212-9566
(210) 225-2243
(210) 225-1980 (fax)
Email: saaf@dcci.com
www.saafdn.org
Contact: Marion T. Lee, Executive Director
Geographic Giving Pattern: Limited to Bexar County Texas and
surrounding counties.
Special Interests: Arts and cultural programs, education, research,
historic preservation, medical care, environment, substance abuse,
youth, aging, homelessness, community development, disabled, and
Catholic agencies.
Assets: $88,595,401 (1998)
Gifts Received: $6,744,072
Grant Total: $4,832,318
Grant Average: $2,500–$15,000
Limitations: No grants to individuals or for deficit financing,
endowment funds, seminars, conferences, or individual churches.
Applications: Initial approach should be by letter or telephone
requesting grant information.

Scanlan Foundation
2401 Fountainview, Suite 312
Houston, TX 77057
(713) 783-3169
Contact: Joseph Johnson, President
Geographic Giving Pattern: Limited to Texas.
Special Interest: Catholic religious, educational, and charitable
organizations.
Assets: $57,472,544 (1997)
Grant Total: $3,816,749 (1996)
Limitations: No grants to individuals.

The Pemmy Smith Foundation
c/o Bank of America
P.O. Box 831041
Dallas, TX 75283-1041

Geographic Giving Pattern: Limited to the Galvaston-Houston, Texas area.
Special Interest: Catholic church support and Catholic agencies.
Assets: $3,466,174 (1999)
Grant Total: $240,000
Grant Average: $28,000
Applications: Contributes to pre-selected organizations only. Applications are not accepted.

South Texas Charitable Foundation
P.O. Box 2549
Victoria, TX 77902-2269
(361) 573-4383
Contact: Rayford L. Keller, Secretary-Treasurer
Geographic Giving Pattern: Primarily Texas.
Special Interests: Human and social services, Catholic church support, Catholic agencies, cancer, and the aging.
Assets: $14,755,454 (1999)
Grant Total: $807,000
Grant Range: $100–$354,224
Limitations: No grants to individuals.
Applications: An application form is not required. There are no deadlines.

Sterling-Turner Foundation
811 Rusk, Suite 205
Houston, TX 77002-2811
(713) 237-1117
(713) 223-4638
Contact: Eyvonne Moser, Assistant Secretary
Geographic Giving Pattern: Limited to Texas.
Special Interests: Arts and cultural programs, historical societies, libraries, literacy, conservation, hospitals, medical research, homelessness, hospices, aging, civil rights, community development, and Catholic agencies and churches.
Assets: $51,962,920 (1999)
Grant Total: $1,993,000
Grant Range: $1,000–$172,667
Grant Average: $5,000–$10,000
Limitations: No grants to individuals.

Applications: Initial approach should be by written request with one copy of proposal. The deadline is March 1.

Strake Foundation
712 Main Street, Suite 3300
Houston, TX 77002-3210
(713) 216-2400
(713) 216-2401 (fax)
Email: foundation@strake.org
Contact: George W. Strake, Jr., President
Geographic Giving Pattern: Primarily Texas, especially Houston.
Special Interest: Catholic-affiliated associations including hospitals, hospices, educational institutions, churches, and social service agencies.
Assets: $61,911,733 (1998)
Grant Total: $2,834,591
Grant Range: $250–$100,000
Grant Average: $1,000–$100,000
Limitations: No grants outside of the U.S. No support for elementary schools. No grants to individuals or for deficit financing, consulting services, technical assistance, or publications. No loans.
Applications: Initial approach should be by brief written proposal. Proposals should be submitted prior to April 1 or October 1.

Stuart-Griffin-Perlitz Foundation
P.O. Box 293580
Kerrville, TX 78029
(512) 896-8964
Contact: James Perlitz. Secretary-Treasurer
Geographic Giving Pattern: Primarily Texas.
Special Interests: Youth services, arts and cultural programs, federated giving programs, education, Catholic church support and Catholic agencies.
Assets: $1,387,713 (1999)
Grant Total: $70,774
Grant Range: $100–$5,500
Limitations: No grants to individuals. Only requests for small, local contributions will be considered.
Applications: Initial approach should be by letter or telephone. There are no deadlines.

Louis H. and Mary Patricia Stumberg Foundation
Tower Life Building, #701
San Antonio, TX 78206
(210) 225-0243
(210) 225-2556 (fax)
Contact: Louis H. Stumberg and Mary P. Stumberg, Trustees
Geographic Giving Pattern: Primarily San Antonio, Texas.
Special Interest: Protestant and Catholic giving, higher education, the arts, and cultural programs.
Assets: $9,661,716 (1998)
Gifts Received: $6,457
Grant Total: $186,475
Grant Range: $10–$77,500
Limitations: No grants to individuals.
Applications: Initial approach should be by letter. The deadline is December 1.

Tex-Trude Charities, Inc.
2001 Sheldon Road, P.O. Box 58
Channelview, TX 77530
(281) 452-5961
Contact: Don L. Lueken, Trustee
Geographic Giving Pattern: Primarily Houston, Texas.
Description: Tex-Trude Charities, Inc. is a corporate foundation.
Special Interest: Secondary education, Catholic agencies, and churches.
Assets: $108,136 (1998)
Grant Total: $9,550
Grant Range: $100–$5,500
Limitations: No grants to individuals.
Applications: Initial approach should be by letter. There are no deadlines.

Art and Eva Camunez Tucker Foundation
230 West Fourteenth Street
San Angelo, TX 76903
(915) 655-4889
Contact: Eva Camunez Tucker, Trustee
Geographic Giving Pattern: Primarily Texas.

Special Interests: Human services, arts, multipurpose centers, secondary education, food services, hospices, Catholic church support and Catholic agencies.
Assets: $2,737,326 (1999)
Gifts Received: $50,000
Grant Total: $129,343
Grant Range: $100–$25,000
Limitations: No grants to individuals.
Applications: Contributes to pre-selected organizations only. Applications are not accepted.

Rachel and Ben Vaughn Foundation
P.O. Box 2233
Austin, TX 78768-2233
(512) 477-4726
Email: rbvf@aol.com
Contact: William R. Ward, Jr., Assistant Secretary-Treasurer
Geographic Giving Pattern: Limited to central and southern Texas.
Special Interests: Arts and cultural programs, education, environment, child development, family planning, healthcare, community development, Catholic federated giving programs, and Catholic agencies and churches.
Assets: $3,926,269 (1998)
Grant Total: $181,010
Grant Range: $500–$15,000
Grant Average: $500–$15,000
Limitations: No grants to individuals.
Applications: Initial approach should be by letter with one copy of proposal. The deadline is September 1.

Lamar Bruni Vergara Trust
106 Del Court
Laredo, TX 78041-2276
(956) 725-5393
Contact: J. C. Martin, III, Trustee
Geographic Giving Pattern: Primarily Laredo, Texas.
Special Interest: Educational human services, and Protestant and Catholic church support and agencies.
Assets: $17,398,166 (1999)
Grant Total: $1,998,973

Grant Range: $1,000–$679,920
Grant Average: $1,000–$50,000
Limitations: No grants to individuals.
Applications: Contributes to pre-selected organizations only. Applications are not accepted.

O'Hanlon Wholly Charitable Trust

c/o Alliance Trust Company, N.A.
P.O. Box 1088
Sherman, TX 75091
Contact: Alliance Trust Company
Geographic Giving Pattern: There are no stated geographical limitations.
Special Interests: Human services, Catholic church support and Catholic agencies.
Assets: $2,784,709 (1999)
Grant Total: $52,257
Grant Range: $3,266–$22,863

UTAH

Marriner S. Eccles Foundation

P.O. Box 45385
Salt Lake City, UT 84145-0385
(801) 532-1500
Contact: Clark P. Giles
Geographic Giving Pattern: Limited to Utah.
Special Interests: Human services, arts and cultural programs, education, medical care, crisis services, community development, youth services, homelessness, and some Catholic giving.
Assets: $140,535,248 (1999)
Grant Total: $5,539,764
Grant Range: $5,000–$400,000
Grant Average: $1,000–$75,000
Limitations: No grants to individuals or for capital expenditures for building projects.
Applications: Initial approach should be by proposal. Seven copies of the proposal are requested. There are no deadlines.

VERMONT

William T. and Marie J. Henderson Family Foundation, Inc.
P.O. Box 600
Mountain Road
Stowe, VT 05672
(802) 253-8428
Contact: William T. Henderson, President
Geographic Giving Pattern: Giving Primarily New Jersey.
Special Interests: Education, healthcare, Catholic agencies and churches.
Assets: $6,761,752 (1998)
Grant Total: $189,250
Grant Range: $500–$33,000
Grant Average: $300–$10,000
Limitations: No grants to individuals.
Applications: Contributes to pre-selected organizations only. Applications are not accepted.

Perrault Family Trust
c/o The Stratevest Group, N.A.
P.O. Box 595, Banknorth Group, Tax Department
Williston, VT 05495-0595
(802) 879-2285
Contact: The Stratevest Group, N.A.
Geographic Giving Pattern: Primarily Vermont and Alabama.
Special Interests: Christian agencies Catholic church support and Catholic agencies.
Assets: $1,243,269 (1999)
Grant Total: $20,300
Limitations: No grants to individuals.
Applications: Contributes to pre-selected organizations only. Applications are not accepted.

VIRGINIA

Aztec Foundation
P.O. Box 16126
Alexandria, VA 22302
(703) 370-4197

Contact: Dr. Joseph V. Braddock
Geographic Giving Pattern: Primarily Virginia and Washington, D.C.
Special Interest: Performing arts, the homeless, and Protestant and Catholic church support and agencies.
Assets: $805,912 (1999)
Gifts Received: $1,002
Grant Total: $34,286
Grant Range: $100–$9,000
Applications: There are no deadlines for grant proposals.

Eric and Marianne Billings Foundation, Inc.
1001 19th Street, 18th Floor
Arlington, VA 22209
(703) 312-9717
Contact: Eric and Marianne Billings
Geographic Giving Pattern: Primarily Washington, D.C.
Special Interests: Diabetes, human services, youth services, Catholic agencies and churches.
Assets: $10,846 (1999)
Gifts Received: $225,000
Grant Total: $250,500
Grant Range: $500–$150,000
Limitations: No grants to individuals.
Applications: Contributes to pre-selected organizations only. Applications are not accepted.

The John C. Fricano Foundation
1601 South Arlington Ridge Road
Arlington, VA 22202
(703) 920-5811
Contact: Msgr. Thomas J. Caroluzza, Manager
Geographic Giving Pattern: Limited to Virginia.
Special Interest: Catholic church and diocesan support, and Catholic agencies.
Assets: $2,537,896 (1999)
Gifts Received: $108,362
Grant Total: $125,000
Grant Range: $3,000–$25,000
Grant Average: $5,000–$10,000

Limitations: No grants to individuals.
Applications: Initial approach should be by letter requesting application guidelines. An application form is required. The deadline is March 1. The application address is c/o Msgr. Thomas J. Caroluzza, 3345 Clubhouse Road, Virginia Beach, VA 23455.

Kentland Foundation, Inc.
c/o Kentland Farms
P.O. Box 879
Berryville, VA 22611
(540) 955-1082
Contact: Helene D. Walker, President
Geographic Giving Pattern: Washington, D.C., Maryland, and Virginia.
Special Interest: Catholic churches, abbeys, religious educational institutions, hospitals, and human services.
Assets: $21,202,352 (1998)
Grant Total: $77,200
Grant Range: $200–$25,000
Grant Average: $1,000–$10,000
Limitations: No grants to individuals.
Applications: Contributes to pre-selected organizations only. Applications are not accepted.

Father John J. McMahon Charitable Trust Fund
600 Yeonas Drive, S.W.
Vienna, VA 22180
(703) 938-0087
Contact: Joseph A. Keating, Managing Trustee
Geographic Giving Pattern: National, with an emphasis on Washington, D.C., Maryland, and Virginia.
Special Interest: Catholic schools and universities, diocesan support, Catholic religious organizations, and Catholic welfare.
Assets: $3,824,020 (1997)
Grant Total: $333,484
Grant Range: $500–$84,200
Limitations: No grants to individuals.
Applications: Initial approach should be by letter. There are no deadlines.

Southern Sewell Foundation
148 Bristol East Road
Bristol, VA 24202-5500
Contact: Geraldine Southern, Secretary
Geographic Giving Pattern: Primarily Virginia.
Special Interests: Protestant agencies and churches Catholic church support and Catholic agencies.
Grant Total: $54,900 (1997)
Limitations: No grants to individuals.
Applications: Initial approach should be by letter. There are no deadlines.

St. Roberto Bellarmin Foundation
c/o Skeen and Johnson
258 East High Street
Charlottesville, VA 22902
(804) 293-9664
Contact: Niklas Schrenck von Notzing, President
Geographic Giving Pattern: National and international.
Special Interests: Catholic priests, chapels, seminaries, and monasteries.
Assets: $289,353 (1999)
Gifts Received: $47,874
Grant Total: $271,157
Grant Range: $473–$184,000
Limitations: No grants to individuals.
Applications: Contributes to pre-selected organizations only. Applications are not accepted.

WASHINGTON

Geneva Foundation
1250 22nd Avenue East
Seattle, WA 98112
(206) 323-3403
Contact: Genevieve Albers, Trustee
Special Interest: Catholic organizations, churches, education, and social services.
Assets: $2,998,354 (1999)

Gifts Received: $100,000
Grant Total: $129,000
Grant Range: $2,500–$30,000
Limitations: No grants to individuals.
Applications: Contributes to pre-selected organizations only.
Applications are not accepted.

GLA Foundation
c/o U.S. Bank Center
1420 5th Avenue, #200
Seattle, WA 98101
(714) 481-5000
Contact: Irwin L. Treiger
Geographic Giving Pattern: Primarily California, New York, and Washington, D. C.
Special Interests: International studies, and Orthodox Catholic agencies, churches, and archdiocesan support.
Assets: $4,182,512 (1999)
Grant Total: $272,250
Limitations: No grants to individuals.
Applications: Initial approach should be by letter. The deadline is January 15. The application address is 949 South Coast Drive, #600, Costa Mesa, CA 92626.

Mabel Horrigan Foundation
1100 University Street, #7C
Seattle, WA 98101
(206) 623-1802
Contact: Mary S. Horrigan, Trustee
Geographic Giving Pattern: Primarily Seattle, Washington.
Special Interests: Human services, elementary, secondary and higher education, hospitals, medical research, youth services, and Catholic federated giving programs.
Assets: $2,669,383 (1999)
Grant Total: $105,000
Grant Range: $100–$7,000
Limitations: No grants to individuals.
Applications: Initial approach should be by proposal. There are no deadlines.

Hudson Charitable Trust
c/o Wells Fargo Bank, N.A.
P.O. Box 21927
Seattle, WA 98111
Special Interests: Catholic agencies and churches, and multiple sclerosis.
Assets: $1,061,098 (1997)
Grant Total: $33,447
Limitations: No grants to individuals.
Applications: Contributes to pre-selected organizations only. Applications are not accepted.

Elizabeth A. Lynn Foundation
PMB 6159
13300 Bothell Everett Highway
Mill Creek, WA 98012-5312
(425) 316-6842
Contact: Diane Titch
Geographic Giving Pattern: Limited to the Pacific Northwest.
Special Interest: Education, Catholic church support, and Catholic agencies.
Assets: $7,910,038 (1999)
Grant Total: $390,482
Grant Range: $750–$25,000
Grant Average: $1,000–$5,000
Limitations: No grants to individuals.
Applications: Initial approach should be by letter. An application form is required. Five copies of the proposal are requested. The deadlines are March 31 and August 31.

The Magdalen Foundation
100655 Northeast Fourth Street, Suite 611
Bellevue, WA 98004-5022
(425) 462-1151
Contact: Nicholas J. Bez, Trustee
Geographic Giving Pattern: Primarily Seattle, Washington.
Special Interests: Performing arts, ballet, higher education, Catholic agencies and churches.
Assets: $4,354,624 (1999)

Grant Total: $250,000
Grant Range: $5,000–$100,000
Limitations: No grants to individuals.
Applications: Contributes to pre-selected organizations only.
Applications are not accepted.

The Norcliffe Foundation

First Interstate Center
999 Third Avenue, Suite 1006
Seattle, WA 98104
(206) 682-4820
Contact: Arlene Hefferline, Secretary
Geographic Giving Pattern: The Pacific Northwest, with an emphasis on Seattle, Washington.
Special Interest: Cultural programs, Catholic church support, religious associations, social service and youth programs, hospitals, education, and historic preservation.
Assets: $72,861,775 (1998)
Gifts Received: $533,296
Grant Total: $6,022,240
Grant Range: $35–$1,033,530
Grant Average: $1,000–$25,000
Limitations: No grants to individuals or for deficit financing, scholarships, or fellowships. No matching gifts or loans.
Applications: Initial approach should be by letter. There are no deadlines.

Riley and Nancy Pleas Family Foundation

2410 Boyer Avenue East, Suite 1
Seattle, WA 98112
(206) 325-3537
Contact: Maureen P. Brotherton, President
Geographic Giving Pattern: Primarily Washington.
Special Interests: Human services, hospices, cystic fibrosis research, nursing education, education, ballet, Catholic church support and Catholic agencies.
Assets: $343,927 (1999)
Grant Total: $90,350
Grant Range: $100–$35,000

Limitations: No grants to individuals.
Applications: Contributes to pre-selected organizations only. Applications are not accepted.

Frost and Margaret Snyder Foundation
c/o Key Trust Company of the Northwest
P.O. Box 11500 MS WA 31-01-0310
Tacoma, WA 98411-5052
(206) 593-3832
Contact: Michael W. Steadman, Trust Officer
Geographic Giving Pattern: Primarily Washington.
Special Interest: Catholic educational and religious associations only.
Assets: $13,967,371 (1998)
Grant Total: $642,655
Grant Range: $10,000–$50,000
Limitations: No grants to individuals.
Applications: Initial approach should be by grant proposal letter. The deadline is September 1.

The Tamaki Foundation
4739 University Way Northeast, Suite 1638
Seattle, WA 980105
(206) 632-6277
Contact: Meriko Tamaki, President
Geographic Giving Pattern: Primarily California, Washington, and some giving in Japan.
Special Interests: Higher education, human services, Catholic agencies and churches.
Assets: $4,480,571 (1998)
Grant Total: $188,737
Grant Range: $55–$100,000
Applications: Initial approach should be by letter. There are no deadlines.

Robert C. and Nani S. Warren Foundation
82 Swigert Road
Washougal, WA 98671
(360) 837-3909
Contact: Penny Guest, Treasurer

Geographic Giving Pattern: There are no stated geographical limitations.
Special Interests: Arts and cultural programs, education, lung diseases, and Catholic agencies and churches.
Assets: $5,390,732 (1998)
Grant Total: $293,931
Grant Range: $25–$105,700
Limitations: No grants to individuals.
Applications: Contributes to pre-selected organizations only. Applications are not accepted.

Whitaker Foundation
1505 N.W. Gilman Boulevard, Suite 1
Issaquah, WA 98027-5329
(425) 392-7583
Contact: John L. Whitaker, M.D., President
Geographic Giving Pattern: Primarily Washington.
Special Interests: Education, human services, and Catholic agencies and churches.
Assets: $2,900,917 (1999)
Grant Total: $165,336
Grant Range: $10–$90,000
Limitations: No grants to individuals.
Applications: Initial approach should be by letter. There are no deadlines.

WEST VIRGINIA

The Frank and Anna Bravchok Foundation
3200 Main Street
Weirton, WV 26062
(304) 748-3200
Contact: Jeffrey J. Rokisky, Trustee
Geographic Giving Pattern: Primarily Ohio.
Special Interests: Education Catholic church support and Catholic agencies.
Assets: $795,227 (1999)
Grant Total: $40,000
Grant Range: $5,000–$12,000

Applications: An application form is not required. There are no deadlines.

D'Annunzio Foundation, Inc.
200 Ferry Street
Clarksburg, WV 26301-2831
(304) 624-9720
Contact: Vincent F. D'Annunzio, Director
Geographic Giving Pattern: Primarily West Virginia.
Special Interests: Education Catholic church support and Catholic agencies.
Assets: $427,362 (1999)
Gifts Received: $113,805
Grant Total: $55,750
Grant Range: $500–$8,500
Applications: Initial approach should be by letter.

John S. Thoner Charitable Family Trust
c/o Diocese of Wheeling-Charlestown
P.O. Box 230
1300 Byron Street
Wheeling, WV 26003
(304) 233-0880
Contact: Most Rev. Bernard W. Schmitt
Geographic Giving Pattern: Primarily Wheeling, West Virginia.
Special Interests: Education and Catholic agencies and churches.
Assets: $5,070,769 (1998)
Gifts Received: $5,321,737
Limitations: No grants to individuals.
Applications: Contributes to pre-selected organizations only. Applications are not accepted.

Vecellio Family Foundation, Inc.
2251 Robert C. Byrd Drive
P.O. Box V
Beckley, WV 25802
(304) 252-6575
Contact: Evelyn P. Vecellio, Manager
Geographic Giving Pattern: Primarily Florida and West Virginia.

Special Interests: Arts and cultural programs, education, scholarship programs, healthcare, human services, youth, and Catholic agencies and churches.
Assets: $7,052,633 (1998)
Gifts Received: $2,619,179
Grant Total: $261,205
Grant Range: $500–$25,000
Limitations: No direct grants to individuals and no loans.
Applications: Initial approach should be by proposal. The deadline is November 15.

WISCONSIN

AMS Fund, Inc.
125 South 84th Street, Suite 110
Milwaukee, WI 53214
(414) 607-6040
(414) 607-6045 (fax)
Contact: Paula N. John, Vice President
Geographic Giving Pattern: Limited to the Archdiocese of Milwaukee.
Special Interest: Catholic giving.
Assets: $70,000,000 (2000)
Grant Range: $5,000–$50,000
Limitations: Contributes to organizations listed in *The Official Catholic Directory* under the Archdiocese of Milwaukee.
Applications: An application form is required. Grants are reviewed two to four months after each deadline. The deadlines are March 1, June 1, September 1, and December 1.

Helen Bader Foundation, Inc.
233 N. Water Street, 4th Floor
Milwaukee, WI 53202
(414) 224-6464
(414) 224-1441 (fax)
Email: info@hbf.org
www.hbf.org
Contact: Daniel J. Bader, President

Geographic Giving Pattern: Primarily the greater Milwaukee, Wisconsin area and Israel.

Special Interest: To advance the well-being of people and promote successful relationships with their families and communities, Alzheimer's disease, education, economic development, and children and youth in Israel.

Assets: $2,184,488 (1999)

Gifts Received: $11,200,000

Grant Total: $12,169,482

Grant Range: $988–$543,000

Grant Average: $10,000–$100,000

Limitations: No grants to individuals. No loans.

Applications: Initial approach should be by letter to request application. The deadlines are July 2 and August 2.

The Lynde and Harry Bradley Foundation, Inc.

P.O. Box 510860

Milwaukee, WI 53203-0153

(414) 291-9915

(414) 291-9991 (fax)

www.bradleyfnd.org

Contact: Michael S. Joyce, President

Geographic Giving Pattern: National and international, with an emphasis on Milwaukee, Wisconsin.

Special Interest: Citizenship, education including Catholic colleges and universities, public policy, foreign policy, the arts, cultural programs, medical centers, and efforts to revive the authority of the traditional institutions of civil society (families, churches, schools, neighborhoods, and entrepreneurial enterprises.)

Assets: $611,173,440 (1998)

Grant Total: $32,664,743

Grant Range: $500–$1,200,000

Grant Average: $25,000–$150,000

Limitations: No grants to individuals. No support for strictly denominational projects or endowment funds.

Applications: Initial approach should be by letter of inquiry. The deadlines for submitting letters of inquiry are March 15, July 15, September 15, and December 15.

Frank G. and Frieda K. Brotz Family Foundation, Inc.
3518 Lakeshore Road
P.O. Box 551
Sheboygan, WI 53082-0551
(920) 458-2121
Contact: The Grants Committee
Geographic Giving Pattern: Wisconsin.
Special Interest: Catholic hospitals, universities, social service programs, and elementary and secondary education.
Assets: $25,057,193 (1999)
Gifts Received: $789,375
Grant Total: $1,028,465
Grant Range: $250–$100,000
Grant Average: $250–$10,000
Limitations: No grants to individuals.
Applications: Initial approach should be by detailed letter of inquiry. There are no deadlines.

Carrie Foundation
P.O. Box 348
Janesville, WI 53547
(608) 756-4588
Contact: George K. Steil, Sr., Manager
Geographic Giving Pattern: Primarily Wisconsin, with an emphasis on Janesville.
Special Interests: Human services, education, higher education, general charitable giving, Catholic church support and Catholic agencies.
Assets: $576,010 (1999)
Gifts Received: $193,750
Grant Total: $70,625
Grant Range: $200–$10,000
Limitations: Contributes to pre-selected organizations only. Applications are not accepted.

Marjorie L. Christiansen Foundation
c/o Bank One Trust Co., N.A.
P.O. Box 1308
Milwaukee, WI 53201-1308
(414) 765-2769

Contact: Roy D. Stewart, Bank One Trust Co., N.A.
Geographic Giving Pattern: Limited to Racine, Wisconsin.
Special Interest: Healthcare programs, and programs for the elderly.
Assets: $4,431,308 (1999)
Grant Total: $179,800
Grant Range: $2,000–$26,000
Applications: Initial approach should be by letter. Four copies of the proposal are requested. There are no deadlines.

William J. Cronin Foundation
P.O. Box 882
Janesville, WI 53547-0882
(608) 756-3151
Contact: James P. McGuire, Trustee
Geographic Giving Pattern: Limited to Janesville, Wisconsin.
Special Interest: Catholic schools, churches, social service agencies, the elderly, and recreations programs.
Assets: $2,683,901 (1999)
Grant Total: $104,100 (1997)
Grant Average: $600–$10,000
Applications: Initial approach should be by letter. The deadline is November 1.

Patrick and Anna M. Cudahy Fund
P.O. Box 11978
Milwaukee, WI 53211
(414) 271-6020
Email: jborcher@ix.netcom.com
Contact: Sr. Judith Borchers, O.S.B., Executive Director
Geographic Giving Pattern: Primarily Wisconsin and Chicago, Illinois for local programs, and Latin America and southern Africa for international (U.S.-based) programs.
Special Interest: Arts, education, youth, international relief, social services, Catholic higher education, Catholic agencies, diocesan support, and churches.
Assets: $30,279,051 (1998)
Grant Total: $2,090,675
Grant Range: $400–$129,110
Grant Average: $1,000–$127,750

Limitations: No grants to individuals or for endowment funds. No loans.
Applications: Initial approach should be by letter. An application form is required. The deadlines vary annually. The application address is 1007 Church Street, Evanston, IL 60201.

James A. Dooley Foundation
622 North Water Street, Number 500
Milwaukee, WI 53202-4978
(414) 273-3939
Contact: Virginia P. Dooley, President
Geographic Giving Pattern: Primarily Wisconsin.
Special Interests: General charitable giving, historic preservation, voluntarism, Catholic church support and Catholic agencies.
Assets: $2,605,635 (1999)
Grant Total: $55,000
Grant Range: $25–$15,000
Limitations: No grants to individuals.
Applications: Contributes to pre-selected organizations only. Applications are not accepted.

John A. Elliot Foundation, Inc.
P.O. Box 2980
Milwaukee, WI 53201
Contact: Marian R. Elliot, President
Geographic Giving Pattern: Primarily LaCrosse Wisconsin.
Special Interests: Arts and cultural programs, education, healthcare, Catholic agencies and churches.
Assets: $6,775,888 (1999)
Grant Total: $284,500
Limitations: No grants to individuals.
Applications: Initial approach should be by letter. The deadline is May 1. The application address is 804 Cass Street, LaCrosse, WI 54601.

Fleck Foundation
2525 North 124th Street, Suite 200
Brookfield, WI 53005
(262) 860-1680
(262) 860-1683 (fax)
Contact: Andrew J. Fleckenstein, Trustee

Geographic Giving Pattern: Primarily Milwaukee, Wisconsin.
Special Interest: Education; primary, secondary, higher and Catholic educational support.
Assets: $22,803,966 (1998)
Grant Total: $1,700,654
Grant Range: $200–$200,000
Limitations: No grants to individuals.
Applications: Initial approach should be by letter. Deadlines are in March, June, September and December.

Greene Manufacturing Company Foundation

1300 North Grandview Parkway
Sturtevant, WI 53177
(414) 884-1144
Contact: James M. Hamilton, Jr., Trustee
Geographic Giving Pattern: Primarily Wisconsin.
Description: Greene Manufacturing Company Foundation is a corporate foundation.
Special Interest: Environment, education, health, welfare, Catholic agencies, and Catholic churches.
Assets: $568,719 (1998)
Grant Total: $69,393
Grant Range: $100–$10,000
Limitations: No grants to individuals. No support for building funds, endowment funds, or scholarships. No support for church or missionary groups unless the project benefits the whole community.
Applications: Initial approach should be by proposal. There are no deadlines.

The Kellogg Family Foundation, Inc.

c/o Godfrey & Kahn
780 North Water Street
Milwaukee, WI 53202
Contact: William S. Kellogg, President and Treasurer
Geographic Giving Pattern: Primarily Milwaukee, Wisconsin.
Special Interests: Health associations, youth services, human services, special populations, Protestant agencies and churches, Catholic agencies and churches.
Assets: $2,704,791 (1998)
Gifts Received: $262

Grant Total: $624,100
Grant Range: $1,000–$401,000
Limitations: No grants to individuals.
Applications: Contributes to pre-selected organizations only.
Applications are not accepted.

Elmore and Alyce Kraemer Charitable Trust

c/o Marshall and Ilsley Trust Company
P.O. Box 2980
Milwaukee, WI 53201-2980
Contact: Marshall and Ilsley Trust Company
Geographic Giving Pattern: Primarily Wisconsin.
Special Interests: Human services Catholic church support and Catholic agencies.
Assets: $1,550,703 (1998)
Grant Total: $65,349
Limitations: No grants to individuals.
Applications: Contributes to pre-selected organizations only.
Applications are not accepted.

Herman W. Ladish Family Foundation, Inc.

790 North Jackson Street, 2nd Floor
Milwaukee, WI 53202-3833
(414) 224-7377
Contact: John H. Ladish, Chair
Geographic Giving Pattern: Primarily Wisconsin, with an emphasis on Milwaukee.
Special Interests: Education, especially Catholic schools, healthcare and the arts.
Assets: $12,987,598 (1998)
Grant Total: $866,000
Grant Range: $1,000–$200,000
Limitations: No grants to individuals.
Applications: Initial approach should be by letter. An application form is not required. There are no deadlines.

Camille A. Lonstorf Trust

777 East Wisconsin Avenue
Milwaukee, WI 53202
(414) 297-5748

Contact: Harrold J. McComas, Treasurer
Geographic Giving Pattern: Primarily Milwaukee, Wisconsin.
Special Interests: Art and cultural programs, secondary and higher education, Catholic federated giving programs, and Catholic agencies and churches.
Assets: $4,757,158 (1999)
Grant Total: $201,000
Grant Range: $1,000–$20,000
Limitations: No grants to individuals.
Applications: Initial approach should be by letter. There are no deadlines.

B. A. Mason Trust
1251 First Avenue
Chippewa Falls, WI 54729
(715) 723-1871
Contact: William Scobie, Trustee
Geographic Giving Pattern: Primarily Chippewa Falls, Wisconsin.
Special Interests: Elementary and secondary education, human services, and Catholic agencies and churches.
Assets: $629,209 (1998)
Grant Total: $581,580
Grant Range: $300–$230,000
Limitations: No grants to individuals.
Applications: Initial approach should be by letter. There are no deadlines.

Mercy Works Foundation
P.O. Box 2518
Appleton, WI 54913
Contact: Robert C. Follett, Trustee
Geographic Giving Pattern: Primarily Appleton, Wisconsin.
Special Interests: Human services, Catholic agencies and churches.
Assets: $8,791,593 (1998)
Grant Total: $1,539,114
Grant Range: $500–$500,000
Limitations: No grants to individuals.
Applications: Contributes to pre-selected organizations only. Applications are not accepted.

Merkel Foundation, Inc.

3712 Bismarck Circle
Sheboygan, WI 53083-2653
Contact: Daniel A. Merkel, Secretary
Geographic Giving Pattern: Primarily Wisconsin.
Special Interests: Human services, youth services, health associations, Catholic church support and Catholic agencies.
Assets: $2,941,431 (1999)
Gifts Received: $107,550
Grant Total: $64,200
Applications: Contributes to pre-selected organizations only. Applications are not accepted.

Rose A. Monaghan Charitable Trust

17100 W. North Avenue
Brookfield, WI 53005-4436
Contact: Walter F. Schmidt, Trustee
Geographic Giving Pattern: Primarily Milwaukee, Wisconsin.
Special Interest: Catholic giving, Catholic welfare, and religious and secondary education.
Assets: $3,148,206 (1999)
Grant Total: $194,500
Grant Range: $1,000–$200,000
Limitations: No grants to individuals.
Applications: Contributes to pre-selected organizations only. Applications are not accepted.

Paul Foundation, Inc.

W4943 CTY Highway G
Necedah, WI 54646
Contact: Marguerite Paul
Geographic Giving Pattern: There are no stated geographical limitations.
Special Interests: Catholic agencies and churches.
Assets: $75,901 (1998)
Gifts Received: $1,215,779
Grant Total: $1,280,051
Grant Range: $4,551–$950,000
Limitations: No grants to individuals.

Applications: Contributes to pre-selected organizations only. Applications are not accepted.

D. B. Reinhart Family Foundation

P.O. Box 2228
La Crosse, WI 54602
(608) 782-4999
Contact: Nancy Hengel, Manager
Geographic Giving Pattern: Limited to Wisconsin, with an emphasis on La Crosse.
Special Interest: Higher education, healthcare, youth, community development, Catholic church support, and Catholic agencies.
Assets: $14,015,860 (1998)
Gifts Received: $7,829,534
Grant Total: $484,555
Grant Range: $75–$80,000
Limitations: No grants to individuals.
Applications: Contributes to pre-selected organizations only. Applications are not accepted.

The Robert J. Sullivan Family Foundation, Ltd.

10180 South 54th Street
Franklin, WI 53132-9184
(414) 421-4747
Contact: Robert J. Sullivan
Geographic Giving Pattern: Primarily Wisconsin.
Special Interests: Education, hospitals, youth, Catholic agencies and churches.
Assets: $4,527,993 (1998)
Grant Total: $190,000
Grant Range: $5,000–$50,000
Applications: Initial approach should be by letter with one copy of proposal. There are no deadlines.

U.S. Oil/Schmidt Family Foundation, Inc.

425 South Washington Street
P.O. Box 25
Combined Locks, WI 54113-1049
(920) 739-6100
(920) 788-9909 (fax)

Contact: Raymond Schmidt, Secretary
Geographic Giving Pattern: Primarily Wisconsin.
Special Interest: Catholic organizations and churches, social service agencies, education, and hospitals.
Assets: $3,498,419 (1999)
Gifts Received: $325,195
Grant Total: $449,909
Grant Range: $50–$25,000
Limitations: No grants to individuals.
Applications: Contributes to pre-selected organizations only. Applications are not accepted.

The Clarence Wallace and Dolores Lynch Wallace Family Foundation

1700 North Viola Street
Appleton, WI 54911-3856
(920) 733-7881
Contact: The Trustees
Geographic Giving Pattern: Primarily Wisconsin.
Special Interests: Food services, secondary education, Catholic church support and Catholic agencies.
Assets: $1,430,421 (1998)
Grant Total: $47,000
Grant Range: $4,000–$15,000
Limitations: No grants to individuals.
Applications: Contributes to pre-selected organizations only. Applications are not accepted.

SECTION II:
CHURCH-BASED AGENCIES

Black and Indian Mission Office

2021 H Street, NW
Washington, D.C. 20006
(202) 331-8542
Contact: Msgr. Paul A. Lenz, Executive Director
Geographic Giving Pattern: Limited to the U.S.
Special Interest: Evangelization; support for Black and Native American missions and programs.
Sources of Income: A national collection.
Grant Total: $7,000,000 (1996)
Grant Range: $1,000–$128,000
Limitations: Grants are awarded directly to the bishop for missions and programs in the diocese. No grants for individuals.

Bureau of Catholic Indian Missions

2021 H Street, NW
Washington, D.C. 20006
(202) 331-8542
Contact: Msgr. Paul A. Lenz, Executive Director
Geographic Giving Pattern: Limited to the U.S.
Special Interest: Catholic, Native American schools.
Sources of Income: Direct mail appeals, wills, and bequests.
Grant Range: $1,000–$60,000 (1996)
Limitations: No grants to individuals. Grants are not awarded to those Catholic, Native American schools which have fundraising offices.
Applications: Initial approach should be by letter. There are no deadlines.

Catholic Charities USA

1731 King Street, Suite 200
Alexandria, VA 22314
(703) 549-1390
(703) 549-1656 (fax)
Contact: Rev. Fred Kammer, S.J., President

Geographic Giving Pattern: National.
Description: Catholic Charities USA was founded to help advance and promote the charitable programs and activities of Catholic community and social service agencies in the United States. Catholic Charities USA is a national Catholic organization which services a network of more than 1,400 agencies and institutions by providing consultation, information, and assistance in planning and evaluating social service programs under Catholic auspices.
Special Interest: Social services, including the provision of food, shelter, counseling, services to children, services to teen parents, services to the elderly, and aid for people and families in need.
Sources of Income: Each local agency has its own fundraising drive.
Limitations: Catholic Charities USA does not administer grant programs. Rather it serves as the coordinating organization for its members, which include the local diocesan Catholic Charities offices.
Applications: Each diocesan Catholic Charities office has its own application process and financial information.

Catholic Church Extension Society

35 East Wacker Drive
Chicago, IL 60601-9987
(312) 236-7240
Contact: Rev. Kenneth Velo, President
Geographic Giving Pattern: National and Samoa, Guam, and Puerto Rico.
Special Interest: American home missions; Support for diocesan seminary education, campus ministry, religious education, and small mission chapels.
Sources of Income: Individual donors.
Grant Total: $12,500,000 (1997)
Grant Average: $25,000–$30,000
Applications: Applications are awarded directly to the bishop of the diocese in which the home mission is located.

Catholic Communication Campaign

3211 Fourth Street, N.E.
Washington, D.C. 20017-1194
(202) 541-3237
Contact: Ramon Rodriguez, Executive Director
Geographic Giving Pattern: National.

Special Interest: Evangelization through the media.
Sources of Income: Primarily a Catholic national collection.
Grant Average: $5,000–$500,000
Limitations: No grants to individuals. No grants for local projects.
Applications: Initial approach should be by letter or telephone. An application form is required. The deadline is the end of September.

Catholic Near East Welfare Association
1011 First Avenue, Room 1552
New York, NY 10022-4195
(212) 826-1480
(212) 838-1344 (fax)
Contact: Msgr. Robert L. Stern, National Secretary
Geographic Giving Pattern: The Middle East, Northeast Africa, India, and Eastern Europe.
Description: Catholic Near East is a papal agency for humanitarian and pastoral support, serving mainly Catholics of the Eastern Rite and seeking to nourish the faith where Catholics are a minority.
Special Interest: Pastoral and religious projects including training of native priests, sisters and brothers; building and maintaining churches, convents, rectories, and clinics; and aid for refugees, women, children, orphans, and the elderly, especially in health, nutrition, sanitation, and housing.
Sources of Income: Individuals, nine percent of the U.S. Mission Sunday national collection, European funding agencies, and U.S. aid.
Grant Total: $20,600,000 (1994)
Applications: Proposals may be submitted in English, French, or Italian and should include an endorsement of the provincial superior or the local bishop.

Catholic Negro American Mission Board
2021 H Street, NW
Washington, D.C. 20006
(202) 331-8542
Contact: Msgr. Paul A. Lenz, Executive Director
Geographic Giving Pattern: Limited to the South.
Special Interest: Poor African-American parish schools.
Sources of Income: Direct mail appeals, wills, and bequests.
Grant Total: $600,000 (1996)
Limitations: No grants to individuals.

Applications: Initial approach should be by letter. There are no deadlines.

Catholic Relief Services (CRS)

209 West Fayette Street
Baltimore, MD 21201
(410) 625-2220
(410) 685-1635 (fax)
crshq@igc.apc
Contact: Kenneth F. Hackett, Executive Director
Geographic Giving Pattern: Africa, Asia, Latin America, Eastern Europe, and the Middle East.
Description: Catholic Relief Services is the official overseas relief and development agency of the U.S. Catholic community and Catholic bishops.
Special Interest: Long-term development projects designed to help people to help themselves and to determine their own future, disaster and emergency relief, refugees, reconstruction, rehabilitation, and reconciliation.
Sources of Income: Catholic church collections, U.S. government, individual contributions, church groups, foundations, and corporations.
Total Program Value: $309,000,000
Grant Total: $231,000,000
Applications: Project proposals should be submitted through local CRS field agencies. There are no deadlines.

Committee on the Home Missions

3211 Fourth Street, N.E.
Washington, D.C. 20017-1194
(202) 541-3450
(202) 541-3322 (fax)
homemissions@nccbuscc.org
Contact: David M. Byers, Executive Director
Geographic Giving Pattern: National.
Special Interest: Evangelization and mission activities, pastoral services, personnel training, and the formation of faith communities.
Sources of Income: A percentage of the Mission Sunday Collection.
Assets: $12,465,794 (1996)
Gifts Received: $4,378,905
Grant Total: $5,293,061

Grant Range: $100,000 or less.

Limitations: No grants to individuals. No support for capital expenses or endowments. No loans.

Applications: Initial approach should be by letter requesting application packet available in early September. An application form is required. Applications are due November 1. Grant decisions are announced in early April for July 1–June 30 funding year.

Holy Childhood Association

1720 Massachusetts Avenue, NW
Washington, D.C. 20036
(202) 775-8637
Contact: Rev. Francis Wright, Director or Emily Dennis, Program Manager.
Geographic Giving Pattern: Africa, Asia, Latin America, the Middle East, and the Pacific.
Description: The Washington D.C. office of the Holy Childhood Association is primarily the fundraising arm of the Pontifical Association of the Holy Childhood, which supports missionaries helping children in developing nations. (See Pontifical Association of the Holy Childhood in Section IV: International Funding Agencies, page 424.)

National Conference of Catholic Bishops
Committee on the Church in Latin America

3211 Fourth Street, N.E.
Washington, D.C. 20017-1194
(202) 541-3050
(202) 541-3460 (fax)
Contact: Rev. John Swope, S.J., Executive Director
Geographic Giving Pattern: Limited to South America, Central America, the Caribbean, and Mexico.
Description: The Committee on the Church in Latin America is a program sponsored by the U.S. National Conference of Catholic Bishops to provide assistance to the bishops and dioceses in Latin America and the Caribbean
Special Interest: Pastoral projects, evangelization, religious formation, religious education, catechesis, lay leadership training, and socio-religious research.

Sources of Income: U.S. Catholic church collection for the Church in Latin America.
Assets: $8,702,287 (1997)
Gifts Received: $4,705,867
Grant Total: $5,179,046
Limitations: Grants are approved on a one-time basis only. No support for operational expenses, land acquisition, equipment, vehicles, construction, or maintenance. Projects should be related to the local bishop's pastoral priorities.
Applications: Preliminary letters should be written in English, Spanish, or Portuguese. An application form is required. The project must be endorsed by the bishop in whose jurisdiction the project will take place. There are no deadlines.

National Religious Retirement Office

3211 Fourth Street, NE
Washington, D.C. 20017-1194
(202) 541-3215
(202) 541-3053 (fax)
Contact: Sr. Andrée Fries, C.P.P.S., National Director
Geographic Giving Pattern: National.
Special Interest: The retirement needs of elderly religious sisters, brothers, and priests.
Sources of Income: National Catholic collection, individuals, and bequests.
Grant Total: $24,500,000 (1996)
Limitations: No grants to individuals directly.
Applications: An application form is required. The deadline is March 21. The National Religious Retirement Office also administers three other smaller grant programs which are the following: The Special Assistance Grant, for community efforts or collaborative projects; The Supplemental Grant; and The Supplemental Identified Need Grant. The deadline is March 31 for the first two listed and August 31 for the last. It is recommended that the applicant call or write for application guidelines.

U.S. Catholic Conference
Catholic Campaign for Human Development

3211 Fourth Street, N.E.
Washington, D.C. 20017-1194
(202) 541-3210
(202) 541-3329 (fax)
www.nccbuscc.org/cchd
Contact: Rev. Robert J. Vitillo, Executive Director
Geographic Giving Pattern: National.
Description: The Catholic Campaign for Human Development is a national social justice program of the United States Catholic bishops. Its mission is to address the root causes of poverty in America through promotion and support of community controlled, self-help organizations and through transformative education of the non-poor.
Special Interest: Projects which aim to attack the basic causes of poverty and empower the poor. CHD-funded projects must have low-income people comprise at least half of the decision-making board of directors and generate cooperation among diverse groups of people. Projects must work to change conditions that create and perpetuate poverty, must directly benefit a large number of people, and must develop a detailed plan for self-sufficiency. CHD also supports community-based economic development and has a business and development grant and loan program.
Sources of Income: Catholic church collections and individuals.
Grant Total: $8,959,210 (1999)
Grant Range: $10,000–$100,000
Grant Average: $30,000
Limitations: No grants to individuals. No support for direct service projects, projects controlled by government, educational or ecclesiastical bodies, research projects, feasibility studies, or individually owned, for-profit businesses.
Applications: Initial approach should be by letter or telephone. A pre-application form is required. The deadline for pre-applications is November 1. Eligible applicants will then be provided with a funding booklet. Full proposals are due January 31. Pre-applications are required for community-based economic development proposals and for business and development projects also. Please contact the CCHD office for guidelines and deadlines.

U.S. Catholic Conference
Office to Aid the Catholic Church in Central & Eastern Europe
3211 Fourth Street, N.E.
Washington, D.C. 20017-1194
(202) 541-3402
(202) 541-3166 (fax)
Contact: Msgr. R. George Sarauskas
Geographic Giving Pattern: Eastern and Central Europe and the
former Soviet Union.
Special Interest: To assist the bishops of Eastern and Central Europe
and the former Soviet Union to restore the pastoral capacity of their
churches. Support for formation and training of priests and religious,
catechetical programs, media and communications apostolates, and
Catholic charitable activities.
Sources of Income: Catholic church collections.
Assets: $4,093,911 (1996)
Gifts Received: $6,408,497
Grant Total: $5,896,926
Applications: Initial approach should be by letter or telephone. An
application form is required. Applications must be submitted to the
local bishop for approval and recommendation. The local bishop will
then submit the applications to the national conference of bishops in
the area of origin. The intent is to screen and prioritize applications at
the local level.

U.S. Catholic Conference
Office of Migration & Refugee Services
3211 Fourth Street, N.E.
Washington, D.C. 20017
(202) 541-3220
(202) 541-3399 (fax)
Contact: Mark Franken, Executive Director
Geographic Giving Pattern: National
Description: The USCC Office of Migration and Refugee Services is
the official agency responsible for carrying out the church's policy on
migration, refugee, and immigration issues.
Special Interest: Support for local Catholic diocesan resettlement
offices in the United States to facilitate self-sufficiency for people
coming to the U.S. from abroad.
Applications: A pre-application form is required.

SECTION III:
RELIGIOUS COMMUNITIES
AND FRATERNAL BENEFIT
SOCIETIES

Adrian Dominican Sisters Alternative Investment Fund
Adrian Dominican Sisters Portfolio Advisory Board
1257 East Siena Heights Drive
Adrian, MI 49221-1793
(517) 266-3523
(517) 266-3524 (fax)
PABcarol@admc-op.org
Contact: Carol DiMarcello
Geographic Giving Pattern: National, and some international
intermediaries.
Description: The Adrian Dominican Sisters Alternative Investment
Fund provides investments and loans to community-based enterprises
which demonstrate a commitment to fostering social justice values
through alternative approaches in the economy.
Special Interest: Housing, small business development, community
development, and economic justice, especially for women and the
poor.
Loan Fund Total: $3,000,000 (1999)
Loan Range: $10,000–$100,000
Loan Average: $35,000
Limitations: No loans to individuals. No loans to for-profit
corporations. All projects must be community-based and reflect the
community in the board membership and workforce. Loans are for one
to five years. No grants are awarded.
Applications: Initial approach should be by letter or telephone. A pre-
application form is required. The pre-application deadline is March 31.
Full applications are due June 1. Decisions are made in August and
September.

Allegany Franciscan Foundation

19329 U.S. Highway 19 North
Suite 100
Clearwater, FL 33764
(727) 507-9668
Contact: Joanne Olvera Lighter
Geographic Giving Pattern: Primarily New York.
Special Interest: The economically disadvantaged, justice and peace, the environment, fostering spiritual development, and Catholic schools.
Assets: $100,000,000 (1996)
Applications: Initial approach should be by letter.

American Association of the Sovereign Military Order of Malta

1011 First Avenue
Room 1500
New York, NY 10022
(212) 371-1522
Contact: Henry Humphreys, Chancellor
Geographic Giving Pattern: National.
Special Interest: Catholic organizations which minister to the sick and the poor.
Applications: Projects should have Knights of Malta volunteers involved.

American Slovenian Catholic Union

2439 Glenwood Avenue
Joliet, IL 60435-5441
(800) 843-5755
(815) 741-2001
(815) 741-2002 (fax)
Contact: Eugene Kogovsek, National President
Geographic Giving Pattern: National.
Description: Fraternal benefit society.
Special Interest: Awards high school and college scholarships for attendance at Catholic private schools and colleges to its student members. Additional scholarships are awarded to those members studying to become priests or nuns.
Assets: $43,385,329 (1999)

The Bernardine Franciscan Sisters Foundation, Inc.
One Bernardine Drive
Newport News, VA 23602-4499
(757) 886-6025
(757) 886-6881 (fax)
Contact: Sr. David Ann Niski, Executive Director
Geographic Giving Pattern: Newport News, Hampton, Poquoson, Gloucester County, and York County, Virgina.
Special Interest: Healthcare, education and social services, with particular attention to the poor and underserved.
Sources of Income: Income generated from the sale of half of the interest of Mary Immaculate Hospital.
Grant Total: $690,000 (1999)
Applications: Initial approach should be by letter or telephone. An application form is required. There are no deadlines.

Catholic Association of Foresters
347 Commonwealth Avenue
Boston, MA 02115-1999
(800) 282-2263
(617) 536-8221
(617) 536-2819 (fax)
Contact: Charles C. Wills, High Chief Ranger
Geographic Giving Pattern: Primarily Connecticut, Florida, Maine, Massachusetts, New Hampshire, Rhode Island, and Vermont.
Description: Fraternal benefit society.
Special Interest: Bishops' charities, Catholic missions, hospitals, and church support.
Assets: $10,054,070 (1999)

Catholic Family Fraternal of Texas
P.O. Box 1884
Austin, TX 78767-1884
(888) 253-2338
(512) 444-9586
(512) 444-6887 (fax)
Contact: Geraldine Nekuza, President
Geographic Giving Pattern: National, with an emphasis on Texas.
Description: Fraternal benefit society, with a Czech heritage.

Special Interest: Scholarships, seminaries, newly ordained priests, children and youth, church and diocesan support, right to life programs, and family ministry.
Assets: $39,958,694 (1999)

Catholic Family Life Insurance

1572 East Capitol Drive
P.O. Box 11563
Milwaukee, WI 53211-0563
(800) 227-2354
(414) 961-0500
(414) 961-2059 (fax)
www.cfli.org
Contact: William L. Eimers, President and CEO
Geographic Giving Pattern: National.
Description: Fraternal benefit society.
Special Interest: Awards Catholic elementary and high school tuition aid grants to members' children. Awards grants for community and parish projects through the society's matching funds program and awards direct grants to several national organizations.
Assets: $213,641,623 (1999)
Grant Total: $1,400,000 (total since 1982) and $1,000,000 in tuition aid (total since 1982).

Catholic Healthcare West's Alternative Investments Program

1700 Montgomery Street
Suite 300
San Francisco, CA 94111
(415) 438-5500
(415) 438-5724 (fax)
Contact: Judy Rimbey, OP, Manager, Alternative Investments
Geographic Giving Pattern: Primarily California, Arizona, and Nevada.
Special Interest: Efforts which empower low-income people to create, manage, and own their own enterprise; employment; management opportunities for chronically unemployed groups; revitalization of decaying urban areas and rural areas; integration; community development; minorities; and women.
Loan Range: $3,500–$250,000

Applications: Initial approach should be by letter or telephone. A pre-application form is required. There are no deadlines.

Catholic Knights of America

3525 Hampton Avenue
St. Louis, MO 63139-1980
(800) 844-3728
(314) 351-1029
(314) 351-9937 (fax)
www.ckoa.com
Contact: John F. Kenawell, President
Geographic Giving Pattern: National.
Description: Fraternal benefit society.
Special Interest: Seminarian scholarships ($250/year for four years), high school scholarships for members' children enrolling in a Catholic high school, right to life programs, and general Catholic charitable giving.
Assets: $47,602,063 (1999)
Applications: Applications for seminarian scholarships must be submitted through the bishop in the resident diocese of the applicant.

Catholic Knights and Ladies of Illinois

2021 Mascoutah Avenue
Belleville, IL 62220
(618) 233-0286
(618) 277-8259 (fax)
Contact: Bernard J. Lengerman, Chair
Geographic Giving Pattern: Primarily Illinois.
Description: Fraternal benefit society.
Special Interest: Awards scholarships to members' children attending Catholic high schools. Contributes to The Education Endowment Trust Fund, which provides assistance to Catholic high schools, and The Continuing Education Fund for priests. Supports youth ministry and retreat programs.
Assets: $34,545,934 (1995)

Catholic Knights Insurance Society

1100 West Wells Street
Milwaukee, WI 53233-2316
(800) 927-2547

(414) 273-6266
(414) 273-2120 (fax)
www.execpc.com/~ckis
Contact: Daniel J. Steininger, President
Geographic Giving Pattern: Primarily California, Florida, Illinois, Indiana, Iowa, Michigan, Minnesota, North Dakota, Pennsylvania, South Dakota, and Wisconsin.
Description: Fraternal benefit society.
Special Interest: Awards Catholic elementary tuition assistance and Catholic high school scholarships to its members' children and awards loans to Catholic parishes and organizations.
Assets: $525,154,393 (1999)

Catholic Knights of Ohio

22005 Mastick Road
Fairview Park, OH 44126
(440) 777-5355
(440) 777-5108 (fax)
Contact: Victor D. Huss, President
Geographic Giving Pattern: Primarily Ohio and Kentucky.
Description: Fraternal benefit society.
Special Interest: Assistance for Catholic high school tuition and education of seminarians.
Assets: $20,138,553 (1999)

Catholic Ladies of Columbia

4480 Refugee Road
Suite 200
Columbus, OH 43232
(800) 845-0494
(614) 868-5336
(614) 868-5221 (fax)
Contact: Theresa A. Gable, President
Geographic Giving Pattern: Primarily Indiana, Kentucky, Michigan, and Ohio.
Description: Fraternal benefit society.
Special Interest: Right to life efforts, evangelization, retired religious, and some scholarship support.
Assets: $16,781,873 (1999)

Catholic Life Insurance
P.O. Box 659527
San Antonio, TX 78265-9527
(800) 262-2548
(210) 828-9921
(210) 828-4629 (fax)
www.catholiclifeinsurance.com
Contact: J. Michael Belz, President and CEO
Geographic Giving Pattern: Primarily Louisiana, New Mexico, Oklahoma, and Texas.
Description: Fraternal benefit society.
Special Interest: Loans for churches, scholarships for seminarians, and grants for Catholic education, colleges, seminaries, the care of retired religious, vocations, and other Catholic activities.
Assets: $386,686,532 (1999)

Catholic Union of Texas
P.O. Box 297
La Grange, TX 78945-0297
(800) 245-8182
(409) 968-5877
(409) 968-5823 (fax)
Contact: Elo J. Goerig, President
Geographic Giving Pattern: Primarily Texas.
Description: Fraternal benefit society.
Special Interest: Catholic church support, Catholic parish schools, scholarships for seminarians, and other charitable activities.
Assets: $23,463,761 (1999)

Catholic Workman
111 West Main
P.O. Box 47
New Prague, MN 56071-0047
(800) 346-6231
(612) 758-2229
(612) 758-6221 (fax)
Contact: James M. Egr, Chair
Geographic Giving Pattern: Primarily Iowa, Kansas, Minnesota, Nebraska, North Dakota, Oregon, South Dakota, and Texas.

Description: Fraternal benefit society.
Special Interest: Youth ministry, education of priests and sisters, support for retired religious, and support for young Catholics in the Czech Republic.
Assets: $32,128,240 (1999)

Central Province Sharing Fund

Missionary Oblates of Mary Immaculate
267 East 8th Street
St. Paul, MN 55101-2374
Contact: The Executive Secretary
Geographic Giving Pattern: International and national.
Special Interest: Formation, ministry programs, evangelization especially of the poor and marginalized, communications, peace and justice, and Hispanic ministry programs.
Sources of Support: Income from the Central United States Province of the Missionary Oblates of Mary Immaculate.
Limitations: No grants to individuals. Eighty percent of funding is for international purposes, 20% for U.S. recipients.
Applications: Initial approach should be by letter. An application form is required. The deadline is September 1. Catholic applicant organizations must include a letter of endorsement from the local bishop or ecclesiastical authority.

Claretian Social Development Fund

Justice and Peace Committee
205 West Monroe Street, Second Floor West
Chicago, IL 60606
(773) 376-3900
TomJoyce@CLARET.org
Contact: Rev. Tom Joyce, CMF
Geographic Giving Pattern: National and Puerto Rico.
Description: The Eastern Province of the Claretians established the Claretian Social Development Fund to promote social justice and peace.
Special Interest: Projects that stimulate, encourage, and assist poor peoples and communities to achieve human dignity. Of highest priority are projects that will initiate long-term activities or establish organizations to change unjust conditions and promote social justice.

Grant Total: $65,000 (1999)
Grant Range: $1,000–$5,000
Limitations: No grants to individuals. Grants are generally awarded on a one-time-only basis. Low priority is given for direct service projects, education, academic research, or the purchase of equipment.
Applications: Initial approach should be by letter requesting procedural guidelines. An application form is required. Five copies are requested. Applications should be submitted between October 1 and October 23.

Croatian Catholic Union of U.S.A. and Canada

One East Old Ridge Road
P.O. Box 602
Hobart, IN 46342-0602
(219) 942-1191
(219) 942-8808 (fax)
Contact: Melchior Masina, National President
Geographic Giving Pattern: National and Canada.
Description: Fraternal benefit society.
Special Interest: Croatian House of Pilgrimage in Rome, Family Life Program of Rome, Croatian refugees assistance, and emergency aid in response to unexpected disasters.
Assets: $7,712,850 (1998)

Czech Catholic Union

5349 Dolloff Road
Cleveland, OH 44127
(216) 341-0444
(216) 341-0711 (fax)
Contact: Mary Ann Mahoney, President
Geographic Giving Pattern: Primarily Illinois, Iowa, Michigan, Nebraska, Ohio, and Pennsylvania.
Description: Fraternal benefit society.
Special Interest: Civic and cultural programs, Catholic social service organizations, and Catholic education.
Assets: $8,602,996 (1999)

Daughters of Charity Healthcare Foundation of St. Louis

231 S. Bemiston, Suite 350
St. Louis, MO 63105-1979

(314) 802-2060
(314) 802-2051 (fax)
Contact: Sr. Joan Kuester, DC, Executive Director
Geographic Giving Pattern: Primarily St. Louis, Missouri.
Special Interest: Youth, families, the economically disadvantaged, community healthcare and clinics, health education, spiritual healthcare, and preventative care.
Assets: $26,700,000 (1999)
Grant Total: $1,700,000
Grant Average: $30,000
Applications: Initial approach should be by letter or telephone. An application form is required. Deadlines are February 1 and August 1.

Daughters of Charity West Central Region Foundation

231 S. Bemiston, Suite 350
St. Louis, MO 63105-1979
(314) 802-2060
(314) 802-2051 (fax)
Contact: Sr. Joan Kuester, DC, Executive Director
Geographic Giving Pattern: Primarily the Midwest.
Special Interest: Youth, families, the economically disadvantaged, community healthcare and clinics, health education, spiritual healthcare, and preventative care.
Assets: $245,288,564 (1999)
Grant Total: $4,000,000
Grant Average: $115,000
Limitations: No giving outside of the U.S.
Applications: Initial approach should be by letter or telephone. An application form is required. The board meets quarterly.

Dominican Sisters of Springfield
Poverty, Justice, and Peace Fund

Stewardship Committee
1237 West Monroe Street
Springfield, IL 62704
(217) 787-0481
Contact: Sr. Linda Hayes, OP
Description: The Poverty, Justice, and Peace Fund was established by the Dominican Sisters of Springfield, Illinois to provide material

support to organizations which represent and serve the poor and to promote and support efforts toward justice and peace.

Special Interest: Self-help efforts for the poor and marginalized.

Limitations: No grants to individuals. Grants are generally made on a one-time-only basis.

Applications: Initial approach should be by letter or telephone. An application form is required. The deadlines are February 1 and August 1.

Dominican Social Action Fund

Aquinas Newman Center
1815 Las Lomas Road, N.E.
Albuquerque, NM 87106-3803
(505) 247-1094
www.domcentral.org
Contact: Rev. Steven Kuhlmann, OP, Director
Geographic Giving Pattern: National and international, with emphasis on the Midwest.
Special Interest: Self-help projects initiated, organized, and implemented by poor and oppressed people so that they can gain an effective voice in and control over decisions which affect their lives.
Sources of Support: Contributions by the communities of the Province and individual brothers.
Grant Total: $17,000 (1998)
Grant Range: $3,000–$5,000
Limitations: No grants to individuals. No more than 10% of funds granted can be used for construction or renovation of physical facilities. No support for academic research.
Applications: Initial approach should be by letter or telephone. An application form is required and is available through the internet by contacting the website listed above and selecting "justice." The deadline is April 1. A letter of recommendation from a member of Dominican Order is required.

Federal Association of the Sovereign Military Order of Malta

1730 M Street, N.W.
Suite 403
Washington, D.C. 20036

(202)331-2494
Contact: Joseph Dempsey, Executive Director
Geographic Giving Pattern: National and international.
Special Interest: Direct assistance to the poor and sick.
Limitations: The organization prefers whenever possible to send in-kind gifts rather than cash grants.
Applications: Initial approach should be by telephone or letter. A grant request form will be provided. Projects should have Knights of Malta volunteers involved.

First Catholic Slovak Ladies Association of the U.S.A.

24950 Chagrin Boulevard
Beachwood, OH 44122
(800)464-4642
(216)464-8015
(216)464-9260 (fax)
www.fcsla.com
Contact: Mary Ann Johanek, National President
Geographic Giving Pattern: National and Canada.
Description: Fraternal benefit society.
Special Interest: Slovak and Catholic charities and organizations.
Assets: $266,678,880 (1999)
Grant Total: $1,600,000 and $67,200 for elementary, high school, and college scholarships.

First Catholic Slovak Union of the U.S.A. and Canada

6611 Rockside Road
Independence, OH 44131
(800)533-6682
(216)642-9406
(216)642-4310 (fax)
www.fcsu.com
Contact: Thomas M. Hricik, President
Geographic Giving Pattern: National and Canada.
Description: Fraternal benefit society.
Special Interest: Preservation of the Slovak cultural and religious heritage, religious orders, and Slovak and Catholic organizations and institutions.
Assets: $115,787,872 (1999)

Incarnate Word Foundation

710 N. Second Street, Suite 400 South
St. Louis, MO 63102
(314) 621-4090
(314) 621-7971 (fax)
iwfdn@swbell.net
www.incarnatewordfund.com
Contact: Sr. Bridget McDermott Flood, Executive Director
Geographic Giving Pattern: National.
Special Interest: Community health, wellness, spiritual healthcare, mental healthcare, and projects that have a lasting influence in ameliorating social problems and improving the life of communities. The foudnation also administers the Annunciation Grant program, which awards grants of $10,000 or less, semiannually.
Assets: $33,000,000 (1999)
Applications: Initial approach should be by letter or by visiting the foundation's website.

Knights of Columbus

One Columbus Plaza
P.O. Box 1670
New Haven, CT 06507-0901
(203) 772-2130
(203) 865-2310 (fax)
www.kofc.org
Contact: Virgil C. Dechant, Supreme Knight
Geographic Giving Pattern: National and international.
Description: Fraternal benefit society.
Special Interest: Vocations, seminarian support, evangelization, Catholic education and schools, promotion of Marian devotion, rosary devotion and Sacrament of Penance, pro-life activities, youth ministry, and family life and ministry. The Knights of Columbus also established the $1,000,000 Father Michael J. McGivney Fund for research in improving Catholic education and the $20,000,000 Vicarius Christi Fund for the Holy Father and his charities.
Assets: $8,063,629,220 (1999)
Grant Total: $108,954,410

Ladies Pennsylvania Slovak Catholic Union

69 Public Square, Suite 922
Wilkes-Barre, PA 18701-2595
(888) 834-6614
(570) 823-3513
(570) 823-4464 (fax)
Contact: Rita M. Simalchik, President
Geographic Giving Pattern: Primarily Connecticut, Illinois, Indiana, Massachusetts, Michigan, New Jersey, Ohio, Pennsylvania, and Slovakia.
Description: Fraternal benefit society.
Special Interest: Church support, seminaries, Catholic organizations, and a fund for churches in Slovakia.
Assets: $15,042,108 (1999)

Leviticus 25:23 Alternative Fund

928 McLean Avenue
Yonkers, NY 10704-4103
(914) 237-3306
(914) 237-3916 (fax)
levf@erols.com
www.Leviticusfund.org
Contact: Patricia Russell, OSU, Loan Officer
Geographic Giving Pattern: Primarily New York, New Jersey, and Connecticut.
Description: The Leviticus 25:23 Alternative Fund is a religiously motivated loan fund which supports community-based development at the service of the economically poor. Primary among the fund's values are participation, local control, more equal distribution of God's gifts, and care for the earth.
Special Interest: Loans to nonprofit organizations which benefit the poor and the powerless and for projects that seek to meet the basic human needs of others. Lending programs are in the following areas: affordable housing, not-for-profit facilities, child day care facilities, and minority and women-owned small businesses.
Sources of Income: Loans from nonprofit organizations, religious orders, church groups, and individuals.
Loan Total: $4,670,832 (1998)
Loan Range: $400,000 or less.

Loan Average: $100,000
Applications: Initial approach should be by letter or telephone. A pre-application form is required. Pre-applications are accepted at any time.

The Louisville Institute
1044 Alta Vista Road
Louisville, KY 40205-1798
(502) 894-3411
Email: infor@louisville-institute.org
Contact: Dr. James W. Lewis, Executive Director
Geographic Giving Pattern: National.
Description: The Louisville Institute seeks to nurture inquiry and conversation regarding the character, problems, contributions, and prospects of the historic institutions and commitments of American Christianity.
Special Interest: Summer research stipends for faculty members, dissertation fellowship support for final year of PhD or ThD, study grants for religious leaders for a period of two or three months, and modest grant support for other religious projects.
Applications: Initial approach should be by letter or telephone. An application form is required.

Loyal Christian Benefit Association
700 Peach Street
P.O. Box 13005
Erie, PA 16514-1305
(800) 234-5222
(814) 453-4331
(814) 453-3211 (fax)
www.lcba.com
Contact: Jacqueline J. Sobania-Robison, National President
Geographic Giving Pattern: National.
Description: Fraternal benefit society.
Special Interest: Deaf and hard of hearing, establishment of the National Catholic Office of the Deaf, and children.
Assets: $82,383,731 (1999)

Marianist Sharing Fund

4301 Roland Avenue
Baltimore, MD 21210-2793
(410) 366-1324
(410) 889-5743 (fax)
Contact: Richard E. Ullrich, Executive Secretary or Darla J. Benton, Program Officer
Geographic Giving Pattern: Limited to the eastcoast of the United States and Puerto Rico.
Description: The Marianist Sharing Fund was established by the New York Province of the Marianist Brothers and Priests (Society of Mary) for the purpose of financing projects of social change which improve the human condition and build community.
Special Interest: Grant interests include social justice, development of community leadership, community organizing, social advocacy, and efforts working directly with the poor and oppressed for social change. Loans are awarded to nonprofit corporations providing community economic development or affordable housing, community development corporations, community land trusts, and worker-owned businesses.
Sources of Support: Allocations from the Marianists' unrestricted income.
Grant Total: $206,600 (1999)
Grant Range: $250–$8,000
Loan Total: $159,171 (1999)
Loan Range: $50,000 and less.
Limitations: Grants are awarded on a one-to-one matching basis. No grants to individuals. No support for direct service projects, research projects, feasibility studies, or partisan political activities.
Applications: Initial approach should be by brief letter. Application forms are required for grants and loans. The deadline for loan applications is February 1. The deadline for grant applications is September 1.

McAuley Institute Revolving Loan Fund

8300 Colesville Road, Suite 310
Silver Spring, MD 20910
(301) 588-8110
(301) 588-8154 (fax)
FGervasi@McAuley.org
www.mcauley.org

Contact: Fred Gervasi, Housing and Community Development Director
Geographic Giving Pattern: National.
Description: The McAuley Institute was established by the Sisters of Mercy to assist local efforts to increase the supply of permanent, affordable housing in the United States. The McAuley Institute provides technical assistance and financial services to individuals, nonprofit organizations, and faith communities interested in local nonprofit housing development. The Institute's services include consulting, advocacy, training for local organizations on housing and community development strategies, providing information, reviewing projects for investors wishing to finance low-income housing development, and providing financial resources for affordable housing through a revolving loan fund.
Special Interest: Nonprofit, low-income housing development, with a special focus on the housing needs of women and children.
Sources of Income: Religious organizations, individuals, and foundations.
Revolving Loan Fund Total: $2,500,000
Loan Range: $1,000–$606,750
Loan Average: $77,319 at 5.5%
Applications: Initial approach should be by telephone to discuss specific need and to request application information. An application fee equal to 1.5 percent of the principal of the loan is required. There are no deadlines.

Mercy Action Foundation

8300 Colesville Road, Suite 300
Silver Spring, MD 20910
(301) 587-0423
Contact: Regina A. Wynn
Geographic Giving Pattern: National.
Special Interest: Direct service programs for the relief of poverty and projects addressing systemic change.
Sources of Income: Religious Sisters of Mercy and Mercy Associates.
Grant Total: $250,000 (1996)
Grant Range: $10,000–$15,000
Limitations: A Sister of Mercy or a Mercy Associate must be involved in the ministry or project.

Applications: Initial approach should be by letter or telephone. An application form is required. The deadline is in February.

Mercy Foundation, Inc.
2700 Stewart Parkway
Roseburg, OR 97470
(541) 677-4818
(541) 677-4891 (fax)
Contact: Dan Hern, President
Geographic Giving Pattern: Primarily Oregon.
Special Interest: Youth, families, the elderly, the economically disadvantaged, community development, community healthcare and clinics, hospital-based healthcare, and terminal illness.
Assets: $907,000 (1996)
Grant Total: $192,739
Grant Average: $1,500
Applications: Initial approach should be by letter.

Mercy Health Services
Emily George Fund for Human Needs
34605 Twelve Mile Road
Farmington, MI 48331-3292
(248) 489-6084
Contact: Nancy Van Zant, Executive Director
Geographic Giving Pattern: Primarily Mercy Grants Services service areas.
Special Interest: Community healthcare and clinics, the economically disadvantaged, youth, the elderly, families, education, housing, social justice, and respect for all life.
Grant Range: $10,000–$50,000
Limitations: Grants are available only to organizations which originate in Mercy Grants Services service areas and/or have the active involvement of a Religious Sister of Mercy or Associate from the Regional Community of Detroit. Grants are awarded on a one-time basis only. No multi-year funding requests will be accepted.
Applications: Grants are awarded every other year. The next call for applications will be in July of 1998. An application form is required. The deadline is October 31.

Mercy Loan Fund

601 East 18th Avenue, Room 150
Denver, CO 80203
(303) 830-3386
(303) 830-3301 (fax)
Contact: Diane Leavesley, Director
Geographic Giving Pattern: Limited to the 48 contiguous states.
Description: Mercy Loan Fund was established by the Sisters of Mercy to provide financial and technical support for housing that benefits low- and moderate-income people. It is sponsored by the Sisters of Mercy of Auburn, Burlingame, Cedar Rapids, and Omaha, and the Sisters of St. Joseph of Peace.
Special Interest: Loans for the development of affordable quality housing for low-income families or persons with special needs.
Loan Range: $2,000–$5,000,000 (1998)
Applications: Initial approach should be by telephone or letter. There are no deadlines.

National Catholic Society of Foresters

320 South School Street
Mount Prospect, IL 60056-3334
(800) 344-6273
(847) 342-4500
(847) 342-4556 (fax)
www.ncsf.com
Contact: Sue Koleczek, National President
Geographic Giving Pattern: National.
Description: Fraternal benefit society.
Special Interest: Catholic grade school and high school grants, Catholic diocesan communications, seminary support and Alzheimer's research.
Assets: $114,143,075 (1999)

Partners for the Common Good 2000 Loan Fund

2507 NW 36th Street
San Antonio, TX 78228-3918
(210) 431-0616
(210) 431-0161 (fax)
Contact: Carol Coston, OP, Director

Geographic Giving Pattern: National; some international support.
Description: Partners for the Common Good is an alternative investment opportunity from Christian Brothers Investment Services, Inc. PCG directs loans and deposits through intermediaries to projects which seek to promote economic justice and social change through modeling alternative approaches to the production of goods and services.
Special Interest: Loans to intermediary agencies which support enterprises owned and/or managed by women and/or racial and ethnic minorities, agencies which support worker co-operatives, and agencies which develop low-income housing projects.
Loan Fund Total : $7,902,000
Loan Range: $30,000–$300,000
Loan Average: $50,000–$100,000
Limitations: All available capital has been lent. The next loan cycle will be in the year 2000.
Applications: Initial approach should be by letter or telephone. A pre-application form is required.

Polish National Alliance of Brooklyn, U.S.A.
155 Noble Street
Brooklyn, NY 11222-9006
(718) 389-4704
(718) 383-8517 (fax)
Contact: Christine J. McMullan, President
Geographic Giving Pattern: Primarily Connecticut, New Jersey, and New York.
Description: Fraternal benefit society.
Special Interest: Parochial schools, seminaries, the clergy, and Catholic church support.
Assets: $7,345,023 (1999)

Polish National Union of America
1002 Pittston Avenue
Scranton, PA 18505-4109
(570) 344-1513
(570) 961-5961 (fax)
www.pnu.org
Contact: Edmund J. Kotula, President

Geographic Giving Pattern: Primarily Connecticut, Illinois, Massachusetts, Michigan, New Hampshire, New Jersey, New York, Ohio, Pennsylvania, and Rhode Island.
Description: Fraternal benefit society.
Special Interest: Missions, seminary support, and women and men's religious societies.
Assets: $24,778,868 (1999)

Polish Roman Catholic Union of America
984 North Milwaukee Avenue
Chicago, IL 60622-4101
(800) 772-8632
(773) 782-2600
(773) 278-4595 (fax)
www.prcua.org
Contact: Wallace M. Ozog, President
Geographic Giving Pattern: National.
Description: Fraternal benefit society.
Special Interest: Religious retreats, clergy support, and church support.
Assets: $94,511,886 (1999)

Providence Association of Ukranian Catholics in America
817-19 North Franklin Street
Philadelphia, PA 19123-2004
(215) 627-4984
(215) 238-1933 (fax)
Contact: Msgr. Thomas Sayuk, Supreme President
Geographic Giving Pattern: New Jersey and Pennsylvania.
Description: Fraternal benefit society.
Special Interest: Scholarships to students and low-interest mortgage loans to religious institutions.
Assets: $13,052,950 (1999)

Salesian Missions
2 Lafevre Lane
New Rochelle, NY 10801
(914) 633-8344
(914) 633-7404 (fax)
Contact: William Sigler, Director, Overseas Development Programs

Geographic Giving Pattern: International.
Special Interest: Support for the approximately 40,000 Salesian men and women working in 100 countries. Provides education and other forms of support to poor, disadvantaged, orphaned, or abandoned youth. Also provides humanitarian aid, relief, refugee resettlement, and emergency and disaster assistance.
Grant Total: $16,979,549 (1991)
Applications: Initial approach should be by letter.

The San Damiano Outreach Fund

Hospital Sisters of the Third Order of St. Francis
P.O. Box 19431
Springfield, IL 62794-9431
(217) 522-3386
Contact: The San Damiano Outreach Committee
Geographic Giving Pattern: Limited to geographical areas where the Hospital Sisters are presently serving.
Special Interest: To support ministries and projects serving the needs of the poor, women, children and minorities.
Grant Range: $1,000–$10,000
Applications: Initial approach should be by letter. An application form is required. Proposals may be submitted semi-annually. The deadlines are February 1 and August 1.

SC Ministry Foundation, Inc.

345 Neeb Road
Cincinnati, OH 45233-5103
(513) 347-1122
(513) 347-1017 (fax)
Contact: Janet Wasser, Executive Assistant
Geographic Giving Pattern: National, with an emphasis on areas where Sisters of Charity of Cincinnati are ministering.
Special Interest: The foundation was established to support the Sisters of Charity of Cincinnati. Grantmaking priorities are projects that further systemic change, support development of alternative services and programs that impact the poor and underserved, promote collaborative initiatives for the extension of services beyond traditional institutional settings and for building healthy communities, and to

sustain and nurture ministries identified with the Sisters of Charity of Cincinnati that are in need of support.

Sources of Income: Income generated from the sale of a Sisters of Charity hospital.

Grant Total: $8,156,337 (1999)

Applications: Pre-applications must be received by the third Friday in August or the third Friday in February. Grants are awarded twice a year in January and July.

Seton Enablement Fund

Sisters of Charity
5900 Delhi Road
Mount St. Joseph, OH 45051
(513) 347-5461

Contact: Sr. Mary Assunta Stang, Administrative Director
Geographic Giving Pattern: National.
Description: The Seton Enablement Fund is a low-interest, revolving loan fund and is a ministry of the Sisters of Charity of Cincinnati.
Special Interest: Loans to enable the economically disadvantaged to develop themselves and their communities through low-income housing development, community development efforts, business ventures, and employment opportunities directly benefiting low-income communities.
Sources of Income: A portion of the Sisters of Charity of Cincinnati congregation's unrestricted funds.
Loan Range: $50,000 or less.
Loan Average: $30,000
Limitations: No loans to individuals. Monies are loaned at a low-interest rate for a maximum of five years. No grants are awarded.
Applications: Initial approach should be by letter. A preliminary application form will be sent. Should the organization qualify, a more detailed application packet will be sent. There are no deadlines.

Sisters of Charity Foundation

2601 Laurel Street
Suite 250
Columbia, SC 29204
(803) 254-0230

Contact: Thomas Keith, Executive Director

Geographic Giving Pattern: Limited to South Carolina.
Special Interest: The relief of poverty.
Sources of Income: Income generated from the sale of half of the interest of Providence Hospital.
Grant Total: $1,000,000 each year for Good Samaritan grants.
Grant Range: $25,000 or less.
Applications: Initial approach should be by letter. Applicants seeking a Good Samaritan Grant should contact the foundation for an application form and guidelines. The deadlines are in March and September. The foundation will soon begin a foundation-initiated grants program totalling approximately $3,000,000 each year.

Sisters of Charity Foundation of Canton
20 Market Avenue South
Canton, OH 44702
(330) 454-5800
Contact: Vicki Conley, Executive Director
Geographic Giving Pattern: Limited to Canton County, Ohio.
Special Interest: Organizations which provide programs for the poor and the under-served, especially in the areas of social services, education, and health.
Sources of Income: Income generated from the sale of a Sisters of Charity hospital.
Assets: $72,500,000 (1997)
Grant Total: 1997 is the first year of grantmaking.
Limitations: No grants to individuals.
Applications: Initial approach should be by letter requesting grant guidelines. The deadlines are March 1, June 1, September 1, and December 1.

Sisters of Charity Foundation of Cleveland
The Hanna Building
1422 Euclid Avenue
Suite 425
Cleveland, OH 44115
(216) 241-9300
(216) 241-9345 (fax)
Contact: Sr. Catherine Lee, CSJ, Executive Director
Geographic Giving Pattern: Primarily Ohio.

Description: There are three foundations administered from this address. They are The Sisters of Charity Foundation of Cleveland, The St. Ann Foundation, and The Good Samaritan Foundation.

Special Interest: Organizations which provide programs for the poor and the under-served, especially in the areas of social services, education, and health.

Sources of Income: Income generated from the sale of a Sisters of Charity hospital.

Limitations: No grants to individuals.

Applications: Initial approach should be by letter or telephone requesting grant guidelines. An application form is required. The deadline is September 3.

The Sisters of Charity of Leavenworth
Health Services Corporation System Mission Fund

4200 South 4th Street
Leavenworth, KS 66048
(913) 682-1338
Contact: Sr. Paulette Krick

Geographic Giving Pattern: Primarily in geographical areas where the Sisters of Charity currently serve.

Description: The SCL/HSC System Mission Fund was designed to fund projects which further the mission of the Sisters of Charity of leavenworth Health Services Corporation.

Special Interest: Projects that address the needs of the economically disadvantaged, human services, and healthcare.

Grant Average: $15,000 or less.

Applications: Initial approach should be by letter. Full proposals can be submitted at any time. The committee meets quartely.

Sisters of St. Francis of Philadelphia
Social Justice Fund

Sisters of St. Francis of Philadelphia
Office for Corporate Social Responsibility
Our Lady of Angels Convent
609 South Convent Road
Aston, PA 19014
(610) 558-7715
(610) 558-6131 (fax)

www.osfphila.org
Contact: Deborah Loyd, Administrative Assistant
Geographic Giving Pattern: National and international.
Description: The Social Justice Fund enables the Sisters of St.
Francis to live out their commitment to the poor and oppressed by
sharing their resources.
Special Interest: Work that promotes social justice at local, national
and international levels. Promotion of self-help and empowerment of
individuals and communities, the poor and the marginalized.
Grant Total: $77,700 (1999)
Grant Range: $500–$5,000
Limitations: Funding for a specific project is limited to two
consecutive years.
Applications: Initial approach should be by letter or telephone. An
application form is required. A letter of endorsement by a Sister of St.
Francis of Philadelphia is recommended. The deadline is the last
Friday in November.
Assets: $51,204,436 (1998)

Sisters of St. Joseph Charitable Fund, Inc.

137 Mount St. Joseph Road
Wheeling, WV 26003-1799
(304) 232-8160
Contact: The Grant Manager
Geographic Giving Pattern: The Calhoun, Jackson, Pleasants,
Ritchie, Roane, Tyler, Wirt, and Wood counties of West Virginia; and
the Athens, Meigs, and Washington counties of Ohio.
Special Interest: Community-wide health promotion, environmental
protection, local development, education, children and adolescents, the
elderly, preventative healthcare, and volunteerism.
Assets: $22,173,030 (1999)
Grant Total: $918,783
Grant Range: $1,000–$50,000
Applications: Initial approach should be by one-page letter.
Application packets will be sent to those the fund would like to invite to
apply.

SOAR! (Support Our Aging Religious)

1400 Spring Street, Suite 320
Silver Spring, MD 20910
(301) 589-9811
(301) 589-2482 (fax)
Contact: Rita Hofbauer, President
Geographic Giving Pattern: National.
Special Interest: The retirement needs of elderly religious sisters, brothers, and priests.
Sources of Income: Individuals and foundations.
Grant Range: $25,000 or less.
Grant Average: $12,000–$15,000
Limitations: Successful applicants must wait three years before applying for funding from the foundation again.
Applications: Initial approach should be by letter by May 1. An application form is required. The deadline is August 1.

St. Elizabeth Hospital Community Foundation, Inc.

1506 South Oneida Street
Appleton, WI 54915
(920) 738-2859
(920) 738-0949 (fax)
Contact: Lisa Weiner, Director
Geographic Giving Pattern: Primarily Wisconsin.
Special Interest: Primarily the poor and medically underserved. Support also for youth, the elderly, community healthcare and clinics, hospital-based healthcare, health education, and preventative care.
Assets: $4,800,000 (1996)
Grant Total: $197,077
Applications: Initial approach should be by letter or telephone. An application form is required. Deadlines are February 1 and August 1.

St. Joseph Health System Foundation

440 South Batavia Street
Orange, CA 92868
(714) 997-7690
(714) 239-6646 (fax)
Contact: Sr. Suzanne Sassus, CSJ, Vice President, Sponsorship
Geographic Giving Pattern: Primarily California.

Special Interest: The economically disadvantaged, community healthcare and clinics, health education, preventative care, families, youth, the elderly, and community development.
Sources of Income: St. Joseph Health System entities.
Assets: $29,000,000 (1996)
Grant Total: $6,600,000
Grant Average: $115,000
Applications: Initial approach should be by letter or telephone.

St. Joseph's Foundation
523 North 3rd Street
Brainerd, MN 56401
(218) 828-7656
(218) 828-3103 (fax)
Contact: Sr. Lynnette Bouta, OSB, Vice President, SJMC
Geographic Giving Pattern: Primarily Minnesota.
Special Interest: Youth, families, community healthcare and clinics, hospital-based healthcare, health education, preventative care, and educational institutions. Some support for the elderly and the economically disadvantaged.
Assets: $1,586,000 (1996)
Grant Total: $67,000
Grant Average: $10,000
Applications: Initial approach should be by letter or telephone.

United Societies of U.S.A.
613 Sinclair Street
McKeesport, PA 15132
(412) 672-3196
(412) 672-3183 (fax)
Contact: Edward M. Boyko, National President
Geographic Giving Pattern: Primarily Indiana, Michigan, New Jersey, Ohio, Pennsylvania, and West Virginia.
Description: Fraternal benefit society formed by Byzantine Rite Catholics.
Special Interest: Catholic charities and seminary support.
Assets: $13,822,263 (1998)

Western Catholic Union
P.O. Box 410
Quincy, IL 62306-0410
(800) 223-4928
(217) 223-9721
(217) 223-9726 (fax)
www.westerncatholicunion.org and
www.wculife.com
Contact: Mark A. Wiewel, FIC, National President and CEO
Geographic Giving Pattern: Primarily Colorado, Illinois, Iowa, Missouri, Texas, and Wisconsin.
Description: Fraternal benefit society.
Special Interest: Catholic education, vocations, and scholarships.
Assets: $40,221,191 (1999)

SECTION IV:
INTERNATIONAL FUNDING AGENCIES

Please note that the international funding agencies included in this section rarely make grants to U.S.-based organizations. Most often they provide support to Catholic church-sponsored efforts in developing nations, or Catholic activities in the country in which the funding agency is located. The grant seeker should be advised that efforts were made to obtain the most current information on the following agencies, but in some cases the information that appears could be dated. Verification of agency information by telephone, fax or email is recommended.

AUSTRALIA

Caritas Australia
19 MacKenzie Street
North Sydney NSW 2060
Australia
(612) 9956-5799
(612) 9956-5782 (fax)
Email: caritas@caritas.org.au
www.caritas.org.au
Contact: Jack de Groot
Geographic Giving Pattern: Africa, Asia, Latin America, the Pacific, Eastern Europe, the Middle East, and Australia.
Description: Caritas Australia is part of the international Catholic network of Caritas agencies.
Special Interest: Community development, poverty relief, justice and peace, human rights, and emergency relief.
Sources of Income: Primarily the Australian Lenten campaign.
Grant Total: $7,200,000
Grant Range: $1,000–$125,000
Limitations: No support for administrative costs, staff salaries, building funds, or vehicles.

Applications: A letter of endorsement from the local bishop is required. The deadline is mid-March or late August.

Paulian Association Lay Missionary Secretariat (PALMS)
P.O. Box 54
Croydon Park NSW 2133
Australia
(612) 642-0558
(612) 742-5607 (fax)
Contact: PALMS Coordinator
Geographic Giving Pattern: Primarily Southwest Pacific (especially Papau New Guinea), Africa, Asia, and Latin America.
Description: PALMS is a lay organization operating out of the Catholic Archdiocese of Sydney, which recruits nationwide. Its aim is to recruit, screen, prepare, and support volunteers overseas.
Special Interest: Skilled development co-workers to work in the fields of medicine, education, agriculture, trades, and development.
Sources of Income: Diocese of Sydney, Paulian Association grants, and individual donations.
Limitations: PALMS is not a funding agency.
Applications: Initial approach should be by letter in English. Letters of application can be submitted at any time.

AUSTRIA

Dreikönigsaktion Der Katholischen Jungschar Osterreichs
Austrian Catholic Youth Organization
Mittersteig 10
A – 1050 Wien
Austria
(43222) 586-6796
(43222) 586-6731 (fax)
Contact: Heinz Hödl
Geographic Giving Pattern: Africa, Asia, the Pacific, and Central America.
Special Interest: Promotion of the individuality of the indigenous churches. Indigenous lay ministry and training, integrated socio-pastoral projects, pastoral formation, human rights, environment, communication, literacy, and evangelization.

Grant Total: $13,000,000
Grant Average: $15,000–$20,000
Applications: Proposals should be written in German, Spanish, Portuguese, English, Italian, or French and may be submitted at any time.

Institute fur Internationale Zusammenarbeit (IIZ)
Institute for International Cooperation
Wipplingerstrasse 32
A – 1010 Wien
Austria
(431) 5334-7860
Geographic Giving Pattern: Western Africa, Asia, the Pacific, and parts of Latin America.
Description: IIZ was founded by the Austrian Section of the International Catholic Peace Movement, Pax Christi.
Special Interest: Provides qualified volunteers to promote socio-economic development in developing countries, especially in rural areas. Expertise includes agriculture, forestry, economics, cooperatives, medicine, education, and planning.
Applications: Proposals should be submitted within the first half of the year.

Katholische Frauenbewegung Osterreichs
Austrian Catholic Women's Movement
Mittersteig 10
A – 1050 Wien
Austria
(43222) 586-6796
(43222) 586-6731 (fax)
Contact: The Project Department
Geographic Giving Pattern: Asia (especially India and the Philippines), Africa, the Pacific, and parts of Latin America.
Special Interest: Socio-economic development, clinics, dispensaries, schools, non-formal education, and programs for women.
Sources of Income: Primarily the Austrian annual Lenten campaign.
Grant Total: $260,000
Grant Range: $15,000–$50,000
Applications: Proposals may be submitted at any time.

Koordinierungsstelle
Coordination Office
Austrian Episcopal Conference for International
Development and Mission
Turkenstrasse 3
A – 1090 Wien
Austria
(431) 340-321
(431) 340-321-85 (fax)
Geographic Giving Pattern: Africa, Asia, Latin America, and the Pacific.
Description: The organization provides information and political advocacy and coordinates the projects of all Catholic aid organizations in Austria which are committed to international development.
Sources of Income: Member organizations and the Austrian Bishops' Conference.
Limitations: Only organized groups or church institutions may apply.
Applications: A letter of support from the local bishop or religious superior is required. Proposals should include an outline of the socio-economic background of the project and should indicate any applications to other agencies. There are no deadlines for proposals.

Österreichische Caritaszentrale
Caritas Austria
Albrechtskreithgasse 19-21
Wien 1160
Austria
(431) 488-31-94-00 (fax)
Email: fkprueller.caritas@netway.at
Contact: Franz Karl Prüeller, Secretary General
Geographic Giving Pattern: Central America, the Sahel, Bangladesh, Philippines, Southeast Asia (except Indonesia and Malaysia), Bolivia, Peru, and Central and Eastern Europe. Disaster relief for all continents except Australia.
Description: Osterrichische Caritaszentrale is part of the international Catholic network of Caritas agencies.
Special Interest: Development aid, especially as it assists self-reliance. Specific areas include the disabled, refugees, leadership

training, cooperatives, nutrition, healthcare, water, and income generation. Also contributes toward disaster relief and emergency aid.
Grant Total: $25,000,000
Applications: Initial approach should be by letter written in German, Spanish, English, or French. Proposals may be submitted at any time. A recommendation by the national Caritas organization or the local bishop where project is located is required.

BELGIUM

Broederlijk Delen
Huidevettersstraat 165
B – 1000 Brussels
Belgium
(322) 502-5700
(322) 502-8101 (fax)
Contact: André Benoit, Director of Project Department
Geographic Giving Pattern: Africa, Asia, Latin America, and the Pacific.
Special Interest: Local community projects, grassroots community development, human rights, cooperatives, literacy, adult education, women, and pastoral projects which address the social, economic, and political struggles of the oppressed.
Sources of Income: Primarily the Lenten campaign in Flanders.
Grant Total: $10,000,000
Grant Average: $28,000
Limitations: Funding preference is for small-scale projects from local communities. Initiatives should incorporate broad local participation and responsibility.
Applications: Proposals should be written in Dutch, Spanish, Portuguese, English, or French and may be submitted at any time.

CIDSE
International Cooperation for Development and Solidarity
Rue Stévin, 16
B – 1000 Bruxelles
Belgium
(322) 230-7722 or (322) 230-7802
(322) 230-7082 (fax)

Geographic Giving Pattern: Africa, Asia, Latin America, and the Pacific.

Description: CIDSE functions as a coordinating agency among the Catholic development agencies in 16 countries. Catholic Relief Services is the development agency in the U.S.A. (See entry in Section II, Church-based Agencies, page 360.)

Special Interest: Agriculture, education, health, and communications.

Grant Total: $527,000,000

Applications: Proposals may be submitted at any time.

DMOS-COMIDE
Dienst Missie en Ontwikkelingssamenwerking
Service de Coopération Missionnaire au Développement

Boulevard Léopold II, 195
1080 Brussels
Belgium
(322) 427-4720
(322) 425-9031 (fax)
Email: dmos.comide@skynet.be

Geographic Giving Pattern: Africa, Asia, Latin America, and the Pacific.

Special Interest: Provides assistance to missionaries and others in preparing project presentations related to socio-economic development for co-financing to proper authorities, especially the Belgian Government and the European Community. COMIDE also provides follow-up financial reports and project activity reports which have been successfully co-financed. Occasionally COMIDE will aid in the purchase and shipment of equipment.

Grant Total: $7,998,908

Limitations: Pastoral projects are not considered.

Applications: Initial approach should be by contacting the regional Development Offices of the organization. The addresses of these offices are available at the DMOS-COMIDE desk in Brussels. Letters should be written in English, Dutch, French, or Spanish. The deadline is prior to May.

Fondation Catholique de Bourses d'Etudes pour Africains (FONCABA)

Rue du Progrès, 333/03
B – 1030 Brussels
Belgium
(322) 201-0383
(322) 201-0400 (fax)
Contact: Mr. Luc Bonte, Secretary General
Geographic Giving Pattern: Africa, with an emphasis on Zaire, Rwanda, and Burundi; also Burkina Faso and Cameroun.
Special Interest: Pastoral and socio-economic development, leadership training, formation of catechists, small Christian communities, evangelization, and scholarships for study in Belgium.
Sources of Income: National collection, individuals, and government contributions.
Limitations: Scholarships for study in Belgium are for applicants recommended through the General Secretariat of the local Conference of Bishops.
Applications: Initial approach should be by typed letter of request in French or Dutch. Applications may be submitted at any time.

Pontifical Missionworks – Belgium

Boulevard du Souverain, 199
B – 1160 Brussels
Belgium
(322) 673-6040
(322) 672-5569 (fax)
Geographic Giving Pattern: Africa, Asia, Latin America, and the Pacific.
Special Interest: Small subsidies for pastoral transportation needs for missionaries and native priests and sisters.
Sources of Income: Lenten contributions from priests and religious communities.
Grant Average: $4,000
Limitations: Only partial funding is available for vehicles. Subsidies generally do not exceed $4,000.
Applications: Initial approach should be by letter. A letter of recommendation from the local bishop or religious superior is required. Please include a documented statement of cost. Proposals may be submitted at any time.

Caritas Secours International Belgique

43 A Rue de aa Charité
Bruxelles 1210
Belgium
(322) 229-3611
(322) 229-3636 (fax)
Email: caritas.sec.int@caritasint.be
Contact: Johan Ketelers, Director
Geographic Giving Pattern: Africa, Asia, Latin America, the
Pacific, Belgium, and Central and Eastern Europe.
Description: Secours International de Caritas Catholica is part of the
international Catholic network of Caritas agencies.
Special Interest: Emergency relief, food aid programs, socio-
economic development, pastoral projects, health centers, and social
services, particularly involving children, the elderly, or the disabled.
Sources of Income: Diocesan collections, individuals, Belgian
government, and EC support.
Grant Total: $35,000,000
Applications: Proposals may be submitted at any time. Authorization
of the local bishop or local Caritas is required.

UNDA
International Catholic Association for Radio and Television

12 rue de l'Orme
1040 Bruxelles
Belgium
(322) 734-9708
(322) 734-7018 (fax)
Geographic Giving Pattern: Africa, Asia, Latin America, and the
Pacific.
Special Interest: UNDA wants to ensure a truly human and Christian
spirit in radio, television, and group media activities, and wants to help
achieve the most effective kind of religious broadcasting at all levels.
UNDA screens broadcasting projects presented to the Propagation of
the Faith for funding.
Sources of Income: Society for the Propagation of the Faith in Rome.
Grant Total: $600,000 each year
Grant Average: $10,000

Applications: An application form is required. Applications should be completed in English, French, or Spanish. The deadline is September 15.

CANADA

Allard Foundation, Ltd.
210-5324 Calgary Trail
Edmonton, AB T6H 4J8
Canada
Contact: Catherine M. Roozen, Secretary-Treasurer
Geographic Giving Pattern: Primarily Edmonton, AB.
Special Interest: Poverty relief, education, hospitals, Catholic churches, Catholic organizations, youth, and sports.
Assets: CAN $12,213,738
Grant Total: CAN $543,700
Grant Range: CAN $200–$200,000
Applications: Initial approach should be by letter.

Canadian Pastoral Fund for Evangelization
Canadian Conference of Catholic Bishops' Missions Office
90 Parent Avenue
Ottawa
Ontario K1N 7B1
Canada
(613) 241-9461
(613) 241-8117 (fax)
Contact: Director, Missions Office
Geographic Giving Pattern: Africa, Asia, Latin America, the Pacific, and Native Canada.
Special Interest: Pastoral projects, evangelization, and formation of church personnel, lay ministers, and pastoral agents.
Sources of Income: Canadian Conference of Catholic Bishops.
Grant Total: $264,260
Grant Range: $1,000–$5,000
Grant Average: $3,000
Limitations: No grants for building projects, staff maintenance, vehicles, equipment, or printing of books. Priority is given for projects

at the national, regional, and diocesan level, although parish projects are sometimes funded.

Applications: Proposals should be written in English, French, or Spanish and deadlines are prior to the end of March and October. A letter of endorsement of the Episcopal Conference of the submitting country is required.

J. A. De Seve Foundation

505 Sherbrooks Street East
Suite 2402
Montréal, PQ
H2L 4N3
Canada
Contact: Robert Trudeau
Geographic Giving Pattern: Primarily Quebec.
Special Interest: Hospitals, healthcare, higher education, the arts, cultural programs, social services, Catholic churches, Catholic organizations, youth, and the disabled.
Assets: CAN $58,020,729
Grant Total: CAN $3,452,600
Grant Range: CAN $1,000–$250,000
Applications: Initial approach should be by letter.

Interchurch Fund for International Development
ICFID

Suite 204
85 St. Clair Avenue East
Toronto
Ontario M4T 1M8
Canada
(416) 968-1411
(416) 231-3103 (fax)
Geographic Giving Pattern: Africa, Asia, Latin America, and the Pacific.
Special Interest: Socio-economic projects and fostering ecumenical partnership with developing country peoples. Prefers projects involving more than one church denomination with a focus on the poorest sectors of society.
Sources of Income: Member churches and the Canadian government.

Grant Total: $2,496,000
Limitations: Strictly pastoral projects and emergency relief requests will not be funded.
Applications: Proposals should be submitted prior to May, September, or December.

Madonna Foundation
McCallum Hill Building
1874 Scarth Street, 10th Floor
P.O. Box 527
Regina, SK
S4P 2G8
Canada
Contact: W.H. Berezan, Secretary
Geographic Giving Pattern: Canada, with an emphasis on Saskatchewan.
Special Interest: Catholic churches, Catholic organizations, secondary education, social services, child welfare, poverty relief, and wildlife.
Assets: CAN $261,425
Gifts Received: $510,590
Grant Total: CAN $323,524
Grant Range: CAN $50–$54,500
Applications: Contributes to pre-selected organizations only. Applications are not accepted.

E. and G. Odette Charitable Foundation
4120 Yonge Street, Suite 410
North York, ON
M2P 2C8
Canada
Contact: Edmund G. Odette, President
Geographic Giving Pattern: Ontario, with an emphasis on Toronto.
Special Interest: The arts (especially galleries and music), Catholic churches, Catholic organizations, healthcare, the mentally disabled, and community services.
Assets: CAN $3,183,321
Grant Total: CAN $327,690
Grant Range: CAN $50–$250,000
Applications: Initial approach should be by letter.

Organisation Catholique Canadienne pour le Developpement et la Paix
Canadian Catholic Organization for Development and Peace
5633 Sherbrooke Street East
Montréal
Quebec H1N 1A3
Canada
(514) 257-8711
(514) 257-8497 (fax)
Contact: Project Officer for appropriate region (see below)
Geographic Giving Pattern: Anglophone Africa, Francophone Africa, South America, Andean Region, Central America, and the Caribbean.
Special Interest: Socio-economic development, women, human rights, environment, preventative care, nutrition, and leadership training. Ten percent of funding is for emergency aid.
Sources of Income: Share Lent campaign, Fall Action campaign, and the Canadian government.
Grant Total: $8,640,000
Limitations: No grants to individuals. No support for formal education, construction, or equipment.
Applications: Proposal and detailed budget should be written in English, French, Spanish, or Portuguese and may be submitted at any time.

Our Lady of the Prairies Foundation
822 Whitewood Crescent
Saskatoon, SK
S75 4L1
Canada
Contact: Patricia J. Sikler, Secretary
Geographic Giving Pattern: Primarily Saskatchewan.
Special Interest: Religious and educational charities, Catholic churches, Catholic organizations, religious education, family and community services, hospitals, healthcare, and housing.
Assets: CAN $3,615,507
Grant Total: CAN $112,364
Grant Range: CAN $1,000-$50,000
Applications: Initial approach should be by letter.

Stephen B. Roman Foundation

P.O. Box 82
Suite 1315
200 King Street West
Toronto, ON
M5H 3T4
Canada
(416) 971-3323
Contact: Julie Lofeodo, Secretary
Geographic Giving Pattern: Canada.
Special Interest: Hospitals, healthcare, the performing arts, higher education, Catholic churches, Catholic religious organizations, and social services.
Assets: CAN $339,214
Grant Total: CAN $54,500
Grant Range: CAN $500–$50,000
Applications: Initial approach should be by letter. The deadline is September 30.

Roncalli International Foundation

1940 Henri Bourassa Boulevard East
Suite 314
Montréal
Quebec H2B 1S1
Canada
(514) 384-5400
(514) 384-9932 (fax)
Contact: Gilles Trahan, Executive Director
Geographic Giving Pattern: Developing nations only.
Special Interest: Health, education, training, aid to churches evangelization, infrastructures, and research.
Applications: Initial approach should be by letter. An application form is required. The board meets four times a year. Applications are accepted at any time.

DENMARK

Caritas Danmark
Vibevej 7 A, 1
Copenhagen 2400
Denmark
(4538) 10-30-49
(4538) 10-53-40 (fax)
Email: caritas@caritas.dk
Contact: René Albeck, Secretary General
Geographic Giving Pattern: Africa, Southeast Asia, Latin America, Eastern Europe, and Denmark.
Description: Caritas Denmark is part of the international Catholic network of Caritas agencies.
Special Interest: Socio-economic development, women, children, the elderly, the disabled, refugees, vocational training, healthcare, nutrition, literacy, rural development, and emergency aid.
Sources of Income: Catholic collections, individuals, legacies, the Danish International Development Agency, and the EC.
Grant Total: $10,000,000
Applications: Proposals should be written in English, French, German, or Spanish and may be submitted at any time.

Nordisk Katolsk Udviklingshjaelp
Nordic Catholic Development Aid
Caritas Danmark
Vibevej 7 A, 1
Copenhagen 2400
Denmark
(4538) 10-30-49
(4538) 10-53-40 (fax)
Contact: René Albeck, Secretary General, Caritas Danmark
Geographic Giving Pattern: Africa, Asia, Latin America, and the Pacific.
Special Interest: Socio-economic assistance to the most needy in developing countries according to each year's theme as decided by the Nordic Catholic Bishops' Conference.
Sources of Income: Lenten collections in the Scandinavian countries.

Grant Total: $302,000
Limitations: Project expenses must be less than $50,000 to qualify for consideration. Proposals must be approved by the local national CARITAS organization.
Applications: Proposals should be written in English, French, German, or Spanish. The application deadline is September 1.

ENGLAND

CAFOD
Catholic Fund for Overseas Development
2 Romero Close
Stockwell Road
London SW9 9TY
England
44 20 7733 7900
44 20 7274 9630 (fax)
Email: hqcafod@cafod.org.uk
Contact: Julian Filochowski, Director
Geographic Giving Pattern: Africa, Asia, Latin America, and the Pacific.
Description: CAFOD is the official organization of the Bishops' Conference of England and Wales and is a member of CIDSE and Caritas International.
Special Interest: Socio-economic development including food production, agriculture, water, AIDS control and prevention, preventative health, vocational training, and non-formal education. Emphasis is placed on ecumenical collaboration.
Sources of Income: Twice a year collections in churches, individuals, voluntary agencies, and the British government.
Grant Total: $27,000,000
Limitations: Funding is limited to programs that come from local NGOs or church networks in southern countires. No support for construction of hospitals, churches, chapels, or seminaries. No support for primary and secondary education or housing programs.
Applications: Initial approach should be by letter requesting application guidelines. Projects are approved three times a year.

Catholic Institute for International Relations (CIIR)

Unit 3 Canonbury Yard
190a New North Road
Islington
London N1 7BJ
England
(44171) 354-0883
(44171) 359-0017 (fax)
Geographic Giving Pattern: South Africa, Somalia, Yemen, Philippines, Hong Kong, Haiti, and the Dominican Republic.
Description: CIIR is an educational charity which recruits and sends skilled and experienced people to work as volunteers in small-scale development projects overseas. CIIR provides personnel, research, information, and solidarity action on justice and human rights issues.
Special Interest: Volunteers participate in programs for rural development, nutrition, urban housing, primary healthcare, agriculture, rural community schools, and forestry.
Limitations: CIIR is not a funding agency.
Applications: Initial approach should be by letter describing need. Letters may be submitted at any time.

Christian Aid

Inter-Church House
35 Lower Marsh
London SE1 7RL
England
(44171) 620-4444
(44171) 620-0719 (fax)
Geographic Giving Pattern: Africa, Asia, Latin America, the Middle East, the Caribbean, and the Pacific.
Description: Christian Aid is the relief and developing agency of 41 sponsoring British churches and works primarily through ecumenical and church-related structures.
Special Interest: Church-based socio-economic development to strengthen the poor, human rights, environment, women, children, refugees, and emergency aid.
Sources of Income: Individuals, the British churches, English and Irish government support, and the EC.
Grant Total: $68,000,000

Applications: Initial approach should be by letter requesting application guidelines. Proposals should be written in English, French, Spanish, or Portuguese and may be submitted at any time. The application address is P.O. Box 100, London SE1 7RT, England.

Volunteer Missionary Movement (VMM)
1 Stockwell Green
London SW9 9HP
England
(44171) 737-3678
(44171) 737-3237 (fax)
Geographic Giving Pattern: Africa.
Description: VMM is an ecumenical movement within the Catholic church which responds to requests from project-holders and tries to match the needs with available volunteers.
Special Interest: Provides volunteers for development projects in educational, medical, technical, community, and pastoral work. The lay missionaries work in Catholic and other Christian mission projects.
Sources of Income: Individuals, voluntary agencies, and host missions.
Limitations: VMM is not a funding agency.
Applications: Proposals should be written in English and may be submitted at any time. Commitment of the volunteer is for a minimum of two years. The costs of recruiting, preparing, and sending a volunteer overseas are shared by VMM and the receiving project.

FRANCE

Comité Catholique contre la Faim et pour le Développment (CCFD)
Catholic Committee Against Hunger and for Development
4, Rue Jean Lantier
75001 Paris
France
(331) 448-28000
(331) 448-28144 (fax)
Geographic Giving Pattern: Africa, Asia, Latin America, and the Pacific.

Special Interest: Socio-economic development, health, sanitation, agricultural development, and leadership training. Special attention is given to those who work for reconciliation, the promotion of peace, and a just distribution of resources.
Sources of Income: Lenten campaign and a public campaign.
Grant Total: $28,000,000
Limitations: No grants for building projects.
Applications: Proposals are accepted at any time.

Oeuvre D'Orient

20 rue du Regard
75006 Paris
France
(331) 4548-5446
(331) 4284-0597 (fax)
Geographic Giving Pattern: The Near East.
Description: Oeuvre D'Orient works in an ecumenical spirit in order to help Oriental populations to bring about the unity of all Christians, to be a living presence of the church, and to support all Catholic activities in the Orient.
Special Interest: Aid to Oriental churches to alleviate the misery and suffering of the poor by means of education, the promotion of human rights, and the advancement of the Faith. Support for building schools, dispensaries, seminaries, hospitals, mission houses, churches, and formation programs for members of religious communities.
Sources of Income: Catholic offerings and collections.
Grant Total: $7,500,000
Applications: Proposals are accepted any time and should be written in English.

Secours Catholique
Caritas France

106, Rue du Bac
Paris Cedex 07
France 75341
(331) 45-49-73-00
(331) 45-49-94-50 (fax)
Email: dir-action-france-international@secours-catholique.assoc.fr

Contact: Jean Celier, Secretary General
Geographic Giving Pattern: Primarily Africa; some support for Asia, Latin America, and the Pacific.
Description: Secours Catholique is part of the international Catholic network of Caritas agencies.
Special Interest: Emergency aid and development assistance especially in the following areas: women, children, the elderly, the disabled, human rights, the environment, leadership training, formal education, literacy, cooperatives, appropriate technology, healthcare, nutrition, rural development, and water.
Grant Total: $30,000,000
Limitations: No grants to individuals.
Applications: Proposals for development must be submitted through the national Caritas organization. Preference is given to broad, multi-year programs rather than limited, small-scale projects. Proposals should be written in French, English, or Spanish and are accepted at any time.

GERMANY

Aid to the Church in Need
Postfach 1209
D – 61452 Konigstein
Germany
(4961) 742-910
(4961) 743-423 (fax)
Geographic Giving Pattern: Africa, Asia, Latin America, the Pacific, Eastern Europe, and the former Soviet Union.
Special Interest: Aid to the persecuted and menaced Catholic church in developing countries. Aid to the Catholic church in the former Soviet Union and the Orthodox church in Russia. Support for training seminarians and laity involved in pastoral work, formation of priests and religious, evangelization, church construction, transportation, provision of religious books, and mass media projects.
Sources of Income: Individuals and private donations.
Grant Total: $56,700,000
Applications: Proposals may be submitted at any time. Approval of the local bishop or local religious superior is required.

Arbeitsgemeinschaft für Entwicklungshilfe e. V. (AGEH)
Association for Development Cooperation
Ripuarenstraße 8
50679 Köln
Germany
(49-221) 8896-0
(49-221) 8896-100 (fax)
Email: AGEH-Mail@t-online.de
www.ageh.de
Contact: Katharina Engels
Geographic Giving Pattern: Africa, Asia, Latin America, and
Eastern Europe.
Special Interest: Placing of personnel for development projects of
local, mainly Catholic, partner organizations in developing countries.
Sources of Income: German Catholic development agencies.
Limitations: The organization is not a funding agency. Development
co-workers will be provided only if financial costs of their commitment
is defrayed by the domestic project head or a relief organization.
Applications: Proposals detailing position(s) needed to be filled,
qualifications desired, and assignments should be submitted first to
cooperating German Catholic relief organizations.

BEGECA
Postfach 109
D – 52064 Aachen
Germany
(49241) 477-980
(49241) 477-9840 (fax)
Geographic Giving Pattern: Africa, Asia, Latin America, and
Eastern and Central Europe.
Special Interest: Provides advice on purchasing and shipping
materials for church-related and charitable groups including vehicles,
medical equipment and supplies, building and printing materials, and
fertilizers. In emergencies BEGECA can rapidly send machines, food,
and tents.
Applications: Initial approach should be by letter expressing need,
description of item required, and precise geographical location. Letters
should be written in English, German, French, or Spanish and may be
submitted at any time.

Bischöfliche Aktion ADVENIAT
Postfach 100152
43001 Essen
Germany
(49201) 175-60
(49201) 175-6111 (fax)
Geographic Giving Pattern: Latin America and the Caribbean.
Special Interest: Evangelization, pastoral development, church support, religious education, apostolic movements, and some support for students.
Sources of Income: Individual donations and a Christmas collection.
Grant Total: $125,000,000
Applications: Application proposals must come directly from Latin America or the Caribbean. Proposals are accepted at any time and should be written in Spanish, Portuguese, English, or French. A letter of endorsement from the local bishop or religious superior is required. The Board of German Bishops meets three times a year to decide on all requests after a formal review by staff.

Catholic Biblical Federation (CBF)
Postfach 105222
70045 Stuttgart
Germany
(49711) 169-240
(49711) 169-2424 (fax)
Contact: General Secretary
Geographic Giving Pattern: Global, especially local churches in developing countries.
Description: CBF is a federation of biblical organizations serving local churches in matters related to the biblical apostolate.
Special Interest: Provides advice and information in the field of biblical-pastoral work.
Limitations: CBF is not a funding agency.
Applications: An agency form is required and should be completed in English, Dutch, German, or Spanish. There are no deadlines.

Catholic Media Council (CAMECO)
Postfach 1912
D – 52021 Aachen
Germany
(490) 241-73081
(490) 241-73462 (fax)
Geographic Giving Pattern: Africa, Asia, Latin America, and the Pacific.
Special Interest: Professional advice and evaluation of media and communication projects.
Sources of Income: Church funding agencies.
Limitations: CAMECO does not award grants nor does it channel projects to other funding agencies. It does, however, aid project leaders in preparing projects and applications.
Applications: Initial approach should be by letter requesting guidelines. Correspondence should be in Dutch, English, French, German, Portuguese, or Spanish. CAMECO may be contacted at any time.

Deutscher Caritasverband
Caritas Germany
Lorenz-Werthmann-Haus, Karlstrasse 40
Postfach 420
D – 79004 Freiburg im Breisgau
Germany
(49761) 20-01-0
(49761) 20-05-72 (fax)
Email: contact@caritas-international.de
Contact: Georg Cremer, Secretary General
Geographic Giving Pattern: Africa, Asia, Latin America, the Pacific, Germany, and Eastern Europe.
Description: Deutscher Caritasverband E.V. is part of the international Catholic network of Caritas agencies.
Special Interest: Socio-economic development, emergency relief, rehabilitation, and strengthening infrastructure.
Sources of Income: Private and church donations, public sources, German government support, and EC support.
Grant Total: $86,000,000
Grant Range: $1,500–$16,000
Applications: Proposals may be submitted at any time.

Katholischer Akademischer Auslander-Dienst (KAAD)
Catholic Service for Foreign Students
Hausdorffstrasse 151
53129 Bonn
Germany
(49228) 917-580
(49228) 917-5858 (fax)
Geographic Giving Pattern: Africa, Asia, Latin America, and
Eastern Europe.
Special Interest: Scholarships for post-graduate university studies
that contain a development factor. Support for Catholic churches in
developing countries in their effort to educate young Christian
academics who can show leadership in their countries' social, cultural,
and intellectual life.
Sources of Income: Donations of German Catholic dioceses and the
German government.
Grant Total: $6,300,000
Limitations: Should the student not return to the home country as
promised, all scholarship grant money must be repaid.
Applications: An application form is required. Applications should be
submitted prior to January 15 or July 15.

Misereor
German Catholic Bishops' Organization for Development
Cooperation
Postfach 1450
D – 52015 Aachen
Germany
(49241) 442-1434
(49241) 442-188 (fax)
Geographic Giving Pattern: Africa, Asia, Latin America, and the
Pacific.
Special Interest: Socio-economic development, human rights, adult
education, health, and social welfare.
Sources of Income: Lenten campaign, church funds, and German
government funds.
Grant Total: $245,000,000
Applications: Proposals should be written in English, French, German,
Spanish, or Portuguese and may be submitted at any time. Local

participation in the project is essential, and projects with long-term solution goals are preferred.

Missio Aachen
Internationales Katholisches Missionwerk
Postfach 1110
D – 5100 Aachen
Germany
(49241) 750-700
(49241) 750-7335 (fax)
Contact: The Project Department
Geographic Giving Pattern: Africa, Asia, and the Pacific.
Special Interest: Pastoral projects, evangelization, youth ministry, leadership training, and scholarships to church personnel from developing countries for studies in philosophy and theology.
Sources of Income: Collections from German Catholics, and church tax through the German Bishops Conference.
Grant Total: $112,000,000
Limitations: Generally does not support construction projects or appeals for vehicles.
Applications: Application proposals should be written in Spanish, German, English, or French and may be submitted at any time.

Missio München
Postfach 20-14-42
D – 80014 München
Germany
(4989) 51620
(4989) 5162-335 (fax)
Contact: Marianne Böld, Director, Project Department
Geographic Giving Pattern: Africa, Asia, and the Pacific.
Special Interest: Pastoral projects, religious formation, church leadership training (clergy and lay), evangelization, communications, and missionary efforts.
Sources of Income: Collections from German Catholics, individuals, and Catholic church groups.
Grant Total: $112,000,000
Limitations: No grants to individuals or for salaries, running costs, endowment funds, or deficit financing.

Applications: Proposals should be written in Spanish, English, or French. A letter of endorsement is requested from the local diocesan bishop or religious superior. Local contribution is required. There are no deadlines.

Päpstliches Missionswerk Der Kinder in Deutschland
Pontifical Society for the Holy Child in Germany

Stephanstrasse 35
52064 Aachen
Germany
(49241) 446-10
(49241) 446-140 (fax)
Contact: Monsignor Poll, Chairman
Geographic Giving Pattern: Africa, Asia, Latin America, and the Pacific.
Special Interest: Pastoral and social aid for poor children, especially in areas of Bible projects, catechesis, schools, water supply, vocational training, day care centers, health, nutrition and relief.
Sources of Income: Donations collected by German churches.
Grant Total: $28,900,000
Grant Average: $15,000
Applications: Proposals should be written in German, Spanish, English, or French. A letter of endorsement is required from the local bishop. The deadlines are April 1 and September 1.

Renovabis
Solidaritatsaktion der Deutschen Katholiken mit den
Menschen in Mittel – und Osteuropa

Domberg 27
D – 85354 Freising
Germany
(498161) 530-90
(498161) 530-911 (fax)
Contact: P. Eugen Hillengass, S.J., Geschaftsfuhrer
Geographic Giving Pattern: Central and Eastern Europe, Russia, and the former Soviet Union.
Special Interest: Training theological students and catechists, feeding the poor, ecumenical projects with the Orthodox church, and nursing.
Sources of Income: Church tax and private donations.

Grant Total: $42,600,000

Applications: Proposals should include an exact description of the project and a financial plan, and must include a letter of support from the local bishop. Proposals may be submitted at any time.

HONG KONG

Asia Partnership for Human Development (APHD)
Suite 3A
Hing Wah Commercial Building
450-454 Shanghai Street
Kowloon
Hong Kong
(852) 2771-7993
(852) 2770-1823 (fax)
Contact: Executive Secretary
Geographic Giving Pattern: Asia (excluding the Middle East).
Special Interest: The poor and marginalized, especially workers, peasants, farmers, fishermen, the urban poor, youth, students, cultural minorities, indigenous peoples, and political prisoners. Support also for women and the environment.
Sources of Income: Grants from member agencies.
Grant Total: $3,500,000
Limitations: No grants for projects of an exclusively pastoral nature. No grants for education, research, equipment, vehicles, or operating costs of schools, churches, and hospitals. No grants for emergency relief or deficit financing. No grants for individuals.
Applications: Proposals should be written in English and may be submitted at any time.

IRELAND

Trocaire - Caritas Ireland
169 Booterstown Avenue
Blackrock
Co. Dublin
Ireland
(3531) 288-5385

(3531) 288-6022 (fax) and
(3531) 288-3577 (fax)
Email: postmaster@trocaire.ie
Contact: Justin Kilcullen, Director
Geographic Giving Pattern: Africa, Cambodia, Laos, Vietnam, and Latin America.
Special Interest: Development projects, education, and emergency relief. Priority is for projects which address inequalities and discrimination and which allow the oppressed to participate in their struggle for self-determination. Specific areas of interest include social services (especially aiding refugees, women, children, the elderly, and the disabled), human rights, leadership, and vocational training, micro-enterprise, literacy, preventive medicine, small rural health schemes, and rural development.
Sources of Income: Lenten campaign, individual donations, Irish government support, and the EC.
Grant Total: $27,800,000
Limitations: No grants for large buildings or institutions.
Applications: Proposals should be written in English, French, or Spanish. There are no deadlines.

ITALY

Agrimissio
International Catholic Rural Association
Piazza San Calisto, 16
00153 Roma
Italy
(3906) 871-23
Contact: Executive Director
Geographic Giving Pattern: Africa, Asia, Latin America, and the Pacific.
Special Interest: Provides agricultural information to help fight hunger. Some modest funds for training farmers and other grassroots projects.
Sources of Income: Catholic individuals.
Applications: Application letters should be written in English, French, or Spanish, and should be submitted in April or October.

Associazione Italiana Amici Di Raoul Follereau (AIFO)
Via Borselli 4
40135 Bologna
Italy
(3951) 433-402
(3951) 434-046 (fax)
Contact: Project Office
Geographic Giving Pattern: Africa, Asia, Latin America, and the Pacific.
Special Interest: Leprosy, especially efforts to control the disease and rehabilitate persons living with leprosy. Some funding for the rehabilitation of persons with other diseases.
Grant Total: $4,500,000
Limitations: Projects must be related to leprosy or rehabilitation, must have the involvement of Italian missionaries, and must have local government approval.
Applications: Proposals should be written in English, French, Italian, or Portuguese. If board accepts proposal in principle, an application form will be provided. Proposals may be submitted at any time.

Conferenza Episcopale Italiana (C.E.I.)
Circonvallazione Aurelia, 50
00165 Roma, Italia
(3906) 663-981
(3906) 662-30-37 (fax)
Contact: Cardinal Camillo Ruini, President
Description: CEI is the Italian Bishops Conference
Special Interest: To advance and support the ministry of the Catholic church, especially evangelization, pastoral care, catechesis, and liturgical life.

Multimedia International (MI)
Via Aurelia 290
00165 Roma
Italy
(3906) 637-1364
Geographic Giving Pattern: Africa, Asia, Latin America, and the Pacific.
Description: MI helps the generalates of religious congregations and international colleges in Rome to understand the modern media and to

bring the media more fully into the church's apostolic and pastoral work.
Special Interest: Pastoral communications and evangelization.
Limitations: MI is not a funding agency.
Applications: Letters requesting further information are accepted at any time.

OCIC Missionary Service
International Catholic Organization for Cinema and Audiovisual

Palazzo San Calisto
00120 Citta del Vaticano
Italy
(3906) 698-87255
(3906) 698-87335 (fax)
Geographic Giving Pattern: Africa, Asia, Latin America, and the Pacific.
Special Interest: Development of cinema, video, and audio-visuals for the purpose of evangelization.
Sources of Income: Pontifical Society for the Propagation of the Faith.
Grant Total: $500,000 each year
Applications: Initial approach should be by letter requesting an application form. A letter of endorsement from the local bishop is required. The deadline is October 1.

Opera Di Promozione Dell'Alfabetizzazione Nel Mondo (OPAM)

Via Monte della Farina 64
00186 Roma
Italy
(3906) 687-5351
(3906) 689-3738 (fax)
Contact: Mons. Carlo Muratore, President or Don Gabriele Fantinati, Director
Geographic Giving Pattern: Africa, Asia, and Latin America.
Special Interest: Socio-economic development, literacy projects with local contributions, women and children, human rights, education, rural development, and technical centers for agriculture and handicrafts.

Grant Total: $578,233
Grant Average: $2,000
Applications: Initial approach should be by letter requesting the agency's application form. Agency forms may be completed in English, French, Italian, or Spanish and may be submitted at any time.

Pontifical Association of the Holy Childhood

Piazza di Spagna 48
00187 Roma
Italy
(3906) 679-6322
(3906) 699-41949 (fax)
Geographic Giving Pattern: Africa, Asia, Latin America, the Middle East, and the Pacific.
Special Interest: Children, especially catechetical education, apostolic movements, maintenance and teaching materials for primary schools, homes for disabled children, orphanages, and child care.
Sources of Income: Donations by children in all countries through diocesan and national associations.
Grant Total: $16,230,370
Applications: An application form is required. A letter of recommendation from the local bishop is required. The deadline is December 15.

Pontifical Council Cor Unum

Piazza San Calisto 16
00120 Citta del Vaticano
(3906) 887-331
(3906) 887-301 (fax)
Email: corunum@corunum.va
Contact: Bishop Paul Josef Cordes, President
Special Interest: To assist the Holy Father to carry out special initiatives and humanitarian activities when disaster occurs; to foster charity; and human development.
Grant Total: $1,237,000

Pontifical Society for the Propagation of the Faith

Via di Propaganda 1/c
00187 Roma
Italy

(3906) 6994-2071
(3906) 6994-2193 (fax)
Geographic Giving Pattern: Africa, Asia, Latin America, and the Pacific.
Special Interest: Pastoral and evangelical projects, religious formation, construction and renovation of buildings, vehicles, and catechetical support.
Sources of Income: Collections in 115 countries by the National Pontifical Society for the Propagation of the Faith.
Grant Total: $120,000,000
Limitations: No support for socio-economic projects, schools, or health projects. The total cost of a project is never funded.
Applications: Initial approach should be by letter requesting application form. Written approval of the local bishop is required. Local bishops should forward applications through the Apostolic Nuncio. Completed applications must reach Rome by December 15.

Pontifical Works of St. Peter Apostle

Via di Propaganda, 1c
00187 Roma
Italy
(3906) 6994-1946
(3906) 6994-2193 (fax)
Geographic Giving Pattern: Africa, Asia, Latin America, and Oceania.
Special Interest: Seminaries in developing countries, scholarships for seminarians and women religious, and pastoral support.
Sources of Income: Church collections, wills, and burses.
Grant Total: $55,000,000
Applications: Project proposals must include written approval of the local bishop. The project should be submitted through the local papal representative. The deadline is prior to December 15.

SEDOS

Via dei Verbiti 1
00154 Roma
Italy
(3906) 574-1350
(3906) 575-5787 (fax)

Geographic Giving Pattern: Africa, Asia, Latin America, and the Pacific.

Description: SEDOS is a membership organization in which religious and missionary institutes of women and men combine their resources in order to serve the Catholic church more effectively in her missionary activity.

Special Interest: Education, experiences, ideas, and practical guidelines relating to missionary work are exchanged through the network.

Limitations: SEDOS is not a funding agency.

Applications: Letters of inquiry regarding membership are accepted at any time.

JAPAN

Japan Lay Missionary Movement (JLMM)
Catholic Center, 6F
2-10-10 Shiomi
Koto-ku
Tokyo 135
Japan

Geographic Giving Pattern: Africa, Asia, Latin America, and the Pacific.

Description: JLMM is a Catholic nonprofit which supports and promotes efforts for self-sufficiency.

Special Interest: Personnel able to provide advice and management services for socio-economic development. The focus is on income generation through cooperatives, appropriate technology, rural development, and agriculture. JLMM is committed to the promotion of appropriate local cultural and technical advancement.

Sources of Income: Donations from Japanese Catholics.

Applications: Initial approach should be by letter outlining the project and personnel need. Letters should be submitted in Japanese or English and may be sent at any time.

LUXEMBOURG

Bridderlech Delen
Lenten Campaign in Luxembourg
5 Avenue Marie-Thérese
L – 2132 Luxembourg
(352) 4474-3258
(352) 4474-3231 (fax)
Contact: Lony Bermes, Desk Officer
Geographic Giving Pattern: Africa, Asia, and Latin America.
Special Interest: Social services, especially benefiting women, children, the elderly, or the disabled. Support also for human rights, formation of church personnel, leadership, vocational training, micro-enterprise, communications, literacy, healthcare, nutrition, and rural development.
Sources of Income: Lenten collection.
Grant Total: $1,600,000
Grant Average: $5,000–$6,000
Limitations: Supports small scale development projects only.
Applications: An application form is required. Proposals should be written in English, French, or German and may be submitted at any time. A letter of recommendation from the local bishop is required.

NETHERLANDS

Advieskommissie Missionaire Aktiviteiten (AMA)
Postbus 75
2340 AB Oegstgeest
Netherlands
(3171) 515-9159
(3171) 517-5391 (fax)
Geographic Giving Pattern: Africa, Asia, Latin America, the Caribbean, and the Pacific.
Special Interest: Parish renewal, pastoral development, lay ministry, religious education, and assistance to religious congregations.
Sources of Income: Contributions of the religious institutions in the Netherlands.
Grant Total: $5,000,000
Grant Average: $7,000

Limitations: Funds pastoral projects only. Generally does not support construction projects or appeals for vehicles.

Applications: Proposals should be written in Dutch, Spanish, Portuguese, English, French, or Bahasa Indonesian. A letter of recommendation from a higher religious authority is preferred but not required. There are no deadlines.

Aktie en Ontmoetins Oosterse Kerken
Apostolate for the Oriental Churches

Dr. Nuijensstraat 4
5014 RL Tilburg
Netherlands
(3113) 536-8985
(3113) 543-9510 (fax)

Geographic Giving Pattern: The Near East, Ethiopia, India, Eastern Europe, and Eastern immigrant churches in the West.

Special Interest: Small pastoral and ecumenical projects of exclusively Oriental Christian communities, both Catholic and Orthodox. The aim of the fund is to contribute to the unity of the church.

Sources of Income: Primarily contributions of Catholics in the Sunday for the Oriental Churches collection.

Grant Total: $60,000

Limitations: Long-term projects are not accepted. Projects must be ecumenical in nature.

Applications: Proposals must be endorsed by local ecclesiastical authorities and should be submitted before April.

Caritas Neerlandica
Stichting Mensen in Nood
Caritas Netherlands

Postbus 1041
NL – 5200 BA's-Hertogenbosch
Netherlands
(3173) 645-6789
(3173) 645-6700 (fax)

Contact: Jaap van Soest, Director

Geographic Giving Pattern: Africa, Asia, Latin America, and Europe.

Description: Caritas Neerlandica Stichting Mensen in Nood is part of the international Catholic network of Caritas agencies.

Special Interest: Emergency relief, refugee aid, food, nutrition, social services, children, and youth.

Grant Total: $43,600,000

Limitations: No pastoral or medical projects are considered.

Applications: Initial approach should be to request the agency's project questionnaire. There are no deadlines.

Centraal Missie Commissie

P.O. Box 16442
2500 BK DEN HAAG
The Netherlands
(3171) 3136700
(3171) 3136777 (fax)
Email: cmcm@antenna.nl

Contact: Janet van der Voort, Secretaresse Communicatie

Geographic Giving Pattern: Africa, Asia, and Latin America.

Description: CMC is mandated by the joint Dutch Catholic religious institutions to operate at the service of missionary activities. CMC screens and selects volunteers in the field of development and pastoral work on behalf of Catholic churches and church organizations. CMC funds pastoral projects through Advieskommissie Missionaire Aktiviteiten – AMA. (See entry in this section, page 427.)

Special Interest: Development and pastoral work.

Sources of Income: Dutch religious institutions and national fundraising.

Applications: Initial approach should be by letter. A questionnaire is required. There are no deadlines.

Centrum Lektuurvoorziening voor Missionarissen ed Kerken Overzee (CLM)

Gasthuisring 54
5041 DT Tilburg
Netherlands
(3113) 422-118
(3113) 441-405 (fax)

Contact: Mrs. R. van Grinsven, Director

Geographic Giving Pattern: Developing countries.

Special Interest: CLM orders books, periodicals, and catechetical materials at the highest discount possible and provides free subscriptions and donations for libraries.

Sources of Income: Dutch collections, Lenten campaign, and the Brothers of Tilburg.

Limitations: CLM is not a funding agency.

Applications: Initial approach should be by letter requesting detailed information. Letters should be written in English, Dutch, French, German, Portuguese, or Spanish. Letters may be sent at any time.

Ecumenical Development Cooperative Society (EDCS)

P.C. Hooftlaan 3
3818 HG Amersfoort
Netherlands
(3133) 463-3122
(3133) 465-0336 (fax)

Geographic Giving Pattern: Africa, Asia, Latin America, and the Pacific.

Special Interest: Loans to aid grassroots efforts to create productive enterprises especially regarding ecumenical projects, women, income generation, cooperatives, agriculture, food production, and equipment.

Sources of Income: Investments by churches, religious orders, and individuals.

Loan Total: $20,000,000

Loan Average: $250,000

Applications: Initial approach should be by letter showing evidence of feasibility study for repayment of loan. Proposals should be written in English, German, French, Portuguese, or Spanish. Applications may be submitted at any time. EDCS local offices which may also be contacted are the following: Asia: 23 Babinda Street, Keperra, Brisbane 4054, Australia. Africa: P.O. Box 1305 Freetown, Sierra Leone and P.O. Box 2340 Harara, Zimbabwe. Central America and the Caribbean: Apto. Postal 1023, 1002 San José, Costa Rica. South America: P. 11 Esc. 1005, Calle Paraguay 1547, Montevideo, Uruguay. Philippines: Rm. 342, J&T Bldg, 3894 R. Magsaysay Blvd, Sta. Mesa, Manila, Philippines. U.S.A.: Rm. 627, 155 N. Michigan Avenue, Chicago, IL 60601, U.S.A.

Interdenominational Foundation for Aid to Missionworkers (IFAM)

Postbus 160
5000 AD Tilburg
Netherlands
(3113) 536-2026
(3113) 542-7489 (fax)
Geographic Giving Pattern: Africa, Asia, Latin America, and the Pacific.
Special Interest: Subsidies for missionary travel by air to and from Europe, Africa, Asia, the Middle East, and Latin America.
Sources of Income: Contributions from church organizations.
Limitations: Subsidies are available for reserved regular fare tickets on selected airlines. Subsidies vary from 10-35% of cost of travel.
Applications: Initial approach should be by letter.

MIVA Netherlands
Missie Verkeersmiddelen Aktie

12 Vijverstraat
4818 ST Breda
Netherlands
(3176) 521-7150
(3176) 520-3530 (fax)
Contact: Dr. Han B. van Peer
Geographic Giving Pattern: Africa, Asia, Latin America, and the Pacific.
Special Interest: Transportation for Catholic Dutch missionaries and their co-workers to be used for pastoral work.
Grant Total: $3,500,000
Grant Range: $10,000 or less.
Limitations: Very rarely is transport aid given to non-Dutch missionaries.
Applications: An application form is required. Application forms are available in Dutch, English, French, Portuguese, and Spanish. Requests should be submitted in the name of the future user of the vehicle, not in the name of the diocese or organization which will become the formal owner. The deadline is February 1.

Solidaridad
Ecumenical Action for Latin America
Goedestraat 2
3572 RT Utrecht
Netherlands
(3130) 272-0313
(3130) 272-0194 (fax)
Geographic Giving Pattern: Latin America, especially Mexico, Guatemala, Honduras, El Salvador, Nicaragua, Costa Rica, Columbia, Ecuador, Peru, Bolivia, Chile, Haiti, Dominican Republic, Brazil, and Argentina.
Special Interest: Socio-economic development. Emphasis is on fair trade, religion, indigenous groups, culture, women's rights, human rights, communications, and building social movements.
Sources of Income: Catholic and Protestant churches and the general public.
Grant Total: $3,000,000
Limitations: No grants to individuals. Grants are for grass roots organizations only.
Applications: Initial approach should be by letter which may be sent at any time.

SCOTLAND

Scottish Catholic International Aid Fund (SCIAF)
19 Park Circus
Glasgow G3 6BE
Scotland
(44141) 354-5555
(44141) 354-5533 (fax)
Email: sciaf@sciaf.org.uk
Contact: Paul Chitnis, Executive Director
Geographic Giving Pattern: SubSaharan Africa, Latin America, and India.
Description: SCIAF is the official overseas agency of the Catholic church in Scotland supporting emergency and development projects with the intention of empowering the poor.
Special Interest: Socio-economic development, preventative healthcare, food production, leadership training, water projects, women, relief work, and AIDS prevention.

Sources of Income: The Catholic community in Scotland, an annual Lenten appeal, the British government, and the EC.
Grant Total: $2,750,000
Applications: Initial approach should be by proposal letter including budget and evidence of local participation. There are no deadlines.

SPAIN

Intermon
Calle Roger De Llúria, 15
08010 Barcelona
Spain
(343) 301-2936
(343) 301-2221 (fax)
Geographic Giving Pattern: Africa, Asia, Latin America, and the Pacific.
Description: Intermon was founded by the Jesuits in 1956 as a non-governmental organization that works for development in the most deprived countries of the world.
Special Interest: Provides funding for socio-economic development projects in the following areas: farming, health, communications, housing, social development, human rights, refugees, emergency relief, and education. Intermon also provides training and information.
Grant Total: $25,000,000
Applications: Initial approach should be by letter. There are no deadlines.

Manos Unidas
Campaña Contra El Hambre
Barquillo 38 3
28004 Madrid
Spain
(341) 308-2020
(341) 308-4208 (fax)
Geographic Giving Pattern: Africa, Asia, Latin America, and the Pacific.
Special Interest: Agriculture, health, social development, and education.
Sources of Income: Catholic collections, and private and government donations.

Grant Total: $70,000,000
Applications: An application form is required. There are no deadlines.

SWITZERLAND

Brücke der Bruderhilfe
Postfach 349
8031 Zürich
Switzerland
(411) 271-0530
(411) 271-0543 (fax)
Geographic Giving Pattern: Africa, Asia, Latin America, and the Pacific.
Special Interest: Preference is for simple, basic projects involving local initiative, socio-economic development, water, agriculture, health, women, job training, and social justice efforts.
Sources of Income: Individuals, the Swiss Catholic labor movement, and Catholic parishes.
Grant Total: $350,000
Applications: Proposals should be written in English, French, or Spanish. Applications are reviewed in February, June, September, and November.

Caritas Schweiz
Caritas Switzerland
Löwenstrasse 3
6002 Luzern
Switzerland
(4141) 419-2222
(4141) 419-2424 (fax)
Email: caritas@caritas.ch
Contact: Krummenacher Jürg , Director
Geographic Giving Pattern: Global with an emphasis on India, Pakistan, Bangladesh, Lebanon, Ethiopia, Sudan, Chad, Mali, Senegal, Uganda, El Salvador, Nicaragua, Columbia, Bolivia, Chile, and Peru.
Description: Caritas Schweiz is part of the international Catholic network of Caritas agencies.
Special Interest: Development and reconstruction, emergency relief, refugees, women and children, micro-enterprise, social services, human rights, and AIDS prevention and care.

Grant Total: $43,500,000
Limitations: No grants for church structures, evangelization, or vehicles. No grants to individuals.
Applications: An application form is required. Applications should be written in English, German, French, Spanish, or Portuguese. A letter of recommendation from the local bishop and local Caritas agency is preferred. Applications may be submitted at any time.

Freres Sans Frontieres (FSF)
Vignettaz 48
CP 129
CH – 1709 Fribourg
Switzerland
(4137) 821-240
(4137) 821-243 (fax)
Geographic Giving Pattern: Africa and Latin America.
Description: FSF is a Catholic lay organization working at the community level in developing countries. Provides French-speaking Swiss development co-workers.
Special Interest: Women, human rights, church-related projects, technology, construction, healthcare, disease prevention, nutrition, sanitation, and rural development.
Limitations: FSF is not a funding agency but does provide travel costs, insurance, and re-adjustment allowances for the co-workers.
Applications: An application form is required. Applications may be completed in French, Spanish, or Portuguese and may be submitted at any time.

International Catholic Migration Commission (ICMC)
Case Postale 96
CH – 1211
Geneva 20 CIC
Switzerland
(4122) 733-4150
(4122) 734-7929 (fax)
Contact: Mr. Thomas Barnes, Director of Operations
Geographic Giving Pattern: Africa, Asia, Latin America, the Pacific, Europe, and the United States.
Special Interest: Migrants, refugees, and displaced persons with a focus on non-material support in crises, especially program

administration, technical assistance and training, rehabilitation programs, repatriation, counselling, healthcare, and income generation.
Grant Total: $16,000,000 for managed programs and 300,000 for sponsored projects
Grant Average: $8,200
Limitations: Projects are not supported longer than two years.
Applications: Initial approach should be by letter requesting format for program submissions. Proposals should be written in English, French, or Spanish and may be submitted at any time.

Interteam
Entwicklungs-Dienst durch Freiwilligen-Einsatz
Untergeissenstein 10/12
CH – 6000 Luzern 12
Switzerland
(4141) 360-6722
(4141) 360-0580 (fax)
Contact: Mr. Klaus Wildisen, Executive Secretary
Geographic Giving Pattern: Kenya, Namibia, Tanzania, Uganda, Zambia, Papau New Guinea, the Phillipines, Bolivia, Colombia, Ecuador, Nicaragua, and Peru.
Special Interest: Provides qualified, experienced Swiss volunteers to work in the fields of socio-economic development, church-related projects, rural development, women and children, human rights, environment, leadership, vocational training, literacy, income generation, cooperatives, construction, healthcare, and technology.
Sources of Income: Swiss Catholic Lenten Fund, individuals, and the Swiss government.
Limitations: Interteam is not a funding agency.
Applications: Application letters detailing personnel need, qualifications, and assignments should be written in German, preferably, and may be submitted at any time.

Swiss Catholic Lenten Fund
Fastenopfer der Schweizer Katholiken
P.O. Box 2856
CH – 6002 Luzern
Switzerland
(4141) 210-7655
(4141) 210-1362 (fax)

Geographic Giving Pattern: Africa, Asia, and Latin America.
Special Interest: Pastoral projects including the development of
Christian communities, training of local catechists and sisters,
catechetical instruction, bible translations, communication projects,
pastoral research, and planning. Support also for socio-economic
development projects including community organizing, non-formal
education, women, and human rights.
Sources of Income: Catholic church collections from the Lenten
campaign and government grants.
Grant Total: $15,000,000
Limitations: No support for individuals.
Applications: Proposals with complete and detailed documentation
regarding the project are accepted at any time.

Swiss MIVA
Missionary Vehicle Association
Postfach 351
CH – 9500 Wil 1
Switzerland
(4171) 912-1555
(4171) 912-1557 (fax)
Geographic Giving Pattern: Africa, Asia, Latin America, and the
Pacific.
Special Interest: Vehicles for religious and lay persons to use for their
pastoral or socio-economic work.
Grant Total: $1,900,000
Limitations: No support for vehicle maintenance costs or for the
purchase of tractors. MIVA provides partial funding for vehicles and
expects the remaining cost to come from the applicant.
Applications: Initial approach should be by letter requesting an
application form. Applications should be completed in English, French,
or German. A letter of endorsement is requested from the religious
superior or the local bishop. There are no deadlines.

UNITED STATES OF AMERICA

Aid to the Church in Need
P.O. Box 576
Deer Park, NY 11729
U.S.A.
(516) 242-8321
Contact: Robert Lulley, Director
Geographic Giving Pattern: Developing nations, Eastern Europe, and the former Soviet Union.
Special Interest: Pastoral activities including the training of seminarians and women religious, reconstruction of churches and chapels, transportation for missionaries, and helping to provide religious books.
Sources of Income: Individuals.
Limitations: The U.S. office of Aid to the Church in Need does not award grants directly, but serves as an information office for its current and potential benefactors.
Applications: Applications should be sent directly to the international headquarters of Aid to the Church in Need in Germany. (See entry in this section, page 413.)

The Lynde and Harry Bradley Foundation, Inc.
See entry in Section I: Foundations, page 347.

The Robert Brunner Foundation, Inc.
See entry in Section I: Foundations, page 226.

J. Homer Butler Foundation
See entry in Section I: Foundations, page 227.

Catholic Medical Mission Board, Inc. (CMMB)
10 West 17th Street
New York, NY 10011-5765
U.S.A.
(212) 242-7757
(800) 678-5659
(212) 807-9161 (fax)
www.cmmb.org
Contact: The Director

Geographic Giving Pattern: Africa, Asia, Latin America, and the Pacific.

Special Interest: Cost-free shipments of urgently needed medicines and equipment to any Catholic institution with the internal capability of using the supplies effectively. CMMB also provides volunteer physicians, registered nurses, and dentists who help in the treatment of the poor.

Sources of Income: Gifts of medicines from pharmaceutical companies, individual donations, and USAID via Catholic Relief Service (for shipping).

Medical Supplies: Valued at $32,000,000

Limitations: CMMB is not a funding agency. Medical supplies must be dispensed to the sick poor without charge, regardless of national origin or religious affiliation.

Applications: Initial approach should be by letter or telephone requesting an application form. Applications should be completed in English and may be submitted at any time.

Catholic Near East Welfare Association
See entry in Section II: Church-based Agencies, page 359.

Catholic Relief Services (CRS)
See entry in Section II: Church-based Agencies, page 360.

Central Province Sharing Fund
See entry in Section III: Religious Communities and Fraternal Benefit Societies, page 372.

Conrad N. Hilton Fund for Sisters
10100 Santa Monica Boulevard, Suite 760
Los Angeles, CA 90067-4011
U.S.A.
(310) 785-0746
(310) 785-0166 (fax)
hltnsister@aol.com
Contact: Sr. Joyce Meyer, PBUM, Executive Director
Geographic Giving Pattern: Global, especially Africa, Asia, Latin America, and the Pacific.
Special Interest: Support for Catholic sisters who minister to the disadvantaged. Emphasis is on the promotion of systemic change and

self-reliance. Projects of interest include job-training, job creation, literacy, health promotion (especially maternal and infant healthcare services), education, agriculture, emergency relief, and refugees.
Sources of Income: The Conrad N. Hilton Foundation. (See entry in Section I: Foundations, page 205.)
Grant Total: $3,000,000 (1999)
Grant Range: $2,000–$15,000
Limitations: At least one member of the Roman Catholic religious congregation of women must be in direct service with the project during the period for which funding is requested. Projects may not receive funding more than twice in a five-year period. No support for retreat programs, prayer centers, catechists, evangelization, or the internal needs of religious congregations (such as formation and retirement), construction, land acquisition, school fees, or projects of U.S. dioceses, parishes, universities, or hospitals.
Applications: Initial approach should be by telephone of by a one-page letter requesting guidelines. The deadlines for completed applications are February 1, June 1, and October 1.

The Cottrell Foundation
See entry in Section I: Foundations, page 105.

Patrick and Anna M. Cudahy Fund
See entry in Section I: Foundations, page 349.

Dolan Family Foundation
See entry in Section I: Foundations, page 232.

The James R. Dougherty, Jr., Foundation
See entry in Section I: Foundations, page 324.

FSC Foundation
See entry in Section I: Foundations, page 109.

The Hackett Foundation, Inc.
See entry in Section I: Foundations, page 211.

Homeland Foundation, Inc.
See entry in Section I: Foundations, page 241.

The International Foundation
See entry in Section I: Foundations, page 212.

W. K. Kellogg Foundation
See entry in Section I: Foundations, page 166.

Kinnoull Foundation
See entry in Section I: Foundations, page 49.

Koch Foundation, Inc.
See entry in Section I: Foundations, page 91.

The Frances and Jane S. Lausche Foundation
See entry in Section I: Foundations, page 279.

Lithuanian Catholic Religious Aid, Inc.
351 Highland Boulevard
Brooklyn, NY 11207-1910
U.S.A.
(718) 647-2434
Contact: Vida Jankauskas, Administrator
Geographic Giving Pattern: Limited to Lithuania.
Special Interest: Catholic schools, youth organizations, summer camps, charities, and help for the economically disadvantaged.
Sources of Support: Individuals.
Assets: $877,318
Grant Average: $2,000
Limitations: No grants to individuals.
Applications: Initial approach should be by letter or telephone. An application form will be provided.

The Loyola Foundation, Inc.
See entry in Section I: Foundations, page 82.

The Henry Luce Foundation, Inc.
See entry in Section I: Foundations, page 246.

The McCaddin-McQuirk Foundation, Inc.
See entry in Section I: Foundations, page 249.

McCarthy Family Foundation
See entry in Section I: Foundations, page 143.

Isabel Medina Charitable Trust
See entry in Section I: Foundations, page 52.

MIVA America
Missionary Vehicle Association, Inc.
1400 Michigan Avenue, NE
Washington, D.C. 20017
U.S.A.
(202) 635-3444
(202) 526-0830 (fax)
mivamerica@aol.com
Geographic Giving Pattern: Africa, Asia, Latin America, and the Pacific.
Special Interest: Vehicles for missioners among the poorest and neediest, especially to bring food to the hungry, and aid to the sick and disabled.
Grant Total: $950,000
Limitations: Applicants are expected to make some contribution toward the cost of the vehicle.
Applications: An application form is required. An endorsement from the appropriate religious authority must be included in the application. Applications are accepted until February 1 for consideration in March, and until August 1 for consideration in September.

National Conference of Catholic Bishops Committee on the Church in Latin America
See entry in Section II: Church-based Agencies, page 361.

Operation Help, Inc.
P.O. Box 134
Hartly, DE 19953
U.S.A.
(302) 492-8985
Geographic Giving Pattern: Africa and Asia.
Description: Operation Help, Inc. supports with grants and advice the most forgotten and neglected missionaries and Catholic native bishops, priests, and sisters working with the poorest people.

Special Interest: Evangelization, formation of church personnel, socio-economic development, basic human needs, and emergency relief. Special attention is placed on those who find it difficult to obtain aid from other agencies due to political persecution.
Sources of Income: Private donors, missionary cooperative plans, and foundations.
Grant Total: $100,000 minimum each year
Applications: Initial approach should be by letter requesting agency's questionnaire. There are no deadlines.

Priester Foundation
See entry in Section I: Foundations, page 69.

Raptim Inservice, Ltd.
501 Madison Avenue
New York, NY 10022
U.S.A.
(212) 486-1250 or (800) 611-6333
(212) 486-7566 (fax)
Geographic Giving Pattern: Global, especially Africa, Asia, Latin America, and the Pacific.
Description: Raptim provides low, negotiated airfares for missionaries and nonprofit travelers.
Applications: Initial approach should be by telephone or letter requesting an application form and guidelines.
Please note: The following are Raptim Representatives: MTS Travel (800) 526-6278 and Christian Brothers Travel Services (800) 807-0600.

Raskob Foundation for Catholic Activities, Inc.
See entry in Section I: Foundations, page 80.

Salesian Missions
See entry in Section III: Religious Communities and Fraternal Benefit Societies, page 385.

Dr. Scholl Foundation
See entry in Section I: Foundations, page 118.

Semper Charitable Foundation
See entry in Section I: Foundations, page 61.

Serra International Foundation
65 East Wacker Place
Suite 1210
Chicago, IL 60601
U.S.A.
(312) 782-2163
Contact: Walter P. Drakis, Executive Director
Geographic Giving Pattern: National and international.
Special Interest: Vocations to the priesthood and religious life.
Sources of Income: Individuals.
Grant Total: $65,000
Grant Range: $2,000–$12,000
Limitations: No grants to individuals.
Applications: Initial approach should be by letter. An application form
is required. The deadline is December 31.

Share Foundation
Salvadoran Humanitarian Aid, Research, and Education
P.O. Box 192825
San Francisco, CA 94119
U.S.A.
(415) 882-1530
(415) 882-1540 (fax)
share@igc.apc.org
Geographic Giving Pattern: Limited to El Salvador.
Special Interest: Humanitarian aid to Salvadoran refugees and
displaced or repopulated communities.
Sources of Income: Individual donors, faith-based congregations,
religious orders, and foundations.
Grant Total: $543,014
Applications: Project proposals may be submitted in English or
Spanish at any time.

St. Roberto Bellarmin Foundation
See entry in Section I: Foundations, page 339.

Vollmer Foundation, Inc.
See entry in Section I: Foundations, page 220.

Alberto Vollmer Foundation, Inc.
See entry in Section I: Foundations, page 221.

SECTION V:
THE FOUNDATION
CENTER COOPERATING
COLLECTIONS NETWORK

Free Funding Information Centers

The Foundation Center is an independent national service organization established by foundations to provide an authoritative source of information on private philanthropic giving. The New York, Washington, D.C., Atlanta, Cleveland, and San Francisco reference collections operated by the Foundation Center offer a wide variety of services and information on foundations and grants. Cooperating Collections are libraries, community foundations, and other nonprofit agencies that provide a core collection of Foundation Center publications and a variety of supplementary materials and services in areas useful to grant seekers.

Many of the network members have sets of private foundation information returns (IRS 990-PF) for their state or region, which are available for public use. A complete set of U.S. foundation returns can be found at the New York and Washington, D.C. offices of the Foundation Center. The Atlanta, Cleveland, and San Francisco offices contain IRS 990-PF returns for the southeastern, midwestern and western states, respectively. Those Cooperating Collections marked with a bullet (•) have sets of private foundation information returns for their state or region.

Because the Collections vary in their hours, materials, and services, it is recommended that you call the Collection in advance. To check on new locations or current information, visit the Foundation Center's website http://fdncenter.org/collections/index.html or call toll-free: 1-800-424-9836.

Where to Go for Information on Foundation Funding

The following is a complete list of reference collections operated by the Foundation Center and cooperating collections:

Reference Collections Operated by the Foundation Center:

The Foundation Center
2nd Floor
79 Fifth Avenue
New York, NY 10003
212-620-4230

The Foundation Center
312 Sutter Street, Suite 606
San Francisco, CA 94108
415-397-0902

The Foundation Center
1001 Connecticut Avenue, NW
Washington, DC 20036
202-331-1400

The Foundation Center
Kent H. Smith Library
1422 Euclid, Suite 1356
Cleveland, OH 44115
216-861-1933

The Foundation Center
Suite 150, Grand Lobby
Hurt Building, 50 Hurt Plaza
Atlanta, GA 30303
404-880-0094

Cooperating Collections
ALABAMA

• Birmingham Public Library
Government Documents
2100 Park Place
Birmingham 35203
205-226-3620

Huntsville Public Library

915 Monroe Street
Huntsville 35801
256-532-5940

- University of South Alabama
Library Building
Mobile 36688
334-460-7025

Auburn University at Montgomery Library
7300 University Drive
Montgomery 36124-4023
334-244-3200

ALASKA

- University of Alaska at Anchorage
Library
3211 Providence Drive
Anchorage 99508
907-786-1848

Juneau Public Library
Reference
292 Marine Way
Juneau 99801
907-586-5267

ARIZONA

Flagstaff City-Coconino County
Public Library
300 West Aspen Avenue
Flagstaff 86001
520-779-7670

- Phoenix Public Library
Information Services Deapartment
1221 North Central
Phoenix 85004
602-262-4636

- Tucson Pima Library
101 North Stone Avenue
Tucson 87501
520-791-4393

ARKANSAS

Westark Community College
Boreham Library
5210 Grand Avenue
Fort Smith 72913
501-785-7200

• Central Arkansas Library System
100 Rock Street
Little Rock 72201
501-918-3000

Pine Bluff – Jefferson County Library System
200 East Eighth
Pine Bluff 71601
870-534-2159

CALIFORNIA

Humboldt Area Foundation
P.O. Box 99
Bayside 95524
707-442-2993

• Ventura County Community Foundation
Resource Center for Nonprofit Organizations
1317 Del Norte Road, Suite 150
Camarillo 93010-8504
805-988-0196

Center for Nonprofit Management in Southern California
Nonprofit Resource Library
315 West 9th Street, Suite 1100
Los Angeles 90015
213-623-7080

Flintridge Foundation
Philanthropy Resource Library
1040 Lincoln Avenue, Suite 100
Pasadena 91103
626-449-0839

• Grant & Resource Center of Northern California
Building C, Suite A
2280 Benton Drive
Redding 96003
530-244-1219

Los Angeles Public Library
West Valley Regional Branch Library
19036 Van Owen Street
Reseda 91335
818-345-4393

Riverside Public Library
3581 Mission Avenue
Riverside 92501
909-782-5201

• Nonprofit Resource Center
Sacramento Public Library
828 I Street, 2nd Floor
Sacramento 95814
916-264-2772

• San Diego Foundation
Funding Information Center
1420 Kettner Boulevard, Suite 500
San Diego 92101
619-235-2300

Nonprofit Development Center
Library
1922 The Alameda, Suite 212
San Jose 95126
408-248-9505

• Peninsula Community Foundation
Peninsula Nonprofit Center
1700 South El Camino Real, R201
San Mateo 94402-3049
650-358-9392

Los Angeles Public Library
San Pedro Regional Branch
913 South Gaffey Street
San Pedro 90731
310-548-7779

Volunteer Center of Greater Orange County
Nonprofit Management Assistance Center
1901 East 4th Street, Suite 100
Santa Ana 92705
714-953-5757

Santa Barbara Public Library
40 East Anapamu Street
Santa Barbara 93101-1603
805-962-1019

Santa Monica Public Library
1343 Sixth Street
Santa Monica 90401-1603
310-458-8600

Sonoma County Library
3rd & E Streets
Santa Rosa 95404
707-545-0831

Seaside Branch Library
550 Harcourt Street
Seaside 93955
831-889-8131

Sonora Area Foundation
20100 Cedar Road North
Sonora 95330
209-533-2596

COLORADO

El Pomar Nonprofit Resource Library
1661 Mesa Avenue
Colorado Springs 80906
719-577-7000

• Denver Public Library
General Reference
10 West 14th Avenue Parkway
Denver 80204
303-640-6200

CONNECTICUT

Danbury Public Library
170 Main Street
Danbury 06810
203-797-4527

• Greenwich Library
101 West Putnam Avenue
Greenwich 06830
203-622-7900

- Hartford Public Library
  500 Main Street
  Hartford 06103
  860-543-8656

  New Haven Free Public Library
  Reference Department
  New Haven 06510-2057
  203-946-7091

DELAWARE

- University of Delaware
  Hugh Morris Library
  Newark 19717-5267
  302-831-2432

FLORIDA

  Volusia County Library Center
  City Island
  Daytona Beach 32114-4484
  904-257-6036

- Nova Southeastern University
  Einstein Library
  3301 College Avenue
  Fort Lauderdale 33314
  954-262-4601

  Indian River Community College
  Learning Resource Center
  3209 Virginia Avenue
  Fort Pierce 34981-5596
  561-462-4757

- Jacksonville Public Libraries
  Grants Resource Center
  122 North Ocean Street
  Jacksonville 32202
  904-630-2665

- Miami-Dade Public Library
  Humanities/Social Science
  101 West Flagler Street
  Miami 33130
  305-375-5575

Orange County Library System
Social Sciences Department
101 East Central Boulevard
Orlando 32801
407-425-4694

Selby Public Library
Reference
1331 1st Avenue
Sarasota 34236
941-316-1181

- Tampa – Hillsborough County Public Library
900 North Ashley Drive
Tampa 33602
813-273-3628

- Community Foundation of Palm Beach & Martin Counties
324 Datura Street, Suite 340
West Palm Beach 33401
561-659-6800

GEORGIA

Atlanta-Fulton Public Library
Foundation Collection – Ivan Allen Department
One Margaret Mead Square
Atlanta 30303-1089
404-730-1909

- United Way of Central Georgia
Community Resource Center
277 Martin Luther King, Jr. Boulevard, Suite 301
Macon 31201
912-738-3949

Savannah State University
Asa Gordon Library
P.O. Box 20394
Savannah 31404
912-356-2185

Thomas County Public Library
201 North Madison Street
Thomasville 31792
912-225-5252

HAWAII

• University of Hawaii
  Hamilton Library
  2550 The Mall
  Honolulu 96822
  808-956-7214

  Hawaii Community Foundation Funding Resource Library
  900 Fort Street, Suite 1300
  Honolulu 96813
  808-537-6333

IDAHO

  Boise Public Library
  715 South Capitol Boulevard
  Boise 83702
  208-384-4024

• Caldwell Public Library
  1010 Dearborn Street
  Caldwell 83605
  208-459-3242

ILLINOIS

• Donors Forum of Chicago
  208 South LaSalle, Suite 735
  Chicago 60604
  312-578-0175

• Evanston Public Library
  1703 Orrington Avenue
  Evanston 60201
  847-866-0300

  Rock Island Public Library
  401 – 19th Street
  Rock Island 61201-8143
  309-732-7323

  University of Illinois at Springfield
  Brookens Library
  P.O. Box 19243
  Springfield 62794-9243
  217-206-6633

- Evansville-Vanderburgh County Public Library
  22 SE 5th Street
  Evansville 47708
  812-428-8200

INDIANA

- Allen County Public Library
  900 Webster Street
  Fort Wayne 46802
  219-421-1200

- Indianapolis – Marion County Public Library
  Social Sciences
  40 East St. Clair
  Indianapolis 46206
  317-269-1733

- Vigo County Public Library
  1 Library Square
  Terre Haute 47807
  812-232-1113

IOWA

Cedar Rapids Public Library
Foundation Center Collection
500 First Street, SE
Cedar Rapids 52401
319-398-5123

Southwestern Community College
Learning Resource Center
1501 West Townline Road
Creston 50801
515-782-7081

Public Library of Des Moines
100 Locust
Des Moines 50309-1791
515-283-4152

Sioux City Public Library
529 Pierce Street
Sioux City 51101-1203
712-255-2933

KANSAS

- Dodge City Public Library
  1001 Second Avenue
  Dodge City 67801
  316-225-0248

- Topeka and Shawnee County Public Library
  1515 SW Tenth Avenue
  Topeka 66604-1374
  785-233-2040

- Wichita Public Library
  223 South Main Street
  Wichita 67202
  316-261-8500

KENTUCKY

  Western Kentucky University
  Helm-Cravens Library
  Bowling Green 42101-3576
  502-745-6125

- Lexington Public Library
  140 East Main Street
  Lexington 40507-1376
  606-231-5520

- Louisville Free Public Library
  301 York Street
  Louisville 40203
  502-574-1617

LOUISIANA

- East Baton Rouge Parish Library
  Centroplex Branch Grants Collection
  120 St. Louis
  Baton Rouge 70802
  225-389-4967

  Beauregard Parish Library
  205 South Washington Avenue
  De Ridder 70634
  318-463-6217

Ouachita Parish Public Library
1800 Stubbs Avenue
Monroe 71201
318-327-1490

• New Orleans Public Library
Business and Science Division
219 Loyola Avenue
New Orleans 70112
504-596-2580

• Shreve Memorial Library
424 Texas Street
Shreveport 71120-1523
318-226-5894

MAINE

Maine Grants Information Center
University of Southern Maine Library
314 Forrest Avenue
Portland 04104-9301
207-780-5029

MARYLAND

• Enoch Pratt Free Library
Social Science and History
400 Cathedral Street
Baltimore 21201
410-396-5430

MASSACHUSETTS

• Associated Grantmakers of Massachusetts
294 Washington Street, Suite 840
Boston 02108
617-426-2606

• Boston Public Library
Social Science Reference
700 Boylston Street
Boston 02116
617-536-5400

Western Massachusetts Funding Resource Center
65 Elliot Street
Springfield 01101-1730
413-452-0697

- Worcester Public Library
  Grants Resource Center
  160 Fremont Street
  Worcester 01603
  508-799-1655

MICHIGAN

Alpena County Library
211 North First Street
Alpena 49707
517-356-6188

- University of Michigan – Ann Arbor
  Graduate Library
  Reference and Research Services Department
  Ann Arbor 48109-1205
  734-763-1539

- Willard Public Library
  Nonprofit and Funding Resource Collections
  7 West Van Burren Street
  Battle Creek 49017
  616-968-8166

- Henry Ford Centennial Library
  Adult Services
  16301 Michigan Avenue
  Dearborn 48124
  313-943-2330

- Wayne State University
  Purdy/Kresge Library
  265 Cass Avenue
  Detroit 48202
  313-577-6424

- Michigan State University Libraries
  Main Library Funding Center
  100 Library
  East Lansing 48824-1048
  517-353-8818

- Farmington Community Library
  32737 West 12 Mile Road
  Farmington Hills 48334
  248-553-0300

- University of Michigan – Flint Library
  Flint 48502-1950
  810-762-3413

- Grand Rapids Public Library
  60 Library Plaza, NE
  Grand Rapids 49503-3093
  616-456-3600

  Michigan Technological University
  Van Pelt Library
  1400 Townsend Drive
  Houghton 49931
  906-487-2507

  Maud Preston Palenske Memorial Library
  500 Market Street
  Saint Joseph 49085
  616-983-7167

- Northwestern Michigan College
  Mark & Helen Osterin Library
  1701 East Front Street
  Traverse City 49684
  616-922-1060

MINNESOTA

- Duluth Public Library
  520 West Superior Street
  Duluth 55802
  218-723-3802

  Southwest State University
  University Library
  North Highway 23
  Marshall 56253
  507-537-6108

- Minneapolis Public Library
  Sociology Department
  300 Nicollet Mall
  Minneapolis 55401
  612-630-6300

  Rochester Public Library
  101 Second Street, SE
  Rochester 55904-3777
  507-285-8002

St. Paul Public Library
90 West Fourth Street
Saint Paul 55102
651-266-7000

MISSISSIPPI

- Jackson/Hinds Library System
300 North State Street
Jackson 39201
601-968-5803

MISSOURI

- Clearinghouse for Midcontinent Foundations
University of Missouri
5110 Cherry, Suite 227
Kansas City 64110-0680
816-235-1176

- Kansas City Public Library
311 East 12th Street
Kansas City 64106
816-701-3541

- Metropolitan Association for Philanthropy, Inc.
211 North Broadway, Suite 1200
St. Louis 63102
314-621-6220

- Springfield – Greene County Library
397 East Central
Springfield 65802
417-837-5000

MONTANA

- Montana State University – Billings
Library – Special Collections
1500 North 30th Street
Billings 59101-0298
406-657-1662

- Bozeman Public Library
220 East Lamme
Bozeman 59715
406-582-2402

- Montana State Library
  Library Services
  1515 East Sixth Avenue
  Helena 59620
  406-444-3004

- University of Montana
  Maureen & Mike Mansfield Library
  Missoula 59812-1195
  406-243-6800

NEBRASKA
University of Nebraska – Lincoln
Love Library
14th & R Streets
Lincoln 68588-2848
402-472-2848

- W. Dale Clark Library
  Social Sciences Department
  215 South 15th Street
  Omaha 68102
  402-444-4826

NEVADA
- Clark County Library
  1401 East Flamingo
  Las Vegas 89119
  702-773-3642

- Washoe County Library
  301 South Center Street
  Reno 89501
  775-785-4190

NEW HAMPSHIRE
- Concord Public Library
  45 Green Street
  Concord 03301
  603-225-8670

- Plymouth State College
  Herbert H. Lamson Library
  Plymouth 03264
  603-535-2258

NEW JERSEY

Cumberland County Library
800 East Commerce Street
Bridgeton 08302
856-453-2210

Free Public Library of Elizabeth
11 South Broad Street
Elizabeth 07202
908-354-6060

• County College of Morris
Learning Resource Center
214 Center Grove Road
Randolph 07869
973-328-5296

• New Jersey State Library
Governmental Reference Services
185 West State Street
Trenton 08625-0520
609-292-6220

NEW MEXICO

• Albuquerque Community Foundation
3301 Menaul, NE, Suite 30
Albuquerque 87176-6960
505-883-6240

• New Mexico State Library
Information Services
1209 Camino Carlos Rey
Santa Fe 87501-9860
505-476-9702

NEW YORK

New York State Library
Humanities Reference
Cultural Education Center, 6th Floor
Empire State Plaza
Albany 12230
518-474-5355

Suffolk Cooperative Library System
627 North Sunrise Service Road
Bellport 11713
516-286-1600

New York Public Library
Bronx Reference Center
2556 Bainbridge Avenue
Bronx 10458-4698
718-579-4257

The Nonprofit Connection, Inc.
One Hanson Place, Room 2504
Brooklyn 11243
718-230-3200

Brooklyn Public Library
Social Sciences/Philosophy Division
Grand Army Plaza
Brooklyn 11238
718-230-2122

• Buffalo and Erie County Public Library
Business, Science & Technology Department
1 Lafayette Square
Buffalo 14203-1887
716-858-7097

Huntington Public Library
338 Main Street
Huntington 11743
516-427-5165

Queens Borough Public Library
Social Sciences Division
89-11 Merrick Boulevard
Jamaica 11432
718-990-0700

• Levittown Public Library
One Bluegrass Lane
Levittown 11756
516-731-5728

New York Public Library
Countee Cullen Branch Library
104 West 136th Street
New York 10030
212-491-2070

Adriance Memorial Library
Special Services Department
93 Market Street
Poughkeepsie 12601
914-485-3445

• Rochester Public Library
Social Sciences
115 South Avenue
Rochester 14604
716-428-8120

Onondaga County Public Library
447 South Salina Street
Syracuse 13202-2494
315-435-1900

Utica Public Library
303 Genesee Street
Utica 13501
315-735-2279

White Plains Public Library
100 Martine Avenue
White Plains 10601
914-442-1480

Yonkers Public Library
Reference Department, Getty Square Branch
7 Main Street
Yonkers 10701
914-476-1255

NORTH CAROLINA

Community Foundation of Western North Carolina
67 Haywood Street
Asheville 28802
704-254-4960

- The Duke Endowment
  100 North Tryon Street, Suite 3500
  Charlotte 28202-4012
  704-376-0291

- Durham County Public Library
  300 North Roxboro
  Durham 27702
  919-560-0110

- State Library of North Carolina
  Government & Business Services
  Archives Building
  109 East Jones Street
  Raleigh 27699-4641
  919-733-3683

- Forsyth County Public Library
  660 West Fifth Street
  Winston-Salem 27101
  336-727-2680

NORTH DAKOTA

- Bismarck Public Library
  515 North Fifth Street
  Bismarck 58501
  701-222-6404

- Fargo Public Library
  102 North Third Street
  Fargo 58102
  701-241-1491

OHIO

  Stark County District Library
  715 Market Avenue North
  Canton 44702
  330-452-0665

- Public Library of Cincinnati and Hamilton County
  Grants Resource Center
  800 Vine Street – Library Square
  Cincinnati 45202-2071
  513-369-6000

Columbus Metropolitan Library
Business and Technology
96 South Grant Avenue
Columbus 43215
614-645-2590

• Dayton and Montgomery County Public Library
Grants Information Center
215 East Third Street
Dayton 45402
937-227-9500 ext. 211

Mansfield/Richland County Public Library
42 West Third Street
Mansfield 44902
419-521-3100

• Toledo-Lucas County Public Library
Social Sciences Department
325 Michigan Street
Toledo 43624-1614
419-259-5245

• Public Library of Youngstown & Mahoning County
305 Wick Avenue
Youngstown 44503
330-744-8636

Muskingum County Library
220 North Fifth Street
Zanesville 43701
614-453-0391

OKLAHOMA

• Oklahoma City University
Dulaney Browne Library
2501 North Blackwelder
Oklahoma City 73106
405-521-5065

• Tulsa City-County Library
400 Civic Center
Tulsa 74103
918-596-7940

OREGON

Oregon Institute of Technology
Library
3201 Campus Drive
Klamath Falls 97601-8801
541-885-1770

Pacific Nonprofit Network
Grantsmanship Resource Library
1600 North Riverside #1094
Medford 97501
541-779-6044

Multnomah County Library
Government Documents
801 SW Tenth Avenue
Portland 97205
503-248-5123

Oregon State Library
State Library Building
Salem 97310
503-378-4277

PENNSYLVANIA

Northampton Community College
Learning Resources Center
3835 Green Pond Road
Bethlehem 18017
610-861-5360

Erie County Library System
160 East Front Street
Erie 16507
814-451-6927

Dauphin County Library System
Central Library
101 Walnut Street
Harrisburg 17101
717-234-4976

Lancaster County Public Library
125 North Duke Street
Lancaster 17602
717-394-2651

- Free Library of Philadelphia
  Regional Foundation Center
  1901 Vine Street
  Philadelphia 19103-1189
  215-686-5423

- Carnegie Library of Pittsburgh
  Foundation Collection
  4400 Forbes Avenue
  Pittsburgh 15213-4080
  412-622-1917

  Pocono Northeast Development Fund
  James Pettinger Memorial Library
  1151 Oak Street
  Pittston 18640-3795
  570-655-5581

  Reading Public Library
  100 South Fifth Street
  Reading 19475
  610-655-6355

  Martin Library
  159 Market Street
  York 17401
  717-846-5300

RHODE ISLAND
  Providence Public Library
  225 Washington Street
  Providence 02906
  401-455-8088

SOUTH CAROLINA
  Anderson County Library
  202 East Greenville Street
  Anderson 29621
  864-260-4500

- Charleston County Library
  404 King Street
  Charleston 29403
  803-723-1645

- South Carolina State Library
  1500 Senate Street
  Columbia 29211
  803-734-8666

  Community Foundation of Greater Greenville
  27 Cleveland Street, Suite 101
  P.O. Box 6909
  Greenville 29606
  864-233-5925

SOUTH DAKOTA

South Dakota State Library
800 Governors Drive
Pierre 57501-2294
605-773-5070
800-592-1841 (SD residents)

Dakota State University
Nonprofit Grants Assistance
132 South Dakota Avenue
Sioux Falls 57104
605-367-5380

Siouxland Libraries
201 North Main Avenue
Sioux Falls 57104
605-367-8720

TENNESSEE

United Way of Greater Chattanooga
Center for Nonprofits
406 Frazier Avenue
Chattanooga 37405
423-265-0514

- Knox County Public Library
  500 West Church Avenue
  Knoxville 37902
  423-544-5700

- Memphis & Shelby County Public Library
  1850 Peabody Avenue
  Memphis 38104
  901-725-8877

- Nashville Public Library
  Business Information Division
  225 Polk Avenue
  Nasville 37203
  615-862-5842

TEXAS

Nonprofit Resource Center
Funding Information Library
500 North Chestnut, Suite 1511
Abilene 79604
915-677-8166

- Amarillo Area Foundation
  Nonprofit Services Center
  801 South Fillmore, Suite 700
  Amarillo 79101
  806-376-4521

- Hogg Foundation for Mental Health
  3001 Lake Austin Boulevard, Suite 400
  Austin 78703
  512-471-5041

  Beaumont Public Library
  801 Pearl Street
  Beaumont 77704-3827
  409-838-6606

- Corpus Christi Public Library
  Funding Information Center
  805 Comanche Street
  Corpus Christi 78401
  361-880-7000

- Dallas Public Library
  Urban Information
  1515 Young Street
  Dallas 75201
  214-670-1487

  Center for Volunteerism & Nonprofit Management
  1918 Texas Avenue
  El Paso 79901
  915-532-5377

Southwest Border Nonprofit Resource Center
1201 West University Drive
Edinburgh 78539
956-384-5900

• Funding Information Center of Fort Worth
329 South Henderson
Fort Worth 76104
817-334-0228

Houston Public Library
Bibliographic Information Center
500 McKinney
Houston 77002
713-236-1313

Nonprofit Management & Volunteer Center
Laredo Public Library
1120 East Calton Road
Laredo 78041
956-795-2400

Longview Public Library
222 West Cotton Street
Longview 75601
903-237-1352

Lubbock Area Foundation, Inc.
1655 Main Street, Suite 209
Lubbock 79401
806-762-8061

• Nonprofit Resource Center of Texas
111 Soledad, Suite 200
San Antonio 78205
210-227-4333

• Waco-McLennan County Library
1717 Austin Avenue
Waco 76701
254-750-9541

North Texas Center for Nonprofit Management
624 Indiana, Suite 307
Wichita Falls 76301
940-322-4961

UTAH

• Salt Lake City Public Library
209 East 500 South
Salt Lake City 84111
801-524-8200

VERMONT

• Vermont Department of Libraries
Reference & Law Information Services
109 State Street
Montpelier 05609
802-828-3261

VIRGINIA

Hampton Public Library
4207 Victoria Boulevard
Hampton 23669
757-727-1312

• Richmond Public Library
Business, Science & Technology
101 East Franklin Street
Richmond 23219
804-780-8223

• Roanoke City Public Library System
Main Library
706 South Jefferson Street
Roanoke 24016
540-853-2471

WASHINGTON

• Mid-Columbia Library
405 South Dayton
Kennewick 99336
509-586-3156

• Seattle Public Library
Fundraising Resource Center
1000 Fourth Avenue
Seattle 98104-1193
206-386-4620

- Spokane Public Library
  Funding Information Center
  901 West Main Avenue
  Spokane 99201
  509-444-5300

  United Way of Pierce County
  Center for Nonprofit Development
  1501 Pacific Avenue, Suite 400
  Tacoma 98401
  253-597-7496

  Greater Wenatchee Community Foundation at the
  Wenatchee Public Library
  310 Douglas Street
  Wenatchee 98807
  509-662-5021

WEST VIRGINIA

- Kanawha County Public Library
  123 Capitol Street
  Charleston 25301
  304-343-4646

WISCONSIN

- University of Wisconsin-Madison
  Memorial Library, Grants Information Center
  728 State Street, Room 276
  Madison 53706
  608-262-4649

- Marquette University Memorial Library
  Funding Information Center
  1415 West Wisconsin Avenue
  Milwaukee 53201-3141
  414-288-1515

  University of Wisconsin – Stevens Point
  Library – Foundation Collection
  900 Reserve Street
  Stevens Point 54481-3897
  715-346-2540

WYOMING

- Natrona County Public Library
  307 East Second Street
  Casper 82601-2598
  307-237-4935

- Laramie County Community College
  Instructional Resource Center
  1400 East College Drive
  Cheyenne 82007-3299
  307-778-1206

- Campbell County Public Library
  2101 4-J Road
  Gillette 82716
  307-687-0115

  Teton County Library
  125 Virginian Lane
  Jackson 83001
  307-733-2164

  Rock Springs Library
  400 C Street
  Rock Springs 82901
  307-352-6667

PUERTO RICO

  Universidad Del Sagrado Corazon
  M.M.T. Guevara Library
  Santurce 00914
  809-728-1515 ext. 4357

SECTION VI:
ADDITIONAL SOURCES OF
INFORMATION

Agencies for Development Assistance, 5th edition. Edited by Pierre Aubin and George Cotter. Provides information on sources of support for community-based socio-economic and religious projects in developing countries. Available from Mission Project Service, 662 Thompson Street, Watertown, NY 13601. (315) 782-2382.

Canadian Directory to Foundations and Grants, 13th edition. This directory is available from the Canadian Centre for Philanthropy, 425 University Avenue, Suite 700, Toronto, ON M5G 1T6. (416) 597-2293, ext. 221.

Catholic Almanac. Compiled and edited by Felician A. Foy, OFM, and Rose M. Avato. A factual volume of basic and contemporary information on an encyclopedic range of subjects pertaining to the Catholic church and its activity in the world. This book is available from Our Sunday Visitor Publishing Division, Our Sunday Visitor, Inc., Huntington, IN 46750.

The Foundation Directory, 22nd edition. Edited by David G. Jacobs. Includes entries arranged alphabetically within states for over 10,400 of the largest foundations. Contains the following information: name, address, contact, statement of purpose and interest, officers, financial data, funding limitations, some phone numbers and some application guidelines. This book is available through the Foundation Center at 79 Fifth Avenue, Dept. CE, New York, NY 10003-3050 or by calling (800) 424-9836. $190, soft cover; $215 hard cover.

Foundation Guide for Religious Grant Seekers, 5th edition. Edited by Kerry A. Robinson. Details 795 foundations which are interested in Catholic, Protestant, Jewish, and interfaith giving. Available from Scholars Press, P.O. Box 6996 Alpharetta, GA 30009. (800) 437-6692. $19.95.

Fund Raiser's Guide to Religious Philanthropy. Details over 1,000 foundations and corporate giving programs interested in religious philanthropy. Available from The Taft Group, 27500 Drake Road, Farmington Hills, MI 48331-3535. (800) 877-TAFT. Current issue is the 2000 edition. $175.

The International Donor Directory. Contains more than 2,000 entries of donor agencies and organizations with an interest in aiding the developing world. This book is available from the International Partnership for Human Development, 12020 Sunrise Valley Drive, #160, Reston, VA 22091.

National Directory of Corporate Giving. Profiles 2,256 companies making contributions to nonprofit organizations through foundations and direct giving programs. This book is available through the Foundation Center at 79 Fifth Avenue, Dept. CE, New York, NY 10003-3050 or by calling (800) 424-9836. $195.

National Guide to Funding in Religion, 5th edition. Edited by Gina-Marie Cantarella. Gives details of 6,745 grantmaking foundations and public charities that have a history of funding churches, missionary societies, religious welfare, religious education programs, and religiously affiliated organizations. This book is available through the Foundation Center at 79 Fifth Avenue, Dept. CE, New York, NY 10003-3050 or by calling (800) 424-9836. $140.

2000 Religious Funding Resource Guide. Details 39 sources of funding for justice and peace efforts. The *Guide* includes ecumenical, Catholic, Episcopal, Jewish, Lutheran, Presbyterian, Unitarian, Methodist, and United Church of Christ funders. Application forms and guidelines for each source are included. Available from Resource

Women, 4527 South Dakota Avenue, NE, Washington, D.C. 20017 or by calling (202) 832-8073. Current issue is the sixteenth edition. $75.

1998 Statistics of Fraternal Benefit Societies. Provides statistical information concerning fraternal benefit societies. Available from National Fraternal Congress of America, P.O. Box 3087, Naperville, IL 60566-7087 or by calling (708) 355-6633. $8.

Index

S